THE UNITED STATES NAVY AND THE VIETNAM CONFLICT

Volume I

The Setting of the Stage to 1959

by

EDWIN BICKFORD HOOPER
DEAN C. ALLARD
OSCAR P. FITZGERALD

Naval History Division, Department of the Navy

Washington, D.C. 1976

Library of Congress Card No. 76-600006

For sale by the Superintendent of Documents, U.S. Government Printing Office
Washington, D.C. 20402 - Price $9
Stock Number 008-046-00070-1

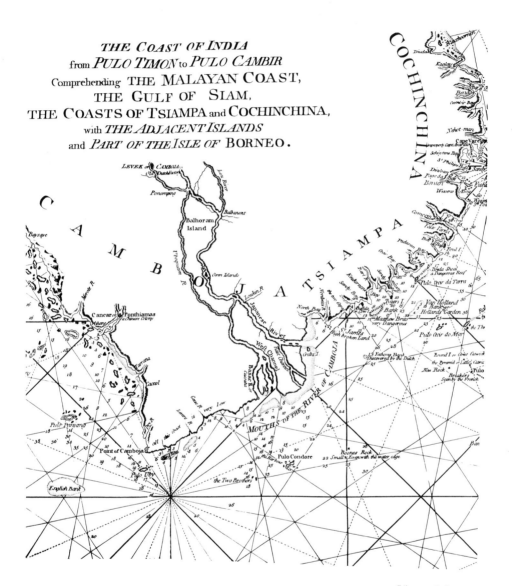

The Coast of India from *Pulo Timon* to *Pulo Cambir* Comprehending The Malayan Coast, The Gulf of Siam, The Coasts of Tsiampa and Cochinchina, with *The Adjacent Islands* and *Part of the Isle of* Borneo.

British chart, 1754.

Preface

This volume, the first of a planned series on the United States Navy and the Vietnam conflict, has a two-fold purpose. First of all, it is intended to provide historical background for the period up to 1959 that will assist readers in understanding naval roles in that conflict, how these roles evolved, their relationships to other forms of power and influence employed in the prolonged and complex struggle, strategic considerations, and the impact of naval power on the course of history associated with the conflict. Secondly, it is intended to trace the story of Vietnam-related actions of the United States Navy through the initial period of American military aid and the first five years that followed the French-Viet Minh War.

In order to gain insights regarding the strategic importance of Vietnam, geographic considerations that affected naval operations along its coast and on inland waters, and some of the local conditions and external relationships that would complicate the conflict, this volume starts with the early history of the area which became Vietnam. In devoting special attention to the maritime influence on that history, an attempt is made to highlight events which will provide perspective for the later period. One example is early operations on inland waters, which were precursors of later naval events. The first two chapters carry the historical background through World War II when the occupation by Japan and the sudden ending of the war provided the Communists a favorable opportunity to establish themselves in a position of power in Vietnam.

Before taking up the story of the subsequent Vietnam conflict, background is laid for understanding the changing United States Navy during the post-World War II period, particularly in regard to its capabilities, employment, direction, and support. This is the primary purpose of the third chapter. Limited coverage is given also to the worldwide roles of the Navy as they evolved in response to the global struggle that followed World War II. Not only were the decisions as to American involvement in the Vietnam conflict strongly influenced by events elsewhere, but the local application of United States naval power in Southeast Asia was only one of many interrelated demands on the Fleet, in the Far East, and elsewhere.

The remainder of the volume encompasses the first fourteen years of the Vietnam conflict, with primary attention being focused on the naval aspects. It includes the history of United States naval operations related to that conflict and the Navy's activities in the aid, advisory, and assistance programs. It also covers French and Vietnamese naval operations, the concepts of which would be further applied during the period of American involvement.

Two specialized works on the United States Navy and the Vietnam conflict have already appeared. One, published by the Naval History Division, is *Mobility, Support, Endurance, A Story of Naval Operational Logistics in the Vietnam War 1965–1968.* Another, written by Richard Tregaskis under the auspices of the Naval Facilities Engineering Command, is *Southeast Asia: Building the Bases,* covering the SEABEES and the Navy's supervision of construction in the Vietnam War.

Together with such specialized works, it is hoped that the volumes in this basic series will serve as useful complements to the historical studies of the other military services, and to studies of the diplomatic, political, and psychological aspects of the Vietnam conflict, and that collectively these will lead to a better comprehension of American involvement in the complex, prolonged, and often controversial struggle.

The volume is the product of a team effort within the Naval History Division. Dr. Dean C. Allard and Dr. Oscar P. Fitzgerald joined me in researching, writing, reviewing, discussing, reorganizing, and revising the material since the start of the project in October 1970. Captain Paul B. Ryan, USN (Retired), was a member of the team until his detachment as Deputy Director of Naval History in June 1972. During tours with the division, Captain Vincent D. Maynard and Commander John C. Bruce carried out research and provided initial drafts on events leading to the initial granting of military aid and on the early advisory years. During a brief assignment in the Division, Dr. Robert H. Levine researched primary source materials on assistance to the Vietnamese Navy in the final period covered by this volume, writing a paper which provided helpful inputs. A special word of gratitude is due Mr. Edward J. Marolda and Ms. Nina F. Statum who carried out the difficult chores of editing final drafts of the manuscript, steering the work through the publication process and preparing the volume's index. The charts were drafted by DM2 Stephen J. Coy working under the supervision of Mr. Marolda. Mr. Charles R. Haberlein, Jr., and Mrs. Agnes F. Hoover aided with the location, selection, and reproduction of pictures for the volume. Under Mr. Walter B. Greenwood, the Navy Department Library staff—particularly Mr. Frederick S. Meigs, Mrs. Rita L. Halle, and Mr. James E. Smith—gave reference assistance to everyone who participated in the project. Miss Barbara A. Gilmore, Mr. Bernard F. Cavalcante, and others of the Operational Archives Branch provided competent and invaluable assistance in the location of source materials. A word of thanks is due the various members of the staff who typed many drafts during the various stages of this project. Senior Chief R. D. Barnett supervised these efforts during most of the later stages. Others deserving of special mention are Chief Glenn N. Pizer, Mrs. T. M. Schuster, Mrs. R. L. Kieltyka, Mrs. P. D. Sherrill, Chief E. J. Moore, and Mrs. Mary M. Edmison.

We are deeply indebted to Dr. Richard W. Leopold of Northwestern University, a member of the Secretary of the Navy's Advisory Committee on Naval History. With remarkable thoroughness, he reviewed a late draft of the manuscript. His scholarly, frank, and perceptive comments both on the overall work and on details were of immense value. These comments led to additional research, rearrangement, and rewording. The product was then reviewed by three other distinguished members of the Committee, Dr. Walter Muir Whitehill, Dr. John H. Kemble, and Dr. Gordon B. Turner. The final revision followed the receipt of their highly constructive comments. I am grateful also to other members of the Committee for their encouragement and advice. At various early stages I sought the advice of Professor William Reitzel, a colleague of mine at the time of establishing the Naval Long Range Studies Project and the Institute of Naval Studies. As always his views were sound and extremely helpful. Useful comments on portions of earlier drafts were provided by Admirals Robert B. Carney and Arleigh A. Burke, by Vice Admiral Lorenzo S. Sabin, and by others associated with events covered by the volume.

The final decisions as to the contents were made by me and the shortcomings are solely my responsibility.

EDWIN B. HOOPER
Vice Admiral, USN (*Ret.*)
Director of Naval History

Contents

Charts and Illustrations

(Illustrations identified by numbers preceded by NH or KN are maintained in the United States Naval Photographic Center, and those preceded by 80G are located in the National Archives and Records Service.)

CHAPTER I

Backdrop To The Stage

From early times history reveals that maritime influence and the application of naval power played decisive roles in shaping the destiny of states in the Indochinese peninsula. This chapter seeks to provide insight as to how control over the region hinged on riverine warfare and amphibious operations along the coast. In particular, French experiences in the nineteenth century provide a useful background for the understanding of strategic possibilities during the Vietnam conflict in the twentieth century and of the role of naval operations at sea and on inland waters during that struggle. Early history also provides background on enduring factors which would complicate the Vietnam conflict—such as the frequent reoccurrence of warfare between north and south, sources of other conflicts between diverse groups within the area, and relationships with China.

Furthermore, the course of history has frequently demonstrated Vietnam's strategic importance. Lying along the South China Sea, on a massive peninsula jutting down between Malaya and China, Vietnam occupies a key position alongside one of the densest shipping lanes of the world. Historically, the relatively narrow span of navigable water beween the southeastern coast of Vietnam and the "dangerous ground" further to the east has been the main trade link between Europe, Africa, the Middle East, South Asia, Singapore, Indonesia, Malaya, Thailand, and Cambodia on the one hand, and China, Japan, the Philippines, and additional East Asian countries on the other. Ships in this lane also proceed between Southeast Asia and North America.

This was the route used by the great Chinese fleets of the Ming dynasty in the first part of the fifteenth century, when China sent seven large sea-going expeditions to exert influence over such far away places as the Persian Gulf, the Red Sea, and the east coast of Africa. Heading south and west from China on the winds of the northeast monsoon of fall and winter, these impressive ships made landfall at Cu Lao Re, an island off the central coast

1

Southeast Asia

of present-day Vietnam, and then stopped in Qui Nhon,[1] later to become a major port for logistics and the location of a small base for coastal patrol craft of the United States Navy. With the coming of the southwest monsoon in the spring, these fleets headed back downwind with their cargoes and with tribute-bearing emissaries to pay homage to the Chinese emperor. During these return voyages, the ships made landfall at Cape Varella (Ke Ga) on the coast of Vietnam, and once again put into the harbor at Qui Nhon.[2]

Vietnam's geography made the area particularly susceptible to the influence of seapower. Even when the many indentations and promontories are not included, the coast measures some 1,500 miles from the Chinese border in the north to Cambodia in the south. As narrow as thirty miles at one point, the S-shaped strip of land that now comprises Vietnam has an average width of only eighty miles. Many rivers wind their way from the mountains down to the sea.

One of these rivers is the mighty Mekong which rises 2,500 miles upstream in the Himalayan Mountains of central Tibet. With a drainage basin larger than the state of Texas, the Mekong proceeds through Yunnan Province of China, forms the border between Laos and Burma and most of Thailand, traverses Cambodia, and at Phnom Penh divides into two arms extending to the South China Sea—the Mekong and the Bassac. Crisscrossed by innumerable waterways, almost the entire region south of Saigon and much of Cambodia consist of a vast delta, the "rice bowl of Asia," formed by the accumulation of silt brought down by the Mekong and its tributaries. Extensive regions of the delta are inundated during the summer months as a result of heavy tropical rains caused by moisture brought from the Indian Ocean by the southwest monsoonal winds. Inland waterways form the main highways in this area for the movement of produce, goods, and

---

[1] The Ming fleet is said to have totaled, at its peak, 400 warships, 400 armed "grain-conveyance" ships, 250 great "treasure ships," each carrying 500 men, 3,000 other merchant ships and 2,500 smaller coastal warships. Sixty-two of the ships were reportedly over 500 feet long and 200 feet wide, designed for long voyages with four decks and watertight compartmentation, and equipped with sails which permitted tacking into the wind. Whatever the specifics, these were impressive ships for their day. Charles P. FitzGerald, *The Southern Expansion of the Chinese People* (New York: Praeger Publishers, 1972), pp. 87–126; Clark G. Reynolds, *Command of the Sea; The History and Strategy of Maritime Empires* (New York: William Morrow and Co., 1974), pp. 102–04.

[2] For an account of the expeditions, see Ma Huan, *Ying-Yai Sheng-Lan: The Overall Survey of the Ocean's Shores,* trans. by Teng Ch'eng-Chun (Cambridge, England: Cambridge University Press, 1970).

people. Oceangoing ships steam through the delta from the sea to Phnom Penh, the capital of Cambodia.

In the north, where the northeast monsoon brings the fall-to-spring rainy season, the predominant waterway is the Red River which rises in Yunnan Province and is navigable all the way from the sea to the Chinese border. The rice-rich delta formed by this river and its tributaries is the most densely populated region of North Vietnam and the site of its capital, Hanoi.

Since the great majority of the inhabitants of Vietnam have lived in the deltas, north and south, and along the coastal lowlands, it was inevitable that inland waterways and their control would, along with maritime influence, play important roles in the history of Vietnam. These roles were in many ways extensions of sea power.

A Divided Land

Future conflict would be influenced by religious, cultural, and political divisions within Vietnam, a country never truly united and under single rule only for brief spans of time. The migration of peoples to Vietnam by sea and inland waters brought additional ethnic strains to those indigenous to the area. Along with traders, missionaries, and conquerors, ships also brought in foreign cultures and religions. The resultant sources of potential conflict between major and minor groupings within the area would persist into the twentieth century. The area where North and South Vietnam would be divided after the French-Viet Minh War was, in particular, the scene of many confrontations and a series of wars spanning the centuries.[3]

To the northern part of Vietnam, came early inhabitants from China down the Red River and along the coast. The predominant strain was a people known to the Chinese as the Yueh, who occupied river and delta regions in early times along the east coast of Asia. Reputedly, they were hardy seafarers skilled in boat building and navigation. Those occupying southern coastal regions were known by the Chinese as Nan (southern) Yueh (Viet), who spread south to occupy the Red River Delta.[4]

---

[3] For a comprehensive discussion of Vietnam's history from early times to the establishment of French Indochina, see Joseph Buttinger, *The Smaller Dragon: A Political History of Vietnam* (New York: Frederick A. Praeger, 1958).

[4] For overviews of the peopling of Southeast Asia and its early history, see Daniel G.E. Hall, *A History of South-East Asia* (London: Macmillan and Co., 1964); and FitzGerald, *Southern Expansion.*

These Nan Yueh in the region later known as Tonkin submitted to the rule of the Ch'in emperor when China became united during the third century B.C., but regained their independence when the dynasty came to an end in 205 B.C. A century later, in 111 B.C., the Han emperor, Wu, conquered Tonkin and Annam. Except for a brief period at the time of Li Bon's revolt in the sixth century A.D., the area would be ruled by China for more than a thousand years. Although the Chinese did not colonize the Red River Delta and the Yueh there were not assimilated to the extent of those further north, the long rule did result in the absorption of Chinese culture and customs, particularly by the political leaders and others of the educated class.

In early history, the area south of Tonkin was the land of the Chams. Largely of Indonesian descent, the inhabitants added cultures and religions imported from India. Controlling regions down to Cam Ranh Bay, the Kingdom of Champa's center of power was near the present city of Danang.

To the area that became Cambodia, came people down the Mekong River from the borders of Tibet. As elsewhere in Southeast Asia, seagoing Indonesians, or Malays, began to arrive several centuries before the Christian era. Ships later brought traders from India, followed by priests. Funan, a pre-Khmer kingdom, governed early Malay settlements along the Mekong between the sites of Phnom Penh, later to be the capital of Cambodia, and Chau Doc, in the Vietnam region of the delta. Additional territories were conquered under Funan's "Great King," Fan Shih-man. The fleet he built was said to have dominated the seas. Funan would be absorbed later into Cambodia.

Warfare between the Chams and the Chinese—contesting the territory between the Hai Van Pass (just north of Danang) and the "Gate of Annam" (at the 18th parallel)—is recorded as early as 248 A.D. Joined by Funan, Champa waged a fourteen-year war against the Chinese-ruled north. By 340 Champa was, for a time, in possession of the contested territory.

China brought its influence to bear on Champa by attacks from the sea. One such attack was repulsed in 431, but fifteen years later the Chinese plundered Hue, returning north with booty. This brought Champa and its tribute-bearing embassies in line for a number of years. Champa renewed its attacks in the sixth century. Once again China raided Hue and seized much of great value.

After a major uprising in 722, China maintained a large army in Tonkin

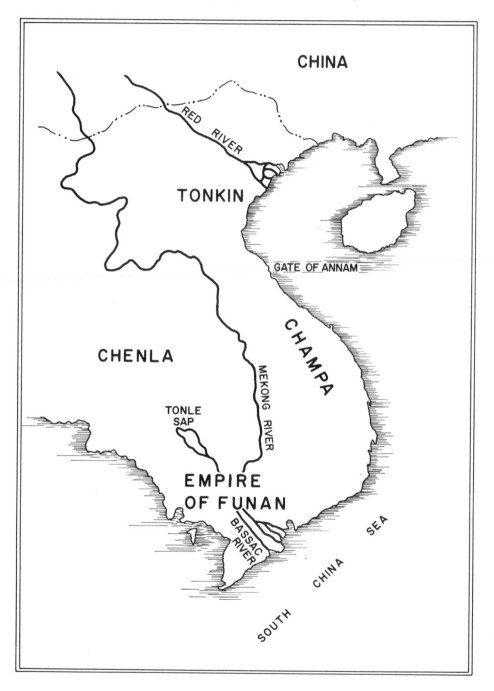

Ancient kingdoms of Indochina.

and renamed the country An Nan (Annam), the "Pacified South." Javanese raids kept Champa occupied during the last half of that century, but once the peril was over, the Chams renewed their attacks against the Chinese who again controlled the contested provinces.

When a rebellion in 934 led to the termination of China's direct rule, Tonkin's relationship with the "Middle Kingdom" became those of a tributary state. As a result, China would continue to exert her pervasive influence until a decisive naval action late in the nineteenth century brought the political relationships to an end. In the light of two millenia of close relationships, it is scarcely surprising that China's support and the threat of her intervention would play key, and perhaps decisive, roles in the Vietnam conflict in the twentieth century and have a major effect on the operations of the United States Navy.

Conflicts between the states in northern and central Vietnam were resumed later in the tenth and eleventh centuries. As result of a series of wars, Annam (the name having been retained) conquered and annexed territory down to the 17th parallel. By 1069 the Annamese had gained control of the entire area later known as North Vietnam.

Another source of conflict was Cambodia (Chenla), which started a series of campaigns against Annam and Champa in 1123. In an early example of riverine warfare, the Chams responded by building ram-equipped galleys. These proceeded up the Mekong River and looted the Khmer capital. Cambodia constructed a similar fleet, won a victory on the country's largest lake, Tonle Sap, and then headed down the Mekong. As a result, Cambodia dominated Champa from 1203 to 1220.[5]

The Extension of Chinese Influence by Sea

Seapower played key roles in China's exercise of suzerainty over lands to the south. Early in the twelfth century, the Southern Sung created the first Chinese navy organized on a permanent basis and functioning as an independent service. By 1237 the Southern Sung navy—equipped with incendiary weapons, rockets, and explosive weapons—had grown to twenty squadrons manned by over 50,000 men. China truly qualified as a naval

---

[5] Reynolds, *Command of the Sea,* p. 100.

power for the next 200 years. Operations by the Sung navy included raids on Annam and Champa.[6]

Naval power was next brought to bear on Vietnam by the Mongols, whose first invasion of Annam, by land in 1257, had been unsuccessful. The Mongols brought about the final collapse of the Sung dynasty by destroying the Chinese fleet in the battle of Yai-shan off the South China coast in 1278. Later that century, 800 ships were employed to invade Annam and Champa. In a campaign mounted by Kublai Khan, a two-pronged attack was launched, as one force struck Annam, the other Champa. A raid by the southern force into northern Cambodia resulted in an offer of tribute and recognition of Mongol suzerainty.

Annamite guerrilla-type actions during this period have been likened to those of the twentieth century. Although waterborne expeditions achieved success, land campaigns often met with frustrations. The terrain was hardly favorable for the usual cavalry tactics of the Mongols and the climate took its toll. When a Mongol force moved north from Champa through swampland and jungles to join the fight against Annam, it was defeated. Then, after Hanoi was taken in 1285, resistance outside the capital continued and the Mongols once again withdrew. Another Mongol invasion two years later met a similar fate.

One of the legends of Vietnamese history relates how Tran Hung Dao ordered his soldiers to drive stakes into the bed of the Red River during one of these attacks. By pretending a frantic flight the Vietnamese lured the Mongol ships upstream at high tide. As the tide ebbed the ships were impaled on the stakes, boarded, and captured. This was the battle of Bach Dang, the inspirational value of which would be exploited in a later era by the Vietnamese as an example of how to defeat a foreign invader.[7]

Seapower played an important part in the decline of Mongol power after the death of Kublai in 1294. One who rebelled against the Mongols was a ruler of the southern provinces of China, Fang Kuo-chen, a former salt merchant. Starting in 1348, his ships, gaining control of southern waters, intercepted rice shipments and tributes enroute to northern Chinese ports.[8]

---

[6] Charles P. FitzGerald. *A Concise History of East Asia* (New York: Frederick A. Praeger, 1966), p. 101; Jung-Pang Lo, "The Emergence of China as a Sea Power during the Late Sung and Early Yuan Periods," *The Far Eastern Quarterly*, XIV, No. 4 (Aug. 1955), pp. 489–503.

[7] FitzGerald, *Southern Expansion*, pp. 26, 82–83; Reynolds, *Command of the Sea*, pp. 98–104; Buttinger, *Smaller Dragon*. p. 130; Vo Nguyen Giap, *Banner of People's War, the Party's Military Line* (New York: Praeger Publishers, 1970), p. xiii.

[8] FitzGerald, *Southern Expansion*, pp. 85–86.

In 1407, during the period of the great Ming fleets, China once again conquered Annam, which now extended as far south as the area of Danang. Following the death of Yung Lo, Chinese seapower declined. An Annamite victory at Lang Son, south of the Chinese border, and the recapture of Hanoi ended a twenty-one year period of Chinese rule.

Although the Chams temporarily regained their northern provinces, they suffered a disastrous defeat in 1471 and Annam annexed territory all the way down to Cape Varella. The area from the Chinese border to the cape was for a time under one ruler, but the basic causes of north-south conflict continued. Finding the lands to the south difficult to control, a viceroy, the head of the Nguyen family, was appointed in 1558 to rule there. His capital was Hue. Later those in the north attempted to oust the Nguyen ruler and in 1627 launched a major attack by land and sea. The south successfuly defended its territory in a prolonged war which ended in a truce in 1673. The area later to be known as Vietnam remained a divided land.

The Beginnings of European Maritime Influence

The arrival of a Portuguese ship in 1535 and the establishment of a trading post at Fai Fo (later known as Hoi An) marked the beginning of European influence in Indochina. Missionaries soon followed. The Mekong Delta was found to be a particularly fertile region for conversions to Catholicism.

With the decline of Portuguese seapower in the early seventeenth century, maritime supremacy in Southeast Asia passed to the Dutch. Predictably, in 1633, Dutch ships arrived at Turon or Tourane (later known as Danang) and four years later traders from Holland set up a factory in Tonkin.

A French missionary, Father Alexandre de Rhodes, visited Cochin China and Tonkin at this time. His belief that the area was excellent for future evangelizing caused him to go to Rome in 1645 to inform the Vatican of the need to expend more resources on Christianizing Indochina. He then visited France on a similar mission. The success of his efforts soon became evident when two French bishops were sent to Indochina as Vicars Apostolic of Tonkin and Cochin China, respectively. As evidence of the diligence of

Father Alexandre and his equally zealous successors, the Vietnamese Christian community soon grew to an estimated 300,000 people.[9]

More than a century later, it would be through the efforts of the Vicar Apostolic of Cochin China, one Monsignor Pigneau de Behaine, that France began to play an important part in the affairs of Vietnam. The occasion was the so-called Tay Son rebellion. When the Tay Son rebels invaded from the north, Nguyen Anh took refuge in Siam. After the Tay Son forces captured Hanoi, a single rule was established over the northern and southern states. Later returning and capturing several provinces, Nguyen Anh was defeated when Tay Son forces were brought in by sea. After a second abortive attempt, Nguyen was advised by Pigneau to seek aid from King Louis XVI. Pigneau's trip to Paris as an emissary resulted in a 1787 treaty providing for military support in return for territorial concessions and a trade monopoly.

The French ministers secretly instructed the French Governor of India at Pondichéry to veto the treaty if, in his opinion, the plan for aid seemed impractical. Having neither the four ships, the 1,650 men, nor the guns and other equipment requested by Pigneau, the governor did not approve the mission. Unable to move the governor, the energetic monsignor approached French traders and merchants and convinced them of the riches to be gained if Nguyen Anh were on the throne granting preference and privilege to his French supporters. The result was that by June 1789 Pigneau acquired two corvettes which he loaded with 100 French and other European mercenaries. They landed in Vietnam, organized a mission to support Nguyen Anh, and taught the men how to cast cannon, build ships, and operate field artillery.[10]

A Vietnamese Navy

With French guidance and assistance a small navy was created. The royal fleet, commanded by Jean Marie Dayot, destroyed the "navy" of the Tay Son rebels in 1792, displayed the flag from the China Sea to the

---

[9] Donald Lancaster, *The Emancipation of French Indochina* (London: Oxford University Press, 1961), pp. 23–27.

[10] Buttinger, *Smaller Dragon*, pp. 233–39; Lancaster, *Emancipation of French Indochina*, pp. 28–29; Bernard B. Fall, "The History and Culture of Vietnam," *Naval War College Review*, XXIII (Feb. 1971), p. 51. For a copy of the treaty, see Eugene Teston and Maurice Percheron, *L'Indochine Moderne* (Paris: Librairie de France, 1931), p. 25.

Bay of Bengal, and reputedly made it respected throughout the Orient. As a result of raids and small invasions along the southern coast and in the Mekong Delta, Nguyen Anh gained control of the delta within ten years. Saigon was captured in 1788. In 1802 occupation of Hanoi ended the Tay Son rule. With the area from the northern border to the Gulf of Siam now under one ruler, the Chinese emperor, to whom Nguyen paid tribute, designated the country Viet Nam.

Significantly, 400 Frenchmen remained in Gia Long's (as Nguyen Anh became known) service. Some like Théodore Lebrun, built the citadel at Saigon and most of the forts throughout Annam.[11]

Alarmed by the growing number of aggressive Western traders in Canton, Hong Kong, and other ports, and fearful that Christian missionary teachings were undermining imperial authority, the Emperor of China initiated a policy designed to push the "barbarians" out of the Middle Kingdom and its tributaries. The new Vietnamese king, Minh Mang, adopted a similar policy of isolation. Becoming convinced that France planned to conquer his people by mass conversion to Christianity, a religion that he believed was at variance with traditional Vietnamese order, Minh Mang began a campaign of persecuting Christians and authorizing the execution of certain French missionaries.[12]

American Attempts to Establish Relationships with Vietnam

During this troubled time, a ship of the United States Navy first visited Vietnam, as America attempted to expand its trade with the Orient. Edmund Roberts, an experienced merchant-ship captain, was appointed as a special diplomatic agent and sent in the American sloop-of-war *Peacock* (Commander David Geisinger commanding) on a cruise to Asia. Roberts's instructions called for him to conclude treaties of commerce and trade with Cochin China (the name then being used by Americans to refer to all Vietnam), with Siam, and with Muscat, a state bordering the Arabian Sea. *Peacock* arrived at Tourane Bay on 1 January 1833. Anchoring off

[11] Teston and Percheron, *L'Indochine Moderne,* p. 26; Buttinger, *Smaller Dragon,* p. 306; Bernard B. Fall, *The Two Viet-Nams: A Political and Military Analysis* (New York: Frederick A. Praeger, 1967), p. 9.

[12] David J. Steinberg *et al, In Search of Southeast Asia: A Modern History* (New York: Praeger Publishers, 1971), pp. 127–30.

Hue or in the roadstead at Tourane was found unsafe because of the north-east monsoon. The ship then proceeded south and found secure anchorage at Vung Lam (Vung Chao), near Qui Nhon. Roberts spent a month attempting to gain an audience with the emperor at Hue, present a letter from President Andrew Jackson, and conduct negotiations. Encountering what were described as "insulting formalities," Roberts terminated the effort.

Sailing in *Peacock* for Siam, Roberts concluded a treaty of commerce and amity with that country. It was the first treaty ever signed by the United States with an Asian nation.[13]

Soon thereafter, France deployed a naval squadron to the Far East. When Minh Mang closed all ports except Tourane to Western ships and pronounced the death penalty for foreign priests, French commanding officers were ordered to protect missionaries, but only if such actions could be carried out without exposing the French flag to possible insult and without resorting to hostilities. It was not long before the French Navy found itself at odds with the king of Annam. The first confrontation came in 1843 when Commandant Lévêque, the commanding officer of a French corvette, appeared at Tourane to obtain the release of five missionaries held captive at Hue.[14]

Two years later the United States Navy had its first introduction to Tourane. This port would become well known in the United States Navy after the passage of another 120 years. The earlier occasion was a visit by the famous frigate *Constitution* which was in the Far East on a round-the-world cruise. The commanding officer of *Constitution* was the contro-versial and colorful Captain John Percival, known in the service as "Mad Jack." Upon anchoring off Tourane in May 1845, Percival learned from a native Christian that a bishop apostolic, Monsignor Lefèbvre, was being held prisoner by the king. Putting ashore a landing force of fifty blue-jackets and thirty Marines, the captain seized five hostages (among them three local officials) and three junks, and held them for almost a week. Whether Percival's tactics, which were later disavowed by the United States, helped to gain the release of the missionary is not clearly established. It is known that, subsequently, a French warship won custody of Lefèbvre and took him from the country. However, the bishop then secretly made

---

[13] A full account is in Edmund Roberts, *Embassy to the Eastern Courts of Cochin-China, Siam and Muscat* (New York: Harper and Brothers, 1837), pp. 6, 171–226, 313.

[14] Steinberg, *In Search of Southeast Asia*, p. 128; Buttinger, *Smaller Dragon*, pp. 304–24; Hall, *History of South-East Asia*, p. 609.

U.S. Frigate Constitution *which visited Tourane in 1845.*

his way back to Hue, where he was again captured by the exasperated mandarins. King Thieu Tri chose not to carry out the death sentence. He deported the brave but reckless clergyman to Singapore.[15]

In 1847 a French frigate and a corvette anchored in the same roadstead. This time the French discovered five Vietnamese corvettes which the king had built to oppose the intruders. The mandarins at Tourane refused to deliver a letter from the senior officer, Captain Lapierre, to the king seeking to negotiate better treatment for Catholics. Frustrated by his inability to communicate with the monarch, the captain decided on direct action and delivered several broadsides, which sank most of the corvettes and killed many Indochinese.[16]

In a sequel to the *Constitution* incident, the king sent a delegation to Joseph Balestier, the American Consul in Singapore, claiming the right to punish Captain Percival. Balestier notified Washington of the Vietnamese demand and of threats issued at the same time to retaliate against other Americans visiting Annam. Subsequently he was ordered late in 1849 by the State Department to proceed to Tourane on board the USS *Plymouth*. Balestier carried with him a note of apology for Percival's actions, but the delivery of this document to the king was impossible due to the familiar obstructions raised by minor Vietnamese officials. Balestier countered Vietnamese threats to punish American citizens visiting Vietnam by stating that, under such circumstances, the President would be "obliged to send a strong armed force" to Annam. Following these acrimonious exchanges, Balestier departed Vietnam early in 1850.[17]

After Commodore Matthew C. Perry's famous expedition to Japan in 1853–1854, that officer's report included the prediction that America's expanding commercial interests would lead the United States to "extend the advantages of our national friendship and protection" to other countries

---

[15] Benjamin F. Stevens, "Around the World in the United States Frigate Constitution in the Days of the Old or Wooden Ships," *The United Service* VII (May 1905), pp. 596–97; Allan Westcott, "Captain 'Mad Jack' Percival," *United States Naval Institute Proceedings,* LXI (Mar. 1935), p. 318; USS *Constitution* Daily Log, 14–16 May 1845; Captains letters received, May 1845, Record Group (RG) 45, National Archives and Records Service; Buttinger, *Smaller Dragon,* pp. 332–33, 391–92.

[16] Buttinger, *Smaller Dragon,* pp. 333, 393.

[17] Quoted in James W. Gould, "American Imperialism in Southeast Asia Before 1898," *Journal of Southeast Asian Studies,* III (Sept. 1972), p. 308.

of the Far East, including "Cochin China." [18] Nevertheless, in the years that followed, American contacts with Vietnam were of a limited nature.

The Evolution of French Indochina

French naval power, at sea and on inland waters, would provide the key to the establishment of controls over Tonkin, Cochin China, Annam, and Cambodia. Naval operations during this period were in many respects indicative of actions that would be required in the Vietnam conflict which would follow World War II.

Napoléon III arranged for his envoy, Louis Charles de Montigny, to open negotiations for trading and religious rights. Arriving in Tourane on 23 January 1857 on board a small steamer, Montigny was highly offended when the king, now Tu Duc, refused to receive him as the emperor's personal representative. In retaliation, the envoy sent a strong warning to Hue that the king's continued maltreatment of Christians could only result in serious consequences. But threats of force by the French only generated more Vietnamese terrorism. It has been estimated that in the years between 1848 and 1860 approximately 25 Catholic missionaries, 300 Vietnamese priests, and 30,000 Vietnamese Christians were put to death.[19]

Faced with an impasse, Napoléon, on the advice of his ministers, decided on a policy which called for a permanent French presence in Indochina, preferably in the form of a protectorate. The decision meant that no longer would the role of naval forces be that of guarding scattered trading posts and missions. Instead, the navy assumed long-range responsibilities for the security of an overseas dominion, including the protection of the ocean routes to these newly won lands, and the control of coastal waters and rivers. To the extent that the navy remained capable of carrying out these tasks, the French colonization of Indochina proceeded apace.[20]

In August 1858 the French Asiatic Squadron, comprising thirteen ships and 2,050 men, sailed to Tourane to occupy the post. Spanish authorities at

[18] Quoted in Ronald Spector. "The American Image of Southeast Asia 1970–1865, A Preliminary Assessment," *Journal of Southeast Asian Studies,* III (Sept. 1972), p. 304.

[19] Teston and Percheron, *L'Indochine Moderne,* pp. 30–31; Buttinger, Smaller Dragon, p. 340; Steinberg, *In Search of Southeast Asia.* p. 128.

[20] Buttinger, *Smaller Dragon,* pp. 342–45; Lancaster, *Emancipation of French Indochina,* pp. 36–37.

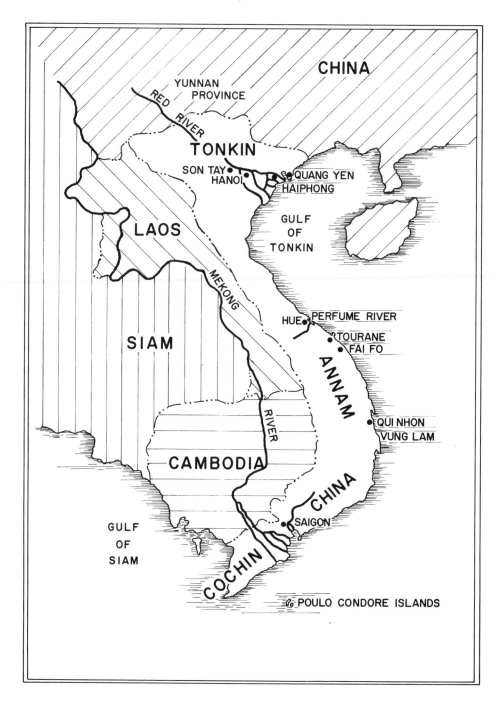

Indochinese Peninsula, 19th Century.

Manila augmented Admiral Charles Rigault de Genouilly's squadron with a ship and 450 troops. The combined force bombarded Tourane and took the city's forts without difficulty. However, the admiral found a largely abandoned city. The lack of a native labor force to convert Tourane into a base, coupled with the presence of disease, discouraged the French from further actions in the area. An assault on the capital at Hue was tempting but Genouilly, finding that the depth of the Perfume (Huong) River restricted passage to ship's boats, decided that a better course was to seize Saigon. On 2 February 1859, the fleet sailed south. Two weeks later the French successfully occupied Saigon, long a center for rice shipments from the southern delta region to the northern cities.[21]

After the French had subjugated much of the Mekong Delta, and foreseeing a serious shortage of rice in his country, the king finally agreed to negotiations. The new concessions wrested from Tu Duc in 1862 by French naval officers, one of whom was Rear Admiral Louis Adolphe Bonard, resulted in the acquisition by France of three provinces around Saigon plus the offshore island of Poulo Condore (Con Son), the right of Catholic missionaries to work among the people, trading privileges for France and Spain in the port of Tourane and several ports near Haiphong, the payment of an indemnity by the Vietnamese government, free ship passage on the Mekong to Cambodia, and finally, the promise of the king not to cede any land to a foreign nation without the agreement of the French government. The French government appointed Admiral Bonard as the first Governor of Cochin China, the French protectorate in the south. Bonard, in turn, organized an administrative command with naval officers acting as "inspectors of indigenous affairs" where they directed administrative, judicial, and financial matters.[22]

A serious challenge to the French arose in 1862 as armed guerrilla bands formed to fight the foreigners in widespread insurrection. Enjoying a superiority in artillery and small arms, the French finally subdued the revolt, forcing Tu Duc to cede even more territory, including disputed land bordering on Cambodia. In 1863, Bonard's successor, Admiral Benoit de la Grandière, forced the Cambodian king to sign a treaty whereby his nation became a French protectorate. Four years later, the King of Siam, who

---

[21] Buttinger, *Smaller Dragon,* pp. 344–46, 351, 404–05; Teston and Percheron, *L'Indochina Moderne,* p. 31.

[22] Lancaster, *Emancipation of French Indochina,* pp. 39–40; Hall, *History of South-East Asia,* pp. 612–13; Buttinger, *Smaller Dragon,* p. 360.

also had an historic claim of suzerainty over Cambodia, recognized Gallic power in a separate treaty with France. As compensation for its concession Siam received two of Cambodia's provinces.[23]

Riverine Operations

The extension of French control to Tonkin was achieved mainly through riverine operations. A pioneer in this form of warfare was Lieutenant Francis Garnier. He had been second-in-command of Lieutenant Doudart de Lagrée's expedition up the river to Cambodia, and after serving as "Inspector of Natives" in Cochin China, Garnier participated in a two year exploration of the Mekong River. Since the Mekong had been found unsuitable for trade with China, attention then focused on the Red River which provided a navigable route to Yunnan Province.[24]

Key points along the river were controlled by bandits and pirates known as the Black Flags. A French arms dealer, Jean Dupuis, pressed the Hanoi mandarins to request that he be allowed to transport his cargo by junk up the Red River without paying custom charges. The king at Hue did not grant the request.[25]

In Saigon the new governor, Admiral Marie Jules Dupré, received a request for help from Dupuis. Tu Duc also asked for assistance, calling on Dupré to uphold the existing treaty and bring the arms dealer to terms. Fortified by Garnier's counsel on the commercial importance of Hanoi, Dupré cabled Paris. His report stated that Tonkin had been opened for commerce by Dupuis and that unless France moved now, China or a European nation might preempt the use of this attractive trade route to Yunnan. Paris replied that, while the government did not object to the occupation of Tonkin, Dupré was not to take action that would result in international complications. The response satisfied Dupré who then instructed Garnier to take command of 3 gunboats and approximately 200 men, to proceed to Hanoi, and open the Red River to French trade.[26]

---

[23] Buttinger, *Smaller Dragon.* pp. 362, 411, 414–15; Lancaster, *Emancipation of French Indochina*, p. 41; Hall, *History of South-East Asia*, p. 613.

[24] Sidney A. Staunton, *The War in Tong-King: Why the French are in Tong-King, and What they are doing there* (Boston: Cupples, Upham and Co., 1884), pp. 15–16; Buttinger, *Smaller Dragon*, pp. 366–71, 415.

[25] Hall, *History of South-East Asia*. p. 620; Staunton, *War in Tong-King*, p. 17.

[26] *Ibid.*, p. 21; Buttinger, *Smaller Dragon*, pp. 368, 416; Lancaster, *Emancipation of French Indochina*, p. 45.

Garnier and his small squadron sailed from Saigon in October 1873 and arrived in Hanoi on 5 November. After several futile attempts to negotiate with the mandarins, Garnier issued an ultimatum—either the king would agree to disarm the forces in the citadel of Hanoi and authorize the French to use the Red River for trade with Yunnan, or the lieutenant would resort to force. When Tu Duc rejected these demands, Garnier and his men stormed the citadel and captured the city on 20 November. His small force then occupied five other fortified towns, including Haiphong. One month later all the delta between Hanoi and the sea was under French control.

The French position was not yet secure. Chinese rebels and coastal pirates moved in on Garnier's lines, launching an attack on 21 December. Rallying his men, the lieutenant counterattacked, charging straight toward the enemy into an ambush and his death. The triumphant rebels cut off his head, an act guaranteed to outrage the French reinforcements who reached Hanoi four days later. Faced with certain defeat by the determined French, Tu Duc sent his emissaries to Saigon where they agreed to Admiral Dupré's terms in a treaty signed on 15 March 1874. Dupré recognized the sovereignty of the king. Tu Duc, for his part, agreed that his foreign policy would conform to that of France. The monarch also recognized the full sovereignty of France over six provinces in the south and acceded to the opening of the Red River to Yunnan for commerce. Finally, the king promised to respect freedom of worship for all Christians.[27]

In a conciliatory mood, and aware of the king's incapacity to maintain order in the face of widespread anarchy, the governor turned over to Tu Duc 5 gunboats, 100 small cannon, 1,000 rifles, and ammunition—to be used against bands such as the Black Flags. More importantly, he provided a naval and military mission to reorganize the king's fleet and army and to build bridges, roads, and other public works. But peace and order were hard to achieve, especially since Tu Duc followed a strategy of encouraging piracy against French shipping.[28]

When a revolt broke out in 1878, Tu Duc appealed to China for help in crushing the insurrection. Only too happy to demonstrate its role as lord and protector of Indochina, Peking sent two gunboats plus troops

[27] Teston and Percheron, *L'Indochine Moderne*, pp. 43–44; Hall, *History of South-East Asia*, pp. 621–22; Staunton, *War in Tong-King*, pp. 23–25; Buttinger, *Smaller Dragon*, p. 372.

[28] Teston and Percheron, *L'Indochina Moderne*, p. 44; Staunton, *War In Tong-King*, pp. 25–27; Hall, *History of South-East Asia*, pp. 622–23.

to help its nominal vassal defeat the insurgents. This challenge to the authority of a French protectorate could not be ignored. The French government responded by sending a naval force to Tonkin, this time under the command of Captain Henri Rivière. On 25 April, with three warships, a French landing force, and a detachment of Cochin Chinese riflemen, Rivière attacked and once again captured the citadel at Hanoi from the forces of Tu Duc. The Black Flags threatened to move on Hanoi. Leading 400 men against a Black Flag stronghold on the Red River just above Hanoi, Rivière followed Lieutenant Garnier's earlier route to Son Tay along the river bank. Like Garnier before him, Captain Rivière was killed in an ambush.[29]

In Paris, news of Rivière's death caused an immediate wave of indignation and a demand for action. In the French Chamber of Deputies, where debate had centered on whether or not to vote funds for an expedition to Indochina, the bill for Tonkin military appropriations passed unanimously. Premier Jules Ferry ordered that an imposing operation be mounted ostensibly against the Black Flags, but in actuality to establish a French protectorate. For this purpose, twenty-nine ships and craft and about 4,250 naval personnel were gathered at Hanoi. From France and New Caledonia came 4,000 infantry troops. With additional artillery forces, the army strength totaled 6,000. Rear Admiral Amédée Anatole Courbet commanded the naval forces, while General Alexandre Eugène Bouët was in charge of army troops.[30]

This impressive invasion force was ready for action by mid-August 1883, at which time Admiral Courbet sailed his ships south to the mouth of the Perfume River. Following familiar tactics, the squadron first bombarded the forts guarding the approach to Hue and then landed the troops. As a result of this action, the Vietnamese sued for peace.[31]

In the month before this French triumph, the death of the aging Tu Duc had generated a dynastic crisis. His successor, Hiep Hoa, signed a new treaty according France full rights of intervention and under which the king agreed to a French protectorate over Annam and Tonkin. The king retained his title but agreed to receive the French commissioner general for private, personal interviews, a right never before granted to any foreigner. The French now controlled the administration, levied taxes and customs,

---

[29] *Ibid.;* Staunton, *War in Tong-King,* pp. 27, 38–40.

[30] Thomas F. Power, Jr., *Jules Ferry and the Renaissance of French Imperialism* (New York: Kings Crown Press, 1944), p. 164; Staunton, *War in Tong-King,* p. 42.

[31] *Ibid.*

manned the forts and military posts on all rivers, and exercised extraterritorial jurisdiction in the courts. As for the French Navy, the treaty made
clear that France alone would suppress the Black Flags and patrol the
Red River.[32]

Following a dispute among the local French administrators, the government placed Admiral Courbet in supreme military command and sent
more troops to Tonkin.[33] With the addition of control over Annam and
Tonkin to that of Cochin China and Cambodia, the greatest of France's
overseas colonies was founded, and senior French naval officers were reminded anew of the navy's responsibility for security of the waters surrounding Indochina and the lines of communication to France.

Limited War between France and China

French consolidation of their position in Tonkin challenged traditional
Chinese suzerainty over their former tributary. A vest-pocket naval war
settled the issue. The Chinese and foreign press carried accounts describing
the strong war feeling in Peking along with reports of military and naval
activity and the movement of troops to the Tonkin border. Twice in June
1884 French and Chinese troops clashed in Tonkin, thus paving the way
for the commander of French forces in Indochina, Admiral Courbet, backed
by Premier Ferry, to announce that France would neither yield her protectorate nor control of the Red River. On 13 July 1884 France presented
an ultimatum to China demanding the immediate withdrawal of its troops
from Tonkin, the payment of an indemnity of 200 million francs, and an
answer to these demands within a week. The Chinese failed to comply.
Rather than attempting a land campaign, Premier Ferry ordered Admiral
Courbet to sail north ready to take retaliatory action.[34]

When Peking still demonstrated that it would not relinquish its suzerainty
over Tonkin, the French squadron was ordered to force an agreement. After
an unsuccessful attack against the port of Keelung on the northern coast
of Formosa, Admiral Courbet steamed to Foochow, where he destroyed the
Chinese southern fleet as it lay at anchor. Subsequently, he returned to
Formosa, and his forces repeatedly attacked the Keelung forts until they

---

[32] *Ibid.,* pp. 42–43; Hall, *History of South-East Asia,* p. 625; Power, *Jules Ferry,* p. 166.
[33] Staunton, *War In Tong-King,* p. 43.
[34] Staunton, *War in Tong-King,* p. 45; Power, *Jules Ferry,* pp. 172–73.

finally capitulated in March 1885. Soon afterwards, Courbet occupied the Pescadores.[35]

Sensing the futility of further fighting, Peking recognized the French claims. Laos, the last Chinese tributary in Indochina, also was destined to become a protectorate, since France claimed that it had "inherited" Vietnamese suzerainty over the territory. This claim resulted in a short conflict with Siam which then relinquished its claim to Laos. The issue was settled when China concluded a convention with France in 1895 recognizing French hegemony in Laos.[36]

Although all of Indochina was now part of the French empire overseas, the arduous task of persuading the people to accept French rule still lay ahead. French forces in Indochina spent the last fifteen years of the nineteenth century attempting to establish order and introducing French institutions. Resistance and rebellion continued even after the French were firmly entrenched. Most of the fighting took place in the mountains or deltas and was led by the mandarins or by local chieftains.[37]

For French troops to reach various points in the delta regions, it was necessary to travel via the inland waterways in naval river gunboats. Predecessors of the "brown water" navies of the next century, these *canonnieres* gave mobility to the French forces, lent authority to their presence, and assured essential logistic support to field units. The river gunboats were indeed a key element in maintaining the French presence in Indochina.

Another visible element of France's status as a great colonial power was its Far Eastern Fleet which by 1900 numbered six cruisers and eleven sloops and gunboats. The shallow-draft, armed sloops were well suited for detached duty on foreign stations.[38]

Against the backdrop of the preceding 2,000 years, the history of Vietnam to 1900 revealed that the maritime element had been decisive. Chinese seapower, particularly during the Ming era, provided one means of gaining and maintaining suzerainty over kingdoms to the south. Later, technical advances in shipbuilding and navigation, coupled with European acquisitiveness and zeal for evangelism, brought Western vessels carrying traders and

---

[35] *Ibid,* pp. 174–76; Hall, *History of South-East Asia,* p. 626.

[36] Buttinger, *Smaller Dragon.* pp. 380–81, 421.

[37] Frank N. Trager, *Why Viet Nam?* (New York: Frederick A. Praeger, 1966), p. 33.

[38] John Leyland, ed., *The Naval Annual, 1900* (Portsmouth, England: J. Griffin and Co., 1900), p. 66.

French and Russian ships at Saigon, late 1880s.

missionaries to Indochina. A small navy, created with the help of French seamen, provided Annam with the means of completing the conquest of Cochin China and the establishment of rule, for a brief period, over all of Vietnam. Sent to protect their nationals, the French Navy played crucial roles in the forcible breaching of the wall of isolation erected by the Vietnamese leaders to defend against expansionist foreign governments. Naval actions gained the acquiescence of China to the establishment of French control over what became known as Indochina. Finally, consolidation of French rule in Indochina flowed from a maritime strategy supported by a combat-ready naval force capable of conducting operations promptly, moving troops swiftly to trouble spots, controlling the sea lanes and trade routes adjacent to Indochina, and operating on inland waters. As long as this seapower remained strong in the Far East, French interests in Indochina flourished.

CHAPTER II

Impact Of The Shifting Balance Of Seapower, 1940-1945

Events over the first four and a half decades of the twentieth century, including two World Wars, would pave the way for the Vietnam conflict. The watershed that was the First World War added stimulus to colonial aspirations for independence and led to the establishment of an Indochinese Communist Party linked to an international movement. Between the wars, the shifting balance of seapower in the Far East would be exploited by Japan to project power by sea onto the continent of Asia and into Southeast Asia. As in earlier history, Vietnam's strategic importance would again be revealed. This time it would be used as a stepping stone in the Japanese conquest of Southeast Asia and play a key role in the events leading to the Pearl Harbor attack. American and Allied victory in the basically maritime war in the Pacific Ocean and in particular in the South China Sea would lead to the elimination of the remnants of French control in Vietnam and then the Japanese surrender, thus providing revolutionary forces with a favorable opportunity to seize power at the end of World War II.

The turn of the century had witnessed the growth of a modern Japanese Navy. By soundly defeating the Chinese Navy in the Sino-Japanese War of 1894–1895, Japan cleared the way for the acquisition of Korea, Formosa, and the Pescadore Islands. Ten years later, the Japanese victory in the Russo-Japanese War of 1904–1905 dramatically demonstrated that Japan was now a first-rate naval power.

As a result of the extraordinary difficulties encountered in the deployment of Vice Admiral Zinovi P. Rozhdestvenski's squadron from the Baltic to the Far East, future Soviet leaders learned the importance of strategically located bases.[1] The last stop of the squadron was made, quite logically, on

---

[1] Sergei G. Gorshkov, *Red Star Rising at Sea* (Annapolis, Md.: United States Naval Institute, 1974), pp. 33–37.

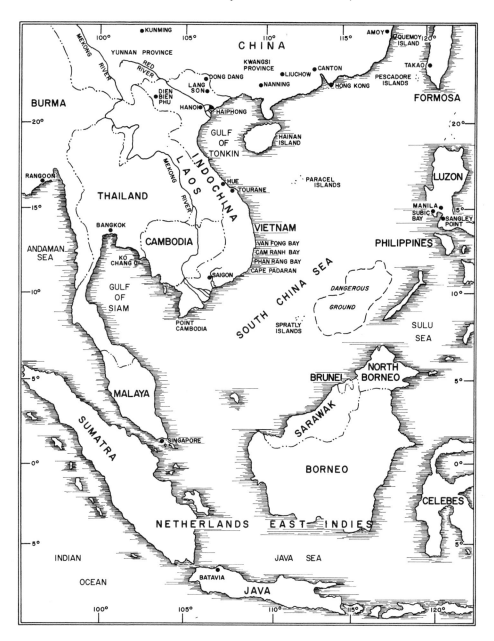

the coast of Vietnam. Rozhdestvenski anchored on 14 April 1905 in Cam Ranh Bay, an extraordinarily fine, large harbor. After the ships had spent a week there, Japan's diplomatic protests led France to send a cruiser from Saigon to request the departure of the Russians, who shifted their anchorage fifty miles northward to Van Fong Bay before continuing the cruise. At dawn on 27 May 1905, while passing through the Strait of Tsushima, the Russians met Admiral Heihachiro Togo's fleet in an engagement which ended in disaster for Czarist Russia and a glorious victory for Japan. Later, in the Vietnam War, Cam Ranh Bay would be the site of a vast American logistic complex and the headquarters of the United States Navy's Coastal Surveillance Force.[2]

A further indication that the balance of power in the Far East was shifting was provided by the Anglo-Japanese Alliance signed in 1902, modified in 1905, and renewed in 1911. Since Britain considered its security needs in European waters to be paramount, and the alliance treaty contained assurances that British interests in Asia would be protected, Great Britain withdrew major portions of its fleet from the Far East in the first decade of the twentieth century. The net effect of the alliance and the transfer of British ships was to allow a freer hand for Japan—to whom Britain tacitly relinquished, for a time at least, naval superiority in the Orient.[3]

The outbreak of World War I further eroded Western naval power in the Pacific. Beset with heavy demands for men and ships in the Mediterranean and in the Atlantic, the French government recalled all but 2,000 of its troops and a small naval contingent from Indochina.[4] At the same time, the reduction of German forces in the Far East provided tempting opportunities to Japan, which had entered World War I in accordance with the provisions of the Anglo-Japanese Alliance. Losing no time, Japanese task forces captured the German-held Marshall, Caroline, and Mariana island groups in the fall of 1914. Then, a Japanese squadron appeared off Tsingtao, China, and seized the German enclaves on the Shantung Peninsula.

The Vietnamese Revolutionary Movement

Of the many direct and indirect results of World War I, two in particular

---

[2] Edwin B. Hooper, *Mobility, Support, Endurance: A Story of Naval Operational Logistics in the Vietnam War, 1965–1968* (Washington: Naval History Division, GPO, 1972), pp. 157–59.

[3] William R. Braisted, *The United States Navy in the Pacific, 1897–1909* (Austin, Texas: University of Texas Press, 1958), pp. 142–43, 183–84; William R. Braisted, *The United States Navy in the Pacific, 1909–1922* (Austin, Texas: University of Texas Press, 1971), pp. 14–15; Arthur J. Marder, *The Anatomy of British Sea Power: A History of British Naval Policy in the Pre-Dreadnought Era, 1880–1905* (New York: Alfred A. Knopf, 1940), pp. 450–53.

[4] Jan Romein, *The Asian Century: A History of Modern Nationalism in Asia* (Berkeley, Calif.: University of California Press, 1962), p. 137.

would influence the chain of events leading to the post-World War II Vietnam conflict and America's involvement. The first was the stimulus to nationalist aspirations within colonies of the European powers. The second was the transformation of a revolutionary Marxist movement into a pragmatic Communist Party, in control of Russia and in a position of leadership over the international Communist movement.

When he asked Congress for a declaration of war in 1917, President Woodrow Wilson reiterated the views of many of his predecessors by associating American national policy with the self-determination of nationalities. According to Wilson, the United States was entering the war:

> for democracy, for the right of those who submit to authority to have a voice in their own Governments, for the rights and liberties of small nations, [and] for a universal dominion of right by such a concert of free peoples as shall bring peace and safety to all nations and make the world itself at last free.[5]

Even if such idealistic goals were not entirely attainable in the world at that time, they endowed the President's decision with a higher purpose, provided inspirational motivation to the American people, and encouraged the support of others. Aside from the utility of the statement, in connection with World War I, it gave expression to a periodic theme of United States policy since the era of the American Revolution.

After the signing of the armistice in 1918, American representatives at the Paris Peace Conference espoused the cause of self-determination for peoples ruled by others. One effect was further encouragement of nationalist movements. Pursuance of similar objectives at the end of World War II would be one of the determinants of United States policy with regard to European colonies. Efforts to accelerate decolonization would have a significant influence on the course of events in the early phases of the Vietnam conflict.

Following the collapse of the Czarist government and the subsequent Bolshevist takeover from the provisional Kerensky government, the Leninist group had gained control of a country of vast natural resources and a large population. In addition to providing a successful example for Marxist revolutionists elsewhere, the Soviet Union became a base for the support

---

[5] "For Declaration of War Against Germany," in Ray S. Baker and William E. Dodd, eds., *War and Peace: Presidential Messages, Addresses, and Public Papers (1917–1924)* of *The Public Papers of Woodrow Wilson* (New York: Harper and Brothers Publishers, 1927), Vol. I, p. 16.

and guidance of their activities. Fully as important, with regard to the long-range effects on the world, were the methods devised by Lenin for exercising political control and the application of power. Lenin's concepts of organization, his use of the Communist Party as a disciplined body for exerting authority, his combination of force with other means of influence to gain his ends, and his utilization of Marxist rhetoric to unify the movement were embraced by Communists in other lands. With the overthrow of capitalism an avowed goal, and expansion of Russian influence abroad a less visible but also important objective, the Communist Party of the Union of Soviet Socialist Republics spearheaded an offensive which, at varying levels of intensity and with diverse means, exploited turmoil in many places. Subsequent American decisions with regard to military assistance and more active involvement in the Vietnam conflict would hinge on judgements as to the relationships of the Vietnamese revolutionaries to the Soviet-led movement.

Founded in July 1919, the Third Communist International (Comintern) provided a mechanism for organizing Communist revolutions abroad. One inviting target was the colonial establishment of "capitalist" nations. In announcing the Comintern's objectives, Lenin criticized socialist groups in capitalist nations which "fail to wage a revolutionary struggle within 'their own' colonies for the *overthrow* of 'their own' bourgeoisie, which do not systematically assist the *revolutionary* work which has already commenced everywhere in the colonies, which do not send arms and literature to the revolutionary parties in the colonies. . . ." [6]

The story of the Communist movement in Indochina is closely intertwined with the life of Ho Chi Minh, who for so many years was to lead the Communist Party in Vietnam. A member of an educated family, Ho was born in 1890 and named Nguyen Sinh Cung. Years later the young man assumed the alias Nguyen Ai Quoc ("Nguyen the Patriot"). While in France during the early 1920s he took the name Nguyen O Phap ("Nguyen Who Hates the French") before finally assuming the name Ho Chi Minh ("He Who Aspires to Enlightenment"). [7]

---

[6] Quoted in Vladimir I. Lenin, *Selected Works* (New York: International Publishers, 1943), Vol. X, p. 46.

[7] David G. Marr, *Vietnamese Anticolonialism: 1885–1925* (Berkeley, Calif.: University of California Press, 1971), p. 253; Ho Chi Minh, *On Revolution: Selected Writings, 1920–66,* ed. Bernard B. Fall (New York: Frederick A. Praeger, 1967), pp. viii-x. At least twenty aliases used by Ho have been identified; see King C. Chen, *Vietnam and China, 1938–1954* (Princeton, N.J.: Princeton University Press, 1969), p. 37–38.

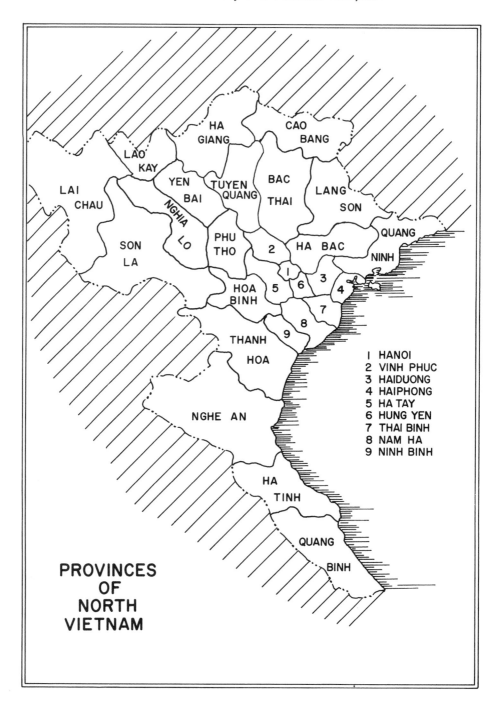

PROVINCES
OF
NORTH
VIETNAM

1 HANOI
2 VINH PHUC
3 HAIDUONG
4 HAIPHONG
5 HA TAY
6 HUNG YEN
7 THAI BINH
8 NAM HA
9 NINH BINH

Ho grew up in Nghe An Province just north of the 17th parallel. His father was a teacher and civil servant who at one time served as an official in the Ministry of Rites. Ho's mother died when he was ten years old. As a youth Ho attended the *Lycée* at Hue where he pursued a program of French studies. In the late nineteenth century his great uncle, a nationalist, had been captured by French troops.

Ho was forced to leave school after his father was removed from his government position by the French. Shortly thereafter, Ho signed on board a French merchant ship as a messboy, serving in that capacity for two years. When World War I broke out he was living in London working at menial jobs. Here he made contact with Fabian socialist groups, closely observed the Irish uprising, and mingled with members of the Chinese Overseas Workers' Association. In 1917 Ho moved to Paris where he met intellectuals, trade unionists, and pacifists. Soon afterward, he began writing articles for *Le Populaire, La Révolution Proletarienne,* and *L'Humanité* on the subject of independence for Vietnam.[8] Ho made his presence in Paris known as World War I drew to a close. In early 1919, Nguyen Ai Quoc, as he then was known, appeared as a spokesman for Vietnamese nationalism at Versailles where, as one of many undistinguished representatives of smaller nations, he hovered on the fringes of the peace conference. His attempts to present a memorandum to the major powers, requesting basic liberties for Vietnamese, proved unsuccessful.

After the signing of the Versailles Treaty, Ho served as one of the representatives at the Eighteenth Congress of the French Socialist Party, which approved the resolution to found the French Communist Party and affiliate it with the Third International. The French Communist Party later arranged to send him as a delegate to Moscow where he was trained in revolutionary methods at the "University of the Toilers of the East." In December 1924, Ho (alias Ly Thuy) arrived in Canton, China, where he served both as an interpreter for Soviet advisors to the Kuomintang, the nationalist political party of China, and as the leader of a small group of expatriate Vietnamese Communists.[9]

Probably Ho's most notable early work was accomplished when, as a member of the Comintern's committee on colonies, he helped to establish the League of East Asian Oppressed Peoples. By 1925 Ho and his followers,

---

[8] Jean Lacouture, *Ho Chi Minh: A Political Biography* (New York: Random House, 1968), pp. 17–18; Fall, *Two Viet-Nams,* p. 87; Marr, *Vietnamese Anticolonialism,* pp. 253–56.

[9] Fall, *Two Viet-Nams,* pp. 88–93; Chen, *Vietnam and China,* pp. 14–23.

still in Canton, had formed the Association of Revolutionary Annamite Youth, some of whose members returned to Vietnam to recruit other followers and set up clandestine political cells. One of the steps taken at this time was the elimination of the greatly respected nationalist leader Phan Boi Chau, now considered by Ho to be a formidable rival. Allegedly, Ho arranged to deliver Chau to the French Security Service for a reward of 100,000 piasters.[10]

Ho Chi Minh and his comrades took a major organizational step on 3 February 1930 when they merged the Communist groups of the north, center, and south of Vietnam into the Communist Party of Indochina. The party then qualified as a national section of the Comintern. Hardly had the party been formed when it launched an offensive. On 1 May, the Communists began to organize mass riots and foment unrest in parts of Annam and Cochin China, efforts that continued into 1933. Predictably, Communist terrorism bred counteraction by the French. The French success in quashing the rebellion was a serious setback to the Indochinese Communist Party and one that almost proved fatal. Ho himself has described the years 1931–1933 as a period of disintegration.[11]

Following these abortive Communist revolts, Ho ordered the party to go underground. He soon was apprehended by the British police in Hong Kong. The French authorities previously had asked for his extradition to Indochina where a death sentence awaited him. Since they viewed Ho as a political refugee, the British refused, Ho then was transferred to a Hong Kong prison hospital because of a worsening of the tuberculosis from which he long had suffered. The last entry made in Ho's file by the French security police read: "died in Hong Kong prison, 1933."[12]

Actually, the "dead" Ho had been slipped out of the prison hospital in 1932 by a British lawyer named Frank Loseby and placed on board a boat bound for Amoy, where he hid for six months. In 1933 Ho resumed his political activities in Shanghai. Some time later, to escape Chiang Kai-shek's hunt for Communists, Ho boarded a Soviet ship which sailed to

---

[10] *Ibid.*, p. 18; Ellen J. Hammer, *Vietnam: Yesterday and Today* (New York: Holt, Rinehart and Winston, 1966), p. 129; Hall, *History of South-East Asia*, p. 719; Marr, *Vietnamese Anticolonialism*, p. 260.

[11] Ho, *On Revolution*, pp. 127, 208; Ralph Smith, *Viet-Nam and the West* (Ithaca, N.Y.: Cornell University Press, 1971), pp. 105–07; Giap, *Banner of People's War*, p. 8; Joseph Buttinger, *From Colonialism to the Vietminh*, Vol. I of *Vietnam: A Dragon Embattled* (New York: Frederick A. Praeger, 1967), pp. 217–20.

[12] Quoted in Lacouture, *Ho Chi Minh*, pp. 62–64.

Vladivostok. From there Ho traveled by train to Moscow. In Moscow, under the name of Livov, he studied at the Lenin Institute, where he also taught Vietnamese history to students in the Asiatic department.[13]

A change in strategy of the world Communist movement gave the Communists in Indochina the chance to accumulate powers on a wider basis. In 1934 the Soviet Union pressed for "collective security" against the threat of aggression by Germany and Japan. The Seventh World Congress of the Comintern was convened in August 1935. Concerned with fascism —particularly its advent to power in Germany—and the danger of an attack on the U.S.S.R., the congress declared that the main and immediate task was to establish a "united fighting front." While long-range goals continued to be the overthrow of capitalism and the victory of the pro-letarian revolution, the united front tactics were to be applied in a new manner in the struggle against fascism. It was deemed the duty of Com-munist parties to seek to "reach agreements with the organizations of the working people of various political trends for joint action on a factory, local, district, national, and international scale." The parties were to partici-pate in election campaigns on a common platform and a common ticket with the anti-fascist front, while reserving for themselves freedom to use the methods of political agitation and criticism. The congress considered it "necessary to draw the widest masses into the national liberation move-ment" in the colonial and semi-colonial countries.[14]

In an effort to create a friendly accord with France, the Comintern directed the French Communist Party to cease its subversive activities against the French armed forces. A popular front government temporarily came into power in France, and a Franco-Russian alliance was signed in 1936.

Ho Chi Minh adapted his party's line to the new Comintern policy, stating:

> For the time being, the Party cannot put forth too high a demand (national independence, parliament, etc.). To do so is to enter the Japanese fascists' scheme. It should only claim for democratic rights, freedom of organization, freedom of assembly, freedom of press and freedom of speech, general amnesty for all political detainees, and struggle for legalization of the Party.

He sought to form a broad "Democratic National Front," including "progressive French" as well as Indochinese "bourgeoisie" and "toiling

---

[13] Lacouture, *Ho Chi Minh*, pp. 64–65; Chen, *Vietnam and China*, pp. 28–30.

[14] Quoted in *VII Congress of the Communist International* (Moscow: Foreign Languages Pub-lishing House, 1939), pp. 570–86.

people." The party was to "win over the elements that can be won over and neutralize those which can be neutralized." Ho Chi Minh stressed that the Indochinese Democratic Front should work closely with the French Popular Front and the French Communist Party. He also urged that the party show itself to the people to be the most active and loyal organ, and thus win the leading position in the Indochinese Democratic Front.[15]

Leaders of the Indochinese Democratic Front in Tonkin were Pham Van Dong, future premier of the Democratic Republic of Vietnam, and Vo Nguyen Giap who, as commander of the North Vietnamese Army in 1954, defeated the French at Dien Bien Phu. According to Giap:

> Our Party [during the 1936–1939 period] cleverly combined the overt, legal, semi-overt, and semi-legal struggles with secret and illegal activities and started a vigorous movement of political struggle in the cities and rural areas, to oppose colonialist reactionaries and the feudalistic king-official clique, to demand freedom, democracy, and a better life, to oppose aggressive fascism, and to protect world peace.[16]

Ho had remained in Moscow since 1933. In the fall of 1938 he returned to China where he wrote articles, using the pen name P. C. Lin, for publication in Vietnam, and was otherwise active in behalf of the Communist revolutionary cause in Indochina.

Japanese Seapower and Indochina

In the decade of the 1930s Japan applied increasing pressure in Southeast Asia. In 1931–1932, the Japanese Navy supported military operations against China in response to that country's boycott of Japanese goods. Aerial bombing of the civilian population, shore bombardment, and infantry actions resulted in thousands of Chinese deaths before the Japanese withdrew their forces. In November 1936, Japan signed an agreement with Germany to cooperate in combating activities of the Communist International.

The following July a skirmish between Chinese troops and a Japanese military detachment stationed near Peking provided Japan with an excuse

---

[15] Ho, *On Revolution,* pp. 130–31.

[16] Giap, *Banner of People's War,* p. 8; Joseph Buttinger, *Vietnam: A Political History* (New York: Frederick A. Praeger, 1968), p. 182.

for outright war. The Japanese immediately blockaded the Chinese coast. However, a land route into China used for supplying badly needed munitions, which began at the French Indochina port of Haiphong and crossed the border into Yunnan Province, remained open. In August 1937, Japan protested the French shipment of munitions through Indochina. A concerned French government sought to placate Tokyo by restricting supplies destined for China to gasoline, trucks, and textiles.[17]

Increasingly it became evident to American policy-makers that the future of Southeast Asia hinged on the ability of Britain and the United States to counterbalance the naval might of Japan. Informal Anglo-American staff conversations, held in London during December 1937 and January 1938, explored the possibility of American and British naval cooperation in containing Japanese expansion. Although no agreement was reached, the discussions dealt with the concept that the Royal Navy would base major forces at Singapore, while the United States Navy would establish a concentration at Pearl Harbor.[18]

The European colonies in Southeast Asia were of particular importance to Japan, both as a source of raw materials, particularly oil, and as a lucrative market for manufactured goods. Late in 1938, in announcing the basis on which Japan expected to make peace, Prince Fuminaro Konoye, the Japanese Prime Minister, spoke not only of military occupation and the development of an economic protectorate in China, but also of the establishment of a "New Order in East Asia." Later the Japanese referred to the "Greater East Asia Co-Prosperity Sphere." [19]

That same year, as part of her continuing attempts to dominate China, Japan advanced south by sea, launching amphibious operations to capture Hankow and Canton. French apprehension for the safety of Indochina mounted in February 1939, when a Japanese naval task force landed troops on the island of Hainan at the entrance to the Gulf of Tonkin. A month later, when the Japanese occupied the nominally French-controlled

[17] For a more detailed description of the Japanese-French negotiation, see Buttinger, *From Colonialism to the Vietminh,* p. 228.

[18] Samuel E. Morison, *The Rising Sun in the Pacific, 1931–April 1942,* Vol. III of *History of United States Naval Operations in World War II* (Boston: Little, Brown and Co., 1948), p. 49; John McVickar Haight, Jr., "Franklin D. Roosevelt and a Naval Quarantine of Japan," *Pacific Historical Review,* XL (May 1971), pp. 203–06.

[19] Richard W. Leopold, *The Growth of American Foreign Policy: A History* (New York: Alfred A. Knopf, 1962), p. 538; Togo Shigenori, *The Cause of Japan* (New York: Simon and Schuster, 1956), pp. 37–42.

Spratly Islands, 300 miles southeast of Indochina, it became clear to France that its Indochinese colonies and protectorates were indeed in jeopardy. Evidence that Japan was furnishing military aid to Thailand, so that the latter could regain territory that then was part of the French protectorate in Cambodia, confirmed these fears.[20]

At this juncture, Britain, facing the increasing probability of war, asked the United States to reopen staff conversations. In May 1939, a British officer informed the Navy's War Plans Division in Washington that the need for naval ships in the Mediterranean would prevent the deployment of a battle force to Singapore. The British suggested that the United States undertake the defense of the Malaya barrier. No longer could American planners count on substantial British naval assistance in the Far East.[21]

On the international scene, the Communists temporarily abandoned the anti-fascist theme when the Soviet Union signed a treaty of non-aggression with Germany on 23 August 1939. Following the German invasion of Poland eight days later and the start of World War II, France outlawed the Communist Party at home and in its colonies. The French Security Service then carried out mass arrests in Cochin China. An uprising initiated by the Communists on 22 November 1940, was crushed by the French who employed troops, police, and aircraft against the insurgents.[22]

At the outbreak of war, France had in Far Eastern waters a small force consisting of 2 cruisers, 6 sloops, 1 surveying ship, and 2 additional auxiliaries, as well as a number of river gunboats.[23] Although the United States Navy was not present in strength in the Far East, it had the only major force in the Pacific capable of challenging Japanese control of the sea.

When Hitler overran Holland and France in 1940, he created almost perfect circumstances for the Japanese to seize then largely defenseless French Indochina. Just prior to the fall of France, Japan demanded that the government newly installed at Vichy terminate all military shipments to China via Haiphong and that a Japanese military control commission be stationed at the Vietnamese-Chinese border to enforce the ban. An impotent French government conceded these demands on 20 June. On 30 August, Vichy recognized Japan's "pre-eminent position" in the Far

---

[20] Buttinger, *Vietnam: A Political History*, p. 185.

[21] Morison, *Rising Sun in the Pacific*, p. 49.

[22] Lancaster, *Emancipation of French Indochina*, p. 85.

[23] Jacques Mordal, *The Navy in Indochina*, trans., N.L. Williams and A.W. Atkinson, 1967, Naval History Division copy (Paris: Amiot-Dumont, 1953), pp. 3–4.

East and agreed to its occupation of certain military transportation centers in Tonkin. Three days later Marshal Henri Philippe Pétain, French head of state, authorized negotiations to establish the terms for Japan's entry into Indochina. When the French colonial governor, Vice Admiral Jean Decoux, protested, Pétain wired him to comply and "give an example of discipline to all Frenchmen." [24]

In the ensuing discussions held at Hanoi, between General Issaku Nishihara and General Maurice Martin, the French general initially followed a policy of delay hoping for a United States naval demonstration that might persuade Japan to ease its demands. The demonstration never occurred. So, an agreement was signed on 22 September 1940 allowing 6,000 Japanese troops to be stationed in Indochina, while another 25,000 were permitted to transit the country. [25]

The primary Japanese objectives were, quite logically, the two most strategic transportation points in northern Indochina—Haiphong and Dong Dang-Lang Son. Despite the agreement, or possibly in ignorance of it, Japanese armed forces struck against both. Haiphong, the major port of Tonkin and the sea terminal for river, road, and rail transportation to the Yunnan and Kwangsi Provinces of China, was bombed. Dong Dang and nearby Lang Son, which controlled the road and rail routes to Nanning and a junction of Indochina's Route 4 paralleling the border, were attacked from China by Japanese troops. All French resistance to the occupation had ceased by 25 September 1940. [26]

The Franco-Thai Naval "War"

A sequel to France's fall in 1940 was another capitulation after a border war with Thailand. In the summer and fall of 1940, taking advantage of the plight of the French and with the encouragement of the Japanese, the Thais demanded the cession of certain Laotian territories on the east side of the Mekong River, as well as three provinces in western Cambodia.

---

[24] Quoted in Ellen J. Hammer, *The Struggle for Indochina: 1940–1955* (Stanford, Calif.: Stanford University Press, 1954), pp. 16–21; Lancaster, *Emancipation of French Indochina,* pp. 91–92; Fall, *Two Viet-Nams,* pp. 42–43.

[25] *Ibid.,* pp. 43–44.

[26] Hammer, *Struggle for Indochina,* p. 22; For events from June through October 1940, see U.S., State Department, *The Far East,* Vol. IV of *Foreign Relations of the United States: Diplomatic Papers: 1940* (Washington: GPO, 1955), pp. 23–180.

All of these areas were claimed as rightfully belonging to Thailand. Japan supported the Thais. Thus emboldened, the Thai prime minister ordered his troops into battle along the Indochinese-Thai frontier in November 1940.[27]

Admiral Decoux decided to mount a naval attack against the Thais. The French force included 1 cruiser (*La Motte Picquet*), 2 large and 2 small sloops, and 8 seaplanes. After assessing the situation, the squadron commander, Rear Admiral Jules Terraux, ordered a surprise attack against the Thai naval force, which comprised 2 coast guard vessels, 2 gunboats, approximately 16 torpedo boats, and other miscellaneous ships and craft located off Ko Chang, an island in the Gulf of Siam.

At dawn on 17 January 1941, the five French ships struck the unsuspecting Thai ships with repeated salvos of gunfire. *La Motte Picquet* also launched three torpedoes, one of which hit a large torpedo boat. After an engagement lasting one hour and forty-five minutes, the French withdrew, leaving behind three torpedo boats and two coast guard vessels of the Thai squadron sunk or destroyed. The Thai air arm, which could have been a threat to the French, appeared only belatedly because of difficulties in establishing radio communications with the surface force. Later in the morning several Thai aircraft did manage to harass the retiring French ships but scored no hits in their attack.[28]

Five days later the Japanese commander in Hanoi advised the French governor general that Japanese warships would proceed along the coasts of Indochina and Thailand and advised him to prevent any incidents from occurring. Following negotiations in Tokyo, the French, on 9 May 1941, ceded to Thailand the territory demanded in Cambodia and Laos.[29]

The small French naval force which returned in triumph to Vietnam slowly dwindled. It had ceased to be a fighting force of any consequence in the Far East.

---

[27] Hammer, *Struggle for Indochina*, p. 25; Mordal, *Navy in Indochina*, p. 21; James V. Martin, Jr., "Thai-American Relations in World War II," *The Journal of Asian Studies*, XXII (Aug. 1963), pp. 452–55.

[28] Mordal, *Navy in Indochina*, pp. 19–49; Hammer, *Struggle for Indochina*, pp. 25–26.

[29] *Ibid.*, p. 26; U.S., State Department, *The Far East*, Vol. V. of *Foreign Relations of the United States: Diplomatic Papers: 1941* (Washington: GPO, 1956), pp. 38–41, 147.

The Viet Minh

Ho returned to Tonkin in February 1941 and exercised his leadership from clandestine locations in the north. He convened a meeting of the Central Committee of the Communist Party of Vietnam on 10 May. The conference lasted until the 19th, by which time the committee decided on a new strategy highlighting the slogan "national liberation." Further, this body established the Viet Minh, changing the names of various mass organizations to "Associations for National Salvation," and decided to step up preparations for an insurrection to be undertaken at the most propitious moment. Decisions were later made to build guerrilla bases and to strengthen leadership of the military and para-military forces. In "a letter from abroad," written soon after the meeting, Ho Chi Minh called for united action to overthrow the Japanese and the French as a means toward achieving victory for "Vietnam's Revolution" and "the World's Revolution." [30] Responding to the call, the Vietnamese Communists staged another uprising against the French on 6 June 1941. Again the Communist effort was suppressed.

When Germany invaded Russia later that month, Soviet foreign policy shifted once more. It was established that the immediate task was to defeat the Axis powers through the combined action of the Soviet Union and its allies. To that end, the whole-hearted support of Communist parties was sought and the Comintern was dissolved.[31]

The 50,000 French and colonial military personnel in Indochina, and the region's 23 million civilian inhabitants, including 40,000 Europeans, faced the bleak future of living under a *de facto* Japanese occupation. On 6 May 1941, Japan and France signed a treaty revealing the commercial benefits that Japan expected to obtain from Indochina. Under its provisions all rice, corn, rubber, coal, and other commodities, which formerly had been exported, were reserved exclusively for Japan and the Japanese occupation forces.[32]

In addition to obtaining these concessions, there were other advantages gained by Japan. Not only were the routes from Haiphong to China blocked, but the Japanese had obtained a Southeast Asian port for their fleet, at

---

[30] *Ibid.,* pp. 51–52; Pham Van Dong, *25 Years of National Struggle and Construction* (Hanoi: Foreign Languages Publishing House, 1970).

[31] Robert V. Daniels, ed., *A Documentary History of Communism* (New York: Random House, 1960), Vol. II, pp. 129–32.

[32] Hammer, *Struggle for Indochina,* pp. 11–14; Buttinger, *Vietnam: A Political History,* p. 189.

Cam Ranh Bay. Only 715 miles from Manila, the bay was centrally located for naval attacks against the Philippines, Borneo, the Netherlands East Indies, Malaya, and Thailand. Furthermore, Cam Ranh Bay provided a well-located base from which to exercise control of the South China Sea.

In persuading the Vichy government to cooperate with them, the Japanese shrewdly satisfied the French desire to maintain some semblance of authority. By retaining nominal power in Indochina, France preserved civic order, thus allowing the Japanese to reap the advantages of occupation with a minimum of effort. Later in World War II the Japanese Army began to "protect" Vietnamese nationalists from the French police. The occupation forces also imported Japanese teachers, cultural counselors, and propaganda officers to win over the Vietnamese people.[33]

Indochina and the Road to Pearl Harbor

As events in the Pacific moved swiftly toward general war, the Japanese occupation of strategically important Indochina became one of the major issues dividing the United States and Japan. In July 1941, the Japanese foreign minister announced that Japan and Vichy had reached an agreement on the joint protection of Indochina. Soon afterward the Japanese demanded the right to occupy airfields in southern Indochina and to use the port facilities at Tourane, Saigon, and Cam Ranh Bay for their fleet. Unlike the 1940 actions, these new demands could not be justified as necessary for cutting off the flow of materials to China. Instead, they portended a deeper drive into Southeast Asia. The American reaction in the summer of 1941 was to freeze Japanese assets in the United States and to enact other economic curbs.[34]

In Imperial Conferences on 2 July and 6 September 1941, the Japanese government made important decisions that would affect the course of negotiations with the United States. The leadership decided not to "decline war with Britain and America" if the United States failed to meet Japanese demands relating to the "Greater East Asia Co-Prosperity Sphere." To these ends the use of French Indochina was considered indispensable.[35]

---

[33] *Ibid.,* pp. 183, 191–93; Hammer, *Struggle for Indochina,* pp. 31–33.

[34] U.S., State Department, *Foreign Relations of the United States, Japan: 1931–1941* (Washington: GPO, 1943), Vol. II, pp. 266–67, 318–22; Togo Shigenori, *Cause of Japan,* p. 51; Lancaster, *Emancipation of French Indochina,* p. 95.

[35] Togo Shigenori, *Cause of Japan,* pp. 351–55, contains the full text of the decision.

On 20 November Special Envoy Saburo Kurusu and Admiral Kichisaburo Nomura, Ambassador to the United States, presented Washington with what proved to be Japan's final offer. Japan proposed to withdraw its troops from southern Indochina and to reposition them in the north in return for the practice of a non-discriminatory trade policy by the United States and the cessation of American military aid to China. Moreover, Kurusu and Nomura claimed that, when Japan had achieved peace in China, all troops would be withdrawn from Indochina and no further advances by the Japanese armed forces would be made into Southeast Asia. This arrangement fell far short of satisfying American policy-makers.

A Japanese carrier force was already on its way toward Hawaii when the Japanese received Secretary of State Cordell Hull's reply of 26 November 1941. Hull demanded, among other things, that Japan withdraw ground, naval, air, and police forces from China and Indochina. The note also called for Japan to conclude with the American, British, Chinese, Dutch, and Thai governments a pledge to "respect the territorial integrity of French Indochina. . . ." Further, the communication proposed that Japan, along with the United States, "give up all extraterritorial rights in China" and endeavor to obtain the agreement of the British and other governments to do the same. In return, Washington promised to lift the embargo and to normalize trading relations with Japan.[36]

In the hours following this diplomatic exchange, the news became even more ominous. Late on 25 November, Washington read intelligence reports indicating that a Japanese expeditionary force with five divisions embarked had steamed south from Shanghai for a possible attack on the Philippines, Indochina, Thailand, the Dutch East Indies, Singapore, or Burma. For the next few days the United States watched the progress of the Japanese task force. Secretary of War Henry L. Stimson wrote in his diary that "if this expedition was allowed to round the southern point of Indochina, this whole chain of disastrous events would be set on foot of going."[37]

In late 1941 no one appreciated the threat posed by Japan's moves to

---

[36] *Ibid.,* pp. 161–63, 171–72, contains an analysis of the Hull note as seen from the Japanese point of view; Cordell Hull, *The Memoirs of Cordell Hull* (New York: The Macmillan Co., 1948), Vol. II, p. 1083; *Foreign Relations of the United States, Japan: 1931–1941,* Vol. II, pp. 755–56.

[37] U.S., Congress, *Hearings Before the Joint Committee on the Investigation of the Pearl Harbor Attack* (79th Cong., 2nd sess.) (Washington: GPO, 1946), pt. 11, pp. 5433–36 (hereafter cited as *Pearl Harbor Hearings*).

the south more than Admiral Thomas C. Hart, Commander in Chief of the small United States Asiatic Fleet. In late November Hart sent his Catalina (PBY) patrol aircraft to scout the area between Manila and the Indochinese coast. During the first week of December, pilots reported a number of transports and other ships at anchor in Cam Ranh Bay.

On 5 December the Office of Naval Intelligence submitted a report on Indochina to the President which revealed that 105,000 Japanese troops were now in Indochina in addition to naval task forces at Saigon and Cam Ranh Bay. Moreover, additional ships were reported in the Hainan and Formosa areas. Following this hard intelligence came a report from Admiral Hart in Manila, confirmed by cables from British sources on 6 December, that a large Japanese naval task force had sailed from Cam Ranh Bay and was steaming past Point Cambodia (Cape Camau), with the Gulf of Siam a possible destination.[38]

Despite continuous pressure from Britain throughout 1941 to gain specific United States assurance of armed support in the event of war with Japan, President Franklin D. Roosevelt refrained from such a commitment. As the situation became more ominous, he told the British ambassador on 1 December that "we should obviously all be together" in case Japan attacked the Dutch or the British. He later indicated that the United States would support the British if war resulted from a Japanese attack on Thailand. Roosevelt sent a message to Japan's Emperor Hirohito on the 6th calling for the evacuation of Japanese forces from Indochina. He considered addressing Congress if this last effort failed, but it was already too late.[39]

The Japanese Offensive

Japanese carrier aircraft struck the American ships in Pearl Harbor on Sunday, 7 December 1941. That same day Japanese aircraft from airfields in Indochina struck at Singapore, the key British naval base in the Far East. Also staging from Indochina, Japanese troops invaded Thailand; Bangkok was occupied soon afterward. An amphibious assault on Malaya

---

[38] *Ibid.*, pt. 14, pp. 1246–47; pt. 15, pp. 1680–81; Morison, *Rising Sun in the Pacific,* pp. 156–57.

[39] Quoted in Raymond A. Esthus, "President Roosevelt's Commitment to Britain to Intervene in a Pacific War," *The Mississippi Valley Historical Review,* L, No. 1, (June 1963), pp. 28–38. For related events, see Leopold, *Growth of American Foreign Policy,* pp. 589–91.

followed. Also on the day of the Pearl Harbor attack, Japanese aircraft from carrier *Ryujo* and from airfields on Formosa commenced a series of strikes against United States naval ships and airfields in the Philippines. Hong Kong was bombarded from the sea and subjected to a naval blockade. The city would fall to the Japanese by Christmas. Britain's *Prince of Wales* and *Repulse* steamed north from Singapore toward the Gulf of Siam with four destroyers seeking to engage Japanese ships. Lacking air cover, both capital ships were sunk on 10 December by Indochina-based aircraft. Japanese amphibious forces landed troops in Borneo on 17 December. Singapore fell on 15 February 1942. By March all opposition from the United States Asiatic Fleet had been eliminated. The Japanese landed troops on Java and soon controlled the Dutch East Indies. American armed forces in the Philippines surrendered on 6 May.[40] There is little wonder that American decision makers would be concerned, decades later, over a "domino effect" in Southeast Asia, should Indochina be seized by the Communists.

The Resistance Movement in Indochina

Ho traveled to China in August 1942 to seek aid for his guerrilla forces. On 28 August, the Kuomintang government, which was aware of Ho's communist activities, took the Viet Minh leader into custody. The Chinese released Ho Chi Minh from detention in September 1943, on the condition that he and the Viet Minh join the expanded "United Front" to make the resistance effort against Japan more productive. The Chinese specifically barred the Indochinese Communist Party from the resistance movement. However, they apparently overlooked the fact that the Viet Minh were controlled by the Communists in Indochina, who had remained operational under the leadership of Ho Chi Minh's two colleagues, Giap in the North and Pham Van Dong in the South.[41]

Eager to initiate this guerrilla warfare against the Japanese, the Kuomintang supplied Ho Chi Minh with funds that he promptly put to use. Soon, he established in Vietnam a network of Communist-dominated Viet

---

[40] Morison, *Rising Sun in the Pacific,* pp. 98–146, 164–83, 187–206, 280–380.

[41] Trager, *Why Viet-Nam?,* p. 57; Chen, *Vietnam and China,* pp. 42, 55, 61, 64–66; Fall, *Two Viet-Nams,* p. 99, provides evidence that American intervention with Chiang Kai-shek on Ho's behalf resulted in his release.

Minh cells that remained apart from the other nationalist groups. The Chinese also supported a Vietnamese "reunification conference" held at Liuchow, China, from 25 to 28 March 1944. With the acquiescence of the Chinese, the Viet Minh attempted to set up a "Provisional Republican Government of Viet-Nam." If the so-called provisional government group did not accomplish much at this time, the favorable impression held by the Chinese of Ho as being cooperative and intelligent was solidified.[42]

In addition to Chinese support, the Viet Minh on several occasions during World War II sought to enlist American diplomatic assistance for their cause. Although their attempts were generally unsuccessful and American officials tended to minimize the importance of the Viet Minh, the Office of Strategic Services (OSS) did provide some American weapons and supplies. The degree of effectiveness of the Viet Minh campaign against the Japanese is not known. However, one observer has noted that, if the intelligence reports supplied by the Viet Minh were not very exact, "they had the merit of being numerous, and this always makes an impression."[43]

A curious sidelight to the assistance rendered Ho by the OSS became known more than twenty-five years after the end of World War II. In July 1945, an OSS team found Ho in a small village approximately seventy-five miles northwest of Hanoi where he apparently was dying from several tropical diseases. One observer described the future ruler of North Vietnam as "a pile of bones covered with yellow dry skin," who was "shaking like a leaf and obviously running a high fever." But, two weeks later an OSS medical corpsman arrived to care for Ho, and the quinine and sulfa drugs that he administered reputedly saved his life.[44]

As later summarized by Giap, the mission of the Viet Minh during World War II continued to be the "preparation of an uprising" to achieve, as its first step, "national liberation." In support of this goal the Viet Minh

---

[42] Chen, *Vietnam and China,* pp. 68–74; Fall, *Two Viet-Nams,* p. 100; Buttinger, *Smaller Dragon,* pp. 441–42.

[43] Quoted in *Ibid.,* p. 442; Fall, *Two Viet-Nams,* p. 100, states that OSS missions in North Vietnam and China employed Vietnamese aides, some of whom later proved to be "good Vietnamese Communists." Additionally, the presence of senior U.S. officers at Viet Minh functions and the flying of the U.S. flag over the American residence helped convince the people that the Viet Minh had "official relations" with the United States. For Viet Minh contacts with American officials during World War II, see Ronald Spector, " 'What the Local Annamites are Thinking': American Views of Vietnamese in China, 1942–1945," *Southeast Asia,* III (Spring 1974), pp. 741–51.

[44] Quoted in R. Harris Smith, *OSS: The Secret History of America's First Central Intelligence Agency* (Berkeley, Calif.: University of California Press, 1972), pp. 331–32.

guerrillas used terrorism and assassination to eliminate leaders of other non-Communist Vietnamese groups. The guerrillas also undertook major propaganda efforts within Southeast Asia and throughout the world. In 1944, Giap formed a platoon-size propaganda unit in his guerrilla army. This act was the start of a program that during the war sought to portray Ho as a nationalist and to establish his reputation as the strongest of all the revolutionary leaders.[45]

United States Naval Operations in Southeast Asia

From the beginning of World War II one of the better hunting grounds for United States submarines was found off the strategically located shore of Indochina in the South China Sea, the location of important Japanese sea lines of communication with Thailand, Malaya, Singapore, and Burma. This was the area through which petroleum and other critical cargos flowed to Japan. Sampans, junks, and steamers also sailed along the coast, carrying rice from the Mekong Delta to Tonkin to feed the people there, and coal south from Tonkin for the power plants of Saigon.

Hardly a week after the Pearl Harbor attack, submarine *Swordfish* (SS–193) sent a Japanese cargo ship to the bottom of the Gulf of Tonkin. By the fall of 1943, the rate of ship sinkings recorded by U.S. submarines in the South China Sea had begun to increase. The sinkings achieved in three and one-half years of war were impressive. In all, American submarines sank approximately 250,000 tons of Japanese shipping, representing more than fifty-five ships and craft along the Indochinese coast.[46]

In view of the long-deferred American decision to use mines off North Vietnam in the 1960s, the mining operations of the Second World War are of particular interest. Between 15 October and 2 November 1942,

[45] Giap, *Banner of People's War*, pp. xii, 8, 27; Fall, *Two Viet-Nams*, p. 101.

[46] Samuel E. Morison, *New Guinea and the Marianas: March 1944–August 1944,* Vol. VIII of *History of United States Naval Operations in World War II* (Boston: Little, Brown and Co., 1953), p. 21; Morison, *Rising Sun in the Pacific,* pp. 191, 304; Theodore Roscoe, *United States Submarine Operations in World War II* (Annapolis, Md.: United States Naval Institute, 1949), pp. 34, 269–72; statistics on submarine successes off the Indochina coast (defined as the area bounded by 08–00 to 20–30N, to 102–00 to 110–30E) are based on U.S., Joint Army-Navy Assessment Committee, *Japanese Naval and Merchant Shipping Losses During World War II By All Causes* (Washington: GPO, 1947); Samuel E. Morison, *The Liberation of the Philippines, 1944–1945,* Vol. XIII of *History of United States Naval Operations in World War II* (Boston: Little, Brown and Co., 1959), p. 281.

NH–84165

Commodore Milton E. Miles on the Chinese coast during World War II.

submarines *Thresher* (SS–200), *Gar* (SS–206), *Grenadier* (SS–210), *Tautog* (SS–199), and *Tambor* (SS–198) planted mines in the frequently used route to Tonkin which passed through Hainan Strait and off Haiphong. Other mines were dropped at points along the routes to Saigon and Bangkok —in the shallow waters near Cape Padaran (Dinh) where the shipping lane hugged the coast and in the approaches to Bangkok. These actions resulted in the sinking of six ships and the damaging of six more. Aerial minelaying by Allied aircraft, begun in Southeast Asia in 1943, included the planting of minefields in Cam Ranh Bay and Phan Rang Bay, and off Saigon and Haiphong.[47]

---

[47] Ellis A. Johnson and David A. Katcher, *Mines against Japan* (Washington: Naval Ordnance Laboratory, GPO, 1973), pp. 90–96.

The campaign against enemy shipping was aided by covert operations within Indochina under the direction of an American naval officer, Rear Admiral Milton E. Miles. Miles, who as a commander had been ordered to China in 1942 to obtain intelligence and make preparations for possible future landings along the Chinese coast, headed the United States Naval Group China, later known as the "Rice Paddy Navy." Along with his other activities, Miles, in a joint effort with the Chinese, created a guerrilla organization and established a network of "coastwatchers." He also set up a similar structure in Indochina under Commander Robert Meynier of the French Navy.[48]

An additional contribution to the Allied war effort resulted from the assignment of a naval mine detail to Naval Group China. The unit readied Navy mines for use by Major General Claire L. Chennault's 14th Air Force and participated in operational missions. Miles and his officers also helped with the planning of these missions.

In October 1943, when coastwatchers reported a convoy of nine or ten ships proceeding to Haiphong, a decision was made to mine that port's channel. Three naval officers participated in the air-mining operation. One enemy freighter struck a mine which had just been laid and the ship blew up in the center of the channel. Later, a second ship was sunk and for the remainder of the war no vessels larger than junks docked at Haiphong.[49]

In May 1944 Miles organized the "14th Naval Unit" at the headquarters of the 14th Air Force. Responsibilities assigned to its head, Commander Charles J. Odend'hal, Jr., included photo-reconnaissance and interpretation, mining, radio intelligence, air combat intelligence, and some guidance from ground to air against specific targets. By exchanging information with the fleet and with the Air Force, Naval Group China and Odend'hal's unit greatly aided coordinated attacks against Japanese ships from sea and air.[50]

By this time the main naval struggle had reached its decisive phase. The weakening of Japanese carrier forces in the battles of Coral Sea and Midway in the spring of 1942 had signified the turning point of the war in the Pacific. Gradually, through a series of naval actions in the Solomons Campaign and through the amphibious seizure of island bases

---

[48] See Milton E. Miles, *A Different Kind of War: The Little-Known Story of the Combined Guerrilla Forces Created in China by the U.S. Navy and the Chinese During World War II* (Garden City, N.Y.: Doubleday and Co., 1967), pp. 186–93.

[49] *Ibid.*, pp. 309–11, 417; Johnson and Katcher, *Mines Against Japan*, p. 97.

[50] Miles, *Different Kind of War*, pp. 309–10.

in the mid-Pacific and the South and Southwest Pacific, the United States offensive gained momentum. In the Battle of the Philippine Sea in June 1944, U.S. forces caused heavy losses of Japanese carrier aircraft and first-line pilots. After the naval actions that occurred during the Leyte campaign, only remnants of a Japanese fleet remained, and these soon would be destroyed by submarine, air, and surface actions. Submarines and mines also exacted an increasingly heavy toll of Japanese merchant shipping. American sea power had become dominant throughout the Pacific.

Miles's organization, including the coastwatchers, made a major contribution to a raid by the carrier task group of Vice Admiral John S. McCain's Task Force 38, for which planning had begun several months earlier. When Admiral William F. Halsey called for information concerning targets along the Indochina coast, Miles alerted port officials, lighthouse keepers, customs officials, and other agents. In a short time Miles's officers in Chungking were receiving photographs and other information on shipping in Haiphong, Cam Ranh, Saigon, and other Indochinese ports. General Chennault's pilots provided additional photographic intelligence. As Admiral Halsey later reported, he had so much information that he was able to "cover the waterfront." [51]

On 9 January 1945 Rear Admiral Gerald F. Bogan's task group (TG 38.2), comprising 4 carriers, 2 battleships, 6 cruisers, and 20 destroyers headed for Indochina. In a typically terse and colorful message, the Third Fleet commander encouraged his forces: "You know what to do—give them hell—God Bless you all. Halsey." Three days later, thirty minutes before sunrise, air strikes were launched against Japanese shipping along the Indochinese coast. In the course of this devastating raid, U.S. naval aircraft sank 44 ships totaling 132,700 tons. Included in the total were 15 combatant ships and 12 oil tankers. The Japanese also had 15 aircraft shot down, 20 float planes sunk, and an estimated 77 land-based planes destroyed on the ground. This raid must stand, as Halsey termed it, as "one of the heaviest blows to Japanese shipping of any day of the war." [52]

Task Force 38's strikes practically eliminated sea traffic along the Indo-

---

[51] *Ibid.*, p. 424; see also Claire L. Chennault, *Way of a Fighter: The Memoirs of Claire Lee Chennault* (New York: G.P. Putnam's Sons, 1949), p. 257; transcript of interview with Ray Kotrla (former Officer in Charge, SACO Office, Kunming, China), 21 Apr. and 1 May 1972 by NHD.

[52] Quoted in Morison, *Liberation of the Philippines,* pp. 165, 169; see also Mordal, *Navy in Indochina,* pp. 75–80; TG 38.2 Action Report, ser 0047 of 26 Jan. 1945.

Japanese tanker aground off Indochina during the Third Fleet's strike, 1945.

chinese coast. Thereafter, some junks managed to make infrequent runs between Haiphong and Saigon. But, so hazardous had the sea route become that the Japanese and the French finally resorted to truck traffic, a slow and inadequate alternative.[53]

The Japanese Coup in Indochina

After the amphibious landings at Leyte and on Luzon and Mindoro, and the carrier task force strikes along the Vietnamese coast, the Japanese decided to execute a contingency plan previously issued by their Imperial General Headquarters regarding the seizure of full control in Indochina. The plan called for "sudden and determined coordinated army and naval attacks on key positions. Particular attention will be given toward the securing of important communication lines, airfields and various installations

---

[53] Mordal, *Navy in Indochina*, p. 81.

as well as the disposition of French Indo-China vessels." On 8 February 1945 Japanese commanders in Southeast Asia received orders to "dispose of French influence in French Indo-China and China after 5 March." [54]

On 9 March, at 2130, the Japanese forces in Indochina launched a lightning coup. Many French troops were disarmed or killed. Responding to radioed pleas from the approximately 13,000 French and Indochinese troops surviving the initial onslaught, and who were seeking to escape into China, Admiral Lord Louis Mountbatten, commander of the Allied Southeast Asia Command, dispatched Royal Air Force transport planes from India to Indochina to parachute in submachine guns, grenades, and mortars. Because of previous orders from President Roosevelt to refuse aid to French forces in Indochina, the United States air commander in the China Theater, Major General Chennault, could not drop supplies. He did, however, increase the number of air strikes on Japanese forces in Indochina. Only on 18 March did Admiral William D. Leahy, Chief of Staff to the President, authorize the American headquarters in China to give direct military aid to the French "provided it involved no interference with our operations against Japan." By this time, however, the Japanese largely had completed their operations and most of the survivors of the French forces, numbering less than 6,000 officers and men, had struggled into southern China. [55]

When the last vestiges of French control were eliminated in the spring of 1945, a barrier to organizational and preparatory efforts by the Indochinese Communist Party was removed. As French military forces departed, arms, ammunition, and military equipment were left behind unattended. The hopes of many Indochinese for decolonization had increased and the people were ripe for exploitation.

The Bao Dai Interlude

On 10 March 1945, during the coup against the French, the Japanese

---

[54] Directive 326 of 28 Jan. 1944 in "Imperial General Headquarters Navy Directives," Vol. II, p. 5; Army Department Order 1266 of 8 Feb. 1945 in "Imperial General Headquarters Army Orders," Vol. III, p. 101.

[55] Albert C. Wedemeyer, *Wedemeyer Reports!* (New York: Henry Holt and Co., 1958), p. 340; Chennault, *Way of a Fighter*, p. 342; William D. Leahy, *I Was There: The Personal Story of the Chief of Staff to Presidents Roosevelt and Truman Based on His Notes and Diaries Made at the Time* (New York: Whittlesey House, 1950), pp. 338–39; Charles de Gaulle, *The Complete War Memoirs of Charles de Gaulle* (New York: Simon and Schuster, 1959), p. 858; Fall, *Two Viet-Nams*, pp. 58–59.

granted the Vietnamese independence, appointing Bao Dai as the new state's nominal head. The ancient city of Hue regained its status as the capital city. Throughout Vietnam, conditions soon degenerated into chaos. Emperor Bao Dai, who was given no real power by the Japanese, failed in his attempts to form a cabinet. Ngo Dinh Diem, his first choice for prime minister, never received the invitation to accept the office, reportedly because the Japanese intercepted the communication. That post eventually was filled by Tran Trong Kim, a famous scholar.[56]

For all underground nationalist groups, the Japanese overthrow of the French in the spring of 1945 was the signal to intensify preparations to gain independence. And, for the Viet Minh, the administrative paralysis and the breakdown of law and order created ideal conditions for a takeover of the country. Despite his pleas, Kim could obtain no help from the Viet Minh. In June 1945, the distracted prime minister described his plight as follows:

> I know that the people are suffering, that the Japanese are going to leave, and I myself, like Emperor Bao Dai, am suffering at the sight of the people starving. But there is nothing we can do. I have been told that there is a party called the Viet Minh. But where is this party? Let it come and I will give it power. The Emperor also asks that. If you know any leaders of the Viet Minh, let them come and I will give them my place.[57]

But Ho Chi Minh, who had been a patient revolutionary for years, remained silent in the early summer of 1945. Ho and his comrades would wait until the Japanese surrendered before moving onto stage center to take the offensive.

The End of World War II

By the summer of 1945, Iwo Jima and Okinawa were secured, the Japanese naval and merchant fleets were virtually eliminated, the Third Fleet and the Air Force were stepping up the tempo of strikes against the Japanese home islands, and American forces were being assembled for the final amphibious assault on Japan. With Japanese seapower virtually

---

[56] Hammer, *Vietnam: Yesterday and Today,* p. 133; Fall, *Two Viet-Nams,* pp. 60–61.
[57] Quoted in Hammer, *Struggle for Indochina,* pp. 49–50; Hammer, *Vietnam: Yesterday and Today,* pp. 133–34.

eliminated, the maritime war in the Pacific was nearing a close.

The end came much sooner than most expected, as the final blows were launched from one of the captured islands, Tinian. On 6 August, a uranium bomb—armed by Captain William S. Parsons, Jr., head of the Los Alamos Ordnance Division, during the flight of an Air Force B–29 (commanded by Colonel Paul W. Tibbets, USA)—essentially destroyed Hiroshima by the release of blast, heat, and nuclear radiation from an explosive force equivalent to 14,000 tons of TNT. Three days later, a plutonium bomb—armed by the bomb commander and weaponeer, Commander Frederick L. Ashworth—inflicted devastating damage on Nagasaki with a blast equivalent to 20,000 tons of TNT. On 15 August Japanese Emperor Hirohito ordered his armed forces to cease fire immediately.

The Allied victory over Japan marked the beginning of a new period, a period when a major influence on the course of events would be the unchallenged strength of the United States upon the sea.

CHAPTER III

The United States Navy
And Postwar Conflict

The United States emerged from World War II as the greatest sea power
the world had ever seen. As long as its naval supremacy was maintained
America would have secure oceanic lines of communication with other
countries. The direct and indirect influence of seapower on the international
scene could be applied by maintaining naval presence in troubled areas,
projecting power overseas, and providing support and assistance to allies
in local crises. America could enjoy the benefits of seapower in the
advancement of its interests abroad and in the rehabilitation of war-torn
nations. The United States Navy could act as a stabilizing factor in a
troubled world and serve as a complement to diplomatic efforts in the
pursuit of national objectives.

Nevertheless, as World War II came to a close there were signs that
the continuing importance of the United States Navy was being questioned.
Some feared that the Navy might be reduced to a point of insufficiency to
support American interests, and that steps might be taken which would
adversely effect the readiness and effectiveness of the Fleet. While facing
the problems of transition from war to peace, the nation became increasingly
concerned over an expanding struggle for power in the post-war world.
Indochina was but one of the areas on the worldwide scene in which
Communists were attempting to exploit instabilities and weaknesses left in
the wake of the most far-reaching war in history. Crises in widely scattered
regions took on the dimension of a global peacetime struggle. The result
was unexpected demands for naval deployments to the Far East and the
Mediterranean.

In view of the declining number of effective units in the Fleet, full
use had to be made of the flexibility and mobility of naval forces and
reallocation of limited resources to meet the varying demands. A process
of change in the composition of naval operating forces, their employment,

their support, and their strategic and tactical direction, and in departmental responsibilities and authority began in the wake of World War II. The process would continue during the prolonged Vietnam conflict. To lay a foundation for understanding the capabilities of the United States Navy during this period some understanding is needed of the evolutionary changes in the Navy brought about by World War II.

In part, the Fleet's extraordinary wartime effectiveness had stemmed from it size, composition, and versatility. It stemmed also from a simple and direct chain of command and from an efficient alignment of departmental responsibilities. The latter provided responsive support to the Fleet with a minimum of overhead and a minimum of diversion of the naval chain of command's attention from its primary tasks of war planning, readiness, and operations. The division of responsibilities within the Navy Department had been the culmination of a process underway since the beginning of the "New Navy" near the end of the nineteenth century, a process influenced by a shift of naval policy from coastal defense and commerce raiding to Fleet actions for control of the sea, and by the experiences and demands of two world wars. The outgrowth of a movement to bring the knowledge and experience of seagoing naval line officers to bear on the management of the affairs of the Navy Department and its direction of the Fleet, resulted in the creation of the position of Chief of Naval Operations in 1915. Rather than establishing a naval general staff with supervisory responsibilities over the entire department, as advocated by a vocal group of naval officers, a congressional act provided that the Chief of Naval Operations would, "under the direction of the Secretary of the Navy, be charged with the operations of the fleet, and with the preparation and readiness of plans for its use in war."[1]

Demands of a "Two-Ocean War"

Prior to the attack on Pearl Harbor, the operating forces were not ideally organized for a global war. There were three fleets—the Pacific Fleet, the Atlantic Fleet, and a tiny Asiatic Fleet. In 1941, the Commander in Chief, U.S. Pacific Fleet, Admiral Husband E. Kimmel, had also been designated Commander in Chief, United States Fleet. He was to assume

---

[1] Quoted in Elting Morison, "Naval Administration: Selected Documents on Navy Department Organization, 1915–1940," 1945, p. II–3.

operational command in the latter capacity only when two or more fleets were concentrated or operated in conjunction with one another. Shortly after America entered the fray, the United States Fleet commander was assigned worldwide responsibilities. Confronted by a "two-ocean war," President Roosevelt issued Executive Order 8984 on 18 December 1941, which provided that the Commander in Chief, United States Fleet:

> shall have supreme command of the operating forces comprising the several fleets of the United States Navy and the operating forces of the naval coastal frontier commands, and shall be directly responsible, under the general direction of the Secretary of the Navy, to the President of the United States therefor.[2]

Admiral Ernest J. King became Commander in Chief, United States Fleet on 30 December 1941 and established his headquarters in Washington.

Insofar as the exercise of operational command was concerned, the Fleet's ability to respond flexibly and effectively to the dynamic needs of World War II was enhanced through the grouping and regrouping of forces in numbered fleets and through the use of a decimal system for designating task forces, groups, units, and elements. This task-oriented system would again prove its value in the Vietnam era.

At the start of World War II the business of the Department of the Navy was distributed among seven bureaus headed by flag officers. Except for those under the operating forces, each facility of the shore establishment was assigned to one of the bureaus.[3] Navy Regulations provided for a mutual exchange of information between the Office of the Chief of Naval Operations and the bureaus, such as in matters requiring cooperation, and the Chief of Naval Operations kept the bureaus and offices of the department informed on matters related to the "war efficiency" of the Fleet. From the time of the establishment of his office, the Chief of Naval Operations had placed major emphasis on obtaining bureau actions responsive to the needs of the operating forces. Having no specific authority over the bureaus, he achieved this responsiveness with leadership and actions subject to the

---

[2] Executive Order 8984 of 18 Dec. 1941 in *Title 3—The President, 1938–1943 Compilation of Code of Federal Regulations* (Washington: GPO, 1968), p. 1046; Julius A. Furer, *Administration of the Navy Department in World War II* (Washington: Naval History Division, GPO, 1959), p. 109; Richard W. Leopold, "Fleet Organization, 1919–1941," 1945, pp. 5–6.

[3] Furer, *Administration of the Navy Department*, pp. 8, 126. The seven bureaus were Aeronautics, Medicine and Surgery, Ordnance, Ships, Supplies and Accounts, Yards and Docks, and Navigation. The latter became the Bureau of Naval Personnel in 1942.

Secretary of the Navy's approval. To meet the urgent demands of World War II, the President's Executive Order 9096 of 12 March 1942 assigned the Chief of Naval Operations direct authority within the Navy Department where Fleet effectiveness was concerned. Under the direction of the Secretary of the Navy, the Chief of Naval Operations was now charged with:

> the preparation, readiness and logistic support of the operating forces comprising the several fleets, seagoing forces and sea frontier forces of the United States Navy, and with the coordination and direction of effort to this end of the bureaus and offices of the Navy Department except such offices (other than bureaus) as the Secretary of the Navy may specifically exempt.

The order stated that the duties of the Commander in Chief, United States Fleet and the Chief of Naval Operations might be assigned to one officer, "who shall be the principal naval adviser to the President on the conduct of the War, and the principal naval adviser . . . to the Secretary of the Navy on the conduct of the activities of the Naval Establishment." It further specified that "duties as Chief of Naval Operations shall be contributory to the discharge of the paramount duties of Commander in Chief, United States Fleet." Two weeks later, on 26 March, Admiral King relieved Admiral Harold R. Stark as Chief of Naval Operations.[4]

As result of the authority assigned under the two positions, the relative freedom from involvement in departmental management and administration, and the delegated authority, King was able to carry out his weighty responsibilities with a remarkably small staff and a minimum of "red tape."

The departmental overhead structure was similarly small, especially when compared with that in the Navy Department and above it in the Office of the Secretary of Defense during the Vietnam era. Throughout World War II, the Navy secretariat consisted of one secretary, an under secretary, and two assistant secretaries. Yet, more than 100,000 ships and craft joined the Fleet during World War II, 80,000 aircraft were accepted over a five-year period, and Marine Corps strength totalled almost a half-million men at the end of hostilities.

The Joint Chiefs of Staff organization which played such an important role during the Vietnam era, had its origin in World War II. This body met formally for the first time on 9 February 1942. The Joint Chiefs re-

[4] Executive Order 9096 of 12 Mar. 1942 in *Code of Federal Regulations*, pp. 1121–22; Furer, *Administration of the Navy Department*, pp. 132–34; Ernest J. King and Walter M. Whitehill, *Fleet Admiral King: A Naval Record* (New York: W.W. Norton and Co., 1952), pp. 356–59.

ported directly to the President. They were responsible for strategic plans to guide the conduct of the war and for coordinating the operations of the armed services. Together with their British counterparts, the Joint Chiefs formed the Combined Chiefs of Staff. In July 1942, the President appointed Admiral Willam D. Leahy as his own Chief of Staff. Leahy also served as Chairman of the Joint Chiefs of Staff.

Unified commands were established to undertake joint Army-Navy campaigns. Based, in general, on whether the effort involved primarily the Army or the Navy, either the Chief of Staff of the Army or the Chief of Naval Operations was designated Executive of the Joint Chiefs of Staff for each unified command. As a result, the Joint Chiefs could focus collectively on strategy, policy, and coordination of critical matters, delegating the details of planning and directing operations to one of the service chiefs.[5]

In the spring of 1942, when the Commander in Chief, United States Pacific Fleet also became Commander in Chief, Pacific Ocean Areas for United Nations forces, the United States Joint Chiefs of Staff were assigned jurisdiction over all matters pertaining to operational strategy in the Pacific. The implementing directive stated that the Commander in Chief, United States Fleet would act as the Joint Chiefs's "Executive Agency" for the Pacific Ocean Areas command. This decision provided the Allies with an efficient chain of command for the direction of the struggle against Japan for control of the Pacific.[6]

As a result of actions such as these to meet the demands of World War II, the assignment of responsibility and authority over the operating forces and for their support were well tailored to meet the requirements for prompt and effective global naval operations with limited resources in response to widely scattered crises. Provision had been made also for the unified control of joint operations involving two or more of the military services.

World War II also produced major changes in the composition and capabilities of the Fleet. Having expanded in response to wartime needs, the United States Navy of 1945 was not only vastly larger than the prewar force, but it was far more diversified and had gained an unparalleled capacity of endurance for combat operations in remote waters. One specific result of the Navy's experience in World War II was the ascendancy of

---

[5] Vernon E. Davis, "Origin of the Joint and Combined Chiefs of Staff," Vol. I of "The History of the Joint Chiefs of Staff in World War II: Organizational Development" (Historical Section, JCS, 1972).

[6] Ltr, SECNAV to distribution list, A16–328 of 20 Apr. 1942.

the aircraft carrier. Screened, supported, and supplied by other ships, this type supplanted the battleship as the primary striking arm of the Fleet. In addition to proving their value in the war at sea, carriers conclusively demonstrated their worth as mobile bases for the launching of air attacks against land targets. Concentrations of carrier air power proved capable of neutralizing enemy airfields. With the introduction of high-performance fighter aircraft, radar, the best antiaircraft fire-control systems in the world, automatically controlled gun mounts, and effective tactical dispositions, the Fleet had gained the capability to withstand enemy air attacks.

In carrying out the island-hopping campaigns of the Pacific war and landing millions of troops on the continents of Africa and Europe, the United States Fleet and its Marine Force had achieved unprecedented advances in amphibious warfare. The limited capabilities and imperfect techniques of the prewar days had been expanded and refined, not only with regard to the assault landings, but also for the softening of enemy defenses by air attack and naval gunfire, the removal of obstacles by underwater demolition teams, close air and gunfire support of forces ashore, and logistic support by sea of subsequent operations.

To sustain ships in combat in distant waters and to support a wide variety of naval forces, the concepts of the fleet train and Base Force had been broadened and developed into the Pacific Fleet Service Force with its extraordinarily effective naval operational logistic system. Significant advances had been achieved in underway replenishment of supplies, ammunition, and fuel. Dependence on fixed bases had been minimized by the extensive mobile capabilities of ships and craft devised to provide repairs, services, and other logistic support. New concepts, techniques, and systems had been developed for the prompt establishment of advanced bases tailored to meet varying requirements. Navy Mobile Construction Battalions (SEABEES) were organized for the construction and maintenance of bases and support of the Marines in combat.[7]

Major progress had been achieved by the United States in submarine warfare and in mining and minesweeping. The serious threat posed by the German U-boat campaign in the Atlantic had forced the assignment of top priority there to antisubmarine warfare. New concepts, tactics, techniques,

---

[7] Worrall R. Carter, *Beans, Bullets, and Black Oil* (Washington: Navy Department, GPO, 1952); Furer, *Administration of the Navy Department;* Hooper, *Mobility, Support, Endurance,* pp. 21–24.

detection devices, weapons, and ship and aircraft systems had been developed to cope with the undersea threat.

Many of the World War II ships and craft would see service in the Vietnam conflict, along with the SEABEES. Concepts such as the Advanced Base Functional Component Systems would prove ideally suited to the establishment of support facilities during the period of American combat involvement with Vietnam. The naval officers advancing to positions of high command responsibilities during the Vietnam era would benefit from their combat experiences in World War II. They would draw upon the knowledge gained from that war both for combat and logistical actions, such as the establishment and operation of mobile support forces and advance bases.

Uncertainties as to the Future

During World War II, one unsettling note, at least insofar as the Navy was concerned, was the advocacy of fundamental revisions in departmental organization and responsibilities and in the control and support of military forces. The proposals were motivated, in part, by advances made in aviation and concepts of "strategic" air power.[8] They also stemmed from differences between the Army and the Navy concerning the direction of the armed forces and the management of their support. The concepts proposed were, in some respects, an outgrowth of a sweeping reorganization of the War Department, initiated by the Army Chief of Staff, General George C. Marshall, shortly after America entered the war. Three commands were established: Army Ground Forces, Army Air Forces, and Services of Supply.[9]

---

[8] As early as 1916, 1917, and 1919, congressional bills had been introduced which would have established a Cabinet-level Department of Aviation to control both Army and Navy aviation and with civil air responsibilities as well. Other proposals were introduced in 1925; one would have abolished the Navy and reconstituted the War Department as a Department of Defense controlling a united Army-Navy Service; another would have placed civil and military aviation under a Department of Defense with undersecretaries for land, sea, and air; another bill would have established an Air Corps within the War Department, in a way similar to that of the Marine Corps in the Department of the Navy. Both the War and Navy Departments were opposed to the degree of autonomy being proposed for aviation under these plans. A summary of the legislative history of unification, beginning in 1921, is contained in Exhibit I of the report to Secretary Forrestal forwarded by Ferdinand Eberstadt on 25 September 1945, entitled *Unification of the War and Navy Departments and Postwar Organization for National Security* (79th Cong., 1st sess.) (Washington: GPO, 1945), pp. 241–51 (hereafter cited as Eberstadt Report).

[9] Forrest C. Pogue, *Ordeal and Hope, 1939–1942*, Vol. II of *George C. Marshall* (New York: Viking Press, 1965), pp. 8, 81–86, 120, 289–301.

In November 1943, Marshall submitted, for consideration by the Joint Chiefs of Staff, a recommendation that a single Department of War be created after the war. Marshall sought a prompt decision to facilitate planning for the postwar period. The justifications advanced for a single department were "real unity of command," centralization of "numerous functions" to eliminate "duplication and overlapping," and "centralized control of the supply of all Services in peacetime. . . ." The single department would be organized into "three major groups: the Ground Forces, the Air Forces, the Naval Forces, together with a general Supply Department." This proposal became the subject of study in the Navy Department and the Joint Staff.[10]

On 24 April 1944 a House of Representatives select committee, chaired by Clifton A. Woodrum of Virginia, began hearings on postwar military policy. The committee made the third agenda item a "study of the development of unity of command," the first order of business. Six Army general officers, the Secretary of War, the Under Secretary of War, and the Assistant Secretary of War for Air, presented well organized and mutually supporting testimony. All the witnesses from the War Department criticized the current organization of the armed forces under the Departments of War and Navy. What the Army witnesses proposed was the establishment of a single Department of the Armed Forces. Under a Chief of Staff, the military would be regrouped into four subdivisions: ground forces, air forces, sea forces, and a common supply and service force.[11]

One of the more significant aspects of the hearings was a recommendation for the consolidation, amalgamation, and centralization of authority of many functions for which each of the two departments were then responsible. If implemented, rather than being in control of all the means and activities essential to the readiness and effectiveness of the Fleet, the Navy would be dependent on others, in competition with the Army and the Air Force. A multitude of centers of functional authority and added complexities in the decision-making processes would result.

Later events would prove these recommendations to be forewarnings of changes during the Vietnam era when unity, elimination of duplication,

---

[10] Memo, COMINCH to SECNAV, GB No. 446, ser 002416 of 4 Nov. 1943; ltr, Chairman, GB to SECNAV, GB No. 446, ser 269 of 17 May 1944.

[11] U.S., Congress, House, Select Committee on Post-War Military Policy, *Hearings on a Proposal to Establish a Single Department of Armed Forces* (78th Cong., 2nd sess.) (Washington: GPO, 1944), pp. 1–111 (hereafter cited as *Single Department of Armed Forces*).

and centralization would approach the status of primary objectives. Recommendations by the witnesses included consolidation of fiscal responsibilities, amalgamation of administrative services, and formation of a common legal service. Also included were unified control of research, development, and design; consolidation of research and development experimental establishments; consolidation of production and engineering supervision; combination of procurement organization under one head; and direct control of production. Other recommendations included a single organization for munitions loading, supplies, research and development, radar, guns, gasoline, textiles, raw materials and food, and auditing; consolidation of storage and issuance of parts and spares, and depot and warehousing functions; and a single petroleum agency. One agency for construction was suggested. Organizations to handle intelligence, weather, photographic work, air charts, and communications were proposed. Administration of medical matters, consolidation of hospitalization and evacuation, and real estate were recommended. A common personnel policy and procurement division, a unified personnel organization, consolidated training establishments, unified schools for intelligence, programming and control, aircraft engineering, and gunnery officers were included. The War Department witnesses proposed the restriction of naval aviation to carriers and ship-based aircraft, a single procurement agency for aircraft, and consolidation of ground organizations for the support of aircraft squadrons and groups.[12]

Four days after the beginning of the congressional hearings in 1944, the first naval officer, Vice Admiral Richard S. Edwards, Chief of Staff to the Commander in Chief, United States Fleet, testified. He expressed opposition to opening the investigation on the assumption that the answers to efficiency could be found only in a single department of defense. Edwards stressed that "the immediate need is to get along with the war," "the present organization is producing effective results," experimental organization "could but interfere with the progress of operations," decisions should be based upon experience in a war "not yet in its final phase," that "no one yet knows what part the United States would play in the peace," and that the services should not leap into a reorganization that might, while correcting some faults, introduce others more serious.[13]

After three weeks of hearings, the committee concluded that it did

---

[12] *Ibid.*, pp. 15, 16, 19, 34. 48, 50–52, 56, 71, 81–85, 91, 94–95, 98, 100–11.
[13] *Ibid.*, pp. 137–38; see also Vincent Davis, *Postwar Defense Policy and the U.S. Navy, 1943–1946* (Chapel Hill, N.C.: University of North Carolina Press, 1962).

"not believe that the time . . . [was] oportune to consider detailed legislation which would undertake to write the pattern of any proposed consolidation, if indeed such consolidation is ultimately decided to be a wise course of action." [14]

As the hearings of the Woodrum committee drew to a close, the Joint Chiefs of Staff convened the Special Committee for Reorganization of National Defense. When Admiral King saw the special committee paper entitled "Point of Departure for Work of Special Committee," two months after it had been approved by deputies of the Joint Chiefs, he concluded that their approval "has set up a situation which bars an objective view of the whole problem of the reorganization of national defense." [15]

The committee report, completed in April 1945, recommended organizing a single department of defense in which the Army, Navy, and Air Force and commanders of areas, theaters, and independent commands would be directly subordinate to a "Commander of Armed Forces." The latter would have his own budget officer and be Chief of Staff to the President. The senior naval representative, Admiral James O. Richardson, submitted a dissenting report.[16]

A Senate bill which proposed a single defense department, a Director of Supply, and other significant features, had been introduced in January 1945, but was not considered until after the war.[17]

The Postwar Navy

During the first two years after World War II, the national defense

---

[14] U.S., Congress, House, Select Committee on Post-War Military Policy, *Report on Post-War Military Policy* (78th Cong., 2nd sess.) (Washington: GPO, 1944), p. 4. According to his biographer, General Marshall was irritated with the President for opposing any proposal for consolidation and with the Navy for its influence on Roosevelt, but the general followed the example of Leahy and King in refraining from appearing before the committee; Forrest C. Pogue, *Organizer of Victory, 1943–1945*, Vol. III of *George C. Marshall* (New York: Viking Press, 1973), pp. 364–65.

[15] Memo, COMINCH to VCNO, ser 5937 of 17 Aug. 1944.

[16] U.S., Congress, Senate, Committee on Military Affairs, *Hearings on Department of Armed Forces Department of Military Security* (79th Cong., 1st sess.) (Washington: GPO, 1945) (hereafter cited as *Department of Armed Forces*), pp. 411–36; ltr, Chairman, General Board to SECNAV, GB No. 446, ser 284 of 15 June 1945.

[17] For a comprehensive discussion of organizational changes which took place in the Army, the Navy, and the Department of Defense from 1900 to 1959, the origins of these changes, and factors influencing the changes, see Paul Y. Hammond, *Organizing for Defense: The American Military Establishment in the Twentieth Century* (Princeton, N.J.: Princeton University Press, 1961).

organizations and the relationships between them would be, in the main, those carried over from wartime. One of the few changes during this period concerned command authority within the Navy. President Harry S. Truman's Executive Order 9635 disestablished, on 10 October 1945, the billet of Commander in Chief, United States Fleet, whose responsibilities were transferred to the Chief of Naval Operations. King, now Fleet Admiral, provided for a smooth transition by transferring the main functions and key staff officers of the former command to the Deputy Chief of Naval Operations (Operations). The new Deputy CNO was Vice Admiral Charles M. Cooke, Jr., who had been Chief of Staff, United States Fleet, under King.[18] In December 1945, when Admiral Cooke was given a well deserved major command at sea, as Commander Seventh Fleet, the new Chief of Naval Operations, Fleet Admiral Chester W. Nimitz, logically chose for Cooke's relief the talented officer who had served in Pearl Harbor since November 1943 as his Deputy Chief of Staff for Plans and Operations, Rear Admiral Forrest P. Sherman.

Wartime experiences were reflected in the postwar "bilinear" relationships in the Navy Department organization. The Chief of Naval Operations exercised command of the Navy (ashore and afloat) and control of the bureau chiefs as related to determining requirements. He coordinated the shore establishment with the operating forces. Although reporting directly to the Secretary of the Navy for decisions on policy, the bureau chiefs were responsible to the under secretary and assistant secretaries for administration and logistic control related to procurement, production, and research.[19]

During the postwar period, United States military programs were largely shaped by the objectives of liquidation of the war and reconversion to a peacetime economy. The American people characteristically viewed war and peace discretely; once the war was over, the need for military readiness tended to be underestimated. As a consequence, the nation shifted quickly from total war to what a relieved populace hoped was total peace. President Truman announced that the armed services were being reduced as quickly as

---

[18] COMINCH, "Commander in Chief, United States Fleet, Headquarters," 1946 in "United States Naval Administration in World War II," pp. 34–37; Furer, *Administration of the Navy Department,* pp. 167–68. The other offices headed by Deputy Chiefs of Naval Operations were Personnel, Administration, Logistics, and Air.

[19] *Ibid.,* p. 12.

possible to the strength required for the tasks of disarming Germany and
Japan and occupying these formerly hostile countries.[20]

The government tended to rely, to a large extent, on continued collaboration between World War II allies for the solution of postwar problems.
Great hope was placed on the developing United Nations organization, and
through it the achievement of world collaboration and well being. The
concept from which the United Nations originated was included in an Inter-
Allied Declaration issued in London—ten days before Germany violated its
nonaggression pact with the Soviet Union in June 1941. "Enduring peace"
was envisaged as being attainable through the collaboration of "free peoples"
working together in peace as well as in war. Those countries then allied
against the Axis powers represented free peoples, as understood in Western
nations.[21] But, this was no longer the case when Russia joined the war against
Germany. The great hopes expressed for the United Nations organization
were not realized. The causes and conditions which bind allies together
in time of peace are far different from those that exist in time of war.

Secretary of the Navy James V. Forrestal was one of those men who
recognized possible limitations to the effectiveness of the United Nations.
Testifying before Congress on 19 September 1945, he recommended that
the United States remain militarily strong. Forrestal highlighted the Navy
as a major contributor to that strength and stated:

> All this sounds as if I did not have confidence in the world organization
> for peace. I have. But that confidence can only be justified if, while these
> organizations are in the process of transfer from paper to living reality, all
> the world knows that the United States will not tolerate the disorder and the
> destruction of war being let loose again upon the world.[22]

Postwar Naval Operations

The months following V-J Day witnessed the hasty demobilization of
U.S. forces. Fleet Admiral Nimitz, in his first annual report as Chief of Naval
Operations, described the situation faced by the Navy during this time:

---

[20] President Truman's First Annual Message to Congress, 14 Jan. 1946 in Fred L. Israel, ed.,
The State of the Union Messages of the Presidents, 1790–1966 (New York: Chelsea House Publishers, 1967), Vol. III, p. 2913.

[21] Quoted in *Everyman's United Nations: A Complete Handbook of the Activities and Evolution
of the United Nations During Its First Twenty Years, 1945–1965*, 8th ed. (New York: United
Nations, 1968), pp. 4–7.

[22] Walter Millis, ed., *The Forrestal Diaries* (New York: Viking Press, 1951), p. 97.

The end of the war found the Navy with all facilities directed toward an invasion of Japan—an unparalleled undertaking that required tremendous reserves of men, ships, aircraft and materials, and imposed unprecedented problems of transportation. For almost four years a large part of the resources of the country and the entire energy of the Navy had been directed toward the building and maintenance of its war machine. New procedures and fresh techniques had been evolved that insured a continuous flow of materials of war. The conduct of war became normal, and when fighting stopped, the situation was abnormal.

* * * * *

The urge of men who have served in war to return to their civil pursuits and the strong desire of families to have service members return home are natural forces of great strength which could not be ignored. In consequence of this factor, the Navy was required to release personnel at a rate much faster than that at which ships could be laid up and arrangements completed for disposal of surplus materials.

* * * * *

Support of United States foreign policy remains a primary responsibility of the Navy. Support of the occupation forces was necessary and is being continued by the Seventh Fleet in the Far East and by the Twelfth Fleet in Europe. It has been necessary to keep those Fleets up to complement during demobilization whatever personnel shortages developed elsewhere.

At the present time the United States Navy stands paramount among the naval forces of the world. To insure that it remains so during the present difficult period of transition and in the future, certain steps have been taken. These steps include a vast reorganization within the limitations of statutory post-war personnel and the continuation of research and development of new equipment and weapons.

* * * * *

The pattern for this period is clear: Reduction, reorganization, training, and preparation for the future.[23]

In the months following V-J Day, the Fleet was hard pressed to fulfill extensive demands for operations in distant areas, primarily in the Pacific. Amphibious operations were needed to land combat, logistic, and administrative units for occupation and disarmament of the former enemy in the

---

[23] CNO, "Annual Report," FY 1946, pp. 1–3.

Japanese home islands. Other naval tasks involved supporting these occupational forces and carrying out such operations as might be needed in nearby waters. One of the most demanding and dangerous tasks was the prolonged effort required to clear the areas where American naval mines had been sown. In the case of China, more than one million Japanese military forces had to be disarmed and evacuated. Disarmament of these troops was China's responsibility, but assistance by the United States was required for associated naval tasks, including the transportation of many Japanese back to their country. In addition to such assignments, the Fleet helped speed the return of American military personnel of all the services back to the United States. In this operation, called *Magic Carpet,* all types of naval ships were involved, including carriers, battleships, cruisers, amphibious types, and auxiliaries. From 1 October 1945 to 1 May 1946, over two million men were returned to the United States by the Fleet. Of the 384 ships involved, all except fifteen were in the Pacific.[24]

Initially, naval operations in the Tokyo area were the responsibility of Commander Third Fleet; soon however, this region was incorporated into the area of responsibility of Commander Fifth Fleet. The latter officer was charged with control of the coastal waters and sea approaches to Japan, and the East China Sea. The Seventh Fleet zone of control encompassed the coastal waters of China, the navigable portion of the Yangtze River, and the Yellow Sea. The North Pacific Force operated north of the 40th parallel.[25]

It soon became apparent that the Seventh Fleet's tasks would be complicated by the struggle for power in China between the Communists and the Chinese Nationalist Government. The outcome of this struggle would influence the Vietnam conflict. Ominous signs had appeared in the Far East when, before its last-minute entry into the war against Japan, the Soviet Union obtained concessions from the Chinese Government with regard to Outer Mongolia and Manchuria. The end of World War II found the Army of the Soviet Union occupying Manchuria. The Russians furnished captured Japanese arms and other equipment to the Chinese Communists who, under Mao Tse-tung, controlled parts of Northern China. Soviet forces occupied the Kurile Islands and Sakhalin. The Cairo Declaration issued by the Allies had promised a unified, free, and democratic Korea. To facilitate

---

[24] *Ibid.,* p. 23.
[25] CINCPAC/POA, OP-PLAN 12–45 (Rev.), of 14 Aug. 1945.

the surrender of the Japanese forces in Korea, it was agreed in Cairo that the U.S.S.R. would occupy that half of the country north of the 38th parallel while the United States would occupy the south. Soviet troops entered Korea on 12 August 1945, two days before the Japanese emperor accepted the Allied terms of peace. Several weeks later the Seventh Fleet transported a United States Army corps from Okinawa to Inchon, Korea. United States proposals to permit freedom of travel between the Korean zones were rejected.[26] And, as will be detailed later, the Indochinese Communist Party initiated efforts to exploit the opportunity and seize control of the nationalist liberation movements in Vietnam..

Shortly after Japan signed the articles of surrender, on 2 September 1945, Task Force 72 carrier aircraft launched flights from the Yellow Sea over the Chinese mainland in a show of force intended to help influence Japanese compliance with peace terms. Seventh Fleet Amphibious Forces, commanded by Vice Admiral Daniel E. Barbey, landed United States Marines at Taku, Chinwangtao, and Tsingtao. Also during this period, flights of aircraft from the Seventh Fleet conducted displays of strength over Shanghai, Dairen, Tientsin, Peiping, Taku, Chefoo, Weihaiwei, Chinwangtao, Tangshan, and the Great Wall.[27] Another operation of the Seventh Fleet in 1945, which will be detailed in a subsequent chapter, was the transportation of Chinese troops from Indochina to northern China.

Because of the presence of the British Fleet in European waters and the fact that the final phase of the land war against Germany had been fought on the continent, few requirements were foreseen in Europe for deployed units of the United States Navy. It was not long, however, before unexpected demands arose as result of Soviet expansion of their zone of control toward the Mediterranean. When areas bordering this sea were threatened, the prompt deployment of United States Navy units complemented diplomatic efforts to contain the advances. In addition to the good will derived from visits by men-of-war to foreign ports, the ships' presence indicated where the

[26] Harry S. Truman, *Year of Decisions*. Vol. I of *Memoirs* (Garden City, N.Y.: Doubleday and Co., 1955), pp. 315–16; James A. Field. Jr.. *History of United States Naval Operations: Korea* (Washington: Naval History Division, GPO, 1962), pp. 16–38; Miles, *Different Kind of War*, pp. 527–48, 565–68.

[27] COM7THPHIBFOR, report, ser 01000 of 22 Dec. 1945; COMNAVFORWESTPAC, "Narrative of Seventh Fleet. 1 September 1945 to 1 October 1946," ser 477 of 20 Feb. 1947; Benis M. Frank and Henry I. Shaw, *Victory and Occupation*, Vol. V of *History of U.S. Marine Corps Operations in World War II* (Washington: U.S. Marine Corps Historical Branch, GPO, 1968), pp. 533–34, 561–63.

line was being drawn; they provided encouraging evidence of American support and the naval strength which gave substance to that support; and they confronted possible aggressors with the potential of formidable military retaliation.

With the dissolution of the Eighth Fleet on 15 April 1945, an independent United States naval command in the Mediterranean had ceased to exist. Its successor became known as United States Naval Forces, Northwest African Waters, and was designated Task Force 125 of the Twelfth Fleet under Admiral H. Kent Hewitt. The operational area of Task Force 125 encompassed the Mediterranean and the waters off the northwestern littoral of Africa. The force's operation plans did not deal with Greece or other parts of the eastern Mediterranean, which then were considered to be largely the strategic responsibility of the British. When participating in operations, such as support of the occupation of Italy and patrols in the Adriatic, the American task force came under the control of the British Naval Commander in Chief, Mediterranean.[28]

The operations in the Mediterranean were closely associated with the beginings of a postwar struggle which would be a major consideration in later decisions concerning American involvement in Vietnam. It has been stated that the Cold War began in Poland when, in February 1945, Soviet Premier Joseph Stalin made clear his intention to maintain in power a government subservient to the Soviet Union. Signs that a confrontation was approaching appeared elsewhere in Europe, as Communist-led partisans in France, Italy, Greece, and Yugoslavia continued efforts to gain power after the war's end. The situation in Poland rapidly became more serious. By September 1945, the seizure of power by the Communists and the Soviet pillage of Polish lands had become matters of major concern to the American Government.[29]

A particularly explosive situation during this period was the Yugoslav-British confrontation at Trieste, a key port located at the head of the Adriatic. Concerned over the crisis, President Truman questioned Admiral King re-

---

[28] COMNAVEU, "Administrative History of U.S. Naval Forces in Europe, August 1945 to March 1947." of 28 Oct. 1947, pp. 108–12.

[29] Dean Acheson, *Present at the Creation: My Years in the State Department* (New York: W. W. Norton, 1969), p. 194; see also John L. Gaddis, *The United States and the Origins of the Cold War, 1941–1947* (New York: Columbia University Press, 1972) which gives a recent interpretation of the origins of the Cold War; *Forrestal Diaries*, pp. 97–98, 103, 111; Edward J. Rozek, *Allied Wartime Diplomacy: A Pattern in Poland* (New York: John Wiley and Sons, 1958), p. 416.

garding the rapid deployment of fleet units to the area. The Fleet was alerted but not then sent.[30]

In Bulgaria and Rumania, the Soviets placed Communists in control of the government at the end of the war. The Russians denied free access into Hungary. Serious problems with regard to the occupation and administration of Germany arose between the Soviets and the Western Allies. In Austria, similar problems, such as Stalin's refusal to let American troops enter Vienna, were encountered. Turkey became increasingly concerned with the threat from Soviet troops in Bulgaria, continuous attacks by the Soviet press, and diplomatic discussions proposing modifications to Turkey's eastern frontier and the establishment of a Soviet base in the Turkish straits. Elsewhere on its southern flank, the Soviet Union delayed the withdrawal of Russian troops from northern Iran and armed a separatist movement, the Tudeh Party, in Azerbaijan Province.[31]

The Role of Naval Power in the Future

Meanwhile, the United States Navy was faced with the problems of determining the size and composition of a Fleet that would best meet the nation's needs and of charting the course of development to meet requirements as they might evolve in the more distant future. Resolution of these problems had to take into consideration the experiences of World War II and the extent to which the lessons would be applicable to the postwar era. Some of the other considerations were changes in the balance of power, potential threats to American interests, the realities of peacetime budgets, technological advances, priorities, and relationships with other military forces. Under the Chief of Naval Operations, planning for the postwar Navy had started in 1943. The first tentative plan was superseded by other plans that were further revised after V-J Day.[32]

The totality of victory in World War II complicated the task of determining and justifying postwar naval requirements. During the earlier years of the twentieth century, proposals concerning the size and composition

---

[30] Truman, *Year of Decisions,* pp. 243–53.

[31] *Ibid.,* pp. 253–54, 297–99, 375–78, 384; Diane S. Clemens, *Yalta* (New York: Oxford University Press, 1970), pp. 70, 303.

[32] For a discussion of the planning efforts and external influences on them, see Vincent Davis, *Postwar Defense Policy and the U.S. Navy, 1943–1946* (Chapel Hill, N.C.: University of North Carolina Press, 1962).

of the United States Fleet had been based primarily on the type and number of ships in the fleets of potential enemies. This criterion was no longer valid at the end of the war. Moreover, the cost of ensuring adequate naval readiness for the future was increasing. Spectacular advances in weapon systems, stimulated by science and technology during World War II, and the likelihood of similar advances by potential enemies necessitated an emphasis on research and development in the postwar era. Naval laboratories were expanded. Many scientists and engineers who had been associated with the Office of Scientific Research and Development or had served in the Navy Department during the war became a part of the Navy's postwar research and development organization or joined its civilian contractors. The major emphasis placed on research and development contrasted sharply with the modest endeavors that had preceded the war.[33]

The absence of opposing surface fleets in the immediate postwar period did not ensure that the United States Navy's control of the sea would continue. Air power was a serious threat. In World War II, carrier aircraft and fleet air defense had been adequate, but further progress in the attack effectiveness of aircraft was inevitable. Still further improvements would be required in the air strike and air defense capabilities of the Fleet. A particularly serious challenge to control of the sea would be that posed by submarines. Despite the vivid lesson of World War I, the Allies had not been well prepared to defeat the greatly improved U-boats of World War II. Impressed by the foreboding implications of the snorkle submarine and new-closed-cycle propulsion systems being developed by the Germans toward the end of the war, and by promises of much greater underwater endurance, naval leaders pressed for advances in antisubmarine warfare.[34] Control of the sea and protection of worldwide American interests would be seriously jeopardized unless the Navy upgraded its capabilities for coping with the undersea threats. If the antisubmarine capabilities were convincing, the use of submarines to contest American control of the sea could be deterred without combat action. If control was contested, antisubmarine forces would have to be adequate to meet the challenge.

The mammoth increase in weapon destructiveness, brought about by the development of the atomic bomb, profoundly influenced postwar strategy and the composition of naval forces. The sudden unveiling and demonstration

---

[33] CNO, "Annual Report," FY 1946, pp. 2–3.
[34] *Ibid.*, p. 23.

of the awesome effects of atomic weapons raised questions, not only of the composition and balance of military forces, but of the very tenets of warfare, strategy, deterrence, and the restraint and control of military operations. The implications of nuclear fission, a process capable of releasing energy a thousand times greater than conventional explosives, were staggering, and this was but the beginning. Smaller, lighter, and more powerful fission weapons were just around the corner. Before long hydrogen bombs would be developed which, through nuclear fusion, would increase the energy release another thousandfold; the potential release of energy would then be a million times that of conventional weapons. It was little wonder that the implications of these fearsome weapons occupied so much of the attention of policy-makers, scholars, military strategists, and others. Concerned with the possibility of nuclear holocaust, the United States Government struggled, without success, to reach accord on some effective means of international control of a weapon that could destroy civilization.

It was recognized early that fear of substantial retaliation could deter the use of atomic weapons.[35] Deterrence of nuclear attack became a major mission of the Air Force. The Navy also recognized the potential of aircraft carriers in such a role and the possibilities of using nuclear power for the propulsion of ships. No one then predicted the key role in deterrence that later would be played by submarine ballistic missile systems.

Alfred Thayer Mahan wrote his famous book, *The Influence of Sea Power Upon History, 1660–1783,* at a time when the transition of navies from sail to steam was underway. Often forgotten is the extent to which he warned of the dangers of assuming that lessons of the age of sail would apply directly to the new era, particularly since "steam navies have as yet made no history which can be quoted as decisive in its teaching." Mahan cautioned that "in tracing resemblances there is a tendency not only to overlook points of difference, but to exaggerate points of likeness —to be fanciful." After World War II the tendency seems to have been the reverse. Many viewed the atomic bomb as having made conventional weapons obsolete and having nullified or radically changed the priniciples of warfare. The call went out for "military authorities . . . to bestir themselves to a wholly unprecedented degree in revising military concepts inherited from the past." "Modern science," it was said, "has utterly changed

---

[35] Bernard Brodie, *The Atomic Bomb and American Security* (New Haven, Conn.: Yale Institute of International Studies, 1945), pp. 10, 12.

the nature of war and is still changing it." As a rule, such thinking largely neglected the probability of lesser wars. Discussing the "military role of traditional armed forces," one respected writer who dealt with military strategy stated: "Obviously, the relative importance of the army and navy in wartime would be considerably diminished if not eliminated by a device which could be operated more or less independently of them and which was capable of producing havoc great enough to effect a decision by itself." He stated, as an essential point, that "it is still possible for navies to lose all reason for being even if they themselves remain completely immune."[36] The roots were already planted for a United States policy of using the threat of atomic weapon strikes to deter conventional as well as nuclear war.

In contrast to these views, Secretary of the Navy James Forrestal noted that

> Seapower did not win this war. Neither did air power, and neither did ground forces. The war was won and the peace is being preserved through the combined striking power of all three, each force being utilized in accord with strategic demands. Because the same combination will be needed to meet or to stamp out any future threat of war, we must preserve all the components in that combination.[37]

In the fall of 1945, Admiral King suggested that the potential of the atomic bomb would lead to "adjustments of both national policy and national defense, probably with increase of complexities and difficulties." At the same time, he concluded that "sea power—which includes naval air power—will continue to play an important part in the history of the world." On the other hand, during congressional hearings some witnesses felt that navies were no longer necessary and therefore that there was no need to "waste" money on the seagoing service of the United States.[38]

In retrospect, it seems remarkable that the requirements for the Navy in the postwar years were recognized so realistically by the Chief of Naval

---

[36] Alfred Thayer Mahan, *The Influence of Sea Power Upon History, 1660–1783* (Boston: Little, Brown and Co., 1928), pp. 2, 5; Bernard Brodie, ed., *The Absolute Weapon: Atomic Power and World Order* (New York: Harcourt Brace and Co., 1946), pp. 81–82; Vannevar Bush, "Scientific Weapons and a Future War," *Life Magazine,* XVI (14 Nov. 1949), p. 113; Brodie, *Atomic Bomb and American Security,* p. 7.

[37] SECNAV, "Annual Report," FY 1945, p. 2.

[38] *Department of Armed Forces;* Davis, *Postwar Defense Policy,* pp. 181–98; U.S., Congress, House, Committee on Naval Affairs, *Hearings on Sundry Legislation Affecting the Naval Establishment, 1945* (79th Cong., 1st sess.) (Washington: GPO, 1946), pp. 1186–99.

Operations. Early in 1946, in testimony before Congress, Fleet Admiral Nimitz stated:

> Our peacetime operating force plan must meet certain requirements for naval forces which will continue whether or not our possible enemies retain battle fleets with which to contest command of the sea. Among these requirements, which can be met by naval forces only, are:
>
> (a) Amphibious forces with which to transport troops to overseas positions and land them against opposition;
>
> (b) Carrier air forces which are the only means of providing a highly effective mobile tactical air force at sea or in coastal areas distant from our own prepared air bases—and which can serve as a striking force for the destruction of specific targets;
>
> (c) Surface fighting ships to support the amphibious forces and carrier forces and to furnish gunfire support for amphibious landings;
>
> (d) Submarine forces of great power and a high degree of technological development;
>
> (e) Antisubmarine and naval reconnaissance forces, surface and air, capable of effectively covering the approaches to our coasts and our essential supply lines at sea and of covering and supporting our ships;
>
> (f) Supply ships and auxiliaries for the logistic support of all forces overseas, including the land armies and land air forces[39]

The capabilities enumerated by Nimitz would prove indispensable to the conduct of the Korean and Vietnam Wars, and lesser crises. One force not highlighted was the mine force. Yet, minesweeping and minelaying would constitute important naval roles in Korea and Vietnam.

Early in 1946, Admiral Nimitz also stressed the importance of preserving a substantial number of World War II ships and craft in a reserve fleet.[40] The United States would draw heavily on these resources to meet the needs of the Korean and Vietnam conflicts.

The Question of Reorganization

By the fall of 1945, the debate over the future organization of the national defense had grown more intense. Despite disagreement among the Joint Chiefs of Staff, the report of their Special Committee for Reorganiza-

---

[39] U.S., Congress, House, Subcommittee of the Committee on Appropriations, *Hearings on Navy Department Appropriation Bill for 1947* (79th Cong., 2nd sess.) (Washington: GPO, 1946), p. 32.

[40] *Ibid.,* pp. 34–35.

tion was forwarded to the President on 16 October 1945. It seemed more than coincidence that the Senate Committee on Military Affairs, which was responsible for War Department matters, began hearings the very next day on two Senate bills—S.84 and S.1482. Senate Bill S.1702 and House Bill HR 550 were also placed on the record. Each bill proposed a single department of defense. S.84 included a Director of Supply. S.1482 proposed six divisions—Scientific Research and Development, Aeronautics, Army, Navy, Procurement, and Military Intelligence. The main provision of both S.1702 and HR 550 was "a separate branch to be known as the Air Force." The former of these two bills, which originated before the United States entered the war, was explicit in including in the proposed Air Force the "Air Corps of the Army, the Navy Flying Corps, and the aviation activities of the Marine Corps, and all that pertains thereto. . . ."

When his time to testify came, Secretary of the Navy Forrestal apprised the committee of a study completed by a group headed by Mr. Ferdinand Eberstadt. Eberstadt's report dealt with broader aspects of national security than had been considered in the reorganization plans. In addition to recommending the establishment of three departments—Army, Navy, and Air— the document proposed a National Security Council to which the Joint Chiefs of Staff and a Central Intelligence Agency would report, and further proposed a National Security Resources Board, a Military Munitions Board, a Military Education and Training Board, and a Central Research and Development Agency.[41]

Lieutenant General J. Lawton Collins, USA, submitted the War Department's plan proposing a single defense department; a single Chief of Staff over Army, Navy, and Air Forces; a Director of Common Supply and Hospitalization; and theater and area commanders. Navy witnesses at the hearings disagreed with basic assumptions in Collin's plan and the congressional bills. Some doubted that the benefits claimed by the proponents would in fact be realized. Particular concern was expressed that implementation of the plan would have a serious impact on the integrity of the Navy and on the preservation of seapower. Such was the concern of Fleet Admiral King, who declared: "I am apprehensive that such an organization would permit reduction in maintenance and use of our sea power by individuals who are not thoroughly familiar with its potentialities, as has happened in several other countries."[42]

---

[41] Eberstadt Report, pp. 1–14.
[42] *Department of Armed Forces,* pp. 124, 156.

A bill, proposed by a subcommittee after the hearings, made no mention of any of the positive factors that had contributed to complete victory in the most extensive war in history. Stating that "our splendid victories were achieved in spite of the shortcomings of our security measures, not because of their virtues," the subcommittee proposed a bill focusing on such alleged deficiencies as the "slow, costly, and erratic industrial mobilization; limited intelligence on the capacities of enemies and allies; incomplete integration of political purpose and military objective, with consequent confusion in command; waste of limited material and irreplaceable human resources. . . ." Also highlighted were "the savage potentialities implicit in scientific developments. . . ." Senators Styles Bridges and Thomas C. Hart submitted dissenting "minority views" stating that, instead of working out a constructive compromise, the subcommittee had adopted the Army's proposals practically unchanged.[43]

On 19 December 1945, President Truman issued a seven-point program for the reorganization of the armed forces. He strongly urged the establishment of a single department with three coordinated branches (Army, Navy, and Air), a Chief of Staff of the Department of Defense, and a commander for each of the branches.[44] Senate Bill S.2044 was adopted by the Military Affairs Committee in April 1946, closely following the President's recommendations. The legislation also incorporated a number of features of the Eberstadt Report, such as mechanisms for civilian-military coordination. The bill was next considered by the Senate Committee on Naval Affairs. The depth of concern felt by naval officers was expressed when Fleet Admiral Nimitz observed that "officers of the Army often lacked adequate appreciation of the capabilities and limitations of naval forces." General Alexander A. Vandergrift, Commandant of the Marine Corps, concluded that "the War Department is determined to reduce the Marine Corps to a position of studied military ineffectiveness," and Admiral John H. Towers, Commander in Chief, United States Pacific Fleet, expressed the fear that the Army Air Forces would absorb naval aviation.[45]

---

[43] U.S., Congress, Senate, Committee on Military Affairs, *Report on Department of Common Defense* (79th Cong., 1st sess.) (Washington: GPO, 1946), p. 2; U.S., Congress, Senate, Committee on Armed Services, *Hearings on National Defense Establishment* (80th Cong., 1st sess.) (Washington: GPO, 1947), p. 6 (hereafter cited as *National Defense Establishment*).

[44] Harry S. Truman, *Years of Trial and Hope,* Vol. II of *Memoirs* (Garden City, N.Y.: Doubleday and Co., 1956), p. 49.

[45] U.S., Congress, Senate, Committee on Naval Affairs, *Hearings on Unification of the Armed Forces* (79th Cong., 2nd sess.) (Washington: GPO, 1946), pp. 80, 90, 106, 147–50, 278.

On 13 May 1946 the President instructed the War and Navy Departments to identify their points of agreement and disagreement on a plan for defense reorganization. The departments listed areas of agreement, disagreement, and "less than full agreement." These issues were set forth in a letter to the President, who then stated his position on the points on which there was less than full agreement and enclosed a proposed executive order which delineated the missions and functions of the Army, Navy, and Air Force.[46] The War and Navy Departments agreed to draft a plan for unification of the military services based on the scope and spirit of the President's proposals. Vice Admiral Sherman and Major General Lauris Norstad, USA, were assigned the task of drawing up the plan. Their plan would provide the basis for an act of Congress in 1947.

Continuing Demands for Naval Deployments

In 1946, the Seventh Fleet faced continuing operational demands in the Far East. The Soviet Union recognized Manchuria as a part of China, subject to the retention of certain rights. The Soviets promised to withdraw their troops from the area by 1 February 1946, but this deadline was not met. Within China, United States efforts to effect a political compromise between the Nationalist government and Mao Tse-tung's Communists failed. Fighting resumed in July, ending a temporary cease-fire. Ships of the United States Naval Forces, Western Pacific command protected United States interests and supported American foreign policy in China. In addition to undertaking periodic visits to Asiatic ports, the United States normally maintained ships on station at Tsingtao and Shanghai.

Vice Admiral Cooke assumed command of the Seventh Fleet on 8 January 1946. Carrying out operations begun in 1945, the fleet's amphibious force repatriated Japanese, Chinese, and Koreans. These operations continued until 8 April, when Japanese and Chinese-manned ships were able to transport the remainder of the troops. By then 321,061 Japanese and 70,108 Koreans from China and 18,965 Chinese from Korea had been returned home in Seventh Fleet ships.

A special diplomatic visit to Manila was conducted by Seventh Fleet aircraft carriers *Antietam* (CV–36) and *Boxer* (CV–21), cruiser *Topeka* (CL–67) and seven destroyers in connection with Philippine Independence

---

[46] Truman, *Years of Trial and Hope*, pp. 50–53.

Day, 4 July 1946, and the inauguration of the new republic's president. By granting independence to these islands, the United States established a precedent for nations which had colonies in Southeast Asia. The naval presence at the time of these ceremonies gave evidence of continuing American support for the Philippines.

In Korea, concern with the movement of Communist personnel and supplies into the zone of American occupation by numerous small craft led to the establishment in July 1946 of an offshore patrol comprising two Seventh Fleet destroyers or destroyer escorts. Korean investigation and armed guard crews, embarked in the patrolling ships, detained fifty-eight craft during the next two months. For the remainder of 1946, operations of the Seventh Fleet were focused mainly on the Chinese coastal area.[47]

By the start of 1946 continued Soviet acts had convinced United States leaders of the need for a strong naval striking force, trained and "ready to operate on short notice as an instrument of national policy anywhere in the Atlantic Ocean Area." Vice Admiral Marc Mitscher was detached as Deputy Chief of Naval Operations for Air and ordered to form a new Eighth Fleet composed of three carriers, cruisers, and destroyers from the Atlantic Fleet.[48] The Eighth Fleet was activated on 1 March 1946. Although manning of ships and training of personnel was made difficult by the mass discharge of wartime crews, the fleet was combat-ready in about two months. By then, United States Naval Forces, Northwest African Waters, consisting of only one cruiser and four destroyers, had been renamed United States Naval Forces, Mediterranean. The force soon expanded, and in October 1946 the command's area of responsibility was extended to include the eastern Mediterranean, the Red Sea, and the Black Sea.

Once Tito's Communist regime was fully established in Yugoslavia that nation became a base of operations for actions against Greece and Trieste. Early in 1946, Albania adopted a constitution based on that of the U.S.S.R. Further east, the Soviet threat to Iran continued to grow more serious. Not until after the United States had promised to support Iran had Soviet troops commenced their withdrawal from Azerbaijan.

---

[47] COMNAVFORWESTPAC, "Narrative of Seventh Fleet;" COMNAVFORWESTPAC, "Summary of Naval Forces Western Pacific 1 October 1946 to 31 March 1947," ser 01324 of 8 May 1947; CNO, "Annual Report" FY 1947, p. 20.

[48] COM8THFLT, "Command Narrative," ser 440 of 23 Dec. 1946. As in World War II, Commodore Arleigh Burke became Mitscher's Chief of Staff and Captain C.D. Griffin became the Operations Officer. As a captain, Burke had only recently taken over the responsibilities of the Assistant Chief of the Bureau of Ordnance responsible for research and development.

80G366179

Battleship Missouri (center) at Istanbul, Turkey, 1946.

The Soviet threats against Turkey became more ominous. On 6 March 1946, Washington announced the decision to send a naval force to Turkey with the remains of the recently deceased ambassador, Mehmet Munir Ertegun. The visit to Istanbul was made by battleship *Missouri* (BB–63), cruiser *Providence* (CL–82), and destroyer *Power* (DD–839) under Admiral Hewitt.

Because of the seriousness of the situation, Secretary of State James F. Byrnes initially sought to dispatch a larger force, including two aircraft carriers. Britain's Prime Minister, Winston Churchill, held similar views and expressed concern that the show of force would not be effective unless a larger task force steamed into the Sea of Marmara. But the visit of even the relatively small force that was sent proved highly successful. This gesture was interpreted by the Turks as proof of the importance the United States attached to Turkey, and the welcome was extraordinarily enthusiastic. *Missouri*—an impressive warship, the ship in which the Japanese had signed the surrender instrument, and a symbol of the colossal naval power that conquered the vast Pacific—had been a wise choice for this mission. Viewing the *Missouri* visit to Turkey as most effective, Secretary of State Byrnes concurred with Secretary of the Navy Forrestal, in June 1946, in a policy of informal and unannounced cruises to the Mediterranean to establish the custom of showing the flag.[49] The application of pressure on Turkey continued as Moscow sent a note to Ankara proposing the cession of certain Turkish territory and urging joint Russo-Turkish control of the straits by the establishment there of a Russian base. In this same note, the Soviets pressed for the revision of the convention governing transit of the passage. This new convention would have been entered into only by those nations bordering the Black Sea, thereby excluding Great Britain and other powers.

In May 1946, the Communists seized power in Hungary. That same month another crisis occurred concerning Trieste. The Soviets supported Yugoslav claims to the area while the United States and Great Britain backed Italy. Toward the end of June, Rear Admiral Bernard H. Bieri, Commander United States Naval Forces, Mediterranean, visited Trieste in the cruiser

---

[49] *Forrestal Diaries,* pp. 144–45, 171; Stephen G. Xydis, *Greece and the Great Powers 1944–1947: Prelude to the "Truman Doctrine"* (Thessalonicki, Greece: Institute for Balkan Studies, 1963), pp. 168–70, 175–78; Truman, *Years of Trial and Hope,* p. 96; see also Jonathan Knight, "American Statecraft and the 1946 Black Sea Straits Controversy," *Political Science Quarterly,* XC (Fall, 1975), pp. 451–75.

80G703134

USS Franklin D. Roosevelt, *Piraeus, Greece, 1946.*

Fargo (CL–106) as a counter-balance to Yugoslav troop demonstrations. An almost continuous American naval presence in the Trieste area would be required from 1946 to 1950, during which period either an Adriatic Task Group or a Northern Adriatic Group (two destroyers or a cruiser) was normally maintained in readiness nearby. By the summer of 1946, the British, weakened by financial woes and demobilization, were having great difficulty keeping their Mediterranean forces up to strength. Great Britain sought increased support from the United States and expressed disappointment that the Eighth Fleet training exercises had not been held in the Mediterranean.[50]

---

[50] Stephen G. Xydis, "The Genesis of the Sixth Fleet," *United States Naval Institute Proceedings,* LXXXIV (Aug. 1958), pp. 44–46; *Forrestal Diaries,* pp. 183–84; ltr, Burke to Hooper, of 28 Jan. 1974.

Following a request by the United States Ambassador to Portugal, the new and larger attack carrier *Franklin D. Roosevelt* (CVB–42) visited Lisbon. The ship then deployed to the Twelfth Fleet. As a result of mounting political tensions in the Mediterranean and Near East, all Twelfth Fleet destroyers were ordered to the inland sea that same month. The French Governor General of Algiers requested visits by ships of the American Fleet because of political unrest in that colony. *Franklin D. Roosevelt's* schedule was revised to include visits to Piraeus, the port for Athens, and Algerian ports. The announcement that a port call would be made in Greece was released just before a plebiscite was held, concerning the retention of the monarchy, on 1 August 1946. During the visit, carrier aircraft conducted an impressive air demonstration.[51] These events occurred during the time when the Soviets were supporting the application of pressure on the Greek border by Yugoslavia and Bulgaria. Simultaneously the Communist-controlled National Liberation Front attempted to seize power in Athens. During a tense period of frontier incidents and guerrilla actions, accompanied by Bulgarian claims to the Greek province of Thrace, destroyers *Warrington* (DD–383) and *Noa* (DD–841) visited Salonika.

On 30 September 1946, the American Government released a statement which stressed the need to maintain American naval units in the Mediterranean. According to press accounts, this "formally linked naval operations with American foreign policy for the first time in the post-war."[52]

Thus it was that the peacetime roles of the United States Navy unfolded. Despite the decline in the strength of the Fleet, the need for deployment of naval forces in the Far East and Mediterranean was well established by 1946.

Now it is time to review events that would lead to the prolonged Vietnam conflict and to the subsequent involvement of the Navy and other American military forces.

---

[51] COMNAVEU, "Administrative History of U.S. Naval Forces in Europe," pp. 125–28; Xydis, *Greece and the Great Powers*, pp. 267–306.

[52] *Forrestal Diaries*, p. 211; *New York Herald Tribune*, 1 Oct. 1946.

CHAPTER IV

The "August Uprising" And Allied Occupation Of Vietnam, 1945-1946

The abrupt ending of World War II presented the Communists in Indochina with extraordinarily favorable opportunities for the seizure of power. After the Japanese coup of March 1945, French military forces had been interned or swept out of the region. Munitions and other military supplies left behind were seized by the Communists. Five months later, Japanese forces stopped combat operations as soon as they received Emperor Hirohito's cease-fire message. A full month would pass before the initial arrival of Allied occupational forces and still more time would pass before these forces would be in position to control key locations in Indochina.

Ho Chi Minh and his fellow Communists had been preparing for such a chance. Shortly after Japan's 10 August message to the Allied governments announcing its willingness to accept the surrender terms, the Vietnamese Communist Party set in motion what they called the "August Uprising." The ensuing struggle for power signified the start of a conflict which would last at least three decades at varying levels of intensity and with a changing list of participants.

On 11 August, Viet Minh forces struck Ha Tinh Province, north of the ancient Gate of Annam. A few days later they attacked Thai Nguyen, at the northern point of the delta, forty miles from Hanoi, and a key point for controlling roads into the mountainous Viet Bac region. The Viet Bac would become the main base area for the Viet Minh.[1]

The Viet Minh Central Committee hastily convened a "National Congress" on 16 August in remote Tuyen Quang Province in the Viet Bac—in such a fashion that few representatives of non-Communist organizations

---

[1] Vo Nguyen Giap, *People's War, People's Army: The Viet Cong Insurrection Manual for Underdeveloped Countries* (New York: Frederick A. Praeger, 1962), pp. 83–85; see also Giap, *Banner of People's War.*

82

were present to express their views. Planning to disarm the Japanese, take over the governing power from them and also from the government of Bao Dai, and assume the role of leading the people, the Communists hoped to present Allied occupation forces with a *fait accompli* when the latter arrived. To direct the struggle, the congress appointed a "National Liberation Committee." Following the conference, Ho called on the Vietnamese people to join and support the Viet Minh Front. Declaring the committee to be the provisional government, he announced that "the decisive hour in the destiny of our people has struck." He called for a united fight for independence and prophesied that the struggle would be long and hard.[2]

On 19 August 1945, the Communists took the initiative in the Tonkin capital of Hanoi. Emperor Bao Dai, under Viet Minh pressure, abdicated three days later. On the 24th, he issued an imperial rescript to the Vietnamese nation in which he advised "all the different classes of people, as well as the Royal Family, to be all united, and to support the Democratic Republican Government wholeheartedly in order to consolidate our national independence."[3]

The U.S. Office of Strategic Services, whose representatives had been in contact with Ho Chi Minh and other Vietnamese leaders for some time, prepared an analysis of the overall Vietnamese political situation at the time of Bao Dai's abdication. This document noted that the provisional government being established by Ho was dominated by the Viet Minh, "a 100% Communist party, with a membership of approximately 20% of the active political native element," and by a diverse coalition of nationalists organized into "six minority parties and a score of independent ones." The OSS stated that these groups sought an American protectorate similar to that established by the United States in the Philippines. Vietnamese activists reportedly hoped that the United States would "intercede with the United Nations for the exclusion of the French, as well as Chinese, from the reoccupation of Indo-China."[4]

Ho continued his drive to seize control in key locations. The Communists

---

[2] Ho, *On Revolution*, pp. 141–42.

[3] "Bao Dai's Rescript on His First Abdication," of 24 Aug. 1945 in Allan B. Cole, ed., *Conflict in Indo-China and International Repercussions: A Documentary History, 1945–1955* (Ithaca, N.Y.: Cornell University Press, 1956), pp. 18–19.

[4] Memo, Director OSS to SECSTATE, of 22 Aug. 1954 in U.S., Defense Department, *United States-Vietnam Relations: 1945–1967* (Washington: GPO, 1971), bk 8, pp. 46–48 (hereafter cited as *U.S.-V.N. Relations*).

stated that they had taken over Hue on the 23rd of August. They also claimed to have assumed control, two days later, of the capital of Cochin China, Saigon, although they exercised little actual authority over the region. At the end of the month, the Viet Minh, with the nominal co-operation of other nationalists, established a formal governmental structure. The president of the new government was Ho Chi Minh. Communists held all the major posts in his cabinet. On 29 August, the "Vietnamese Liberation Army," commanded by Giap, entered Hanoi, and seized weapons from Japanese stocks.[5]

On 2 September 1945, the same day the formal signing of the Japanese surrender took place on board battleship *Missouri,* Ho issued, as president of the provisional government in Hanoi, a "Declaration of Independence" not only for Tonkin, but for the "whole population of Vietnam." In keeping with the American declaration of 1776, upon which it was partially modeled, this document denounced past French colonial policies. It concluded by noting that "the French have fled, the Japanese have capitulated, Emperor Bao Dai has abdicated," and in lieu thereof, the Vietnamese have "established the present Republican Government."[6]

General Giap later claimed that this "August Revolution was the first success of Marxism-Leninism in a colonial and semi-feudal country." Ho Chi Minh and his cohorts had wasted no time. In the three weeks between Japan's acceptance of the terms of peace and the surrender ceremony, they had gained some measure of control over the capitals of Tonkin, Annam, and Cochin China, claimed independence, and announced the establishment of their revolutionary government over all of Vietnam.[7]

American Policy and the Future of Vietnam

During much of World War II, President Roosevelt left no doubt concerning his strong personal objections to continued French rule in Indochina. Elliott Roosevelt reported that, at the Casablanca Conference in January 1943, his father expressed his feelings in these terms: "The native Indo-

---

[5] Giap, *People's War, People's Army,* pp. 51–52, 84–85; Lancaster, *Emancipation of French Indochina,* pp. 120–21.

[6] Quoted in John T. McAlister, Jr., *Viet Nam: The Origins of Revolution* (New York: Alfred A. Knopf, 1969), pp. 193–94.

[7] Giap, *Banner of People's War,* p. 9; see also Hammer, *Struggle for Indochina,* pp. 98–105 and McAlister, *Viet Nam: The Origins of Revolution,* pp. 185–98.

Chinese have been so flagrantly downtrodden that they thought to themselves: Anything must be better, than to live under French colonial rule! Should a land belong to France? By what logic and by what custom and by what historical rule?"[8]

In March 1943, in a conversation with British Foreign Minister Anthony Eden, the President suggested that a trusteeship be established for Indochina. Soviet Premier Joseph Stalin, in a discussion with Roosevelt at the Tehran Conference in November 1943, asserted that France should not be permitted to regain control of Indochina and that, "the French must pay for their criminal collaboration with Germany." The President stated that "he was 100 percent in agreement" with the Soviet marshal. Roosevelt added that he had discussed with Chiang Kai-shek the possibility of creating a trusteeship for Indochina prior to granting independence to the indigenous peoples, perhaps twenty or thirty years later. Stalin also favored the idea.[9]

Ten months later, in January 1944, President Roosevelt stated to Secretary of State Hull: "France has milked it [Indochina] for one hundred years. The people of Indo-China are entitled to something better than that." Roosevelt further explained that he saw no reason to "play in with the British Foreign Office in this matter. . . . They have never liked the idea of trusteeship because it is, in some instances, aimed at future independence."[10]

Aware of Roosevelt's desire to keep the French out of Indochina, Under Secretary of State Edward Stettinius advised the President on 2 November 1944 that a French military mission had arrived in Ceylon, received American recognition, and parachuted officers into Indochina to support a resistance movement. The American leader reacted sharply, and on 3 November directed Stettinius to "not give American approval to any French military mission. . . . We have made no final decisions on the future of Indo-china. . . ." Stettinius also quoted the report of an Office of

---

[8] Elliott Roosevelt, *As He Saw It* (New York: Duell, Sloan and Pearce, 1946), p. 115; for a general discussion of President Roosevelt's views on Indochina, see Gary Hess, "Franklin Roosevelt and Indochina," *Journal of American History*, LIX (Sept. 1972), pp. 353–58.

[9] Roosevelt, *As He Saw It*, p. 115; minutes of meeting, JCS at White House, 7 Jan. 1943 in U.S., State Department, *Conferences at Washington, 1941–1942, and Cassablanca, 1943* of *Foreign Relations of the United States: Diplomatic Papers* (Washington: GPO, 1968), p. 514; minutes of meeting of 28 Nov. 1943 in U.S., State Department, *The Conferences of Cairo and Tehran, 1943* of *Foreign Relations of the United States: Diplomatic Papers* (Washington: GPO, 1961), p. 485.

[10] Memo, President to SECSTATE, of 24 Jan. 1944 in U.S., State Department, *The British Commonwealth and Europe,* Vol. III of *Foreign Relations of the United States: Diplomatic Papers, 1944* (Washington: GPO, 1965), p. 773.

Strategic Services representative with the British-led Southeast Asia Command:

> There can be little doubt that the British and Dutch have arrived at an agreement with regard to the future of Southeast Asia, and now it would appear that the French are being brought into the picture. . . . It would appear that the strategy of the British, Dutch and French is to win back and control Southeast Asia, making the fullest use possible of American resources, but foreclosing the Americans from any voice in policy matters.

Roosevelt warned Stettinius again on 1 January 1945 that he did not want "to get mixed up in any military effort toward the liberation of Indochina from the Japanese." Finally, during a press conference on 23 February, the President commented:

> With the Indo-Chinese, there is a feeling they ought to be independent but are not ready for it. I suggested . . . to Chiang, that Indo-China be set up under a trusteeship—have a Frenchman, one or two Indo-Chinese, and a Chinese and a Russian because they are on the coast, and maybe a Filipino and an American—to educate them for self-government.[11]

Roosevelt's hopes of establishing a trusteeship for Indochina aroused serious British opposition that climaxed at the Yalta Conference. As a result, on 3 April 1945, Secretary of State Stettinius, announced a new policy approved by the President that trusteeships should only apply to prewar mandated territories, lands taken from the Japanese, and "other territories as might be voluntarily . . . placed under trusteeship." Roosevelt was then in Hot Springs, Georgia, as a result of deteriorating health. By the time of his death on 12 April, the President was aware of British and French plans to occupy Indochina at the end of hostilities.[12]

During a State Department review of the trusteeship policy, between 20 and 23 April, other reasons for abandoning the proposed trusteeship status for Indochina came to light. The specialists on the European desk adamantly

---

[11] Memo, Under SECSTATE to President, of 2 Nov. 1944 and President to Under SECSTATE of 3 Nov. 1944 in *Ibid.,* pp. 778–80; Presidential Press Conference, of 23 Feb. 1945 in Cole, *Conflict in Indo-China,* p. 48; President to SECSTATE, of 1 Jan. 1945 in U.S., State Department, *The British Commonwealth and the Far East,* Vol. VI of *Foreign Relations of the United States: Diplomatic Papers, 1945* (Washington: GPO, 1969), p. 293.

[12] *U.S.—V.N. Relations,* bk 1, p. A–20; Hess, "Franklin Roosevelt and Indochina," pp. 354, 363; Walter LaFeber, "Roosevelt, Churchill, and Indochina: 1942–1945," *American Historical Review,* LXXX (Dec. 1975), pp. 1277–95.

opposed a policy that would antagonize the French or run counter to the United States policy of reconstituting France as a world power. Raising the specter of Russian domination of Europe, the experts in the European section concluded that "now is the time for us to cooperate wholeheartedly with France." The review ended with a decision not to revise the policy adopted on 3 April. A State Department cable, signed four months later on 30 August by Acting Secretary of State Dean Acheson, contained an authoritative statement of American policy with regard to Indochina. In this dispatch Acheson stated flatly that the:

> US has no thought of opposing the reestablishment of French control in Indochina and no official statement by US Govt has questioned even by implication French sovereignty over Indochina.

But this assertion was accompanied by another proviso indicating that positive U.S. support for the French might be severely limited:

> However, it is not the policy of this Govt to assist the French to reestablish their control over Indochina by force and the willingness of the US to see French control reestablished assumes that French claim to have the support of the population of Indochina is borne out by future events.[13]

Occupation by Allied Forces

As the Communists gained power in Vietnam, the military efforts of the United States in the Far East were focused primarily on the occupation of Japan and on bringing hostilities to a conclusion in China, where the Japanese occupation force totaled more than one million men. At the Potsdam Conference in July 1945, the Combined Chiefs of Staff agreed that a large part of the Southwest Pacific Area, including the southern portion of Indochina, should pass to British control during the last phase of World War II. In order to protect the flank of projected operations in China, the Combined Chiefs stipulated that the northern portion of Indochina would, for a time, remain in the China Theater area of responsibility. As a consequence, armed forces in the north were subordinated to Chiang Kai-shek. This arrangement entailed a degree of United States involvement, since

---

[13] Memo, Assistant SECSTATE to Under SECSTATE, of 23 Apr. 1945 in *U.S.—V.N. Relations,* bk. 8, p. 18; msg, Acting SECSTATE, of 5 Oct. 1945 in *Foreign Relations of the United States, 1945: Diplomatic Papers,* Vol. VI, p. 313

Lieutenant General Albert C. Wedemeyer, USA, served both as Chiang's Chief of Staff and as Commanding General, United States Forces, China Theater. The southern sector of Indochina became the responsibility of the Supreme Allied Commander, Southeast Asia, Admiral Lord Louis Mountbatten.[14]

Initially, the 15th parallel was designated the dividing line between the British and Chinese spheres in Indochina. This boundary later was moved north to the 16th parallel, south of Tourane, as a result of the final recommendations made by the Combined Chiefs of Staff at the Potsdam Conference.[15]

Although the critical issue of the postwar political organization of Vietnam was not dealt with at the Potsdam Conference, the subsequent implementation of the Allied occupation plan would have a profound effect on this matter. Ho Chi Minh clearly appreciated this fact, as did the French, who repeatedly and strenuously asserted that their sovereignty over Indochina had in no way been modified by the events of World War II. An indication of French thinking came late in August, when France requested that General of the Army Douglas MacArthur, Commander in Chief Allied Powers, Southwest Pacific, place all Indochina in a single occupation zone controlled by the British, hoping that this step would facilitate later French reoccupation. Although the Allies had discussed such a proposal at the conference in July, the Department of State now chose to let the French, British, and Chinese make the final decision. American authorities added that the provision for dividing Indochina into two zones, initially, was based purely on "operational" grounds, and that "military" factors should continue to prevail while the war lasted.[16]

In September 1945, American naval authorities responded to a French plea for minesweepers to clear Indochinese ports by suggesting that the request be resubmitted through diplomatic channels. Captain Alexander S.

---

[14] S. Woodburn Kirby, *The Surrender of Japan*, Vol. V of *The War Against Japan* in *History of the Second World War: United Kingdom Military Series* (London: Her Majesty's Stationery Office, 1969), pp. 224–25; memo, U.S. Chiefs of Staff, of 17 July 1945 and report, Combined Chiefs of Staff, of 24 July 1945 in U.S., State Department, *The Conference of Berlin (The Potsdam Conference), 1945* of *Foreign Relations of the United States: Diplomatic Papers* (Washington: GPO, 1960), Vol. II, pp. 1313, 1465.

[15] *Conference of Berlin*, Vol. II, pp. 1313, 1465, 1470–71.

[16] Msgs, Acting SECSTATE, of 9 May and 2 June 1945 in *Foreign Relations of the United States: Diplomatic Papers, 1945*, Vol. VI, pp. 307, 312; msg, CINCAFPAC ADV Yokohama 050017 Sept. 1945; Giap, *People's War, People's Army*, p. 85; *Conference of Berlin*, Vol. II, p. 1465; msg, OPD WD 312126 Aug. 1945.

McDill, Aide to the Chief of Naval Operations, assessed this procedure as an expression of uncertainty concerning the current national policy. In a memorandum to Fleet Admiral King, he concluded that this "only draws the thin veil of tactical timidity over the major issue but in view of lack of policy on Indo-China the State Department should furnish guidance in the premises." [17]

By late October, little doubt existed among American military authorities that United States policy continued to be that of seeking to avoid participation in matters dealing with restoration of French control in Indochina. To underscore this position, the United States publicly announced that it had withdrawn from Mountbatten's Southeast Asia Command. In January 1946, State Department sources asserted that the United States Government would adhere to the principle of providing "no arms or ammunition" for French use in Indochina. The employment of American ships to transport troops to Indochina also was barred. One result was that ships of the French Navy were sent from Southeast Asia for time-consuming round trips to France to transport men and equipment.[18]

Only one minor deviation from the American policy regarding aid to the French in Indochina occurred. In January 1946, President Truman indicated to State Department officials that he had no objections to the proposed transfer from the British occupation forces to the French of 800 jeeps and trucks provided originally to the United Kingdom through American lend-lease. The President noted that this transfer did not introduce new supplies into Indochina, and that in any event the removal of the equipment from Indochina was impractical.[19]

Even though military aid was not supplied initially to the French in Indochina, the French Navy did utilize ships provided to France through the wartime lend-lease program of 1944. Included in this group were 1 escort carrier, 6 destroyer escorts, 30 smaller escorts, 30 minesweepers, 50 submarine chasers, 5 coastal tankers, and miscellaneous yard craft. Of these French vessels, the escort carrier *Dixmude,* which had recently been on loan to Britain, 3 destroyer escorts (*Senegalais, Algérien,* and *Somali*), at least 4 minesweepers, 2 coastal tankers, and several small

---

[17] Memo, ASM (CAPT A. S. McDill) to CNO, of 18 Oct. 1945.

[18] Msg, OPD WD 151631Z Jan. 1946; NA Paris, report, 739–46 of 26 Dec. 1946, JN 4933, box 34, FRC.

[19] Ltr, Matthews to Acheson and note, Acheson to Matthews, of 18 Jan. 1946 in *U.S.—V.N. Relations,* bk 8, p. 52.

escorts served in Indochina immediately after World War II. Most of the minesweepers and submarine chasers were not used in Indochina during this period because they were engaged in sweeping the extensive minefields sown in European waters during World War II.[20]

The Southern Occupation Zone

In August 1945, Admiral Mountbatten was assigned the mission of reoccupying the southern area of French Indochina in order to secure effective control and enforce the surrender and disarmament of Japanese forces. Because of the generally cooperative attitude demonstrated by the Japanese military leaders, once they had received their emperor's orders, the second objective of Mountbatten's mission posed few problems. The first objective was quite another matter, since the Viet Minh had already struck and Ho's "August Revolution" was under way.

From the earliest stages of their occupation of southern Indochina, the British stated that they intended to assist the French in resuming control of this region as soon as possible. The British policy, which stood in stark contrast to that of the Chinese forces north of the 16th parallel, was summarized in a message sent to the United States War Department on 11 September 1945. In this communication, Lieutenant General Raymond A. Wheeler, USA, Commanding General, United States Forces, India-Burma Theater, reported that Admiral Mountbatten foresaw two phases in the fulfillment of his task. The first was the occupation of key locations by British and French forces. Then, as soon as French forces were strong enough to maintain law and order, British troops would withdraw and transfer "all military and civil functions" to the French.[21]

By mid-September, the British and French had designated key officials to oversee Indochinese operations. Major General Douglas Gracey was named to command the British and Indian occupation forces allocated by Admiral Mountbatten. Gracey also controlled other Allied forces in South Vietnam, including those provided by the French. The senior French political official in Indochina, holding the title of High Commissioner, was

---

[20] Report of Conference, 25 May 1946, at the French Admiralty concerning the disposition of lend-lease ships in NA Paris, report, 30–S–46 of 5 June 1946, JN 4993, box 7, FRC; NA Paris, report, 320–46 of 22 Apr. 1946, JN 4993, boxes 33–34, FRC.

[21] Msg, CG U.S. Forces, India-Burma Theater 110926 Sept. 1945.

Vice Admiral Georges Thierry d'Argenlieu, former head of the French Admiralty Board. The commander of French military forces being dispatched to the area was General Philippe Leclerc. Prior to General Leclerc's arrival in Saigon, early in October, Colonel Jean Cédile acted as the senior French military official.[22]

The situation in the region south of the 16th parallel, as reported by General Gracey upon reaching Saigon on 13 September, was anarchical. The 17,000 Japanese troops in the area had ceased hostilities, but were either unwilling or unable to maintain order. There were reports that both the Viet Minh and the French colonials were equipping themselves with Japanese arms in preparation for civil war. Gracey learned that a riot already had erupted in Saigon on 2 September. Bands of Vietnamese were reported to be roaming the area bent on anti-French action and sabotage, while virulent propaganda against both the British and French flowed from the Vietnamese press. According to one account, "no legal process was operative—inactive mob rule was the only proper description of the situation."[23]

Although General Gracey was charged with restoring order south of the 16th parallel, the forces initially available to him for this purpose were extremely limited. Within ten days of Gracey's arrival, fewer than 4,000 British troops had arrived by air, and most of these were concentrated in the Saigon region. As yet, no additional French forces had reached Vietnam, although a small French contingent of approximately 1,200 men, mainly composed of French Army and Navy personnel recently freed from Japanese internment, was available.[24] An additional constraint on Gracey was the stated British policy of seeking to avoid entanglement in local Indochinese politics.

Despite these restrictions, Gracey took immediate actions to gain control. On 16 September, he began using British forces to disarm insurgents. Three days later, the British general announced his plan to issue a proclamation suspending publication of all newspapers in Saigon because of their continuing propaganda campaign. On 23 September, he directed the numeri-

---

[22] Senior U.S. Navy Liaison Officer, British East Indies Station, "Monthly Report," ser 0069 of 4 Oct. 1945; Kirby, *Surrender of Japan,* pp. 298–99, 305. Leclerc was an adopted name; actually his name was Philippe de Hautecloque.

[23] Senior U.S. Navy Liaison Officer, British East Indies Station, "Monthly Report," ser 0069 of 4 Oct. 1945; msg, SACSEA (quoting a message from Gracey), 232045Z Sept. 1945.

[24] Msg, SACSEA 241205 Sept. 1945; Kirby, *Surrender of Japan,* p. 298.

cally weak French forces in Saigon to seize the facilities of the local police, as well as those of the *Garde Civil*, which the general described as the "armed forces of the Viet Minh Provisional Government." Finally, Gracey commanded Colonel Cédile to "immediately start means to effect proper resumption by French of all administrative control" in Saigon. More than two decades later, this action of 23 September 1945 was characterized by the authors of the "Pentagon Papers" as a *"coup d'etat."* [25] However, at no time did the British formally recognize the Viet Minh in southern Indochina as a political entity.

Whatever the nature of these events, there followed a new series of disorders in the vicinity of Saigon. On the night of 24–25 September, Vietnamese mobs rampaged through the Tan Dinh area of the city assaulting, killing, and kidnapping hundreds of French and Eurasian civilians.

One of the earliest combat actions engaged in by the French Navy in postwar Vietnam took place at this time, when a group of French sailors repulsed a force of rebels along the banks of the Chinese Arroyo, a major tributary flowing into the Saigon ship channel. On 28 September, the same naval unit came to the rescue of hard-pressed Gurkha troops of the British 20th Infantry Division. General Gracey later commended these men, noting "the splendid work of the Navy who arrived quickly and in the nick of time bringing aid to the British troops, [who] promptly re-established the situation." [26]

Nevertheless, conflict in Cochin China continued. The Viet Minh threw up roadblocks on many thoroughfares in the Saigon region. Terrorism against French civilians continued, accompanied by sabotage of public utilities. General Gracey reacted by directing the Japanese to provide more effective assistance in maintaining law and order. Early in October, he obtained Admiral Mountbatten's permission to use Spitfire aircraft against the Viet Minh roadblocks. Casualties sustained by the British, French, and Japanese amounted to twenty-three men killed and forty-six wounded between 10 and 21 October, many having been inflicted in enemy ambushes. [27]

In essence, the successful pacification of South Vietnam depended on the speedy buildup of Allied forces south of the 16th parallel. The first sizeable

[25] Msgs, SACSEA (quoting Gracey) 241217 and 232045 Sept. 1945; *U.S.-V.N. Relations,* bk 1, pt. IA.1, pp. 22, 24, pt. IB.2, pp. 36–37.
[26] Hammer, *Struggle for Indochina,* p. 118; Kirby, *Surrender of Japan,* pp. 299–300; Mordal, *Navy in Indochina,* pp. 127–28.
[27] Kirby, *Surrender of Japan,* pp. 299–303.

reinforcements, consisting of two brigades of British troops, arrived at Saigon on 29 September in two transports escorted by frigate *Waveney.* As this force, commanded by Captain Scott Bell, Royal Navy, entered Vietnamese waters, both transports triggered mines laid by American forces off Cape Saint Jacques during World War II. Only one of these ships was able to proceed to Saigon; the other had to be towed to Singapore for repairs.[28]

As the designated British naval commander in southern Vietnam, Captain Bell also controlled 9 minesweepers, 3 landing craft, tank (LCT), 1 repair ship, and 1 oiler in addition to the frigate and the transports.

The first large increment of French reinforcements debarked at Saigon on 3 October 1945. This 1,000-man force consisted of French units transported from Ceylon in two British steamers, *Princess Beatrix* and *Queen Emma,* escorted by the 35,000-ton French battleship *Richelieu* and destroyer *Triomphant.* Landing parties, drawn from the ship's company of these units, also went ashore at this time.[29]

The major French force designated for Indochina duty was an Expeditionary Corps, under the direct command of General Leclerc. It was composed of the 2nd Armored Division, the 9th and 3rd Colonial Infantry Divisions, and a sizeable naval component, the Far East Naval Brigade. During the summer of 1945, Leclerc's corps was in the process of organizing and training at bases in metropolitan France and on the island of Madagascar. Originally formed for the proposed 1946 Allied invasion of Japan, this corps was operational when the sudden Japanese surrender appeared to clear the way for an immediate French return to Indochina.[30]

General Leclerc, his staff, and advance elements of the reinforcements from France reached Saigon on 5 October. Later in the month, other components of his corps were brought to the area in French naval ships, including transports *Ville De Strasbourg* and *Quercy,* aircraft carrier *Béarn,* cruisers *Gloire, Suffren,* and *Fantasque,* destroyer escorts *Somali* and *Senegalais,* and sloops *Annamite* and *Gazelle.* The arrival of additional forces swelled the number of French military personnel available in southern

---

[28] Mordal, *Navy in Indochina,* pp. 12, 129.

[29] *Ibid.,* p. 129; Paul Auphan and Jacques Mordal, *The French Navy in World War II* (Annapolis, Md.: U.S. Naval Institute Press, 1959), p. 365; Robert Kilian, *History and Memories: The Naval Infantrymen in Indochina* (Paris: Editions Berger-Levrault, 1948), pp. 11–12.

[30] For the arrangements made prior to the end of hostilities regarding the deployment of these forces, see *Foreign Relations of the United States: Diplomatic Papers 1945,* Vol. VI, pp. 307–11; *Conference of Berlin,* Vol. II, pp. 1465–66.

Vietnam to 21,500 by early December 1945. The British force comprised 22,000 officers and men, the majority of them assigned to the 20th Infantry Division.[31]

As Allied forces south of the 16th parallel increased in strength, British and French commanders formulated a basic agreement on the employment of their respective units which called for the concentration of British forces in the Saigon region. Small detachments also would be stationed at Phnom Penh in Cambodia and at Cape Saint Jacques, the strategic peninsula that flanked the entrance to the waterways connecting Saigon with the sea and close to the mouth of the Mekong River. Until the British withdrew from Vietnam, the primary mission of the French Expeditionary Corps would be restoration of authority in the interior of the country. In this task, the French would be assisted by British and Japanese troops. To make Japanese assistance possible, Admiral Mountbatten found it necessary, early in October, to defer the former enemy's disarmament for several months.[32]

Riverine Operations

In view of the subsequent development of United States riverine capabilities in the 1960s, the operations of the French Far East Naval Brigade are of particular interest. The Naval Brigade, initially commanded by Captain Robert Kilian, attained a strength of approximately 3,000 officers and men by January 1946. Naval infantry units, trained for amphibious assault operations similar to those undertaken by marine organizations of other navies, composed a major part of this brigade. In addition to the troop units, the brigade contained about fifty landing craft and thirty junks, scows, and launches obtained within Indochina. Also included in the brigade were paratrooper-trained commando units and communication, repair, river base, and medical elements.[33]

Early objectives of the Naval Brigade in the Mekong Delta were three

---

[31] Auphan and Mordal, *French Navy in World War II*, p. 366; Kilian, *Naval Infantrymen*, p. 14; Kirby, *Surrender of Japan*, pp. 302–03; msg, CG U.S. Forces, India-Burma Theater 081100 Dec. 1945; memo, British Chiefs of Staff, CCS 644/38 of 21 Dec. 1945.

[32] Msgs, SACSEA 241402 Sept. and 022131 Oct. 1945; msg, CG U.S. Forces, India-Burma Theater 081100 Dec. 1945.

[33] Kilian, *Naval Infantrymen*, pp. 5, 225–28. The French Navy did not have a separate marine organization. See NA Paris, reports, 403–47 of 9 Oct. 1947 and 253–50 of 7 June 1950.

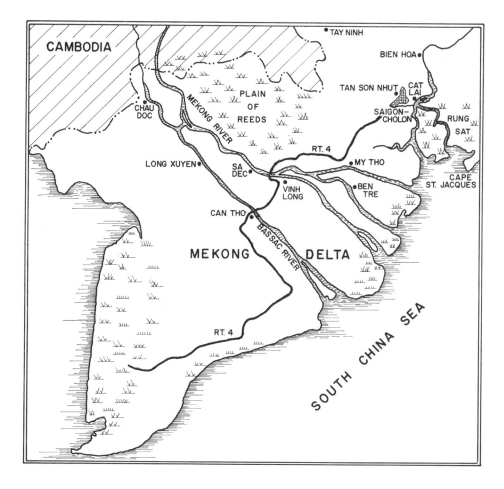

Mekong Delta.

strategically located provincial capitals, their populations numbering from 45,000 to 80,000 people. Each of these cities would later become a site for an American naval base. The first objective was My Tho, capital of Dinh Tuong Province. My Tho, situated at the juncture of several highways, including strategic Route 4 from Saigon, is on the north bank of the main shipping channel to Phnom Penh. The second objective was Vinh Long, capital of the province with the same name, a river port and transshipment center. Vinh Long is located at a point where the Mekong diverges into several outlets to the sea. The third objective was Can Tho, the capital of Phong Dinh Province, a center of rice production, a trading point, a principal inland port, and center of the Hoa Hao religious sect. Can Tho lies along Route 4 at the confluence of the Can Tho and Hau Giang (Bassac) Rivers and is near the center of the intricate waterway network serving the Mekong Delta.

French Army units moving overland from Saigon via Route 4 had initially been detailed to seize My Tho from the Viet Minh. However, the French column found the road sabotaged, and their vehicles repeatedly bogged down in the sponge-like delta terrain. Thus, the reoccupation of My Tho during the last week in October was effected by units of the Far East Naval Brigade, transported there in small river craft.[34]

On 29 October, in a joint operation with army troops, who advanced overland, another contingent of the Naval Brigade embarked in the sloop *Annamite,* and took control of Vinh Long. Then, on 30 October, a ninety-man force from the brigade overcame enemy resistance at Can Tho and captured that city. Operating from Can Tho, the small French force conducted patrols, ambushes, and river raids against rebel concentrations south of the Bassac River to create the illusion that the French had sizeable forces at their disposal. By mid-November, after a second unit of the Naval Brigade arrived in Vietnam, the French were able to extend the operational area to a twenty-five kilometer radius around Can Tho. They seized four towns in that sector, capturing ammunition and equipment.[35]

The initial success achieved by the Naval Brigade in restoring French control impressed General Leclerc. In November, he directed one of the brigade's unit commanders, Captain Jaubert, to establish within the force a permanent flotilla of small boats and a self-contained landing force of naval infantry, with the capability to undertake sustained operations throughout southern Indochina. The task of this new riverine amphibious force, initially designated the Naval Infantry River Flotilla, was to reestablish a French presence along the Bassac and Mekong Rivers. The force also was ordered to assist in occupying and securing a zone extending south from Saigon to My Tho and Vinh Long.[36]

---

[34] Kilian, *Naval Infantrymen,* p. 18; Commander in Chief, French Forces Indochina, *Lessons of the War in Indochina,* trans. by V. J. Croizat (France: 1955), Vol. II, p. 348.

[35] Kilian, *Naval Infantrymen,* pp. 19–21; Mordal, *Navy in Indochina,* pp. 137–38.

[36] E. Le Breton, "The Marines in Indo China," *La Revue Maritime,* XXX (Oct. 1948), trans. by Remote Area Conflict Information Center, pp. 3–5; Guy Hébert, "The Birth of a Flotilla," *La Revue Maritime,* XLII (Oct. 1949), trans. by Remote Area Conflict Information Center, pp. 3–5; Kilian, *Naval Infantrymen,* p. 10; Mordal, *Navy in Indochina,* pp. 132–33.

NH–79375

French River Assault Group.

Within a few weeks, Jaubert had obtained and armed 5 small vessels, including 2 former Japanese junks acquired from the British Navy and 3 armored craft, and barges, launches, and steamers captured from the Viet Minh. In early December French aircraft carrier *Béarn* delivered to Vietnam a flotilla of 14 landing craft, assault (LCA) and 6 landing craft, vehicle and personnel (LCVP), purchased from the British at Singapore. Small boats and junks provided living quarters for Jaubert's landing force, which was composed of two companies of naval infantry (about 400 men), augmented by a small detachment from *Béarn.* Throughout December, while preparing for extended campaigns, these units conducted mopping-up operations near Saigon.[37]

Captain Jaubert's Naval Infantry River Flotilla was the embryo which developed into the well known French naval assault divisions (*dinassauts*).

---

[37] Hébert, "Birth of a Flotilla," pp. 6–8; Le Breton, "The Marines in Indo China," pp. 4–5.

The United States Mobile Riverine Force, established in 1967, would represent a further development of the *dinassaut* concept.

By December 1945, the combined efforts of the British and French ground and naval forces restored relative stability to the Saigon region. Following a visit to Saigon in December, Admiral Mountbatten reported that the Cholon-Saigon area was "quiet and likely to remain so, apart from the continuation of occasional sniping, outrages against French Nationals and grenade throwing." The admiral noted that the French were gradually assuming control of major towns outside Saigon, although "the intervening country is not yet pacified." [38]

Coastal Operations

Meanwhile, important land and sea operations were underway in other parts of southern Indochina. A key French objective on the coast of Annam was the city of Nha Trang. This provincial capital was controlled by the Viet Minh, and rebel reinforcements were believed to be available in the area. Further, a garrison of 1,000 Japanese troops was stationed in the vicinity. Despite evidence of Japanese-Allied cooperation in other regions of Vietnam, the reaction of the former enemy at Nha Trang to the arrival of British and French units could not be predicted. [39]

On 15 October, General Gracey dispatched a combined force, composed of one British landing craft, infantry (LCI) and the French destroyer *Triomphant,* to occupy Nha Trang. When a sixty-man landing party from the French ship entered the city, the local Viet Minh commander issued an ultimatum threatening an armed attack on the detachment unless it was withdrawn. The British naval commander, headquartered in Saigon, authorized the French to remain. On 22 October, the Viet Minh launched an assault on the French which was repulsed with the assistance of the Japanese garrison. Later in the month, the French battleship *Richelieu* arrived offshore, ready to support the forces on land with her eight 15-inch and twenty 5-inch guns. By early November, additional French reinforcements had arrived, and Nha Trang appeared secure. Nevertheless, the Viet

---

[38] Msg, CG U.S. Forces, India-Burma Theater (quoting Mountbatten) 081100 Dec. 1945; see also Mordal, *Navy in Indochina,* pp. 146–47.

[39] *Ibid.,* pp. 142–43.

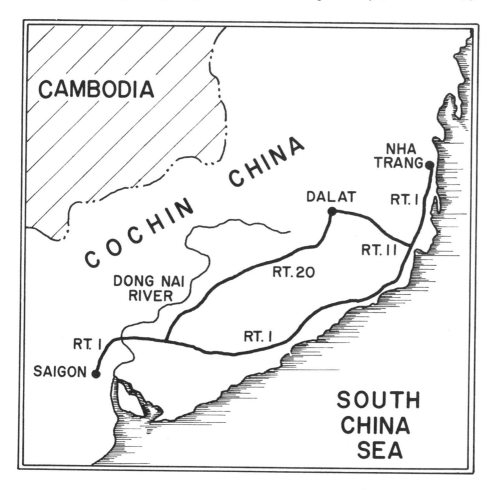

Area of operations northeast of Saigon.

Minh controlled the roads into the city and maintenance of the French position in Nha Trang depended on support from the sea.[40]

Another major campaign, launched in January 1946 by nearly all elements of the Expeditionary Corps, had the objective of controlling the land lines of communication extending north from Saigon into Annam. In order to secure a reliable base to support these operations, the Far East Naval Brigade, then almost at full strength, was assigned the mission

---

[40] *Ibid.*, pp. 144–46.

of patrolling the rivers and canals to the northeast and east of Saigon. The largest operation was an advance up the Dong Nai River and its tributaries, from 20 to 25 January, that employed two armored scows, eight landing craft, and amphibious assault forces drawn from Captain Jaubert's Naval Infantry River Flotilla. On the 25th, Captain Jaubert was mortally wounded while directing an attack north of Saigon. Despite the death of this aggressive and imaginative leader, the naval forces accomplished their mission and succeeded in opening transportation routes north into Annam.[41]

At the same time, the French Army cleared the enemy from the road into Dalat, from there proceeded to the sea, and then turned north, securing the coastal road to Nha Trang by the end of January 1946. The ground advance along the coast was facilitated by naval gunfire from French warships which also established a coastal blockade to interdict Viet Minh junks and sampans attempting to transit the area.[42]

French Army and Navy units conducted successful operations elsewhere along the central Vietnamese coast, and by early 1946 the major population centers and lines of communication south of the 16th parallel were in French control.[43]

The successful outcome of the combined French-British operations enabled the British to implement the planned withdrawal of their forces from southern Indochina. On 19 December 1945, the British transferred responsibility for administering the Saigon region to the French, completing a process begun in October. Subsequently, Captain Bell turned over to the French the former British naval headquarters in addition to a number of landing craft. Finally, on 1 January 1946, a statement issued jointly by Admiral Mountbatten and Admiral d'Argenlieu proclaimed that the French would have sole responsibility for maintaining law and order throughout southern Indochina, except for the control and repatriation of Japanese troops.[44]

---

[41] Kilian, *Naval Infantrymen*, pp. 31–45.

[42] *Ibid.*, pp. 36–45.

[43] Vo Nguyen Giap, *The Military Art of People's War: Selected Writings of General Vo Nguyen Giap* (New York: Monthly Review Press, 1970), pp. 82–83.

[44] Kirby, *Surrender of Japan*, p. 305.

Occupation of the North

Above the 16th parallel the situation was far less favorable than in the South, insofar as restoration of French rule was concerned. The initial bases of the Viet Minh paramilitary forces, the first regular platoon, and a propaganda unit, were quite logically established in a jungle-covered, mountainous region contiguous to the Chinese border known as the Viet Bac. The bases were located in several districts of three Indochinese provinces—Lang Son, at the juncture of Routes 1 and 4, Cao Bang, further to the northwest at the juncture of Route 3 with Route 4, and Bac Kan, to the south along Route 3. Lang Son had been one of the strategic points seized by the Japanese in September 1940.

The initial effort to reestablish a French position in the north was made by two small French Navy ships, *Frézouls* and *Crayssac*. Evading capture at the time of the Japanese coup against the French in March 1945, the ships had taken refuge along the Chinese coast. On 15 August 1945, the day after Hirohito issued the cease-fire order, the two ships, commanded by Lieutenant Jean Blanchard, steamed up the river to Haiphong. Four days later, Lieutenant Blanchard, in *Crayssac,* attempted to proceed to Hanoi via the Bamboo Canal. While underway, the lieutenant observed that the houses on the high banks of this waterway were flying the new flag of the Viet Minh. Viet Minh forces revealed their intentions when they directed heavy, small-arms fire against the French from positions along the canal. Blanchard was forced to turn back temporarily, but a few days later he was able to reach Hanoi with the protection of a Japanese escort. There, the lieutenant made a fruitless attempt to free French military personnel who had been interned by the Japanese.[45]

Faced with Chinese and Viet Minh opposition to the establishment of any substantial force in the heartland of Tonkin, subsequent French military operations during 1945 were concentrated in the coastal regions. Special attention was devoted to securing Along Bay because of its extensive and exceptional sheltered anchorages and its harbor, Hon Gay. This bay, twenty miles east of Haiphong and seventy miles southwest of the Chinese border, had been utilized historically by France as a base to support opera-

---

[45] Auphan and Mordal, *French Navy in World War II,* pp. 366–67; Mordal, *Navy in Indochina,* pp. 148–50.

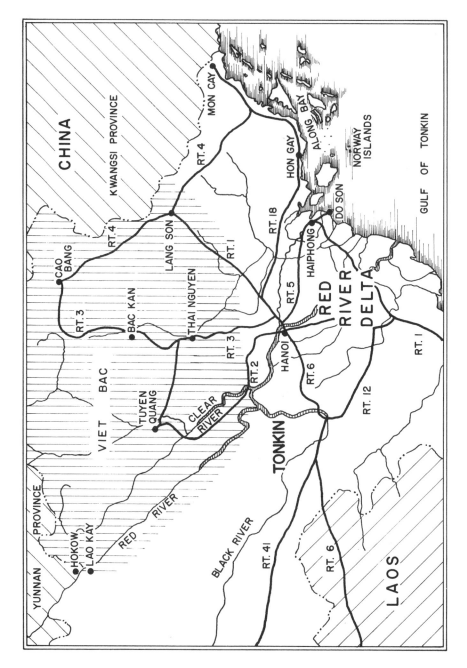

Northern Tonkin, 1945–1946.

tions in Tonkin. Aside from its military importance, many French civilians lived in the area.[46]

By mid-October, French naval and ground forces had succeeded in establishing garrisons at two key locations in Along Bay. These posts were in jeopardy, however, due to hostility from a variety of forces that included not only the Viet Minh, but also Chinese irregular troops and Vietnamese pirates and smugglers. Chinese officials ordered a French withdrawal from these locations, citing prior Allied occupation agreements as authorization for their demands. However, the French refused to evacuate these posts, despite such pressures, and maintained a perilous foothold in the north.

In this maritime environment, the French ability to maintain a position depended upon naval support. On one occasion in November *Senegalais*, one of three lend-lease destroyer escorts operating in Indochina during this period, assisted French troops on an island in the bay in repulsing an amphibious assault by Viet Minh units.[47]

Two months previously, in mid-September, the four armies of the First Chinese Army Group, commanded by General Lu Han, had arrived at their assigned occupation zones in the Hanoi, Haiphong, and Tourane regions. Although the Chinese used some river craft to transport troops up the Red River, the occupation primarily was accomplished by an overland march. As a result of the difficulty of this march, some Chinese units arrived in Vietnam "in very poor shape." To these forces, General Wedemeyer assigned United States Army advisory and liaison teams, commanded by Brigadier General Philip E. Gallagher, USA.

The Viet Minh policy at this time was to avoid all conflicts and to seek friendly relations with the Chinese. This policy was reciprocated by the Chinese general who acknowledged with reluctance the presence of a French mission in Hanoi, headed by Jean Sainteny.[48]

The extent of Lu Han's opposition to the French was revealed during the formal Japanese surrender ceremony held in Hanoi in late September. More than a month earlier, American military officials had endorsed French requests that a representative be present at the ceremony. However, the Chinese general refused to allow the French to attend in an official capacity

---

[46] *Ibid.*, pp. 151–57.
[47] *Ibid.*, pp. 157–61.
[48] Ltr, Gallagher to McClure, of 20 Sept. 1945, Gallagher Papers, CMH.

and Lu Han refused to fly the French flag during the ceremony, even though this gesture had been requested by American officials, and reportedly, even by his Chinese superiors.[49]

Lu Han took a number of other steps that increased French suspicion regarding Chinese intentions. Not until 5 October, after several weeks of repeated French and American requests, did the Chinese consent to free French soldiers and sailors formerly interned by the Japanese, and then only with the stipulation that these personnel not be rearmed. Commissioner Sainteny repeatedly asked for Chinese protection against Viet Minh harassment and terrorism aimed at the 30,000 Frenchmen living in the northern zone. In spite of the efforts of General Gallagher to persuade the Viet Minh and the Chinese to halt such actions, anti-French depredations continued. Among other charges, French officials claimed that China was plundering the north and manipulating Vietnamese currency in a manner designed to yield enormous profits for the occupation officials.[50]

At the same time, developments thousands of miles from Indochina were laying the basic for the withdrawal of Lu Han's forces. It was soon evident that the Chinese Communists were seeking to dominate north China and Manchuria. To counter these moves, Chiang ordered the redeployment of Chinese Nationalist troops, including some from Lu Han's command. Such an operation entailed participation of the United States Navy, since American forces in the Far East had orders to support the Chinese Nationalist occupation of strategic positions in the China Theater.[51]

Withdrawal of Chinese Troops from Indochina

On 15 September 1945, Chiang Kai-shek conveyed to General Wedemeyer his urgent request that the Chinese 52nd Army be transported from Haiphong to Dairen, Manchuria. The proposal was approved in Washington

---

[49] Msg, OPD WD 150130Z Aug. 1945; McAlister, *Viet Nam: The Origins of Revolution,* pp. 228–29.

[50] *Ibid.,* pp. 226–30; ltr, Gallagher to McClure, of 20 Sept. 1945 and "French Indochina 14 Sept. 1945–12 Dec. 1945," Gallagher Papers, CMH.

[51] CINCPAC/POA, "Report of Surrender and Occupation of Japan," ser 0395 of 11 Feb. 1946, pp. 120–22; msg, OPD WD 132252 Sept. 1945.

and Wedemeyer then called upon Vice Admiral Thomas C. Kinkaid's Seventh Fleet to plan and execute the operation.[52]

Before the actual transportation of these forces could begin, it was necessary to take several preliminary steps. The Seventh Fleet's area of operation initially did not include any part of Indochina. Therefore, on 27 September 1945, Admiral Kinkaid requested that the Commander in Chief, Pacific Fleet (Admiral Raymond A. Spruance) move the Seventh Fleet's operational boundary southward to the 16th parallel. Kinkaid noted that such a step would "place all coastal waters contiguous to the China Theater under a single naval command which is already charged with the support of that theater." Although Spruance's approval was not forthcoming until 28 October, Kinkaid proceeded to plan for the operation.[53]

Admiral Kinkaid ordered Rear Admiral Elliott Buckmaster, commander of the South China Force (Task Force 74), to plan and coordinate the embarkation of the Chinese in United States Navy ships. Previously, Buckmaster's forces had operated in the Yangtze River and around Hong Kong in order to "support the U.S. China Theater Forces and to control the coastal waters of South China."[54] Commander Seventh Fleet Amphibious Force (Task Force 78), Vice Admiral Barbey, was directed to provide ships for the transportation of the Chinese troops. Barbey in turn assigned this responsibility to Commander Transportation Squadron 24, Commodore Edwin T. Short, whose command comprised 28 ships (7 Liberty Ships, 15 attack transports (APA), and 6 attack cargo ships (AKA)), organized into three transportation divisions. On 14 October Commodore Short issued the operation order and detailed three liaison officers from his staff to proceed to Haiphong. These representatives were assigned to temporary duty with Admiral Buckmaster in order to develop detailed plans for the impending operation.[55]

Commodore Short's operation order contained an interesting estimate of the internal situation in North Vietnam. According to the intelligence officers of Transportation Squadron 24, the strong "independence move-

---

[52] Msg, CG U.S. Forces, China Theater 151032 Sept. 1945; COMNAVFORWESTPAC "Narrative of Seventh Fleet."

[53] Msgs, COM7THFLT 270836 Sept., 180912 Oct., and CINCPAC 280205 Oct. 1945.

[54] Commander South China Force, OP-PLAN 1–45, ser 0001 of 2 Sept. 1945; USCGC *Ingham* (Buckmaster's flagship), war diary Oct. 1945.

[55] Ltr, COMTRANSRON 24 to distribution list, ser 288 of 14 Oct. 1945, South China Force Files, FRC Mechanicsburg, Pa.; COM7THPHIBFOR, OP-PLAN A1704–45, ser 00163 of 5 Oct. 1945; COMTRANSRON 24, report, ser 042 of 25 Nov. 1945, encl A.

ment" then underway in North Vietnam was guided by the belief that this was the

> one and only opportunity to cast off the French yoke. . . . The Communist sentiment is also strong and the present ruler of Annam, Tongking and Cochin-China is Ho Chin [sic.] Minh, a strong Communist leader. . . . The French Government, seeing what is in the wind, has offered to make certain concessions and it is possible that . . . some form of self government [would be established].[56]

On 16 October 1945, following a passage from Hong Kong in his flag-ship, Coast Guard cutter *Ingham* (AGC–35), Admiral Buckmaster reached the Haiphong area. The admiral then established liaison with the repre-sentatives of Transportation Squadron 24, with Brigadier General Gallagher, with the other members of the small American advisory staff assigned to General Lu Han, and with officers of the Chinese 52nd Army. Additionally, contacts were made with the Chinese 62nd Army, which recently had received orders to deploy from Indochina in American ships.[57]

Because the first group of American transports would not arrive until later in October, Buckmaster first devoted his attention to ascertaining the availability of ports or other possible loading sites in the Haiphong area. Prior to his departure from Hong Kong, the admiral had received a report from the former French harbor master of Haiphong, which indicated that large ships were unable to use the port due to the threat of Allied minefields. The former French official further noted that navigational lights and buoys had been destroyed and that two ships had been sunk in the main channel. For these reasons, the basic operation order for the trans-portation of the Chinese 52nd Army designated as the point of embarkation an anchorage off the town of Do Son. Located on a peninsula, Do Son was twenty-three miles southeast of Haiphong and connected to that city by a good road.[58]

As would be the case more than twenty years later, in the Vietnam War, mines had been laid in the seaward approaches to Haiphong, and

---

[56] *Ibid.,* encl C, pp. 3–4.

[57] USCGC *Ingham,* war diary, Oct. 1945; ltr, Gallagher to McClure, of 26 Oct. 1945, Gallagher Papers, CMH.

[58] Ltr, Marcel Hulin (former Harbor Master, Haiphong) to Chief American Mission Haiphong, of 27 Sept. 1945 in ltr, COM7THFLT to Commander South China Force, ser 686 of 12 Oct. 1945, South China Force Records, FRC Mechanicsburg, Pa.; COMTRANSRON 24, report, ser 042 of 25 Nov. 1945. encl C, p. 11.

Admiral Buckmaster ordered that minesweepers be deployed to the area in advance of Commodore Short's transports. Since Admiral Buckmaster had the general responsibility for opening ports to shipping and for clearing mines throughout his command area, he also considered minesweeping the river channel into Haiphong.[59]

To undertake sweeping operations in the entire region, the admiral had operational control of Mine Squadron 106 (Task Group 74.4), commanded by Commander Strauss S. Leon, USNR, and composed of several divisions of 136-foot auxiliary motor minesweepers (YMS). In addition, the admiral discovered that Japanese forces in the Haiphong area had two 70-foot, wooden-hulled trawlers available for limited mine-clearing operations.[60]

According to General Gallagher, both Admiral Buckmaster and he considered the broader implications of clearing the Haiphong channel. The general noted that this step would remove a major obstacle to the restoration of French authority in northern Vietnam. Conversely, at one point, he also observed that the continued presence of obstacles in this channel "would tend to prevent French aggression." Owing to such considerations, Gallagher stated that, as late as 29 October, Admiral Buckmaster had considered limiting minesweeping activities only to the Do Son approaches.[61]

It does not appear, however, that there was communication between Admiral Buckmaster and his naval superiors regarding the political implications of clearing the channel into Haiphong. On 17 October, Buckmaster forwarded to Admiral Kinkaid a technical summary detailing the condition of the river approaches to that port. Observing that twenty-three magnetic mines were still unaccounted for in this area and citing the hazards associated with navigating the shallow depths of the channel, Buckmaster stated that if clearance operations were undertaken, he preferred to use the smaller, wood-hulled Japanese trawlers already located in the area. He

---

[59] COM7THFLT, OP-PLAN 13–45, ser 000222 of 26 Aug. 1945.

[60] Msg, CTF 74 170330 Oct. 1945; COMINRON 106, report, ser 0810 of 23 Nov. 1945.

[61] Ltr, Gallagher to McClure, of 26 Oct. 1945 and Gallagher memo for record, of 29 Oct. 1945, Gallagher Papers, CMH.

concluded his message, copies of which were sent for information to the Pacific Fleet commander and to the Chief of Naval Operations in Washington, by asking, "do you desire channel swept? If so will leave 1 minesweeping officer in Haiphong to direct Jap sweeping. . . ." [62]

The following day, Kinkaid directed Buckmaster to undertake minesweeping of the Haiphong channel with the Japanese trawlers. By the 22nd, the Japanese had begun exploratory operations in this area under the overall direction of an officer from Commander Leon's staff. On the 24th, regular sweeps were initiated. Routine descriptions of these events were included in the comprehensive daily "Presidential Summaries," describing naval operations throughout the world, that the Navy submitted to the White House on 24 and 25 October 1945. These brief statements contained no reference to the possible political significance of the operations that had been foreseen by General Gallagher. [63]

On 22 and 23 October, as the Japanese-manned units began operations in the river leading to Haiphong, four American minesweepers (YMS–4, YMS–336, YMS–363, and YMS–392) from Commander Leon's Mine Squadron 106 swept the proposed transport zone off Do Son and, from 23 to 29 October, the sea lanes near the Norway Islands (Xuy Nong Chao). Active mines were located in neither of the areas. Beginning on 30 October, these forces contributed to opening a critical coastal line of communication by check-sweeping the West Hainan Strait, but again no mines were found. Early in November, upon completion of these operations, Leon committed the same craft, and additional American LCVPs to help the Japanese finish clearing the approaches to Haiphong. On 23 November, Admiral Buckmaster's minecraft commander reported that five American magnetic

---

[62] Various message files of the Office of the Chief of Naval Operations and the Commander in Chief, Pacific Fleet, held in the Operational Archives, plus records of the South China Force, held in the Federal Records Center, Mechanicsburg, Pa. were searched. Message files of the Seventh Fleet for the period do not appear to be extant. Admiral Kinkaid's "The Reminiscences of Thomas Cassin Kinkaid" (Columbia University, Oral History Research Office, 1961) makes no reference to U.S. naval operations in Indochina. After a review of this section early in 1971, Admiral Buckmaster notified the Director of Naval History (letter of 11 February 1972): "I don't believe there is anything I can add to it. I kept no diary or personal records, so I have to rely on my memory for events that happened more than 25 years ago;" msg, CTF 74 170330 Oct. 1945.

[63] Msg, COM7THFLT 180116 Oct. 1945; msg, CTG 74.4 221031 Oct. 1945; msgs, "Presidential Summaries," of 24 and 25 Oct. 1945; msg summaries, COM7THFLT, 22 Oct.—11 Nov. 1945.

(Mark 13) mines had been swept and that the channel was considered "safe for all types of craft. . . ."[64]

Well before the completion of this final minesweeping task, the Chinese 52nd Army had begun embarking in United States Navy ships at the anchorage near Do Son. The first element of Transportation Squadron 24 reached this area on 26 October. On the following day, the embarkation of Chinese forces in landing craft over the beaches of Do Son began and by 30 October, 12,000 Chinese troops were on board the transports which then set sail for the north. The other two elements of the squadron arrived at the loading area on 2 November and departed two days later carrying the remaining 11,000 officers and men of the Chinese army.[65]

The medical aspect of this operation was of particular concern to the crews of the American transports. According to the final report of Commander Transportation Squadron 24, the Chinese troops had marched 500 miles overland into Tonkin through areas notorious for the prevalence of malaria, cholera, and other diseases. Further, the arrival of the squadron in Indochina coincided with the "usual fall cholera epidemic," a point impressed on the medical officers of the squadron when one Chinese soldier in the first element died from this disease within seven hours of reaching an American ship. In the interest of protecting both American crews and Chinese troops, medical officers carefully screened embarkees, rejecting approximately five percent of them as too sick to make the sea voyage. Nonetheless, 35 Chinese died during the voyage north and approximately 350 more were discovered to have dysentary or cholera. Not surprisingly, Commodore Short noted that the medical problems of this mission were "unparalleled in the experience of this command."[66]

Although the original destination of the Chinese troops had been Manchuria, threatened opposition by local Russian and Chinese Communists to their debarkation there resulted in the rerouting of the convoy to

---

[64] COMINRON 106, reports, ser 0758 of 4 Nov. 1945 and ser 0810 of 23 Nov. 1945; CTG 74.4, report, ser 0759 of 4 Nov. 1945. Despite the minesweeping operations, General Gallagher continued to have the impression as late as January 1946 that magnetic mines in northern ports of Indochina "would continue to help keep the French from undertaking large-scale landing operations in that area"; see memo of conversation, Division of Southeast Asian Affairs, of 30 Jan. 1946 in U.S., State Department, *The Far East,* Vol. VIII of *Foreign Relations of the United States: Diplomatic Papers 1946* (Washington: GPO, 1971), p. 20.

[65] COMTRANSRON 24, report, ser 042 of 25 Nov. 1945.

[66] *Ibid.,* pp. 3–5, encl F; COM7THPHIBFOR. report, ser 01000 of 22 Dec. 1945, encl B, p. 8; Admiral Buckmaster made similar remarks in his letter to the Director of Naval History, 11 Feb. 1972.

Chinwangtao, North China. Shortly before the landing of the Chinese at Chinwangtao, Rear Admiral Buckmaster returned to Hong Kong from Indochina. Prior to leaving Vietnam, he arranged for the transportation of the Chinese 62nd Army from the Haiphong region to Formosa. When preparations were almost complete, Chiang Kai-shek decided that this force of 20,166 officers and men could be more usefully employed in Manchuria. However, General Wedemeyer, pointing out that the units were not equipped for winter operations, persuaded the Chinese to follow the original plan. Between 15 November and 6 December, tank landing ships (LSTs), APAs, and AKAs of the Seventh Fleet, assisted by several chartered Liberty Ships, transported this force to Takao, Formosa.[67]

In December 1945, as the bulk of the Chinese occupational forces were withdrawn, General Wedemeyer directed General Gallagher to leave Indochina with his advisory group because of "unsettled conditions" in the area. Before the month was out, 5,700 more Chinese troops were withdrawn by sea. These troops, of the Northeastern Garrison, were transported to northern China by six American Liberty Ships and three LSTs. Soon thereafter the Chinese 93rd Army returned across the border into southern China.[68]

In the south, some British forces still remained to carry out their overall occupational responsibilities. However, except for control and repatriation of the Japanese, the responsibility for law and order had been delegated to the French. With the help of riverine and amphibious operations, France was increasing its degree of control at key points below the 16th parallel.

In the north, the French started negotiations which would authorize their return to Tonkin. Meanwhile, the departure of major Chinese units was providing the Viet Minh with favorable conditions for strengthening their political and military position in Tonkin.

---

[67] COM7THPHIBFOR, report, ser 01000 of 22 Dec. 1945, encl B, pp. 47; Daniel E. Barbey, *Mac Arthur's Amphibious Navy: Seventh Amphibious Force Operations: 1943–1945* (Annapolis, Md.: U. S. Naval Institute, 1969), pp. 336–41; COMNAVFORWESTPAC, "Narrative of Seventh Fleet," p. 10; msg, HQ China Theater, CM-in-1868 of 5 Nov. 1945; LST GRP 42, war diary, Nov. 1945.

[68] COMNAVFORWESTPAC, "Narrative of Seventh Fleet," p. 10; msg, HQ China Theater CM-in-1868 of 5 Nov. 1945; msg, Assistant Chief, Division of Southeast Asian Affairs, of 24 Feb. 1946 in *Foreign Relations of the United States, 1946: Diplomatic Papers Vol. VIII*, p. 28; ltrs, Gallagher to McClure, of 26 Oct. and 9 Nov. 1945, Gallagher Papers, CMH.

CHAPTER V

The Outbreak Of Hostilities And First Phase Of The French-Viet Minh War, 1946-1950

Starting with a major amphibious landing and riverine operations, the French would reestablish positions in Tonkin in the spring of 1946. The last of the British forces would depart and the U.S. Seventh Fleet would withdraw most of the remaining Chinese troops. A struggle between the French and the Vietnamese Communists would intensify in northern Vietnam, resulting in open hostilities as the year came to a close. This would mark the start of the French-Viet Minh War, a war which would be a forerunner of the Vietnam War of the 1960s. Experiences of French Union Forces would be similar in many respects to problems the Americans later would encounter.

In January 1946 a proposal to remove southern Vietnam from Admiral Lord Mountbatten's strategic control prompted the cautious reentry of American policy-makers into the Indochina situation. United States authorities expressed their opposition to the proposed shift, noting that the British had not completed the disarmament and repatriation of Japanese forces in accordance with occupation agreements established for the postwar period. On 27 February, as a result of American objections,[1] a compromise was reached by which Lord Mountbatten continued to have responsibility for disarming and evacuating Japanese troops, while the French assumed strategic control of southern Indochina.

On 28 February, the French Ambassador to China and the Chinese Foreign Minister reached agreements in several separate but interconnected accords. In one agreement the French conceded to the Chinese unhindered use of the port of Haiphong and the Haiphong-Kwangsi railroad for trans-

---

[1] Memo, OP–35 to OP–03, of 25 Jan. 1946.

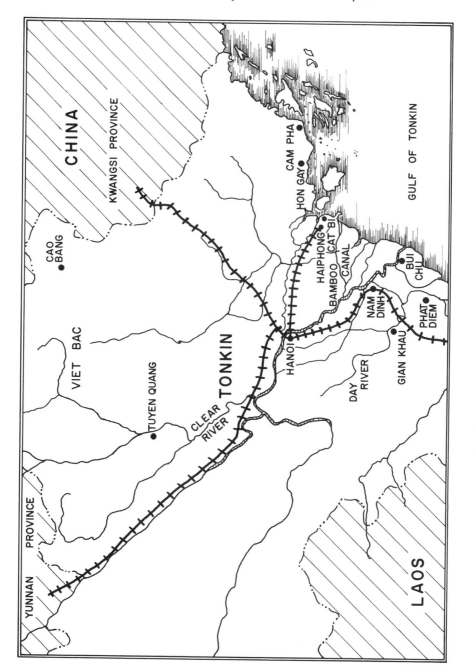

Northern Tonkin, with main rail lines.

porting goods into South China. They transferred to the Chinese ownership of that section of the railroad running between Kunming and Hokow, in southern China. These concessions represented the price paid by the French for a separate agreement, completed on the same day, by which the Chinese promised to withdraw all their forces from northern Indochina and relinquish control there by the end of March 1946. One French official expressed the opinion that the decision to withdraw occupational forces from northern Indochina was based also on the Chinese hope that this action would set an example for the Soviets, who continued to occupy positions in Manchuria.[2]

For months prior to the signing of the Sino-French accords, parallel negotiations had been underway in Hanoi between Sainteny and Ho Chi Minh, the latter continuing to claim the title of President of the Democratic Republic of Vietnam. Typically, the Communists welcomed negotiations as a means toward achieving their objectives, taking "advantage of the contradictions between the French and Chiang Kai-shek forces. . . ."[3] The fact that these negotiations were conducted constituted *de facto* recognition of Ho's revolutionary government. Such recognition bolstered Ho's claims of his regime's legitimacy and enhanced beliefs held by many people that the Viet Minh movement provided the most likely prospect for attaining independence from colonial rule.

While Sainteny attempted to gain Viet Minh concurrence to restoring at least some degree of French influence in northern Indochina, Ho sought not only to obtain Vietnam's independence but also to gain the right for his government to rule all three sections of the country. According to an American diplomat who visited Hanoi at this time, Sainteny responded to the Viet Minh demands by offering "complete independence within [the] French community." Ho, in turn, informed the United States representative of his suspicions that such a formula represented only "new language to describe usual French control . . . [of Vietnamese] affairs."[4]

Meanwhile, the French Navy had assembled at Saigon and other Vietnamese ports almost all of its seagoing units in the Far East in order to

---

[2] "Franco-Chinese Agreement Concerning Sino-Indochinese Relations," of 28 Feb. 1946 in Cole, *Conflict in Indo-China*, pp. 7–9; msg, U.S. Embassy, China, of 1 Mar. 1946 in U.S., State Department, *The Far East*, Vol. VIII of *Foreign Relations of the United States, 1946* (Washington: GPO, 1971), pp. 28–31.

[3] Giap, *People's War, People's Army*, pp. 90-91.

[4] Msg, Assistant Chief, Division of Southeast Asian Affairs, of 27 Feb. 1946 in *Foreign Relations of the United States, 1946*, Vol. VIII, pp. 26–27.

form an amphibious force. This consisted of 3 cruisers, 7 destroyer types, a transport group of 8 ships (including aircraft carrier *Béarn*, which operated as a supply and troop ship), and a unit of 2 LSTs and 8 LCIs. By 28 February, embarkation of 21,700 men of the landing force and their arms, ammunition, vehicles, and equipment was essentially completed. The French amphibious force got underway for Tonkin on the following day. The 6th of March would be the last day, for two weeks, in which tides would be high enough to permit these French ships to transit the Haiphong channel.[5]

As usual, power and diplomacy played complementary roles. It hardly seemed coincidental that Sainteny reached an agreement with Ho the same day that the French flotilla steamed up the Haiphong channel, which had been cleared the previous fall by Rear Admiral Buckmaster's minesweepers. The Preliminary Agreement recognized "the Republic of Vietnam as a free state, having its own government, parliament, army and treasury. . . ." A proviso stipulated that the new state would be part of "the Indo-Chinese Federation and . . . the French Union." [6] The French and Viet Minh agreed to abide by the results of a referendum of the people of Cochin China to to determine if they desired to be unified with Annam and Tonkin.

The Viet Minh pledged to "accept amicably the French army when, in conformance with international agreements, it relieves the Chinese forces." However, in an annex to the basic agreement, French forces in northern Indochina were limited to a mere 15,000 men, fewer than the number already in the Haiphong area with the amphibious expedition. The annex further stipulated that, within five years, all French forces, except those charged with the defense of naval and air bases, would be relieved by the Vietnamese Army. Both parties were required to "stop hostilities immediately" and "to create the favorable climate necessary to the immediate opening of friendly and frank negotiations" on a number of matters reserved for future resolution. These matters included "the diplomatic relations of Vietnam with foreign states; the future status of Indo-China; and French economic and cultural interests in Vietnam." [7]

Hours before Ho Chi Minh and Sainteny signed these documents in Hanoi, the French Expeditionary Force, commanded by General Leclerc,

---

[5] Mordal, *Navy in Indochina*, pp. 164–68; Kilian, *Naval Infantrymen*, pp. 52–62.

[6] "Franco-D.R. Vietnam Agreements," of 6 Mar. 1946 in Cole, *Conflict in Indo-China*, pp. 40–42.

[7] *Ibid.*

prepared to land at Haiphong. At 0840 on 6 March, as French landing craft reached a point approximately 2,000 meters east of Haiphong, a heavy volume of artillery and small-arms fire was encountered. Amazingly, this attack was launched by the Chinese—not the Viet Minh. Return fire by the French ships was withheld for more than an hour. Then, a half-hour of "very effective" bombardment followed, highlighted by a direct hit that demolished an ammunition depot. The Chinese called a truce and sent officials to destroyer *Triomphant* to negotiate a settlement. The intensity of the action was indicated by the 439 holes later counted in her superstructure. French losses during the engagement totaled 24 dead and about 100 wounded. Later, Chinese officials claimed that they had failed to receive orders to implement the Sino-French accords of 28 February, under which French landings were authorized.[8] Following further Sino-French discussions on board *Triomphant* French forces began to land on 7 March without opposition. Not until 16 March 1946 would Chinese officials allow French troops to enter Hanoi.

On 8 March 1946, in a separate Anglo-French arrangement, the French agreed to take on Mountbatten's duties. Faced with this development, the Combined Chiefs of Staff, on 28 March, formally designated the French military commander in Indochina the Allied agent for Japanese repatriation. In the words of a British official historian, this decision meant that Great Britain "ceased to have any responsibility whatever in French Indo-China. . . ."[9] The agreement expedited the withdrawal of all British forces from Indochina, a process completed by April.

On 10 April, the American Joint Chiefs of Staff, acting with their British counterparts as the Combined Chiefs of Staff, stated through diplomatic channels that they had "no objection to the relief of Chinese troops in northern French Indo-China by French forces, since they consider that such arrangements are a matter for determination by the Governments of France and China." The Combined Chiefs added that "since the Franco-Chinese agreement completes the reversion of all Indo-China to French control," the French military commander in the area should assume all "duties and responsibilities for disarmament and evacuation of Japanese in Indo-China."[10]

---

[8] Mordal, *Navy in Indochina*, pp. 167–77; Kilian, *Naval Infantrymen*, pp. 67–73.

[9] Kirby, *Surrender of Japan*, pp. 305–06.

[10] Msg, SECSTATE, of 10 Apr. 1946 in *Foreign Relations of the United States, 1946*, Vol. VIII, p. 34–35.

The first of the follow-on negotiations, agreed to on 6 March, began in mid-April when a preliminary conference of Viet Minh and French leaders convened in Dalat. It soon became evident that little progress could be made at this conference delineating the authority of the "free state" of Vietnam. Even less headway was made in scheduling the referendum in Cochin China. One of the issues complicating these negotiations was the Communist charge that the limited French military actions in Cochin China represented a breach of the truce. Against such a background of mutual hostility and distrust, the Dalat conference was concluded in May without any real success except for an agreement to reopen negotiations in France later that summer.[11]

The Chinese 60th Army was redeployed from Haiphong to Manchuria at the end of April by twenty-seven United States Navy LSTs. Even then, a few small Chinese units remained in Indochina and there were reports of scattered armed clashes between Chinese and French troops. This dangerous situation did not end until August, when the final units of Chiang Kai-shek departed.[12]

The Republic of Cochin China

Vietnamese nationalist leaders in Cochin China—many of whom opposed union of that region with the Democratic Republic of Vietnam—had been seeking to establish a separate government. On 30 May Vice Admiral d'Argenlieu recognized the Republic of Cochin China as a provisionally autonomous state. D'Argenlieu's recognition was contingent upon the referendum in the South (already agreed to in principle by both sides) and ratification by the constitutional body of the French Union. The Viet Minh claimed that this recognition violated the accords previously signed with the French.[13]

In Tonkin, the signing of the Preliminary Agreement on 6 March 1946 had not resulted in an amicable acceptance of the French Army in Tonkin, the complete cessation of hostilities, or the creation of a favorable climate

---

[11] *Ibid.;* Lancaster, *Emancipation of French Indochina,* pp. 154–55; Giap, *People's War, People's Army,* p. 91.

[12] *Foreign Relations of the United States, 1946,* Vol. VIII, pp. 33, 36–37, 42–43; COMNAV-FORWESTPAC, "Narrative of Seventh Fleet," p. 11; Mordal, *Navy in Indochina,* pp. 188–89; Edgar O'Ballance, *The Indo-China War, 1945–54: A Study in Guerrilla Warfare* (London: Faber and Faber, 1964), p. 64.

[13] Lancaster, *Emancipation of French Indochina,* pp. 156–58.

for further negotiations. Characterizing the accord as "making peace to go forward," the Viet Minh undertook to reduce the opposition and to consolidate their power in the north. And to that end, they would employ violent as well as non-violent means. Their stated intent, "to exterminate the reactionary colonialists and the traitors," made clear the extent to which they were willing to go to achieve their goals. It was thus not surprising that the Preliminary Agreement was followed by a period of increasing strife in the South as well as in the North, as terrorists carried out acts of assassination and "armed propaganda." When French authorities reacted to terrorism by apprehending suspects and destroying houses where terrorists sought refuge, Ho Chi Minh charged that the French were taking "political prisoners" and undermining "democratic liberties." He demanded that such actions be halted as a precondition for the resumption of more tranquil conditions in the North.[14]

The Viet Minh used the period after the signing of these accords to dispose of the Vietnamese armed forces of the non-Communist nationalist party known as the Dai Viet Quoc Dan Dang, or simply the Dai Viet, which occupied certain areas along the Chinese border and in the midland of North Vietnam. In April, the Viet Minh ambushed a road convoy bringing the crew of a French naval patrol plane from Cat Bi Airfield into Haiphong. The following two months witnessed attacks against river convoys between Haiphong and Hanoi.[15]

As they issued public statements designed to enlist sympathy for their cause in France, the United States, and other nations, the Communists sought further concessions in an extension of the Preliminary Agreement. Meanwhile, French Navy and Army units were overcoming political and military opposition in reestablishing French authority in population centers, including Hon Gay and Cam Pha, along the northern coast of Tonkin.[16]

Under these stormy conditions, the French and Viet Minh resumed

---

[14] Giap, *People's War, People's Army,* pp. 41E, 90–95; msgs, U. S. Consul Saigon, of 4 May 1946 and U. S. Vice Consul Hanoi, of 1 Nov. 1946 in *Foreign Relations of the United States, 1946,* Vol. VIII, pp. 39–40, 62; see also O'Ballance, *Indo-China War,* pp. 62–68; Hammer, *Struggle for Indochina,* pp. 159–62.

[15] The Dai Viet Party had been suppressed by the French in 1940, but was reestablished with Japanese support following the *coup de force* of March 1945. The Dai Viet's military wing had maintained its existence throughout World War II; see McAlister, *Vietnam: The Origins of Revolution,* pp. 168–78; Giap, *People's War, People's Army,* p. 91; Kilian, *Naval Infantrymen,* pp. 99–100, 107–09.

[16] *Ibid.,* pp. 95–104; Mordal, *Navy in Indochina,* pp. 185–88.

negotiations on 6 July 1946 at Fontainebleau, France. Once again, the principal discussions concerned the degree of independence to be accorded Ho Chi Minh's Democratic Republic of Vietnam within the French Union, and the geographic limits of its power. Ho Chi Minh and his representatives at Fontainebleau saw the French Union as restricted to making recommendations to member states. The French delegates viewed the union as a federation in which unified control would be exercised by France over the diplomatic relations and armed forces of each member state. On the issue of Cochin China's political future, neither side questioned the desirability of eventually polling the people of that area for their opinion, but no progress was made in establishing the date or circumstances under which a referendum would be held.[17]

In August, while discussions continued in Fontainebleau, Admiral d'Argenlieu called for a second Dalat Conference to discuss the organization of an Indochinese Federation. The admiral invited representatives from Cochin China, Cambodia, Laos, and a portion of southern Annam where there was an active separatist movement. The Viet Minh protested that their representatives were not included and voiced suspicions that the new conference was an effort to weaken politically the Democratic Republic of Vietnam. They accused d'Argenlieu of undermining the proceedings in France.[18]

Within Hanoi and Haiphong, Viet Minh militia (known as the Tu Ve) undertook a variety of psychological and armed actions against the French. They erected barricades and other fortifications in key locations, a step that French forces periodically resisted. Early in August, in one of the most serious incidents of 1946, Giap's troops ambushed a French supply convoy near Hanoi, inflicting fifty-two casualties.[19]

A few weeks later it became evident that no further progress would be achieved in the discussions at Fontainebleau. On 14 September 1946, on the eve of his departure from France, Ho Chi Minh signed a temporary agreement with the Minister for Overseas France, pending further negotiations. It called for negotiations on a "general final treaty" to begin no later

---

[17] Hammer, *Struggle for Indochina*, pp. 165–74; Lancaster, *Emancipation of French Indochina*, pp. 157–63.

[18] Hammer, *Struggle for Indochina*, pp. 171–72.

[19] Memo, Chief, Division of Southeast Asian Affairs to Director, Office of Far Eastern Affairs, of 9 Aug. 1946 in *Foreign Relations of the United States, 1946*, Vol. VIII, pp. 52–54; Kilian, *Naval Infantrymen*, p. 106.

than January 1947. Once again, both parties agreed that "all acts of hostility and violence on both sides will cease," and that "the exercise of democratic liberties . . . will be reciprocally guaranteed." [20]

The Growing Crisis

Yet another ominous step in these tangled events came in late October 1946 when, shortly before Ho Chi Minh's return, General Giap arrested all nationalist members of the Constituent Assembly of the Democratic Republic of Vietnam who might have opposed Communist goals. This purge was preliminary to the formation of a new government in November that was controlled by the Communists even more openly than before. Renewed efforts of the Viet Minh militia to build fortifications at key locations in the cities of Haiphong and Hanoi and the evacuation of many Vietnamese to the countryside were further signs of trouble ahead. In Cochin China, a new wave of political assassinations, ambushes, and river mining was reported.[21]

A lengthy dispute over a critical issue with maritime implications—control of the customs service in the port of Haiphong—was laying the foundation for armed action. To prevent the smuggling of Communist war supplies through this major port, and to dry up the source of funds by which additional munitions could be purchased for Giap's forces, the French seized control of imports and exports at Haiphong in October and carried out patrols to cut off Viet Minh supplies coming in by water.

On 20 November 1946, a small French patrol craft captured a Chinese sampan carrying contraband cargo, precipitating a crisis. As tension mounted, the Communist forces set up roadblocks in certain sections of the port city. Heavy fighting broke out when the French began to use bulldozers to remove the barricades. It was only on the following day that French and Viet Minh officials could agree to keep their troops apart in the city to avoid further clashes.[22]

---

[20] The text of the *modus vivendi* is in Cole, *Conflict in Indo-China,* pp. 43–45.

[21] O'Ballance, *Indo-China War,* p. 71; Kilian, *Naval Infantrymen,* pp. 127–28, 186–89; Lancaster, *Emancipation of French Indochina,* pp. 168–69.

[22] Fall, *Two Viet-Nams,* pp. 75–76; Mordal, *Navy in Indochina,* pp. 193–95; Hammer, *Struggle for Indochina,* pp. 182–83.

In the aftermath of these events in Haiphong, the French stiffened their policy towards the Viet Minh. Admiral d'Argenlieu, who was in Paris at the time of the Haiphong incident, suggested retaliation. The High Commissioner's proposal was approved by Premier Georges Bidault and authorization was given to Colonel Debès, commander of French troops in Haiphong, to "use all the means at your disposal" to make himself the "complete master" of the city.[23]

Accordingly, on 23 November Debès issued an ultimatum to the Viet Minh demanding that they evacuate specified sections of the city and reply to his demand in two hours.[24]

The Viet Minh failed to comply and, an hour after the deadline, the 5.5-inch guns of sloop *Savorgnan de Brazza* opened fire on rebel concentrations, while French ground and naval forces moved in to take the enemy positions. By the 27th, French forces had ejected the Viet Minh from the city and serious fighting ceased. Throughout these actions, the French lost twenty dead and thirty wounded. The French naval bombardment inflicted heavy casualties in Haiphong.[25]

The Haiphong affair, continuing violence in other parts of Vietnam, the diplomatic impasse, and the scheduled expiration of the Fontainebleau *modus vivendi* at the end of 1946 indicated to the United States, and all other parties concerned with Southeast Asia, that a general conflict was near at hand. To this time, American diplomats primarily played the role of neutral, but increasingly concerned observers of the growing crisis. In early December, Washington decided that, at the very least, it should urge both sides to achieve a peaceful resolution of their differences. Acting upon instructions from the State Department, the United States Ambassador to France, Jefferson Caffery, emphasized to Paris officials the need for a pacific settlement of Viet Minh-French differences. Among the dangers foreseen, should a complete rupture in relations occur, according to Acting Secretary of State Acheson, was the possibility that the Vietnamese might turn "irrevocably against West and toward ideologies and affiliations hostile

---

[23] Quoted in *Ibid.*, p. 183.

[24] *Ibid.*

[25] Kilian, *Naval Infantrymen*, p. 142; Fall, *Two Viet-Nams*, p. 76 and Lancaster, *Emancipation of French Indochina*, p. 171 state that it was the heavy cruiser *Suffren* which bombarded Haiphong, but according to Mordal's *Navy in Indochina*, pp. 194–95, *Suffren* did not arrive with troops from Saigon until after the bombardment.

[to] democracies which could result perpetual forment [*sic.*] Indochina with consequences all Southeast Asia." [26]

In Indochina, a similar plea for moderation was made to the Viet Minh and to local French authorities by Abbot L. Moffat, Chief of the State Department's Division of Southeast Asian Affairs, who had come to Indochina for a first-hand view of the situation. It is of interest to note a portion of the instructions forwarded to Moffat by Acting Secretary of State Acheson on 5 December, although this message apparently was not received until after the diplomat's conversations with Ho. Acheson had warned:

> Keep in mind Ho's clear record as agent international communism, absence evidence recantation Moscow affiliations, confused political situation France and support Ho receiving French Communist Party. Least desirable eventuality would be establishment Communist-dominated, Moscow-oriented state Indochina in view Dept, which most interested info strength noncommunist elements Vietnam.[27]

The results of American representations, both in Paris and Hanoi, were discouraging. On 17 December, Secretary of State James F. Byrnes issued a pessimistic summary of the situation. It began by noting that the Vietnam government continued to be controlled by "a small Communist group possibly in indirect touch with Moscow and direct touch" with Chinese Communist leaders. Byrnes pointed out that the Vietnamese should have realized that it was to their benefit to have continuing French influence in the region, "not only as an antidote to Soviet influence but to protect Vietnam and SEA [Southeast Asia] from future Chinese imperialism." The secretary concluded this appraisal with the following enumeration of the overwhelming problems of Franco-Vietnamese relations:

> (a) complete mutual distrust, (b) failure of the French to resolve their own views on "free state within French Union", (c) almost childish Vietnamese attitude and knowledge of economic questions and vague groping for "independence." Agreement cannot be reached by trying to reach accords on incidental problems. Basic Vietnam powers and relations with France must

---

[26] Msg, Acting SECSTATE, of 5 Dec. 1946 in *Foreign Relations of the United States, 1946,* Vol. VIII, pp. 67–69.

[27] U.S., Congress, Senate, Committee on Foreign Relations, *The United States and Vietnam: 1944–47* (92nd Cong., 2nd sess.) (Washington: GPO, 1972), pp. 12–13; msg, Acting SECSTATE, of 5 Dec. 1946 in *Foreign Relations of the United States, 1946,* Vol. VIII, pp. 67–69.

first be established. Not only new faces are needed but neutral good offices or even mediation may be essential.[28]

By now, time had run out for further negotiations.

The Start of the French-Viet Minh War

On 19 December 1946, the Viet Minh attempted a lightning coup in the capital city of Tonkin. At eight in the evening, bands of insurgents signaled the start of open conflict throughout Vietnam by cutting off electricity and water in Hanoi and launching indiscriminate attacks on French military and civilian personnel. Nevertheless, due in part to a last-minute warning of the impending coup from intelligence sources, French forces repulsed the enemy after several days of heavy fighting and reestablished firm control in Hanoi.[29]

At the same time, Ho Chi Minh appealed to "compatriots all over the country" to "rise up" and "fight the French colonialists." He ordered:

> Those who have rifles will use their rifles; those who have swords will use their swords; those who have no swords will use spades, hoes, or sticks. Everyone must endeavor to oppose the colonialists and save his country.
> Armymen, self-defense guards, and militiamen!
> The hour for national salvation has struck! We must sacrifice even our last drop of blood to safeguard our country.[30]

Unlike the Haiphong incident of the previous month, the attempted coup in Hanoi was accompanied by similar Viet Minh attacks at other locations in Tonkin, Annam, and Cochin China. As the French Overseas Minister, Marius Moutet, assessed the situation early in January 1947: "Before any negotiations today, it is necessary to have a military decision."[31] A war that would last almost eight years was underway.

---

[28] Msg, SECSTATE, of 17 Dec. 1946 in *Ibid.*, pp. 72–73.

[29] Fall, *Two Viet-Nams*, pp. 76–77; Kilian, *Naval Infantrymen*, pp. 149–53.

[30] "Appeal to the Entire People to Wage the Resistance War," of 20 Dec. 1946 in Ho, *On Revolution*, p. 172; Pham Van Dong uses the date of 19 December in his *25 Years of National Struggle and Construction*, p. 21.

[31] Quoted in Hammer, *Struggle for Indochina*, p. 194.

French military operations in the first phase of the war against the Viet Minh were shaped, to a large extent, by geographical considerations and maritime capabilities. France could bring troops and supplies in by sea and move them from one point to another on the long, indented coastline, projecting them ashore and up inland waterways by amphibious operations. Within extensive regions of Indochina, movement by water far exceeded that by land. Naval ships and craft could extend control over major water routes and the traffic that flowed on them and intercept enemy movements along coastal waters. The limiting factor would be the composition and size of naval forces operating in the Indochinese area.

Under Commander in Chief French Naval Forces, Far East, Vice Admiral Philippe Auboyneau, the main fleet units were assigned to Commander Naval Division, Far East. At the start of the war in December 1946, the naval units consisted of 3 heavy cruisers, 3 colonial sloops, 4 minesweeper-corvettes, 4 frigates, and 1 division of minesweepers. Auboyneau's other major subordinate was Commander French Naval Forces, Indochina, who commanded approximately 100 craft (ranging in size from 192-foot LCTs to 41-foot assault landing craft (LCAs) and small native craft) and the Far East Naval Brigade. On 1 January 1947, the Naval Amphibious Force was organized under Naval Forces, Indochina. It had two flotillas, one in Tonkin and one in Cochin China. Five sections of naval commandos were assigned to Tonkin and two to Cochin China.[32]

France's overall military plan of action envisaged three phases, namely:

1. The control of an area's key road and waterway lines of communications and the establishment of one or more secure bases in order to provide for the free movement and logistical support of French armed forces.

2. The control of the total area by systematically seizing additional lines of communications and by creating a dense network of additional bases or strong points. The effect of this so-called "oil slick" technique was to saturate an area with friendly forces and hence to eject or destroy the enemy.

3. The ultimate pacification of the area, a stage that was marked by the elimination of subversive sentiments among the population, the restora-

---

[32] Kilian, *Naval Infantrymen*, pp. 227–38.

tion of the authority of the legal government, and the active participation by the indigenous people in defending themselves against the Viet Minh.

Under this strategy, first priority was assigned to the deltas and coastal regions, the most densely populated areas and the location of cities and centers of industry, trade, and communications. These regions provided the country with most of its food. These were also the areas where naval power, in all its forms, could be brought to bear. The French occasionally raided more remote parts of the country, but these raids were judged to be only of "incidental" importance when compared with the "real and continuous struggle [that] took place in the regions we wished to control, namely, the two deltas and certain portions of the central coast where there was a high population density and the most fertile lands."[33] It is worthy of notice, however, that the French violated this principle with disastrous effects when they occupied the isolated outpost at Dien Bien Phu in 1953.

Confronted by superior regular army forces, air forces, and naval power, the Viet Minh would undertake a wide development of guerrilla warfare, combining economic, political, cultural, and propaganda actions with those of a military nature, overthrowing local officials, and eliminating the opposition. The Viet Minh sought to indoctrinate and mobilize the people, to consolidate Communist control, and to counter the French efforts to attract Vietnamese to their side. Toward these ends, full use was made of the extensive political infrastructure that the Communists had established to control and influence the Vietnamese people and to direct and coordinate revolutionary actions. This took form as an intricate network of administrative committees. At the base were villages grouped into intervillages. The latter were subordinated to districts and these, in turn, to provinces. Groups of provinces were organized into zones and further into six interzones encompassing all Vietnam.

On the international scene the Communists attempted to "win over the support of progressive people throughout the world, particularly to closely co-ordinate with the struggle of the French people and those in the French colonies. . . ." Means were employed to sabotage the French economy, to prevent French use of Vietnamese manpower and wealth, and to "use war

---

[33] *Lessons of the War in Indochina,* Vol. II pp. 51–52, 63, 83–84, 90, 110, 112; see also Bernard Fall's commentary in *Two Viet-Nams,* pp. 106–07.

to feed war." Publicizing their interim goal of independence from French colonial rule did much to influence the opinion of many in France and other parts of the world. It attracted varying degrees of support to Viet Minh efforts against the French from many Vietnamese who did not share the ultimate goals of the Communists. The support of international communism did not include, at the start of the war, any substantial supply of arms and munitions. It was, however, helpful in the fields of international politics and propaganda. Within France, a strong Communist party attempted to disrupt the effort against the Viet Minh, to gain sympathy for their cause, and to erode the French resolve.[34]

According to Giap, the war "became a people's war."[35] The form of warfare that would be adopted was along the lines of the concepts of a "people's war" as set forth more than a century before by the noted strategist, General Karl von Clausewitz. The conditions he cited for such a war were:

> That the War is carried on in the heart of the country.
> That it cannot be decided by a single catastrophe.
> That the theatre of War embraces a considerable extent of the country.
> That the national character is favourable to the measure.
> That the country is of a broken and difficult nature, either from being mountainous, or by reason of woods and marshes, or from the peculiar mode of cultivation in use.[36]

Inland Waterways

Particularly notable were the operations of the French Navy on the inland waterways of Vietnam. French naval officers writing of this period often noted that these activities were reminiscent of those undertaken by such men as Rivière, Courbet, and Garnier in the 1870s and 1880s.[37] There also are striking similarities between these operations and the inshore and

---

[34] For a discussion of Communist strategy during the French-Viet Minh War, see Giap, *People's War, People's Army.*

[35] *Ibid.,* p. 43.

[36] Karl von Clausewitz, *On War* (London: Kegan Paul, French, Trubner and Co., 1908), Vol. I, p. 33, Vol. II, pp. 341–50. Mao Tse-tung later prescribed similar actions.

[37] Mordal, *Navy in Indochina,* p. 209; Jean Mauclère, *Sailors on the Canals* (Paris: J. Peyronnet, 1950), p. 20.

NH–79374

French LCM in Indochina.

riverine warfare conducted by American and South Vietnamese forces during the Vietnam War that began in 1965.

Some operations were mounted up the rivers which flowed into the sea along the Annamese coast. A greater effort was devoted to the waterways of Cochin China, where a particular concern was the protection of civilian convoys carrying rice and other supplies into Saigon. But the most crucial riverine region was in Tonkin, where the Viet Minh had their greatest strength and the level of combat was usually at its maximum intensity.[38]

At the outbreak of hostilities in December 1946, a particularly hard-pressed French position in the north was Nam Dinh, the third largest city

---

[38] *Lessons of the War in Indochina,* Vol. II, pp. 352–54; see also ONI, "The Dinassaut Units of Indochina," *The ONI Review, Supp.* (Autumn 1952), pp. 26–34.

in Tonkin, which is located in the delta southeast of Hanoi. Here, a garrison of approximately 500 men and a French civilian population of between 200 and 300 people were holding out against determined Viet Minh attacks. By early January 1947, it became obvious that the evacuation of the civilians in Nam Dinh and the reinforcement of French forces were imperative.

After considering the hazards of an overland expedition, the French developed a plan for mounting a cordinated assault by riverine and airborne forces from Haiphong. The naval forces, consisting of 2 LCTs, 1 LCI, and 4 LCMs (landing craft, mechanized), under the command of Lieutenant François, were assigned the task of transporting artillery, tanks, supplies, and additional troops to the beleaguered garrison of Nam Dinh. The relief force was expected to arrive via the narrow Nam Dinh canal, adjoining the Red River, at dawn on 6 January 1947, within hours of a scheduled drop of 400 paratroopers. The airborne forces had the task of establishing two beachheads on the canal, where Lieutenant François could land his waterborne troops and supplies.

The most direct inland water route from Haiphong to the Red River was the Bamboo Canal. However, this waterway lay in a region controlled by the enemy and the expedition's commanders elected to enter the Red River at its mouth on Tonkin Gulf. Sailing from Haiphong on the night of 4 January, the flotilla narrowly succeeded in crossing the shallow bar at the mouth of the Red River at high tide on the following morning. Beyond lay the enemy, who opened heavy fire at several points during the passage of the French force up the river, but failed to halt it. Early in the morning on 6 January, under cover of darkness and heavy fog, the riverine amphibious force approached Nam Dinh.

The paratroop elements, which were only partially landed due to heavy antiaircraft fire, became widely scattered during the drop and were unable to seize the designated beachheads. Then, heavy enemy fire erupted from both banks of the waterway, sinking one LCM and killing Lieutenant François. Under these critical conditions, Lieutenant Garnier succeeded to the command of the force and took decisive action by landing his embarked troops on the other side of the river from the planned beachheads. He supported these troops with a heavy volume of gunfire from his landing craft. Within a short time, the enemy's positions on the near side of the canal were neutralized, and the French concentrated their fire on the opposite bank, from which the enemy soon fled. By noon, the way was clear for the entry of French forces into Nam Dinh. At 1630, its mission accomplished in a highly satisfactory manner, Lieutenant Garnier's flotilla departed for Haiphong after embarking French civilian evacuees.

The completion of the January 1947 mission did not end the Navy's involvement at Nam Dinh, for it soon became evident that the enemy was continuing to concentrate forces in the area. In March, two additional supply and reinforcement convoys were dispatched to the city. Each succeeded in its mission, despite enemy ambushes from waterway banks. Thereafter, monthly or bi-monthly convoys to Nam Dinh continued on a regular basis. Although logistical operations were recognized as essential, one naval writer observed that the recurring operations absorbed a large percentage of the Navy's resources in Tonkin, often precluding assault operations elsewhere in the north.[39]

The specific problem of the Nam Dinh convoys was related to a general complaint by the French Navy that the Army officers who controlled naval operations in Indochina tended to use river forces all too seldom for aggressive strikes at the enemy. Instead, they claimed, the Army favored patrol missions that supported the overall effort to control lines of communication. In addition to noting the relative lack of outright assault missions, official critiques of the war concluded that the effectiveness of river assault divisions was hampered by the absence of integral landing forces of sufficient strength to assure the control of contested riverbanks. As a result, one of the major naval recommendations emerging from the war called for the establishment of a powerful amphibious corps under a single commander, composed of riverine craft, sizeable ground forces, and artillery. It was further suggested that this force, foreshadowing the Mobile Riverine Force later established by the United States in the Vietnam War, should be assigned the responsibility for maintaining security within a specified territorial zone.[40]

Realistic appraisals by the French of the shortcomings of their river forces included recommendations for specially constructed craft with greater speed and armament than the converted Allied landing craft that typically were used. The French further acknowledged the enemy's ability to plan assaults on river forces, his skill in exploiting support and intelligence gained from the local people, and his ingenuity in using the watercraft that

---

[39] Mordal, *Navy in Indochina,* pp. 208–17; Kilian, *Naval Infantrymen,* pp. 168–78; NA Paris, report, of 11 Dec. 1950.

[40] *Lessons of the War in Indochina,* Vol. II, pp. 348–58.

abounded in the deltas in order to "infiltrate everywhere and break out of our most carefully deployed formations." [41]

One writer has suggested that the creation of the *dinassauts* "may well have been one of the few worthwhile contributions of the Indochina war to military knowledge." A senior French Army commander, who had a direct appreciation of these forces, summarized the importance of their role in the following words: "For the first time, our armed forces have created a flexible, strategic instrument, thanks to the diversity of its materiel, capable of action in every region without being tied by the bonds of territorial security." [42]

Amphibious Operations

When the Viet Minh launched their offensive in December 1946 the port city of Tourane just north of the 16th parallel was threatened and the French forces there placed in jeopardy. As was the case years later when American forces were deployed to the area, the major road and railway connections to this region were among the first targets of the Viet Minh, who easily obstructed the land routes by destroying bridges or excavating whole sections of the highway.

The situation in the Tourane area was brought under control by troops brought in by sea and supported by gunfire from ships of the French Navy, including heavy cruisers *Suffren* and *Tourville,* during the period 20 December 1946 to 8 January 1947. Once the security of that city was assured, the French mounted a series of amphibious operations to recapture Hue, then held by the Viet Minh. These landings were undertaken despite the seasonal peak of the northeast monsoon which brought periods of rough seas, pounding surf, and limited visibility.

Between 18 and 21 January 1947, the French Navy landed troops at four separate points north of Hai Van Pass, where the road and railroad from Tourane to Hue hug the coast. More than 1,500 troops were landed under the protection of naval gunfire, and supplies built up for the overland advance to Hue. Then, on 4 February, the second phase of this operation began, when a flotilla of ten landing craft, with troops embarked, entered

---

[41] *Ibid.,* pp. 173–75.

[42] Quoted in Mordal, *Navy in Indochina,* p. 239; Bernard B. Fall, *Street Without Joy* (Harrisburg, Pa.: Stackpole Co., 1964), p. 44.

NH–79392

French amphibious operation north of Nha Trang late in the French-Viet Minh War.

the lagoons separating the approaches to Hue from the open sea. A frontal assault by the landing force and French Army columns moving up from the south led to the recapture of Hue by 9 February.

Over the next two months, equally successful amphibious operations were launched in the Fai Fo region, just south of Tourane, and at several points on the southern Tonkin coast. By the end of March, the French had reestablished control over most of the major population centers along the coastal sections, although the Viet Minh still controlled pockets in the area.[43]

---

[43] Mordal, *Navy in Indochina,* pp. 217–20.

Air support of an amphibious assault at Fai Fo, on 16 and 17 March 1947, marked the first combat use of aircraft carriers in French history. The ship from which the missions were launched was *Dixmude* which, as HMS *Biter,* had served in the British Royal Navy during World War II. Less than 500 feet in length and with a maximum speed of 16.5 knots, *Dixmude* was an escort carrier converted in the United States from a C–3 merchant-ship hull. The ship carried Dauntless aircraft, originally designed as United States Navy dive bombers. Ten days after the Fai Fo operation, *Dixmude* provided close air support for the forces that had landed. She then proceeded north into Tonkin Gulf, and on 2 April her aircraft struck Viet Minh base areas near Tuyen Quang, a road junction in the mountains northwest of Hanoi. Thus, in her first actions, *Dixmude* had demonstrated the importance of a carrier's ability to move freely from one area to another and concentrate air power wherever it was needed. Such a capability was particularly important in view of the small number of airfields in Vietnam and their limited facilities to support aircraft.[44]

As a consequence of actions such as these in the delta and along the coast, the initial Communist attacks against population centers in Vietnam were repulsed and overrun positions were promptly regained by French forces. Giap withdrew his troops to remote inland regions, where he built bases to prepare for guerrilla warfare and the development of regular army units. He continued to use the Viet Bac for his main base area and established smaller bases in the provinces of Thanh Hoa, Nghe An, and Ha Tinh—south of the Red River Delta. In addition to providing safe havens for the training of troops, the manufacturing of munitions in small plants, and the stockpiling of arms, these base areas were also the location of political headquarters.[45]

French Riverine and Coastal Operations, 1947-1949

In October 1947 the French launched an offensive, Operation *Lea*, which sought to deal a decisive blow to the enemy. The specific goals of Operation *Lea* included capture of the Viet Minh leadership, destruction of the main

---

[44] *Ibid.,* pp. 220, 284–86; *Lessons of the War in Indochina,* Vol. II, pp. 337–38; see also *The ONI Review,* IV (Nov. 1949), p. 40 and V (May 1950), p. 210. For the overall effect of French air power on the Viet Minh, see O'Ballance, *Indo-China War,* p. 98.

[45] O'Ballance, *Indo-China War,* pp. 66–67.

NH-79379

French patrol ship cruising in Along Bay.

force of Communist regular troops, and seizure of positions that would facilitate the sealing of the Chinese border across which supplies were flowing.

This French offensive achieved only limited success. A paratroop assault against the Viet Minh headquarters in the Viet Bac failed to capture either Ho Chi Minh or General Giap. The subsequent advance of the French Army into the Viet Bac did not result in contact with the elusive Communist main force, which avoided engagement. A combined amphibious and ground thrust up the Red and Clear River valleys into northwestern Tonkin did succeed in securing pockets of territory for the French, but again the enemy's principal forces largely eluded the French. Only in northeastern Tonkin, at the border town of Cao Bang and other points along Route 4, were specific objectives achieved.[46]

A more successful French operation was carried out early in 1948, when

---

[46] Fall, *Street Without Joy,* pp. 28–31.

a naval force composed of four LCMs and two LCAs embarked two companies of Army troops and naval commandos to raid Viet Minh positions near Gian Khau. The objective, sixty-five kilometers from the *dinassaut* base at Nam Dinh, had to be approached through enemy infested territory via the Day River. Nevertheless, the force advanced under cover of darkness and achieved strategic, if not tactical, surprise. On 2 February, with minimal opposition, landing parties swept through four enemy villages, destroying a number of Viet Minh installations.

After anchoring in the Gian Khau area overnight, the flotilla sailed downriver on the morning of 3 February, fully expecting an enemy ambush. To meet this threat, the French deployed their forces in two columns, with the LCAs 500 meters in advance of the LCMs. The lead boats were instructed to scan the banks for the controlled mines often used by the Viet Minh. In the event of attack, the commanders of both types of landing craft were directed to land the embarked troops as speedily as possible on the enemy's flanks, while their guns opened heavy fire into the Viet Minh positions.

On the same day, at exactly noon, the anticipated attack was initiated from Viet Minh positions scattered on both sides of the river. But the French executed the planned counterattack and achieved excellent results. Within twenty minutes, the Viet Minh were driven back with losses of more than 100 men and a number of weapons, including 1 37-millimeter gun, 3 mortars, and 12 rifles.

The Gian Khau operation and the earlier *dinassaut* missions to Nam Dinh demonstrated some of the general lessons that the French had derived from their experiences in riverine combat. As at Gian Khau on the night of 2 February 1948, naval mobility often gave the French the element of suprise.[47]

The French plans for the expected ambush of 3 February indicated their respect for the enemy's use of controlled mines, which often initiated an ambush, or which, in many instances, were employed in conjunction with barricades thrown across waterways to obstruct river movement. Yet the actual attack, on 3 February, revealed the tendency of the Viet Minh to vitiate the effectiveness of their firepower by failing to concentrate it. The French counterattack demonstrated the importance of responding as quickly as possible with a concentrated and heavy volume of gunfire.

---

[47] *Lessons of the War in Indochina,* Vol. II, pp. 173–75; NA Paris, report, 590–50 of 11 Dec. 1950, pp. 8–13.

For the remainder of 1948, both sides consolidated their positions. The Viet Minh continued to train and equip their main forces in remote areas, to develop local militia and regional forces, and to establish political footholds in rural regions. Aided by their Navy, the French won or retained predominant influence in the heavily populated and strategically important delta and coastal regions of Vietnam. Notable successes were achieved in Cochin China, where Viet Minh actions resulted in the alienation of two strong religious sects—the Cao Dai, in the Tay Ninh Province area northwest of Saigon, and the Hoa Hao, in the region around Can Tho. The French exploited this situation by offering the sects substantial autonomy in return for a pledge to resist the Viet Minh. In Tonkin, strongly Catholic regions near Bui Chu and Phat Diem, which previously had attempted to maintain a perilous neutrality between the contenders in the war, began to swing to the French side.[48]

At the end of the year, the cruise of *Arromanches* showed again the major contributions aircraft carriers could make in a limited war. *Arromanches,* formerly HMS *Colossus,* a light carrier of British design, had been lent to France by the United Kingdom in August 1946 for a five-year period. With her full-load displacement of 18,000 tons, length of 695 feet, and speed of 25 knots, she was far better suited for combat operations than escort carrier *Dixmude.*

Making full use of her mobility during the short time on station, from 29 November 1948 to 4 January 1949, *Arromanches* and her obsolescent Dauntless aircraft carried out as many air support and strike sorties against the enemy as had been flown by the entire French Air Force in Indochina during all of 1948.[49]

Because of her mobility, the carrier was able to select launching and recovery points, thus avoiding adverse northeast monsoonal weather conditions which often grounded land-based air units. As United States forces would learn later, weather in Vietnam exerted a major influence on military actions, particularly air operations in the north. Late September is the beginning of the autumnal transition from the southeast to the northeast monsoon. Soon thereafter, cooling of the northern part of the vast continent

---

[48] O'Ballance, *Indo-China War,* pp. 83–92; *Lessons of the War in Indochina,* Vol. II, p. 17.

[49] ONI, "French Naval and Air Operations in Indochina," *The ONI Review,* VI (Nov. 1951), p. 437; Mordal, *Navy in Indochina* pp. 284–91; Norman Polmar, *Aircraft Carriers: A Graphic History of Carrier Aviation and Its Influence on World Events* (Garden City, N.Y.: Doubleday and Co., 1967), pp. 564–67.

NH–74146

SB–2C Helldivers landing on Arromanches *in the Gulf of Tonkin.*

of Asia develops a wide, high-pressure area which increases in intensity. In the Northern Hemisphere, the air spirals clockwise out of the high pressure area. Although cold and dry at the source region over China, the northeast monsoon is greatly modified as it passes over the South China Sea and the Gulf of Tonkin, arriving over northern Vietnam as a warm, humid air mass. The result is increased rainfall and cloudiness east of the Annam mountains. This is the period of the *Crachine,* a phenomenon which occurs periodically until spring, generally persisting for two to five days at a time, with clouds 3,000 to 5,000-feet thick. Ceilings are usually below

1,000 feet and frequently below 500 feet. Often accompanied by fog and drizzle or light rain, visibility is generally reduced to less than two miles and frequently to less than a half-mile.

The transitional periods from late September to early November and from mid-March to mid-May are characterized by changeable weather, bringing frequent showers and thunderstorms as the zone of convergence between the two monsoons transits the area. In the summer, when heavy rains from the southwest monsoon are falling over the southern portion of Indochina, northern Vietnam enjoys its dry season.

Monsoonal weather also had an impact on naval operations along the coast, particularly in northern Annam and southern Tonkin, where high seas were produced by winds of the northeast monsoon sweeping across the full reach of the South China Sea. In addition to affecting French amphibious operations, seasonal weather influenced the introduction of Communist men and material into South Vietnam by sea, their movement from point to point along the coast, and the French efforts to prevent such operations.

Even without the problem of weather, the French Navy faced difficult problems in its maritime surveillance campaign. The legitimate activities of Vietnamese fishing and other small craft provided natural camouflage for the enemy's efforts to move men, arms, and supplies within Indochina, or to introduce these sinews of war from China. A French naval officer once related how, from a single point off the Annamese coast, he counted more than 500 small craft whose sails appeared to touch "each other," giving the appearance of a "white sea."[50] The formidable problem, in these circumstances, was to identify which, if any, of the myriad of small craft were operating in the service of Ho Chi Minh.

The task of interdiction was further complicated by effective Viet Minh control of a number of islands in the Gulf of Siam, coastal regions near Vinh in Tonkin, between Tourane and Nha Trang in Annam, and Cape Camau in Cochin China. Geographic factors compounded the problem, since the tortured coastline of much of Indochina offered numerous hiding places.

During the northeast monsoon season from October through March, the French considered the seas off the northern part of Indochina too rough to allow extensive waterborne traffic. During that time, naval leaders diverted their major attention to southern waters. When favorable weather

---

[50] Quoted in Mordal, *Navy in Indochina*, p. 275; Hammer, *Struggle for Indochina*, p. 232.

returned to the north, the French shifted their patrol units to the coasts of northern Annam and Tonkin.[51]

French ships and craft were placed under regional operational commands. For inshore and riverine activities, two of these commands were organized under the operational control of Commander Naval Forces (*COMAR*), Indochina and designated *COMAR* Tonkin and *COMAR* Mekong, the latter in the Cochin China region. Regional commands for offshore surveillance were established under Commander Naval Division, Far East. These were, *SURMAR* (a French acronym for *Surveillance Maritime*) Tonkin, covering the sector from the Chinese border to 18° north, and *SURMAR* Annam, which controlled the area extending from 18° north to 10°30' north to the Thailand border.[52]

To increase the effectiveness of their maritime patrol efforts, the French established a third subordinate command, Commander Naval Aviation, under *COMAR* Indochina. The former was assigned land-based squadrons of Sea Otter observation aircraft and Catalina amphibian patrol planes, based near Saigon at Cat Lai and Tan Son Nhut respectively. Catalinas also were based near Haiphong at Cat Bi. Although used primarily for observation and coastal surveillance missions, the naval air units were under the operational control of the French Air Force commander in Indochina.[53]

The French were convinced that conducting small-scale amphibious raids against Viet Minh supply points along the coast was one effective means of interdicting the enemy's logistics. These operations resulted in a number of successes in destroying small enemy craft beached on the coast or the personnel facilities and supply depots that supported these units. Nevertheless, in their critique of the war, French officers noted that one of the frustrating aspects of such operations was the ability of the enemy to escape before contact was made. For this reason, French tacticians emphasized the need for the utmost speed of execution directly against predetermined locations of enemy forces. These authorities noted that encirclement tactics were

---

[51] Mordal, *Navy in Indochina*, pp. 276–77.

[52] NA Saigon, report. 1-S-50 of 21 July 1950, JN 11285, box 6, FRC; ONI. "French Naval and Air Operations in Indochina" p. 431.

[53] NA Saigon, report, 1-S-50 of 21 July 1950, JN 11285, box 6 FRC; *Lessons of the War in Indochina*, Vol. II, p. 336; Naval Section, "Area Report on Southeast Asia by the Military Group of the Joint State-Defense Survey Mission to Southeast Asia," 22 Nov. 1950, encl 8, p. 2 (hereafter cited as Melby-Erskine Report).

typically unproductive in the face of the enemy's skillful ability to avoid combat when it was in their interest to do so.[54]

By the middle of of 1950, the French naval units involved in the war increased to approximately 165 ships and craft. French naval personnel totaled about 12,000, 10,000 of whom were assigned to the riverine, amphibious, and logistic components of *COMAR* Indochina. The seagoing forces included only 1 combatant ship of destroyer size or larger (a light cruiser) and 7 major auxiliary ships (1 transport; 2 oilers; 1 repair ship; 3 LSTs), with a carrier occasionally on the scene. The balance of the French forces was composed of patrol and landing craft, minesweeping units, and utility types. Approximately 40 of the landing craft, and a number of naval commando units were organized into 6 *dinassauts,* 4 of which operated in the delta regions of Cochin China and Cambodia and 2 in Tonkin.

A cruiser, 7 corvettes, 6 minesweepers, 2 escort ships, 3 launches, and 2 squadrons of naval observation aircraft had the formidable task of patrolling a coastline measuring approximately 1,500 nautical miles in length,[55] an assignment that obviously could not be completely fulfilled without additional ships and inshore craft. Nevertheless, the French Navy reportedly achieved considerable success. Between 1,200 and 1,800 suspicious junks and sampans were hailed each quarter. Intelligence assessments indicated that Viet Minh infiltration by sea along the coast, by 1950, had been drastically reduced and perhaps eliminated in certain areas.[56]

After three years, the first phase of the French-Viet Minh War was drawing to a close. During this time, naval power along the coast and on inland waters had made it possible for the French to make major progress toward winning the war. They had ejected the Communists from centers over which they had gained control at the start of the French-Viet Minh War. French forces had been reinserted in Tonkin and were increasingly extending their control in the populous delta and coastal regions.

On the other hand, as will be covered later, Communist successes in China and events elsewhere on the worldwide scene were already drastically changing the situation.

---

[54] *Lessons of the War in Indochina,* Vol. II, pp. 185–87.

[55] As calculated by Coast and Geodetic Survey using Base Line method.

[56] Mordal, *Navy in Indochina,* pp. 277–83; ONI, "French Naval and Air Operations in Indochina," pp. 435–36.

CHAPTER VI

Declining Naval Power, Defense Changes, And Increasing Tension

As 1949 drew to a close, mainland China was in Communist hands. The Viet Minh would now have a sanctuary north of the border for the training and equipping of their Army. China could act as a base for the injection of supplies by land across the border, or by sea, into positions along the coast. In addition, there was the possibility that the Chinese Communists might intervene militarily.

Southeast Asia was but one of many trouble spots on the world scene. Throughout the first phase of the French-Viet Minh War, instabilities in the wake of World War II had continued elsewhere in the Far East and in the European area. Crisis situations in both regions were often caused or accompanied by Communist efforts to expand their control or influence. Cold War associated events posed increasing threats to countries bordering the Mediterranean. These threats, accompanied by a rapid decline in the British Navy, led to expanding requirements for American naval presence in that region. In the Far East, the struggle between the forces of Chiang and Mao in China, the split of Korea into two occupation zones with the Communists in control of the north, the war in Indochina, and the unsettled conditions in other parts of Southeast Asia placed continuing demands on the United States Pacific Fleet. American policy-makers devoted increased attention to steps which might be taken to prevent further Communist gains.

Reductions in overall defense funding and the increasing emphasis on capabilities for the delivery of atomic bombs had resulted in a major decline in the strength of the Navy and other conventional forces during this period. As a result of the top priority accorded to Europe, force levels in the Far East were reduced to the point where capabilities no longer matched commitments.

The period also witnessed a fundamental alteration in the United States organization for the national defense, followed shortly by other changes which represented, in many respects, even more drastic departures from earlier assignments of responsibilities.

Decisions on the fiscal year 1947 budget (covering 1 July 1946 to 30 June 1947) had not taken into account the extent of requirements to be placed on the Navy in remote waters. At the end of this fiscal year, Fleet Admiral Nimitz reported that "despite numerous difficulties the Navy has maintained its forces in Europe and the Far East, often at great sacrifice to the remainder of the Naval Establishment, but in so doing has fulfilled its primary mission in support of United States Foreign Policy." [1]

Efficient utilization of the limited naval forces in the Pacific was complicated by a Unified Command Plan placed in effect on 1 January 1947 whereby operational control of units of the Pacific Fleet would be divided between three unified commands. The Chief of Naval Operations would be the Joint Chiefs of Staff Executive Agent for one, and the Chief of Staff of the Army would be the agent for the other two.

The plan was an outgrowth of a proposal by the Army Chief of Staff, the purpose of which was "to attain a greater degree of unified command than now exists." The proposal brought to a head one of the basic differences between Army and Navy operations: on land, command was usually divided, quite logically, into areas determined by political-military-geographical considerations; at sea, boundaries drawn on a map for command purposes detracted from the flexibility of Fleet operations and from the efficient utilization of naval ships. A continuous naval presence was not always required to exert naval influence or to control specific maritime regions. Highly mobile naval forces can range the vast expanse of the oceans, exercise overall command of the sea, and regroup as necessary to respond promptly to local situations.

As Chief of Naval Operations, Admiral Nimitz recommended that the Atlantic Fleet and Pacific Fleet commanders should continue to operate "under the CNO in time of peace and as determined by the JCS in the event of hostilities." A major issue was the division of responsibility between General MacArthur and the Pacific Fleet commander. Admiral Leahy, Chief of Staff to the President and Chairman of the Joint Chiefs, did not believe that the general could adequately discharge responsibilities for far-flung operations in the Pacific, in view of General MacArthur's major responsibilities in Japan. He proposed the appointment of "an individual

---

[1] CNO, "Annual Report," FY 1947, p. 2.

over-all commander in a delimited Central Pacific Ocean Area who will be neither General MacArthur nor the Commander in Chief of the Pacific Fleet." [2]

Nimitz finally agreed to a compromise Joint Chiefs of Staff plan which received the approval of President Truman. As a result, the world was divided into areas, each under a Unified Commander in Chief who had operational control over all the Army, Army Air Force, and Navy forces within his assigned area. In European waters, command of naval operations was exercised by the Chief of Naval Operations (the Joint Chiefs of Staff Executive Agent) directly through Commander United States Naval Forces, Eastern Atlantic and Mediterranean, with logistic support provided by the Atlantic Fleet. Three unified commands were established in the Pacific; the Alaskan Sea Frontier Forces of the Navy were placed under the operational control of Commander in Chief, Alaska, an Army Air Force officer; General MacArthur was designated Commander in Chief, Far East, and a new command, Naval Forces, Far East, was established under MacArthur's operational control; and Admiral Towers became Commander in Chief, Pacific. Staff layering was minimized since Towers continued to serve as Commander in Chief, United States Pacific Fleet. As directed by the Chief of Naval Operations, the Commander in Chief, Pacific Fleet assigned units to the other unified commands, provided logistic support, and carried out naval command functions other than operational control.

Normally assigned one cruiser, four destroyers, and miscellaneous logistic support ships and smaller craft, Commander Naval Forces, Far East assumed responsibilty for the patrols off Korea which had formerly been under control of the Seventh Fleet.[3] Ships assigned to this command were frequently rotated with those under the Pacific command, so that all could gain training and experience in task force operations. While awkward and far from ideal, this measure was necessary to ensure that the deployed naval forces were in the highest possible state of readiness for fleet actions which might be required on short notice.

Under CINCPACFLT, Commander Naval Forces, Western Pacific was responsible for protecting United States interests and supporting American policy in China and in other areas not under the Commander in Chief,

---

[2] JCS, "Decisions Leading to the Establishment of Unified Commands;" CINCPACFLT, "Semi-annual Summary of 1 October 1946–31 March 1947," 18 Apr. 1947; CNO, "Annual Report, FY 1947," pp. 15–16.

[3] *Ibid.*

Far East. Normally comprised of one cruiser division, three destroyer divisions, a small amphibious task group, and logistic support ships, Naval Forces, Western Pacific conducted protective patrols, as in the Taiwan Strait, and periodically visited important Asiatic ports. Station ships continued to be located at Tsingtao and Shanghai.

By 1947, the Cold War in the Mediterranean had become more critical. The United States weighed the consequences if Greece or Turky came under Soviet domination. Matters were brought to a head when Britain informed the United States, on 24 February, that it could not extend financial and economic support to Greece and Turkey beyond the end of the fiscal year.[4] Threatened internally by a strong guerrilla force and externally by Communists who controlled countries along her northern border, Greece's government might not long survive. In the case of Turkey, there was no serious internal threat, but, in response to continuing Russian pressures, the nation had kept its armed forces fully mobilized since the end of World War II. Unaided, it was questionable if the weak financial and economic condition of Turkey could continue to support this high state of readiness.

President Truman promptly took action to fill the gap that would result from British withdrawal of assistance. He obtained $400 million in aid to Greece and Turkey and gained congressional permission to send civilians and military personnel there for supervision and training. The policy statements in his message to Congress had implications far beyond those of responding to a local emergency. In what became known as the Truman doctrine of "containment," he stated:

> I believe . . . it must be the policy of the United States to support free peoples who are resisting attempted subjugation by armed minorities or by outside pressures.
> I believe that we must assist free peoples to work out their own destinies in their own way.

Visits by United States Navy ships to Greek ports increased sharply. A large portion of the United States Naval Forces, Mediterranean either operated nearby or was so positioned that other ships of the force could reach the area on short notice. At the request of the President, carrier *Leyte* (CV–32) and nine other ships were dispatched to Greece "as a token of our

---

[4] See U.S., Congress, Senate, Committee on Foreign Relations, *Hearings on a Bill to Provide for Assistance to Greece and Turkey* in series *Legislative Origins of the Truman Doctrine* (80th Cong., 1st sess.) (Washington: GPO, 1973).

intention, hoping to persuade the British to stay on, at least until our aid to Greece became effective." When, in July 1947, the situation took a serious turn, with paramilitary forces crossing the border, Truman asked Secretary of the Navy Forrestal, "how large a part of our Mediterranean fleet [could be moved] to Greek ports?" Forrestal responded that a large group could be sent on short notice.[5]

In the same month, half-way around the world, Commander Task Force 38, Rear Admiral Samuel Ginder, with carrier *Antietam,* cruiser *Duluth* (CL–87), and a destroyer division visited Manila on 4 July for the first anniversary of the independence of the Republic of the Philippines. Soon thereafter, in response to a request from the Philippine Government for ships and material and in compliance with a Presidential directive in June, the United States Naval Advisory Group, Philippines was established. As confirmed by an agreement signed on 14 March 1947, the United States retained bases at Sangley Point, Bagobantay, Subic Bay, and Baguio.[6] Later, Sangley Point and Subic Bay provided important support of naval operations related to the Vietnam conflict.

Reorganization of American Defense

On 26 July 1947, Congress enacted a law changing the way in which the common defense had been organized for 149 years. This was but the beginning of a long series of statutory and executive changes over the next decades.[7] As stated by Congress, the intent was: "a comprehensive program for the future security of the United States," "integrated policies and procedures," "three military departments," "authoritative coordination and unified direction under civilian control," "effective strategic direction of the armed forces," "their operation under unified control," and "integration into an effective team of land, naval, and air forces." A new echelon was created

---

[5] Truman, *Years of Trial and Hope,* pp. 106–09.

[6] CNO, "Annual Report," FY 1947, p. 25; COMNAVPHIL, "A Narrative History of U.S. Naval Forces, Philippines from 1 September 1945 until 1 January 1948," 19 Feb. 1948, pp. 10–11; SECNAV, "Annual Report," FY 1948, p. 8.

[7] For an overview of changes in the first decade after passage of the National Security Act of 1947, see Timothy W. Stanley, *American Defense and National Security* (Washington: Public Affairs Press, 1956). For management implications, see John C. Reis, *The Management of Defense: Organization and Control of the U.S. Armed Services* (Baltimore: The Johns Hopkins Press, 1964).

between the President and the departmental secretaries. A council was formed "to advise the President with respect to the integration of domestic, foreign, and military policies relating to national security." The Joint Chiefs of Staff now received directions from another official in addition to the President. Headed by a Secretary of Defense, the resultant National Military Establishment consisted of three departments (Army, Navy, and Air Force), a War Council, the Joint Chiefs of Staff, a Munitions Board, and a Research and Development Board.

During the hearings before the newly organized Senate Committee on Armed Services and the House Committee on Expenditures in the Executive Department that spring, one of the issues had been the power to be granted the Secretary of Defense.[8] Some witnesses emphasized the need for decisions and advocated strong powers for the secretary, even to the point of giving him power to change the functions of the military services, subject to the direction of the President. Others were concerned with the secretary's power over the budget, the broad authority granted to one man, the lack of a clear definition and delineation of his powers, and the overall results if a super-ambitious man was appointed to the job. One point of view was that the secretary's proper role should be that of a policy-maker, exercising controls of a very broad nature. Under this concept, he would be a coordinator or a planner. Another point of view was that the secretary should act as a representative, or deputy, of the President rather than as a representative of the military services to the President.

Under the 1947 act, the Secretary of Defense was directed to:

(1) Establish policies and programs . . . ;
(2) Exercise direction, authority, and control . . . ;
(3) Take appropriate steps to eliminate unnecessary duplication or overlapping in the fields of procurement, supply, transportation, storage, health and research;
(4) Supervise and coordinate the preparation of the budget estimates . . . ; formulate and determine the budget estimates for submittal to the Bureau of the Budget; . . . and supervise . . . the budget programs. . . .

---

[8] For especially pertinent testimony on this and other related issues, see *National Defense Establishment,* pp. 30, 68, 75, 101, 113, 139, 148, 155, 200, 203, 222, 241, 325, 348, 412, 458, 522, 577; see also U.S., Congress, House Committee on Expenditures in the Executive Departments, *Hearings on the National Security Act of 1947* (80th Cong., 1st sess.) (Washington: GPO, 1947), pp. 218, 240, 265, 348, 357, 454, 580, 668, 669 (hereafter cited as *National Security Act of 1947*).

In addition, the Secretary of Defense was designated Chairman of the War Council, with "the power of decision." Other members of the council were the Army, Navy, and Air Force secretaries, the Chief of Naval Operations, and the Chiefs of Staff of the Army and Air Force. Primarily, the council was to "advise the Secretary of Defense on matters of broad policy." Limitations were placed, however, on his authority. The Secretaries of the Army, Navy, and Air Force were to administer their organizations as "individual executive departments and retain all powers and duties not specifically conferred upon the Secretary of Defense." They were authorized, after first informing the Secretary of Defense, to present any report or recommendation to the President or Director of the Budget.

Still encompassing the United States Navy, including naval aviation and the Marine Corps, the Department of the Navy was ostensibly to continue much as before. The Navy was to be "organized, trained, and equipped primarily for prompt and sustained combat incident to operations at sea." In particular, the act specified that "the Navy shall generally be responsible for naval reconaissance, antisubmarine warfare and protection of shipping."

The Joint Chiefs of Staff became a statutory body under the direction of the Secretary of Defense as well as the President. They were to "act as the principle military advisors" to both. "The Chiefs of Staff to the Commander in Chief, if there be one" was a member. During World War II, President Roosevelt had "refused to issue a formal definition of JCS duties and functions, arguing that a written charter might hamper the Joint Chiefs of Staff in extending their activities as necessary to meet the requirements of the war." Now they were assigned specific duties, namely:

(1) to prepare strategic plans and to provide for the strategic direction of the military forces;

(2) to prepare joint logistic plans and to assign to the military service logistic responsibilities in accordance with such plans;

(3) to establish unified commands in strategic areas when such unified commands are in the interest of national security;

(4) to formulate policies for joint training of the military forces;

(5) to review major material and personnel requirements of the military forces, in accordance with strategic and military plans; and

(6) to provide United States representation on the Military Staff Committee of the United Nations. . . .[9]

---

[9] *National Defense Establishment.* p. 13; William A. Hamilton, "The Decline and Fall of the Joint Chiefs of Staff." *Naval War College Review,* XXII (Apr. 1972), p. 53. For a comprehensive study of the Joint Chiefs, see Davis, "Origin of the Joint and Combined Chiefs of Staff."

One of the duties assigned by the bill, that of reviewing major material and personnel requirements of the military forces, would involve them in peacetime controversies.

During the hearings, Admiral Sherman stated that the purpose of some sections of the proposed bill was to make certain that neither the Secretary of National Defense nor a military chief could act as a "single military commander: and to prevent the establishment either of a large military staff or a large bureaucracy over the three military departments." He envisaged "a small executive force . . . to consist of 15 to 25 '$10,000-a-year-men'. . . ." Proponents of centralization predicted substantial savings through "elimination of duplication." Other witnesses were undecided whether economies would in fact result. A few predicted higher costs, as from increased overhead. In the final bill, the Secretary of Defense was authorized only three special assistants and was forbidden a military staff. The Joint Chiefs were restricted to a staff of 100.[10]

In addition to provisions for the National Defense Establishment, the National Security Act established a National Security Council, a Central Intelligence Agency (under the council), and a National Security Resources Board. The council was to be composed of the President, the Secretaries of State and Defense, the secretaries of the military departments, and the Chairman of the National Security Resources Board. Later, the National Security Council and its staff would be deeply involved in the decision to aid the French and the Associated States of Indochina, and in many subsequent decisions concerning such matters as military assistance, national strategy, and involvement of combat forces.[11]

After passage of the 1947 act, the Navy Department continued to run its affairs basically as it had in the past, with no major changes in organization or internal responsibilities. It soon became apparent, however, that complications had been added to processes of administration, management, and justification of programs and budgets. One of the impacts would be the diversion of a far greater percentage of the efforts by the Navy's leadership to external relationships. Heretofore, the two departments had dealt directly with the President and his Bureau of the Budget as they determined the levels of budget submissions, balanced the needs of the departments, and

---

[10] *National Defense Establishment.* pp. 16, 155.

[11] For National Security Council background, see Alfred D. Sander, "Truman and the National Security Council: 1945–1947," *The Journal of American History,* LIX (Sept. 1972), pp. 369–88.

passed judgements on major programs. Now, before policies, programs, and budget estimates were submitted to the President, they were subject to supervision, coordination, formulation, and decision by the Secretary of Defense. The creation of a third military department, by splitting the War Department into Departments of the Army and the Air Force, meant more administrative complexities. Before 1947, the Military Affairs Committees had been the focal points of congressional matters related to the War Department and the Naval Affairs Committees for the Navy Department. Now, the functions were merged into Armed Services Committees. As a consequence of all these changes in the executive and legislative branches of the government, many more individuals and groups were involved in the review and approval of programs and budgets. Differences of professional opinion and detailed arguments in competing for resources were aired at additional levels within the national military establishment and in congressional hearings. The increasingly austere peacetime military budgets accentuated the difficulties. After a year's experience, the new Secretary of the Navy, John L. Sullivan, summarized the far-reaching effects when he reported that "the approval of the National Security Act on 26 July 1947 dominated the events of the fiscal year 1948, and there have been few activities of the Navy which have not felt its influence in some degree."[12]

Soon thereafter, the Secretary of the Navy and the Chief of Naval Operations moved their offices from the Main Navy Building to the Pentagon. Prior to the move, collocation of these officials with the chiefs of the material bureaus had facilitated dialogue between responsible officials in the department and had simplified internal direction and coordination. Thus, such improvements as may have been achieved at the joint level were at the cost of the ease and efficiency of internal management of the Navy Department and its activities.

Continuing Crises

While these changes were taking place on the domestic scene, the Fleet responded to crises abroad. In Italy, a strong Communist party was making an all-out bid to gain control. Visits by United States ships were scheduled

---

[12] SECNAV, "Annual Report," FY 1948, p. 1.

to provide a stabilizing influence. Shortly after the Italian Peace Treaty became effective on 15 September 1947, Yugoslavia threatened the occupation of Trieste.[13] That same month, the Communist parties of the U.S.S.R., Poland, Czechoslovakia, Hungary, Yugoslavia, Bulgaria, Rumania, Italy, and France established the Bureau of Information of the Communist and Workers' Parties (COMINFORM). Elections were held in Poland in October. Despite an agreement with the United States and Britain to hold free elections, international supervision was rejected. The Communist takeover in Poland was, after two years, essentially complete. In Rumania, the National Democratic Front, headed by the Communist party, displaced the National Peasant Party and proclaimed a "People's Republic" on 30 December. King Michael was forced to abdicate. These events had no direct impact on naval operations, but they did accentuate the importance of maintaining a United States naval presence in European waters.

In the Netherlands East Indies a rebellion had been underway since shortly after World War II. In March 1947, the Dutch recognized the Indonesian Republic under President Sukarno. They promised full independence and coequal status in a Netherlands-Indonesian Union by 1 January 1949, but fighting continued. In November 1947 Commander Naval Forces, Western Pacific, Vice Admiral Cooke, was directed to send a ship to receive, quarter, and support a United Nations Good Offices Committee which had been directed to seek a peaceful settlement. *Renville* (APA–227), Captain David M. Tyree commanding, arrived at Batavia, Java, on 2 December, thus providing a neutral site for the discussions. The truce agreement, signed on 17 January 1948, became known as the Renville Agreement.[14]

Capabilities versus Commitments

Despite the extensive commitments abroad, the United States Navy was undergoing further reductions as part of an overall decline in conventional military capabilities. The Navy was particularly hard hit because of the need for expensive technological advances, especially in antisub-

[13] *Forrestal Diaries,* pp. 312–13.

[14] COMNAVFORWESTPAC, "Semiannual Summary of Naval Forces Western Pacific, 1 October 1947 to 31 March 1948," 17 Apr. 1948, pp. 2–3.

marine warfare. Increasingly, it became apparent that the Soviet Union had learned from German experiences and was building the largest submarine force in the world's history. Secretary of Defense Forrestal stated that he considered the solution of antisubmarine warfare of first importance to the nation's security.[15]

The Joint Chiefs of Staff became increasingly concerned over the growing imbalance between conventional warfare capabilities as compared with commitments. Director of the Joint Staff, Major General Alfred M. Gruenther, USA, highlighted the imbalance in an 18 February 1948 presentation to the President. He compared available U.S. military strength with present and possible future commitments, stating that the Army shortage would be 165,000 men by the end of 1948, that the Navy now had an acute personnel shortage, and that only the personnel situation in the Air Force was satisfactory. He identified Greece, Italy, Korea, and Palestine as possible explosive points.[16]

Forrestal requested an increase in authorized personnel, predominately for the ground forces. As a result, the downward trend of military manpower was, for a time, reversed. Within the next six months, Army personnel strength increased by almost 15 percent, the Air Force went up 10 percent, and the Navy and Marines 6 percent.

Subsequent events proved this modest expansion to be short-lived. Despite the ominous signs abroad, the manpower increase authorized in the spring of 1948 was reversed in fiscal year 1949, when major budgetary cuts were imposed. In the air power portions of the budget, naval aviation bore the major share of the cuts. Attack carrier strength had declined from twenty-four at the end of 1945 to eleven in 1948. Further reductions were in the offing.

Once organizational questions were resolved, for the time being at least, by passage of the National Security Act of 1947, the administration focused major attention on such matters as force levels, balance of forces and functions of the services, and on the strategic considerations, upon which decisions on military programs and budgets would be based. One of the inputs into these decisions was an Air Policy Commission under the chairmanship of Thomas K. Finletter (later to become Secretary of the

---

[15] U.S., Defense Department, *First Report of the Secretary of Defense: 1948* (Washington: GPO, 1948), p. 12; CNO. "Annual Report," FY 1948, p. 17.

[16] *Forrestal Diaries,* pp. 374–77.

Air Force). In his letter appointing the commission, Truman stated that "the rapid development of aviation in recent years has made many of our former concepts out of date." Concerned over aircraft production and the aircraft industry, he expressed "an urgent need at this time for an evaluation of the course which the United States should follow in order to obtain, for itself and the world the greatest possible benefits from aviation." He sought "a guide for formulating a carefully considered national air policy."

In its report, "Survival in the Air Age," dated 1 January 1948, the Finletter Commission first took up "the problem of national security." It concluded that:

> Relative security is to be found only in a policy of arming the United States so strongly (1) that other nations will hesitate to attack us or our vital national interests because of the violence of the counterattack they would have to face, and (2) that if we are attacked we will be able to smash the assault at the earliest possible moment.

While recognizing that adequate naval aviation must be maintained as a supplement to the Air Force, the commission concluded that "our military security must be based on air power." A new strategic concept was recommended, since it was predicted that "the mass-destruction weapons which now exist and almost surely will be developed within the next few years . . . radically change the strategic needs of the United States." The commission fixed the "target date by which we should have an air arm in being capable of dealing with a possible atomic attack on this country at January 1, 1953."

This was the basis on which the commission recommended an increase of the Air Force from fifty-five to seventy groups, organized, equipped, and ready for service by the end of 1952. Rather than additional planes for the Navy, the report recommended procurement of new replacement aircraft. The result was a proposed program which recommended budgetary increases of 91 percent for the Air Force and 12.5 percent for the Navy over a three-year period, with the Army budget remaining level.

Other recommendations were made regarding mobilization planning, the aircraft manufacturing industry, aeronautical research and development, civil aviation, and governmental organization with regard to aviation. One of the areas addressed which would lead to changes in responsibilities was military air transportation. The commission reported that 366 Air Force aircraft (22,000 personnel) had flown an average of about 10 million ton-miles per month during the year, and that 84 Navy aircraft (6,300 personnel) had flown an average of 8 million ton-miles. Consolidation of the Air Transport Command and the Naval Air Transport Service into one Military Air Transportation Service was recommended. Later in 1948, responsibilities for air transport were assigned to the Air Force, and the Military Air Transport Service was formed.[17]

The fiscal year 1950 budget, then being reviewed, would eliminate a quarter of the planned operational aircraft for the Navy; the number of attack carriers was to be reduced to seven. Early in 1949 the Air Force cut back procurement of other aircraft types and reallocated funds to procure a substantial additional number of B–36 bombers. On 18 April, the Navy laid the keel of a new carrier, *United States* (CVA–58), designed to handle the high-performance aircraft of the future. Louis A. Johnson, who had replaced Forrestal as the Secretary of Defense, requested that the Joint Chiefs consider the advisability of continuing work on the carrier. However, the Joint Chiefs were unable to reach agreement and, on 23 April, the newly appointed secretary decided to abandon the project.[18]

The Department of Defense

As a result of a 10 August 1949 congressional amendment to the National Security Act of 1947, the National Military Establishment became the Department of Defense. The Secretary of Defense was given greatly increased powers and his staff and that of the Joint Staff were increased. The roles and authority of the secretaries of the military departments were drastically reduced.

Even while the 1947 hearings were in progress, General Alexander A. Vandergrift, USMC, had spotlighted the basic problem, when he described the bill "as an attempt to reconcile two entirely divergent philosophies which had gone into the framing of this bill." He did not believe that these two philosophies had been truly resolved. The fact that basic differences remained unresolved became all the more evident when the Chief of Staff

[17] President's Air Policy Commission, *Survival in the Air Age: A Report by the President's Air Policy Commission* (Washington: GPO, 1948), pp. v, vi, 3, 6, 8, 15, 19, 25, 26–27.
[18] Naval History Division, "Tabulation of Attack Carrier Strength," 5 Aug. 1969; for background on these events and those that followed, see Paul Y. Hammond, "Super Carriers and B-36 Bombers: Appropriations, Strategy and Politics," *American Civil-Military Decisions, A Book of Case Studies,* Harold Stein, ed. (Birmingham, Alabama: University of Alabama Press, 1963), pp. 465–567.

of the Army, General of the Army Dwight D. Eisenhower, made it clear that he considered the establishment of the Office of the Secretary of Defense as constituting "the most feasible effective step," that he opposed "any attempt at this time to prepare a detailed legislative pattern for unification," that the "bill makes a great start," and that he still believed in a single Chief of Staff but that, because of fears, it "would be wrong for the moment."[19]

As Secretary of Defense, Forrestal had opinions different from those he held as Secretary of the Navy. He soon considered it necessary to resolve "profound differences . . . over internal policies from becoming topics of public debate. . . ." The differences continued to be debated. One was the controversy over air power. As stated by the secretary:

> Many officers in the Air Force honestly believe that the carrier will have a limited use in any war that we may fight in the future, and, therefore, challenge the maintenance of the important carrier task forces. These misgivings are honestly held, as undoubtedly are the Navy's regarding the capabilities of the long-range bomber.[20]

By March 1948 Secretary of Defense Forrestal had begun to show physical and mental signs of stress. Impatient to reach unified solutions to problems involving divergent professional opinions, the secretary was already suggesting statutory changes to materially strengthen his authority; add an under secretary; no longer require a Chief of Staff to the President; transfer responsibilities to the Joint Chiefs of Staff and designate a responsible head over them; remove or raise the personnel ceiling of the Joint Staff; provide that the Secretaries of the Army, Navy and Air Force no longer be members of the National Security Council; provide that the Secretary of Defense be the only representative of the National Military Establishment; and clarify the secretary's "authority with respect to personnel, including authority for the establishment and organization of appropriate staff facilities. . . ."[21]

Forrestal had played a key role in establishing what came to be known as the Hoover Commission (Commission on Organization of the Executive Branch of the Government), of which he was a member. The commission,

---

[19] *National Security Act of 1947*, pp. 240, 272–89.

[20] SECDEF, *First Report of the Secretary of Defense* (Washington: GPO, 1948), pp. 8–11.

[21] *Ibid.*, pp. 2–4, 6; Arnold A. Rozow, *James Forrestal: A Study of Personality, Politics, and Policy* (New York: Macmillan, 1963), p. 306.

which initially excluded consideration of the National Military Establishment from its deliberations, expanded its scope when Forrestal sought stronger powers. Even though Forrestal took no part in the preparation of the report on the National Security Organization, his views were well known to the commission.[22] Not surprisingly, the majority recommendation of a Task Force on National Security Organization, organized under Ferdinand Eberstadt, was closely aligned with the secretary's views.[23]

On 5 March 1949, President Truman sent recommendations to Congress along the lines of major conclusions of the Hoover report and somewhat beyond those envisaged by Forrestal. Nineteen days later, Forrestal appeared as the first witness at hearings before the Senate Committee on the Armed Services concerning a bill to implement the President's recommendations. Forrestal's statement recognized that the chief objection would be vesting "too great a concentration of power" in the Secretary of Defense. He felt, however, that the checks and balances in the governmental structure would prevent misuse of the additional authority. Questioning of the secretary was brief, for the committee members knew that he had already submitted his resignation. Nevertheless, in one exchange, Senator Leverett Saltonstall expressed the fear that, if "there is perhaps an unwise appointment of a Secretary of Defense, this bill will give him very substantial and arbitrary power." Forrestal concurred that there was such a risk.[24]

The next witness, Eberstadt, testified "as an individual, not on behalf of our committee." He urged caution with regard to the temptation to cure defects in policies and personnel through "organizational expedients," and stated that "the attempt . . . will not only fail of its purpose, but may injure a sound organization." He suggested "that great care be exercised lest the Office of the Secretary of Defense, instead of being a small and efficient unit which determines the policies of the Military Establishment and controls and directs the departments, feeding on its own growth, becomes a separate empire." While endorsing the objectives, Eberstadt expressed specific reservations concerning some of the means by which the bill proposed to achieve these objectives.[25]

---

[22] *Forrestal Diaries.* pp. 324, 433, 465. 497.

[23] U.S., Congress, Commission on Organization of the Executive Branch of the Government, *National Security Organization* (81st Cong., 1st sess.) (Washington: GPO, 1949).

[24] U.S., Congress, Senate, Committee on Armed Services, *Hearings on the National Security Act Amendments of 1949* (81st Cong., 1st sess.) (Washington: GPO, 1949), pp. 9, 16.

[25] *Ibid.,* pp. 48–70.

The amendment resulting from hearings by the Senate and House of Representatives was a major departure from some of the principles of the original National Security Act. The National Military Establishment became an executive department, renamed the Department of Defense. The Departments of the Army, Navy, and Air Force lost their status as executive departments with representation in the Cabinet and became separate military departments within the Department of Defense. The Secretary of Defense was given unqualified power of "direction, authority and control" over the entire department. Provision was made for the growth of the Office of the Secretary of Defense and three additional Assistant Secretaries of Defense. A full-time chairman was assigned to the Joint Chiefs of Staff; the President would no longer have an officer on his staff acting in that capacity. The Joint Staff was authorized an increase in personnel from 100 to 210.

During Senate hearings concerning the bill, Forrestal noted that: "What I call the philosophy of the act is essentially different under this concept than it is under the act of 1947 . . . one is based on the idea of coordination. The other is the present bill, and is based on the concept of straight line authority." [26] Reportedly Forrestal envisaged the role of the Secretary of Defense as becoming that of an administrative manager. The secretary would indeed be in the line of authority to the President, but subsequent actions would depart from straight line authority within the new department, as decisions in functional areas were delegated to staff members and others who reported to the Secretary of Defense. As Johnson saw it, the result was "greater control being exercised over the affairs of the military departments . . . the resolution of . . . matters without the delays previously experienced," and the placing of emphasis "on the responsibility of staff agencies. . . ." Based on the new authorities granted by the amendments, the secretary eliminated the War Council and substituted an Armed Forces Policy Council, to which the Under Secretary of Defense and Chairman of the Joint Chiefs of Staff were added. He issued new charters giving the power of decision to the Chairman of the Research and Development Board and the Munitions Board, and brought certain joint boards under the control of his staff assistants. Johnson created the positions of Comptroller, Administration and Public Affairs, and Legal and Legislative Affairs for the new assistant secretaries. He also established an Assistant to the Secretary for Foreign Military Affairs and Military Assistance, an official who exercised

---

[26] Ries, *Management of Defense*, p. 143.

extensive authority with regard to aid and assistance in subsequent phases of the Vietnam conflict.[27]

Adjustments within the Navy

Once again the Navy Department adjusted to the changes without major alterations to its organizational structure or departing from the "bilinear" divisions of responsibility. However, with the diminution of the powers of the Secretary of the Navy and the superimposing of additional centers of functional authority over the military departments, gradual revisions took place in the Navy Department organization and its administrative processes. One of the most notable of these was the demise of the General Board.

Established by Secretary of the Navy John D. Long in 1900, and initially headed by Admiral of the Navy George Dewey, the General Board had exerted a strong and persuasive influence during the first four decades of the century. Headed by senior officers who had proven their capabilities in top command and often were nearing retirement, the board had provided the secretaries with independent advice of great value. Its prestige had helped shape national policy and assisted in the justification of programs. Some of the board's functions had been transferred after establishment of the Chief of Naval Operations in 1915, but it continued to be the key body in the formulation of ship construction programs and the determination of ship characteristics until the Ship Characteristics Board was organized within the Office of the Chief of Naval Operations in 1945. When termination of the General Board had been considered early in 1946, Admiral King recommended its continuance. To Forrestal, he commented that the board

> should be considered on the basis that it is an agency of the Secretary— to advise him on matters of policy—and implementation thereof in broad terms—covering the whole field of naval activities—not only those which are assigned to C.N.O. but also to the Secretary himself and the Under and Assistant Secretaries.

[27] U.S., Defense Department, *Semiannual Report of the Secretary of Defense,* July–Dec. 1949 (Washington: GPO, 1950), pp. 28–33.

In King's opinion:

> there is need for a competent agency to view, impartially and objectively, the many matters of policy—and their broad implementation. Such an agency would obviate . . . the need for the numerous ad hoc boards, etc., (now generally employed) which have, for the most part, not the time for a broad outlook on naval matters (being charged with ad hoc matters) and lack the perspective which would enable the several matters to be considered as parts of a whole.

King felt that the board's conclusions and recommendations "should—as has been the practice—be reached after ascertaining the facts, weighing the views . . . on the matter in hand, and due deliberation (which is what they have time for)." He noted that the advice was "the result of impartial and objective consideration by a body of senior officers whose functions do not include executive and/or routine duties." [28]

Sound as Admiral King's advice may have been in 1946, the impatience of the 1950s and tendencies to submerge differences of opinion hardly provided a conducive environment for such a full-time body. Secretary of the Navy Francis P. Matthews abolished the General Board in 1951.

Shifting Priorities and Declining Resources

The budget for fiscal year 1950 forced further cutbacks in naval forces. As Admiral Sherman, then Chief of Naval Operations, assessed the situation a year later, "after World War II terminated, the Naval Establishment went through a period of demobilization, a year and a half of shrinkage, about a year of moderate expansion, and about a year of rapid cutback." [29]

The Pacific Fleet was particularly hard hit because of the top priority accorded to Europe. Pacific Fleet units scheduled for inactivation included 2 aircraft carriers, 6 light cruisers, 4 minesweepers, 17 amphibious ships, and several Service Force types. In addition, 16 destroyers, 2 attack transports and 4 major Service Force ships were scheduled for redeployment to the Atlantic. Of 8 attack carriers then in the active fleet, only *Boxer* (CV–21) and *Valley Forge* (CV–45) were to remain in the Pacific during fiscal year 1950, which precluded the operation of one constantly in the

---

[28] Memo, King to Forrestal, GB No. 401 of 16 May 1946.
[29] CNO, "Annual Report," FY 1950, p. II-1.

Western Pacific. The Pacific Fleet would be assigned 3 of the 7 escort carriers (CVEs) but none of the small aircraft carriers (CVLs).[30] The single cruiser assigned to Naval Forces, Far East would be withdrawn in the spring. The Fleet Marine Force (2 landing teams, 1 fighter squadron, and 1 transport squadron) of Naval Forces, Western Pacific, would also be withdrawn.

Meanwhile, the buildup of the Soviet submarine force continued and the United States Navy allocated still more resources to antisubmarine warfare. Step by step it was becoming apparent, as coastal-type submarines were augmented by fleet types, that the Russian objectives included more than coastal defense. The Soviet Navy was estimated to have at least 370 submarines.[31] Rather than resulting in an overall funding increase, the need for antisubmarine capabilities—so vital to the nation's security— had to be accommodated within a budget which continued to decline. The decrease in the total defense budget, the escalating demands of such areas as nuclear warfare and antisubmarine warfare, and the increasing cost of new weapon systems combined to reduce markedly the United States Navy's ability to fight in the early stages of a conventional war.

In the spring and summer of 1949, the forces of Mao Tse-tung were accelerating progress toward their conquest of mainland China, and Communist insurgencies continued in Southeast Asia. To insure a more effective presence in light of the deteriorating situation in the Far East, the Seventh Task Fleet was established on 1 August. Under the Commander in Chief, United States Pacific Fleet, it was assigned the following tasks:

> Operate in Western Pacific and Southeast Asia waters in order to support US policy and interests X maintain readiness for operating in accordance with approved emergency plans X conduct evacuation operations as required and as practicable X and make good will visits to ports as appropriate in the areas controlled by friendly powers.[32]

The Naval Forces, Western Pacific command was dissolved on 28 August.

In September 1949, the world was shocked by the announcement that the

---

[30] SECNAV, "Annual Report," FY 1949; CINCPACFLT, "Semi-annual summary of CINC-PACFLT command narrative for the period 1 April 1949–30 September 1949," 8 Nov. 1949.

[31] CNO, "Annual Report," FY 1949, p. 12; *Jane's Fighting Ships: 1950–1951* (London: Sampson Low, Marston and Co., 1951), p. 332.

[32] Msg, CNO 192133Z July 1949; SECNAV, "Semi-annual Report," July–Dec. 1949, pp. 167–70.

Soviet Union had exploded an atomic device. Such a test had been expected, but ignorant of the leaks of security information to the Soviets by Klaus Fuchs and others, official estimates put the probable date further in the future. The next month Congress appropriated funds for fifty-eight air groups for the Air Force, ten more than had been requested by the President. Meanwhile, there had been indications that the number of attack carriers might be reduced to six or even four.

As the already severe competition for limited funds allocated to the total national defense effort intensified, differences between Air Force and Navy proponents were increasingly aired in the press and magazines with regard to roles, strategy, the need for carriers, and the effectiveness and vulnerability of the B–36.[33]

In the heated testimony during congressional hearings that fall, tasks in addition to those involving atomic bombs were discussed. Nevertheless, most witnesses seemed to have assumed that the next war would be a total one involving use of atomic weapons. A notable exception was Fleet Admiral King who, in commenting on the idea that the atomic bomb had changed everything, concluded:

> A likely possibility now is that there will be some kind of stalemate unless both sides expect to destroy each other, or a situation might develop similar to that in the last war when both sides were prepared to use toxic gases but none was willing to loose the inevitable terror and destruction.[34]

Others within the Navy, including Fleet Admiral Nimitz, expressed similar views.

The Navy was assigned an additional responsibility when the Military Sea Transportation Service (MSTS) was established on 1 October 1949. Under the direction and control of the Chief of Naval Operations, as executive agent for the Joint Chiefs of Staff, Commander MSTS had the same relationship to the Chief of Naval Operations as that of a task fleet commander operating directly under the latter's command. The Chief of Naval Operations also was responsible for management, technical, and fiscal matters integral to the transport operation. Initially, MSTS was com-

---

[33] Field, *History of United States Naval Operations: Korea*, pp. 31–34; U.S., Congress, House, Committee on Armed Services, *Hearings on the National Defense Program—Unification and Strategy* (81st Cong., 1st sess.) (Washington: GPO, 1949), pp. 22, 109–11, 481, 526–27.

[34] *Ibid.*, pp. 238, 251, 294.

prised of the government-owned ships assigned to the Army and Navy for ocean transportation of personnel and material, together with the personnel, facilities, and equipment to support such operations. The command was not responsible for ships assigned to the Navy's combatant fleets or "those required by the individual services in harbors or inland waterways." MSTS was authorized to acquire additional merchant-type ships by permanent assignment or charter.[35] Heavy demands would be placed on MSTS during the Korean and Vietnam wars.

By the latter part of 1949 the fall of Nationalist China was imminent. On 1 December, Admiral Sherman ordered that a carrier be permanently deployed to the Western Pacific. *Boxer* joined the Seventh Task Fleet on 29 January 1950, the first carrier to be so assigned since the summer of 1947. The task fleet was redesignated the Seventh Fleet on 11 February 1950. A few months later, this small fleet was desparately needed in an emergency effort to help stem Communist aggression in Korea, and to deter war between the mainland Chinese Communists and the Taiwan-based Nationalists.

These events and others on the worldwide scene had been imparting an increased sense of urgency to the question as to whether or not the United States should furnish military and economic aid to the French Union Forces in Indochina.

---

[35] SECNAV, "Semi-annual Report," July–Dec. 1949, pp. 176–77.

CHAPTER VII

American Military Aid

Until 1950, the French, insofar as the United States was concerned, were on their own in the war against the Viet Minh. Repeatedly France—struggling to recover from the effects of World War II and the German occupation, and beset with troubles elsewhere—had sought American arms, munitions, naval ships and craft, and other military equipment. Although support was provided to assist metropolitan France, the United States continued to withhold aid for the reestablishment of control over Indochina.

From the beginning of the Marxist revolutionary movement, one of its doctrines had been the exploitation of suitable "wars of national liberation," and one of its assumptions had been that conflicting objectives of "capitalist" nations would weaken their resistance to the movement. Events added substance to that assumption when, after World War II, two objectives complicated American policy toward Indochina. One objective, stemming from the principle of self-determination, was progress toward independence of the Indochinese peoples from colonial rule. The other, resulting both from this principle and from the cumulative threat of international communism, was maintenance of the area's freedom from Communist control. Both objectives were consistent, and conceivably could have been accommodated in a long-range plan of action. Balancing of the two objectives did, however, pose problems as to priorities, and was complicated by uncertain assessments of the Vietnam conflict. The result was indecision and ambiguity in the American position. As Secretary of State Acheson later evaluated the situation:

> Both during this period [prior to 1950] and after it our conduct was criticized as being a muddled hodgepodge, directed neither toward edging the French out of an effort to re-establish their colonial role, which was beyond their power, nor helping them hard enough to accomplish it or, even better, to defeat Ho and gracefully withdraw. The description is accurate enough.[1]

---

[1] Acheson, *Present at the Creation,* pp. 672–73.

160

On 8 January 1947, three weeks after the Viet Minh attacks which triggered the war, the State Department had notified the American Ambassador in Paris that the sale of arms and armaments to France would not be approved "in cases which appear to relate to Indochina." Yet, early the next month, the State Department said it wanted to avoid the appearance that the United States was in any way endeavoring to undermine the posiion of full recognition of French sovereignty, stating that the "French should know it is our desire to be helpful and we stand ready to assist [in] any appropriate way we can to find [a] solution for [the] Indochinese problem." No overall solution for the problem was suggested. On the one hand, expressing concern over "continued existence dangerously outmoded colonial outlook and methods in area," the United States urged France to be "more than generous in trying to find a solution." On the other hand, recognizing the association of Ho Chi Minh with the international Communist movement, the United States told France that "we are not interested in seeing colonial empire administrations supplanted by philosophy and political organizations emanating from and controlled by Kremlin. . . ."[2]

From the earliest days of the war, the French had sought "more moderate" leaders than Ho. The key figure in the French plan was former Emperor Bao Dai, head of the short-lived government which the Japanese had established in the wake of their Indochina coup in March 1945. When Bao Dai abdicated under Viet Minh pressure in August 1945, he accepted an appointment as the Supreme Political Advisor to the Democratic Republic of Vietnam. However, after departing for Hong Kong, where he resided for more than a year, Bao Dai took no active role in Indochinese affairs. Then, in January 1947, the French asked him to form a broadly based coalition of Vietnamese nationalists. Bao Dai demanded, as a precondition for his active leadership of Indochinese affairs, firm assurance of support for the longstanding goals of the Vietnamese nationalists for independence and unity. He reportedly told one French representative that he would demand as much or more of the French than Ho Chi Minh.[3]

Despite the expressed American desire for a non-Communist Vietnamese government, the French move did not receive Washington's unqualified

---

[2] Quoted in *U.S.-V.N. Relations.* bk 1. pt. 1. pp. A44–A46.

[3] Msg, U.S. Ambassador France, of 22 Jan. 1947 in U.S., State Department, *The Far East* Vol. VI of *Foreign Relations of the United States, 1947* (Washington: GPO, 1972), p. 66; Lancaster, *Emancipation of French Indochina,* pp. 175, 179; Hammer, *Struggle for Indochina,* pp. 207–08.

support. Some policy-makers viewed Ho Chi Minh as the only leader with broad-based backing in Vietnam and characterized Bao Dai as a potential French "puppet." One of the interesting consequences of this attitude arose in August 1947 when the Assistant Naval Attache in Thailand, Commander Alfred W. Gardes, Jr., proposed a good-will visit to Vietnam by United States naval units. Although the visit was endorsed by Charles S. Reed, the American Consul in Saigon, by Admiral Robert Battet, Commander in Chief French Naval Forces, Far East, and by the French High Commissioner, Émile Bollaert, officials in Washington vetoed the proposal. One concern was that such an operation might imply American endorsement of French support of Bao Dai.[4]

That same month Vietnamese nationalists, comprising a National Union Front, appealed to Bao Dai to return to Indochina for negotiations with the French. In October, as another pessimistic estimate of the viability of a Bao Dai government was issued by American diplomats, the former emperor gave a favorable response to the renewed appeal of Vietnamese leaders that he open negotiations with the French for a new government. Bao Dai specifically pledged that in his bargaining with France, "I want first of all to get independence and unity for you. . . . Then I shall exert the full weight of my authority to mediate in the conflict which has put you one against the other."[5]

In December 1947, Bao Dai flew from Hong Kong to Along Bay for a conference with Bollaert in the cruiser *Duguay-Trouin* concerning the establishment of such a government. At the conclusion of the conference, both parties initialed a joint French-Vietnamese declaration recognizing Vietnam's right to independence. Yet, upon returning to Hong Kong, Bao Dai discovered that, while his advisors were in agreement about approving the declaration, they rejected the secret protocol which accompanied it. This protocol seriously restricted Vietnamese independence in diplomatic and military spheres.[6]

The French continued their attempts to define a satisfactory relationship upon which to base a new government and meet American prerequisites

---

[4] Msgs, SECSTATE, of 13 May 1947 and U.S. Ambassador China, of 18 Oct. 1947, and memo, Assistant Chief, Division of Southeast Asian Affairs to Deputy Director, Office of Far Eastern Affairs, of 4 Aug. 1947 in *Foreign Relations of the United States, 1947*, Vol. VI, pp. 95–97, 128–29, 143–44; NA Bangkok, report, R 123–47 of 28 Aug. 1947, JN 5694, box 6, FRC.

[5] Quoted in Hammer, *Struggle for Indochina*, pp. 210–11, 214.

[6] Lancaster, *Emancipation of French Indochina*, pp. 181–85.

for aid. In May 1948, Bao Dai, although still refusing to return to Southeast Asia, concurred in the establishment of a provisional central government for Vietnam under Nguyen Van Xuan, who previously had served as Prime Minister of the Provisional Government of Cochin China. Xuan and Bao Dai met in Along Bay with French authorities on 5 June and formally approved a second agreement guaranteeing Vietnamese independence and unity, subject to continuing French authority in specified areas and to the approval of the French Assembly in Paris.[7]

Indochina and the Cold War

In the debate as to whether the United States should furnish aid to the French in Southeast Asia, one of the questions continued to be the relationship of the Indochina struggle to the Cold War. Some American assessments, while indicating little doubt as to the Communist domination of the Viet Minh, raised questions as to Moscow's role. In July 1948, the State Department informed the Ambassador in China:

> 1. Depts info indicates that Ho Chi Minh is Communist. His long and well-known record in Comintern during twenties and thirties, continuous support by French Communist newspaper *Humanite* since 1945, praise given him by Radio Moscow (which for past six months has been devoting increasing attention to Indochina) and fact he has been called 'leading communist' by recent Russian publications as well as *Daily Worker* makes any other conclusion appear to be wishful thinking.
> 2. Dept has no evidence of direct link between Ho and Moscow but assumes it exists, nor is it able evaluate amount pressure or guidance Moscow exerting. We have impression Ho must be given or is retaining large degree latitude. Dept considers that USSR accomplishing its immediate aims in Indochina by (a) pinning down large numbers of French troops, (b) causing steady drain upon French economy thereby tending retard recovery and dissipate ECA [Economic Cooperation Administration] assistance to France, and (c) denying to world generally surpluses which Indochina normally has available thus perpetuating conditions of disorder and shortages which favorable to growth communism. Furthermore, Ho seems quite capable of retaining and even strengthening his grip on Indochina with no outside assistance other than continuing procession of French puppet govts.[8]

---

[7] Hammer, *Struggle for Indochina,* pp. 215, 221, 224–25; Lancaster, *Emancipation of French Indochina,* pp. 186–88.

[8] Quoted in *U.S.-V.N. Relations,* bk 1, pt. 1, p. A49.

The United States then concentrated diplomatic efforts on urging France "unequivocally and promptly" to approve "the principle of Viet Independence" and to take concrete steps in achieving this goal. With regard to financial aid for Indochina, the American ambassador informed the French Foreign Office, in September 1948, that the United States "could not give consideration to altering its present policy in this regard unless true progress [was] made in reaching non-Communist solution in Indochina based on cooperation of true nationalists of that country." [9]

As the Democratic Republic of Vietnam more openly allied itself with the world Communist movement, American foreign affairs officials took a harder look at the real nature of Ho Chi Minh's regime. In September 1948, Acting Secretary of State Robert A. Lovette pointed out that "to win support and allies in their drive for power, Communist leaders have consistently pretended to champion cause of local nationalists and have attempted to identify communism with nationalism in minds of people in area." He noted the Cominform's criticism of Yugoslav Communist leaders as being guilty of nationalism. [10]

A less certain assessment was a survey by the Department of State's Office of Intelligence Research in the fall of 1948 that concluded:

> Since December 19, 1946, there have been continuous conflicts between French forces and the nationalist government of Vietnam. This government is a coalition in which avowed communists hold influential positions. . . .
>
> To date the Vietnam press and radio have not adopted an anti-American position. It is rather the French colonial press that has been strongly anti-American and has freely accused the U.S. of imperialism in Indochina to the point of approximating the official Moscow position. . . .
>
> If there is a Moscow-directed conspiracy in Southeast Asia, Indochina is an anomaly [*sic.*] so far. Possible explanations are:
>
> 1. No rigid directives have been issued by Moscow.
> 2. The Vietnam government considers that it has no rightest elements that must be purged.
> 3. The Vietnam Communists are not subservient to the foreign policies pursued by Moscow.
> 4. A special dispensation for the Vietnam government has been arranged in Moscow.
>
> Of these possibilities, the first and fourth seem most likely. [11]

---

[9] Quoted in *Ibid.,* pp. A47–A48.
[10] Msg, Acting SECSTATE, of 22 Sept. 1948 in *Ibid.,* bk 8, pp. 141–42.
[11] *Ibid.,* bk 1, pp. A49–A50.

Later writings of General Giap suggested that, whether or not the North Vietnamese Communists were under the direction of Moscow, they fully shared the objectives of world communism. Giap's rhetoric—including such phases as introducing Vietnam to a "path to socialism," "one of the great historic events . . . in the period of transition from capitalism to socialism," "struggle of the world people," "proletarian internationalism," and "to win complete victory for socialism and communism in our country as well as in the world"—was indicative of the Viet Minh leaders' ultimate intentions.[12]

Creation of the State of Vietnam

Continuing American pressure on the French to make real progress toward Indochinese independence was part of the background to the Élysée Accords that elaborated upon the earlier agreements reached at Along Bay on 8 March 1949. In an exchange of letters at the Élysée Palace in Paris, France promised to grant independence to Vietnam, Cambodia, and Laos within the French Union. Vietnam would be unified under its own autonomous administration with the exception of French control of the armed forces and foreign relations.

Certain Vietnamese leaders, including Ngo Dinh Diem, who at this juncture was refusing to participate in the Vietnamese government, continued to suspect the sincerity of French intentions to implement the substantial grant of independence promised in the accords. Nevertheless, Bao Dai returned to Indochina in April 1949 to take active leadership.

Meanwhile, Mao Tse-tung was making major gains in China. Nanking, Hankow, and Shanghai fell to the Chinese Communists in May. Policymakers in Washington considered the possible impact of successes by Chinese Communists on the French-Viet Minh War.

On 2 April 1949, the Viet Minh announced that "the first elements of the Chinese forces of liberation have registered great activity recently at the Sino-Vietnamese frontier." They referred to "important support which the Vietnam forces have received as a result." [13] On 10 May, the American

---

[12] Giap, *People's War, People's Army,* pp. 37, 112, 126, 150; Giap, *Banner of People's War,* p. 9.

[13] U.S., State Department, *Foreign Relations of the United States, 1949* (Washington: GPO, 1975), Vol. VII, pt. 1. p. 17.

Consul in Saigon was informed that the United States desired the "Bao Dai experiment" to succeed. The State Department further advised that "it must be clear that France will offer all necessary concessions to make the Bao Dai solution attractive to the nationalists . . . in view of the possibly short time remaining before Communist successes in China are felt in Indochina." [14]

Bao Dai assumed from Xuan the prime minister's portfolio for the government of Vietnam. On 14 June 1949, France formally merged Cochin China, Annam, and Tonkin into the State of Vietnam. [15]

Secretary of Defense Johnson expressed increasing alarm over the advance of communism in large areas of the world and particularly over their successes in China. He requested that the National Security Council review United States policy toward Asia. Five months later, the National Security Council concluded: "it is now clear that Southeast Asia is the target of a coordinated offensive directed by the Kremlin." [16]

Between April and September 1949, the United States, backed by Britain, pressured the French government to implement the Élysée Accords. The United States-United Kingdom position was that their assistance would not be forthcoming until the accords had been ratified by the French National Assembly; supplementary agreements had been made transferring administrative functions; relationships between the three Indochinese governments and France had been shifted from the Overseas Ministry to that of Foreign Affairs; and a statement had been issued that the Élysée Accords were only a first step toward a treaty to be made with a duly elected Vietnamese government. [17]

The relationship of the Cold War in Europe to the French efforts in Indochina added yet another dimension to be considered in the aid decision. In 1949, the United States entered into firm commitments for the defense of Europe. The North Atlantic Treaty, signed by the United States, Canada, and ten European nations, which took effect on 24 August 1949, declared that an armed attack against one or more of the signatories in Europe or North America would be considered an attack against all. One result was

---

[14] Quoted in *U.S.-V.N. Relations,* bk 1, pt. 1, p. A48.

[15] O'Ballance, *Indo-China War,* p. 92; Fall, *Two Viet-Nams,* p. 241; Hammer, *Struggle for Indochina,* p. 243.

[16] *U.S.-V.N. Relations,* bk 1, pt. 1, pp. A54–A55; memo, SECDEF to NSC, of 10 June 1949 in *Ibid.,* bk 8, p. 218.

[17] Acheson, *Present at the Creation,* p. 672.

concern over the extent to which expenditures in Indochina were reducing French contributions to the security of the European theater. Indeed, the Indochina War absorbed half the French defense budget for 1949. It forced France to commit one-fourth of her naval strength and all of her Naval Academy graduates that year.[18]

The Mutual Defense Assistance Act

President Truman, in July 1949, recommended congressional legislation authorizing military aid to free nations. His primary concern was for Western European countries, although aid to Greece, Turkey, Iran, Korea, and the Philippines was also included. As Congress debated the President's bill, Senator William F. Knowland pressed for the appropriation of funds to assist the Nationalist Chinese. The administration did not choose to support such a provision.[19]

In October 1949, Congress passed a compromise Mutual Defense Assistance Act. It was based on a congressional finding that "additional measures of support" were required "based upon the principle of continuous and effective self-help and mutual aid." These measures included American military assistance in connection with arrangements for individual and collective self-defense. The act coupled military and economic aid, stating that "economic recovery is essential to international peace and security and must be given clear priority." An amendment introduced by Senator Knowland authorized $75 million for the President's discretionary use "in the general area of China," an amount suggested in congressional testimony by Vice Admiral Oscar C. Badger.[20] The sum was provided to the President as an emergency fund. Rather than being reserved solely for military assistance, it might be "expended to accomplish in that general area the policies and purposes declared in this Act." Also, Congress expressed "itself as favoring the creation by the free countries and the free peoples of the Far East of a joint organization, consistent with the charter of the

---

[18] Melby-Erskine Report, Ann. E., p. 5; NA Saigon, report, 56-S-52 of 24 Mar. 1952, JN 15531, box 32, FRC; *U.S.-V.N. Relations* bk 1, pt. 1, p. A51.

[19] *Harry S. Truman: 1949* in series *Public Papers of the Presidents of the United States* (Washington: GPO, 1964), pp. 395–400; *U.S.-V.N. Relations,* bk 1, pt. 1, p. A51.

[20] Formerly Commander Naval Forces, Western Pacific, with additional duty as Commander Seventh Task Fleet, Admiral Badger served in the Navy Department as a consultant and advisor on Far Eastern matters until May 1950, when he became Commander Eastern Sea Frontier.

United Nations, to establish a program of self-help and mutual cooperation designed to develop their economic and social well-being to safeguard basic rights and liberties and to protect their security and independence." [21]

The coupling of military programs and economic recovery, the world-wide scope of the program, the multinational aspects, and the changes taking place in the Department of Defense led to administrative complexities, additional levels of review, approval, and direction, and longer response times. In January 1950, President Truman directed the Secretary of State "to perform the functions and exercise the . . . authority vested in the President by the Act. . . ." Truman did, however, retain the decision-making authority with regard to the section on the "general area of China." [22]

For interdepartmental administration, the Foreign Military Assistance Steering Committee was formed. Its members were the Secretary of State, the Secretary of Defense, and the Administrator for Economic Cooperation. Direction of the program was carried out by a working-level Foreign Military Assistance Coordinating Committee. A Director, Military Assistance Program was established in the State Department with programming and control staffs. Within the Department of Defense, Secretary Johnson established an Office of Military Assistance, with Major General Lyman P. Lemnitzer, USA, as its first director. Later, under President Eisenhower, the responsibilities would be carried out by a civilian Deputy to the Assistant Secretary of Defense (International Security Affairs). Both the Joint Chiefs of Staff and the Munitions Board were involved in the program. The Joint Chiefs designated the Chief of Staff of the Army as their executive agent for the Mutual Defense Assistance Program.

Rather than Army, Navy, and Air Force missions in the various countries that previously had reported to their respective department, military assistance and advisory groups, jointly manned under senior officers of one of the military services, were created. Previously, the Office of the Chief of Naval Operations had processed foreign requests received from U.S. Naval Attaches directly with the technical bureaus. Now inquiries had to be processed through the advisory groups and, "because of the different

---

[21] U.S., Congress, House, *1st Semi Annual Report of the Mutual Defense Assistance Program, October 1949–April 1950* (81st Cong., 2nd sess.) (Washington: GPO, 1950).
[22] Executive Order 10099 of 27 Jan. 1950.

procedures and laws under which military supplies and equipment must now be processed," special procedures and additional staffing within OPNAV were deemed necessary.[23]

Functional centralization was carried one step further when the Army Chief of Staff was designated JCS Executive Agent for MDAP. Secretary of State Johnson directed that he "act as the coordinator of the administrative operation and support of Defense MDAP overseas." "With respect to these administrative matters," he was to "present consolidated information and recommendations to the Secretary of Defense." The Office of the Secretary of Defense reserved authority "with respect to the substantive matters of development of military assistance programs or the implementation of approved programs." [24]

The People's Republic of China

Mao Tse-tung had formally proclaimed the People's Republic of China on 1 October 1949. In November, his troops began to occupy positions along the Tonkin border. The triumphant Chinese Communists unfurled their red flag at the international bridge linking Mon Cay with Chinese territory while French forces looked on. By the end of the year, the Nationalist Government had withdrawn to Taiwan. Now in control of all mainland China, the Chinese Communists could provide a secure haven and extensive military supplies for Viet Minh forces. General Giap later gave his assessment of the impact of the transfer of mainland China to Communist control, stating:

> This great historic event which altered events in Asia and the world, exerted a considerable influence on the war of liberation of the Vietnamese people. Viet Nam was no longer in the grip of enemy encirclement, and was henceforth geographically linked to the socialist block.[25]

---

[23] Memo, OP–41 to OP–32, ser 534P411 of 25 Apr. 1950.

[24] Memo, SECDEF to Secretary of the Army, of 11 Mar. 1950. For a discussion of military assistance during this period, see Stanley, *American Defense and National Security;* see also Robert H. Connery and Paul T. David, "The Mutual Defense Assistance Program," *The American Political Science Review* (June 1951), pp. 321–47; and Harold A. Hovey, *United States Military Assistance: A Study of Policies and Practices* (New York: Frederick A. Praeger, 1965).

[25] Giap, *People's War, People's Army,* p. 22; O'Ballance, *Indo-China War,* p. 103; Hammer, *Struggle for Indochina,* p. 250.

In initiating studies concerning mutual defense aid, Secretary of Defense Johnson defined the general area of China to include Indochina. Recognizing that the $75 million for aid provided an opportunity for implementation of an approved Asian policy, the Joint Chiefs recommended, on 28 December 1949, that an integrated program be developed, approved, and executed as a matter of urgency. Two days later, the National Security Council concluded that "the United States should act to develop and strengthen the security of the area from Communist external aggression or internal subversion." That same day France took major steps in directions that had been urged by the United States. One was the announcement of transfer of responsibilities for internal affairs to the Vietnamese government. Another was the conclusion of a French-Vietnamese Military Agreement, whereby the role of the Vietnamese army and the location of bases were defined.[26]

President Truman approved National Security Council recommendations concerning the general area of China—although he refused at that time to spend the $75 million. "A program will be all right," he said, "but whether we implement it depends on circumstances." [27]

Worldwide Priorities

Trouble spots were erupting at scattered locations throughout the world and there were usually Communist overtones as efforts were made to stir up trouble, capitalize on grievances, and take advantage of conflicts whatever the source. These incidents were placing increased demands on the United States Navy to provide naval presence as a stabilizing and deterring influence. To meet threats along the southern border of Europe and in the Near East, units of the hard-pressed Pacific Fleet were transferred to the Atlantic theater. The Mediterranean Fleet, which had become the Sixth Task Fleet in 1948, was strengthened and redesignated the Sixth Fleet on 12 February 1950.

The commitments to Europe, the changes taking place in Asia, and reductions in conventional forces were accompanied by reappraisals of United States strategy. In his address to the National Press Club on 12

---

[26] Memo, OP–007 to CNO, ser 1541–49 of 28 Dec. 1949; memo, OP–007 to CNO, ser 44–50 of 16 Jan. 1950; Cole, *Conflict in Indochina*, pp. 81–82; SECDEF, *Semiannual Report, July 1 to December 31, 1949*, pp. 22–23; *U.S.-V.N. Relations*, bk 1, pt. 1, p. A57.

[27] Memo, OP–007 to CNO, ser 19–50 of 9 Jan. 1950.

January 1950, Secretary Acheson gave public expression to the changing policy with regard to Asia. Russian encroachments in Asia, particularly in North China and Mongolia, were considered inimical to American interests. Acheson described these as "fundamental realities . . . out of which our relations and policies must grow" in Asia.[28] The United States was determined to hold the defensive perimeter running from the Aleutians, Japan, and the Ryukyus to the Philippines. Nations not within that perimeter were told they must rely initially on their own resources pending action by the United Nations.

Ho Chi Minh proclaimed that his Democratic Republic of Vietnam was the only lawful government in Vietnam, to which the People's Republic of China extended recognition on 18 January 1950. On 20 January, the American Joint Chiefs of Staff concluded that "first priority [for aid within the "general area of China" should] be given to FIC [French Indochina], and that $15,000,000 [should] be tentatively allocated for political and military assistance to that area."[29] Russia added its recognition of Ho's government on the 30th, followed by other Communist countries.

On 2 February 1950, the French National Assembly ratified the Élysée agreement and Secretary of State Acheson recommended United States recognition of Vietnam, Laos, and Cambodia. The reasons he advanced were:

> Encouragement to national aspirations under non-Communist leadership for peoples of colonial areas in Southeast Asia; the establishment of stable non-Communist governments in areas adjacent to Communist China; support to a friendly country which is also a signatory to the North Atlantic Treaty; and as a demonstration of displeasure with Communist tactics which are obviously aimed at eventual domination of Asia, working under the guise of indigenous nationalism.[30]

The National Security Council noted: "The presence of Chinese Communist troops along the border of Indochina makes it possible for arms, material and troops to move freely from Communist China to the northern Tonkin area now controlled by Ho Chi Minh." Citing evidence that arms were already being delivered across the border, the council concluded that "the Departments of State and Defense should prepare as a matter of priority

---

[28] Dean Acheson, "Crisis in Asia—An Examination of U.S. Policy," *The Department of State Bulletin*, XXII (23 Jan. 1950), pp. 111–18; Acheson, *Present at the Creation*, p. 355.

[29] Memo, OP–35 to OP–03, of 10 Feb. 1950.

[30] Memo, SECSTATE to President, of 2 Feb. 1950 in *U.S.-V.N. Relations*, bk 8, pp. 276–77.

a program of all practicable measures designed to protect United States security interests in Indochina." The Department of State now considered it "a matter of the greatest urgency that the Department of Defense assess the strategic aspects of the situation and consider, from the military point of view, how the United States can best contribute to the prevention of further encroachment" in the area of Indochina and the rest of Southeast Asia.[31] Two weeks later, the French urgently appealed for American military and economic assistance.

In 1950, for the first time, Giap launched Viet Minh regular forces in relatively large-scale attacks against the French. He later described this period as "the opening of a new phase in the evolution of our long Resistance." While guerrilla actions continued at scattered locations throughout Indochina, mobile warfare became, for a time, the Viet Minh's main military strategy in the north. Giap defined "mobile warfare" as a form of fighting in which the principles of regular warfare gradually appeared. He described it as:

> The fighting way of concentrated troops, of the regular army in which relatively big forces are regrouped and operating on a relatively vast battlefield, attacking the enemy where he is relatively exposed with a view to annihilating enemy manpower, advancing very deeply then withdrawing very swiftly, possessing to the extreme, dynamism, initiative, mobility and rapidity of decision in face of new situations.[32]

The targets of Giap's offensive were, quite logically, the key French outposts along the Chinese border. First to fall was Lao Kay, where the Red River enters Vietnam. When the Viet Minh gained control of this strategic location in February 1950, the upper reaches of the historic river route fell into Communist hands.

In its assessment of the situation in late February and early March the Department of State viewed the threat to Indochina as being "only one phase of anticipated communist plans to seize all of Southeast Asia." Southeast Asia was considered "in grave danger of Communist domination as a consequence of aggression from Communist China and of internal subversive activities." Being in the most immediate danger, Indochina was judged "the most strategically important area of Southeast Asia."[33]

---

[31] Quoted in *Ibid.*, bk 1, pt. IVA.2, pp. 2–4, 6–8.
[32] Giap, *People's War, People's Army*, pp. 22, 106.
[33] Quoted in *U.S.-V.N. Relations*, bk 8, pp. 283, 288.

On 6 March 1950, Secretary Johnson advised the President: "The choice confronting the United States is to support the legal governments in Indochina or to face the extension of Communism over the remainder of the continental area of Southeast Asia and possibly westward. . . ." Four days later, President Truman approved $15 million of aid in principle.[34]

Soon thereafter, destroyers *Stickell* (DD–888) and *Anderson* (DD–786) proceeded to Saigon, in response to a State Department request, arriving there on 16 March 1950 and remaining until the 20th. The fact that the Seventh Fleet commander, Vice Admiral Russell S. Berkey, was embarked in *Stickell* underscored the importance the United States attached to the visit. During the stay of the ships at Saigon, sixty planes from carrier *Boxer* staged an aerial parade over the city.[35]

In response to a definitive list for military aid submitted by Paris on 15 March, the Joint Chiefs estimated that French requirements through June 1951 for equipment, supplies, and spare parts would total approximately $100 million. To fulfill their naval needs, the French sought immediate delivery of 36 LCVPs, 6 river craft (shallow draft with speeds greater than 12 knots), 14 harbor tugs, 13 submarine chasers, 10 Catalina aircraft, and the loan of a troopship. For delivery before 1 October they desired 75 more LCVPs, 20 more amphibian aircraft, 2 LSDs (dock landing ships), 7 LCTs, 3 LCIs, 55 LCMs, 3 small tugs, 1 gasoline barge, and an escort carrier.[36]

An expression of urgency came from another quarter, in the form of a mission that Secretary Acheson sent to Indochina and other Asian countries to study the types and approximate value of assistance the area might need in the form of economic aid. Robert A. Griffin, a former Deputy Chief of the China Mission under the Economic Cooperation Administration, headed the group. On 22 March, after a ten-day stay in Indochina, Griffin submitted his report. He recommended American aid for a program of rural development, a limited amount of commodities and industrial equipment, and technical assistance. The Griffin Report also suggested that the "psychological shock of ships with military aid material in the immediate future" would be of more benefit than many large shiploads over a long period.[37]

---

[34] Quoted in *Ibid.,* bk 1, pt. IVA.2, p. 8; "MDAP Newsletter" No. 4, of 27 Mar. 1950, p. 5.

[35] Memos, OP–35 to OP–03, of 1 Mar. 1950 and 6 Feb. 1950.

[36] "Dossier Relatif a l'Aide U.S." in Melby-Erskine Report, background papers; *U.S.-V.N. Relations,* bk 1, pt. IVA.2. p. 9.

[37] *Ibid.,* p. 8; see also Samuel P. Hayes, ed., *The Beginning of American Aid to Southeast Asia: The Griffin Mission of 1950* (Lexington, Mass.: D.C. Heath and Co., 1971).

Bao Dai now submitted his own requirements to State Department officials in Saigon. His list, forwarded to Washington on 25 March 1950, included a request for ten gunboats, six dispatch boats, and "a few destroyers." The Navy Department concluded, however, that the earlier French list reflected a truer picture of the Indochinese military requirements and was the only one with sufficient detail to permit pricing and availability review.[38]

In an apparent effort to prevent further delay, Secretary of the Navy Francis P. Matthews recommended that American aid be furnished to the French commander with the understanding that representatives of the Indochinese states participate in its distribution. The French were opposed to direct military aid for the Vietnamese. General Marcel Carpentier, the French military commander in Indochina, declared:

> I will never agree to equipment being given directly to the Vietnamese. If this should be done I would resign within twenty-four hours. The Vietnamese have no generals, no colonels, no military organization that could effectively utilize the equipment. It would be wasted, and in China the United States has had enough of that.

Faced with French intransigence and recognizing the lack of military experience on the part of the Vietnamese, the United States decided to grant military aid directly to the French who then, in turn, would allocate some of it to the Vietnamese. Economic aid, however, would go directly to the Vietnamese.[39]

At this time, Captain Howard E. Orem, head of the Office of the Chief of Naval Operations's International Affairs Division, expressed general agreement with comments of the Army concerning problems in the administration of the aid program. The existing structure and procedures of the Military Defense Assistance Program were not" 'well adapted' to permit maximum progress in future implementation." The Department of State was supervising the military operational aspects of the program, as well as those to do with foreign policy. The former could best be handled by the military services. Undue delays should be avoided by decentralizing the controls of MDAP. As phased by Orem, "even minor decisions, many of which are extremely technical, must now be referred through various

---

[38] Memo, OP–007 to CNO, ser 361–50 of 8 Apr. 1950; memo, SECNAV to SECDEF, ser 00032P35 of 28 Mar. 1950.

[39] Quoted in *U.S.-V.N. Relations,* bk 1, pt. II, pp. A18, A22, A38; memo, SECNAV to SECDEF, ser 00032P35 of 28 Mar. 1950.

channels to the Department of State for decision." Reference was made to the Greek-Turkish program when elaborate organizations had not been superimposed to administer it.[40]

Throughout the long American decision process on the aid program, more and more aid flowed to the Viet Minh from "fraternal socialist countries," particularly the People's Republic of China, which increased the support started in 1949. In April 1950, the People's Republic of China and the Democratic Republic of Vietnam publicized the signing of a formal agreement for arms and supplies. Pack howitzers, antiaircraft guns, and heavy mortars were appearing in the hands of the Viet Minh. In Yunnan Province, rest camps safe from French pursuit were in evidence and in Kwangsi Province, seasoned Chinese advisors trained Giap's troops.[41]

On 5 April 1950, the Joint Chiefs of Staff expressed to the Secretary of Defense their view that the situation in Southeast Asia had deteriorated and that, without American assistance, this deterioration would be accelerated. Considering the military situation to be of "pressing urgency," particularly in Indochina, they recommended the provision of military aid at the earliest practicable date, utilizing the $15 million allocated in principle for this purpose, and the immediate establishment of a small military aid mission in Indochina.

The initial $15 million would suffice to fulfill the first three of the fifteen priority categories requested by the French. Of this sum, about $2 million was programmed for 12 LCVPs and 6 LSSLs (support landing ship, large), and about $6 million for 40 naval aircraft. Admiral Sherman, the CNO, suggested that the French escort carrier *Dixmude,* scheduled to load F6F Hellcat fighters and SB2C Helldiver bombers on 25 April for delivery to France, should be diverted to Vietnam, subject to French concurrence. He also suggested that the Navy Mobile Training Team, scheduled to train the French in the use of the planes at Bizerte, Tunisia, should be sent instead to Indochina for about two months.[42]

The long-awaited decision finally was reached on 1 May 1950, when President Truman approved the allocation of $10 million to cover the immediate shipments of urgently needed items to Indochina provided for

---

[40] Ltr, OP–35 to OP–03B, of 7 Apr. 1950.
[41] Giap, *Banner of People's War,* p. 36; Fall, *Street Without Joy,* p. 32; O'Ballance, *Indo-China War,* pp. 104–06.
[42] *U.S.-V.N. Relations.* bk 1, pt. IVA.2, pp. 5, 7–10; memo, SECNAV to SECDEF, ser 00032P35 of 28 Mar. 1950.

in Section 303 of the Mutual Defense Assistance Program. The approval of funds for the Hellcats, made soon after a meeting between U.S. Military Assistance representatives and French authorities in Paris, brought the total to $16 million. Then, Secretary of State Acheson, on 8 May, announced after a meeting with the French Foreign Minister in Paris:

> The Foreign Minister and I have just had an exchange of views on the situation in Indochina and are in general agreement both as to the urgency of the situation in that area and as to the necessity for remedial action. We have noted the fact that the problem of meeting the threat to the security of Viet Nam, Cambodia, and Laos which now enjoy independence within the French Union is primarily a responsibility of France and the Governments and peoples of Indochina. The United States recognizes that the solution of the Indochina problem depends both upon the restoration of security and upon the development of genuine nationalism and that United States assistance can and should contribute to these major objectives.
> The United States Government, convinced that neither national independence nor democratic evolution exist in any area dominated by Soviet imperialism, considers the situation to be such as to warrant its according economic aid and military equipment to the associated states of Indochina and to France in order to assist them in restoring stability and permitting these states to pursue their peaceful and democratic development.[43]

During this time, Dong Khe, at the juncture of one of the roads from Kwangsi Province with Route 4 in Tonkin, fell to the Viet Minh on 25 May 1950. French paratroopers dropped into the area and drove them out two days later. Giap drew back to continue training and equipping his forces.

At a conference of the Military Assistance Coordinating Committee in Washington on 31 May, it was reported that the programs for French Indochina aid had at last been approved. When the Navy representatives asked for more information regarding this approval, it developed that the programs were approved by the State Department in principle only. By 6 June only $1,656,000 had been received by the Navy to rehabilitate twelve LCVPs and six LSSLs (support landing ship, large). French Minister of Defense René Pleven expressed concern to various American officials regarding inadequate information on deliveries of Mutual Defense Assistance Program (MDAP) material and the slow shipment of the aid. General

---

[43] Dean Acheson, "Economic and Military Aid Urged for Indochina," 8 May 1950, *The Department of State Bulletin*, XXII (22 May 1950), p. 821; *U.S.-V.N. Relations*, bk 1, pt. IVA.2, p. 10.

Lemnitzer, aware of the problem, exhorted the services to work continually toward faster deliveries of aid material. Later that month, Secretary of the Navy Matthews complained to the Secretary of Defense that the detailed information required on military aid "is entirely excessive and unnecessary and results in unjustifiable overhead costs." [44]

While Washington grappled with the question of aid to France and the Associated States, events were moving rapidly in Asia. During the spring of 1949, as the Communists took over more and more key locations in China, French military officers had become increasingly aware of the vulnerability of their outposts just south of the Chinese border. An overall study of the situation in Indochina, completed in June by General Georges Revers, the French Chief of Staff, essentially called for consolidation before any attempt was made to extend French positions. Noting the vulnerable and extended French supply lines to the northeastern frontier posts of Cao Bang and Lang Son, Revers called for their abandonment. He urged the French to concentrate upon the pacification of the Red River Delta region and recommended that the formation of Vietnamese armed forces be expedited. Later events, including French defeats at Cao Bang and Lang Son, would prove the soundness of his recommendations, but they were not then accepted. Instead, during the last half of 1949, the French extended their control to a series of towns north of Hanoi. As they concentrated on keeping lines of communication open to the positions just south of the Chinese border, they faced a never-ending task of reacting to Viet Minh attacks which became increasingly bold.[45]

At 0400 on Sunday morning, 25 June 1950, the North Korean People's Army launched its attack across the 38th parallel. On 27 June, President Truman directed "acceleration of the furnishing of military assistance to the forces of France and the Associated States in Indochina and the dispatch of a military mission to provide close working relations with those forces." This order was accompanied by the President's approval of a Joint Chiefs' recommendation to increase military aid for Indochina to $31 million for fiscal year 1950. The Navy's share of the total was $13.5 million, permitting an increase in the LCVPs initially programmed, as well as in other small craft and equipment.[46]

---

[44] Ltr, OP–35, of 31 May 1950; memo, OP–35 to OP–03, ser 000120 of 6 June 1950; ltr, SECNAV to SECDEF, ser 0324P411 of 27 June 1950; memo, OP–35, ser 0040 of 14 June 1950.

[45] *Lessons of the War in Indochina.* Vol. II, p. 18; O'Ballance, *Indo-China War,* pp. 93–94.

[46] Quoted in *U.S.-V.N. Relations,* bk 1, pt. IVA.2, pp. 10–11; memo, OP–4C to OP–35, ser 000103 of 6 July 1950; memo, OP–35 to OP–03, ser 000120 of 6 June 1950.

On that same day, President Truman reported to the American people that he had taken a number of steps to meet Communist aggression not only in Korea but also in Taiwan, the Philippines, and Indochina. With the sanction of a United Nations' Security Council resolution denouncing the breach of the peace, the United States entered the fray. Truman named General George C. Marshall "from civilian life" to the position of Secretary of Defense.

Superimposed on Korean War tasks was the additional mission assigned by President Truman to the Seventh Fleet to prevent a possible invasion of Formosa by Chinese Communist forces. At the same time, the Seventh Fleet was directed to prevent Nationalist attacks from Formosa against mainland China. The forces immediately available were meager. To carry out tasks assigned by General MacArthur, the units under Commander Naval Forces, Far East, Vice Admiral C. Turner Joy, then consisted of 1 anti-aircraft cruiser, 1 destroyer division, 1 mine squadron, 4 amphibious ships, 1 fleet tug, and 1 submarine. Under the operational control of Commander in Chief, Pacific, Admiral Arthur W. Radford (who served also as Commander in Chief, United States Pacific Fleet), the Seventh Fleet, commanded by Vice Admiral Arthur D. Struble, had 1 attack carrier, 1 heavy cruiser, 1 destroyer squadron, 2 aircraft patrol squadrons, 1 submarine division, and 5 logistic ships.[47]

The Seventh Fleet's striking force, including carrier *Valley Forge* (CV–45) and other units in Southeast Asian waters, was ordered north for the Formosan and Korean tasks and placed under the operational control of Admiral Joy. Together with the small force already in nearby waters, they were hard-pressed to carry out even the most vital tasks until help arrived from the Eastern Pacific and the Atlantic, the Naval Reserve, and the Reserve Fleet.

Initial Deliveries of Military Aid

The first shipment of American military aid to the French in Indochina comprised eight Dakota aircraft (C–47s), transferred to the French in Saigon on 29 June 1950. A Military Assistance Advisory Group (MAAG)

---

[47] Field, *History of United States Naval Operations: Korea*, pp. 41–47.

arrived in Saigon on 3 August. Its Navy Section consisted of Commander James B. Cannon and a staff of seven officers and men.

The Army portion of priority items, enough to equip twelve battalions, arrived in commercial ships by mid-August. About the same time, *Dixmude* departed France and proceeded to Alameda, California, to pick up the F6F aircraft. As a result of more debate on types of aircraft, *Dixmude* did not leave California until the end of September, arriving at Saigon on 28 October. French LST *Rance,* escorting six LSSLs and carrying the first shipment of LCVPs, reached Saigon late in November.[48] On 23 December 1950, the United States signed military aid agreements with the governments of Vietnam, Laos, Cambodia, and France.

At long last, American aid was flowing to the hard-pressed naval forces engaged in the French-Viet Minh War.

---

[48] "Dossier Relatif a l'Aide U.S.," pp. 2–3, 6, 17; NA Saigon, reports, 34–50 or 13 Nov., 39–C–50 of 22 Nov., and 42–C–50 of 30 Nov. 1950, JN 11284, box 13, FRC; "Estimate of the Situation for Indochina," Navy Member Report to Melby-Erskine Mission, 31 July 1950, encl. 8, p. 1; P. Ortoli, "The French Navy in Indochina," *La Revue Maritime,* trans. by Remote Area Conflict Information Center, LXXX (Dec. 1952), pp. 1497–1505.

CHAPTER VIII

The War Intensifies, 1950-1953

By the time American military aid had begun to arrive, the French situation had become precarious. As the summer of 1950 ended, the expected Viet Minh offensive was well underway against French positions south of the border with China's Kwangsi Province. Initiating his attack near the end of the southwest monsoon season, Giap recaptured Dong Khe in September. This was more than an isolated victory, for it severed the French line of communication to the northwest along Route 4. Since supplies and reinforcements could no longer reach the French stronghold at Cao Bang, that post was evacuated. As the 1,500-man garrison retired to Lang Son, which anchored the southern end of the Cao Bang ridge paralleling Route 4, the Viet Minh ambushed the French column repeatedly in the mountains and cut it to pieces. Subsequently, the Viet Minh captured other positions along Route 4, leaving Lang Son precariously exposed. This strategic point on the line of communication from China also was abandoned by the French.[1]

The only French success along the northern front was at Mon Cay, where seapower was brought to bear. Deploying all available naval forces to the Tonkin region, Vice Admiral Paul Ortoli, Commander French Naval Forces, Far East, landed the badly needed reinforcements when the Viet Minh threatened the last of the French border positions. Supplied by sea and under the protective guns of their navy, the French continued to repulse Viet Minh efforts to take the town.[2]

Naval Requirements

As the French withdrew from their northern outposts, the United States evaluated the assistance needs of the Southeast Asian area as a whole.

---

[1] O'Ballance, *Indo-China War,* pp. 114–16.
[2] NA Saigon, reports, 31–C–50(A) of 8 Nov. 1950 and 36–C–50 of 15 Nov. 1950, JN 11284, box 13, FRC.

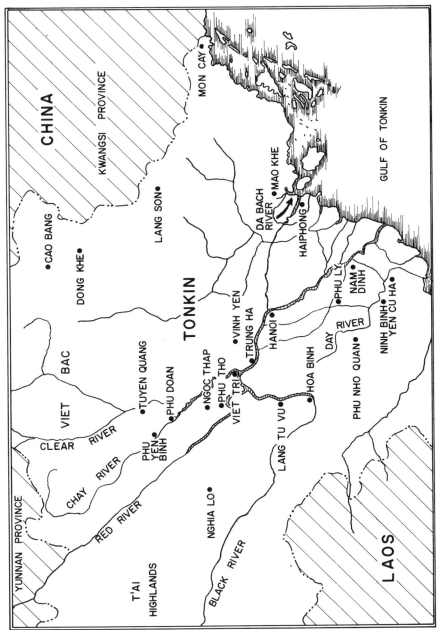

Area of the French–Viet Minh War in Tonkin.

A Joint State-Defense Survey Mission had been sent to the area two days after the President's announcement of accelerated aid to Indochina. The chairman of the mission was John Melby, who had served with the American Embassy in China from 1945 to 1949. Major General Graves B. Erskine, USMC, headed the Military Group. One of the mission's tasks was "to survey, evaluate and make recommendations as to the desirable type and scope of U.S. military assistance that should be provided to the countries of Southeast Asia, including the organization required for properly handling such assistance." [3]

The Military Group's report of 22 November 1950 to the Joint Chiefs of Staff, on the subject of Mutual Defense Assistance Programs for countries of Southeast Asia, judged the military problem to be "one dealing mainly with quelling internal communist inspired uprisings and maintaining internal security." The group concluded:

> At the present time the situation in Indo-China warrants major consideration since it is the keystone in the arch of Southeast Asia, without which, the balance of the area will likely fall. It is also the most active theater within the area. [4]

The report noted Chinese Communist assistance to the Viet Minh in the form of supplies, equipment, training, and provision of a refuge. A considerable increase in the combat efficiency of the Viet Minh troops also was reported. Of particular interest, in view of subsequent events, was the observation that:

> The Commander-in-Chief has not been granted full authority commensurate with that of a theater commander in a theater of operations, apparently on account of the complicated political situation existing within Indo-China and the desire of the Paris office to have final approval of military operations. Unless the present political and military relationships are modified, resources increased and the state of mind improved, the French will not only be unable to restore order but will probably be decisively defeated. [5]

Erskine's group recommended that Indochina receive first priority and Thailand second, followed by the Philippines, Indonesia, and Malaya. The total cost of military aid for Indochina, in addition to programs already

---

[3] Melby-Erskine Report, p. 1.
[4] *Ibid.*, p. 2.
[5] *Ibid.*, p. 3.

approved, was assessed as $298 million to take care of the immediate need for equipment, supplies, and training. In the case of the French Navy in Indochina, a $50 million program was proposed which emphasized spare parts, maintenance facilities, and training—in that order. The Navy members of the group, Captain Mervin Halstead and Commander Ralph J. Michels, identified two aspects of the naval war, as follows:

War on the open sea. There are three major objectives here. *First* to prevent the enemy from using the open sea for carrying supplies and ammunition from foreign countries to those sections of the Indochina coast which are occupied by the enemy. *Second* to use the open sea to support combined operations against the enemy held coast. *Third* to use the open sea to supply French forces as necessary.
River warfare. Here again there are three main objectives. *First* to deny the enemy the use of the rivers and to prevent arms traffic. *Second* to protect French river traffic from enemy mines, ambushes and attacks. *Third* to support combined military operations against enemy troops, installations, and shipping which latter consists only of sampans and junks. Commando raids are made frequently for harassing and morale effect.

The Navy members concluded that the "French Naval Forces in the Far East are not prepared for a naval war" and that they would need American or British assistance against a strong naval power. The members reported that the French "want us to block off Tonkin Gulf and South China Sea to enemy forces which might attempt landing." They also noted requirements for port development, which the French were expected to accomplish without aid. One item was for the construction of a wharf in Tourane Bay to permit the docking of Liberty Ships. Regrettably, no deep-draft pier would be constructed until the fall of 1966, after a year and a half of extraordinary logistical difficulties in support of American Marines and other forces deployed to this area.[6]

To the Navy members of the Erskine group, the most pressing naval requirement was for the delivery of ten Privateer or Liberator long-range patrol planes with high-discrimination, air-search radar for surveillance of coastal waters. They rejected, for the present, the escort carrier requested by the French, citing as reasons the lack of enemy planes or ships, France's shortage of trained personnel, and the existence of airfields controlled by

---

[6] *Ibid.*, pp. 2–3, 7, 10, Ann. B., pp. 1–2, 5; U.S.. Defense Department, Joint Logistics Review Board Report, "Logistic Support in the Vietnam Era," 1970, Vol. II, p. 240; Hooper, *Mobility, Support, Endurance*, p. 88.

the French. Actually, the air base capabilities ashore were very limited. At the time, there existed only three major airfields, at Saigon, Bien Hoa, and Hanoi, plus a smaller one at Haiphong.[7]

The Navy members also recommended small craft suited for operations in the immediate coastal region. They felt that the river patrol capability of the French should be expanded by the provision of a variety of different craft suited to Indochina's river system. Specifically mentioned were 158-foot LSSLs and fast shallow-draft units for use in the lower reaches of the inland waters. A landing ship dock was placed low on the priority list because of the lack of manpower for amphibious operations.

With the aid envisaged, Admiral Ortoli was confident of the ability of his forces to carry out their naval missions against the Viet Minh. His capabilities for a war at sea were another matter. During the briefings for the Erskine group, Ortoli, fully appreciating the importance of control of the sea, said that the "threat from another Navy could not be met without help from somewhere."[8]

Defense of the Red River Delta

Following their successes in the North, the Viet Minh intensified their guerrilla activities and prepared for a campaign to reduce the French zone of control. American naval aid arrived in Vietnam none too soon. Emboldened by the Viet Bac victories and now in control of land lines of communication from China, General Giap prepared his army for a drive down from the mountains into the Red River Delta. The French ability to repulse the offensive hinged on their control and use of the extensive waterways and on naval support of army operations. Prior to receipt of amphibious craft, equipment, and other aid from the United States, the French Navy in Indochina lacked the required strength. Moreover, many of the riverine units, having operated at a high tempo for four years, had deteriorated and needed replacement. Now, naval aid from the United States permitted the French to form two new *dinassauts*. Four continued to operate in the Mekong Delta of Cochin China and Cambodia, and the two new *dinassauts* reinforced the two already operating in Tonkin.[9]

---

[7] The Air Force members considered the fields adequate for current efforts but not for expanded operations; Melby-Erskine Report, Air Force Section, pp. 6–7.

[8] *Ibid.*, Ann. B, pp. 2–3, 10–11.

[9] OP–002, "The Military Assistance Advisory Group in Indo-China," 23 Nov. 1953.

With a name derived from the color of the silt suspended in its waters and a flow double that of the Nile, the Red River carried approximately 130 million tons of soil downstream each year to build up the rich agricultural lands of its delta. The delta was heavily populated; the location of the capital, Hanoi, and the port city of Haiphong; and the industrial center of the northern portion of Vietnam. The Red River connected China's Yunnan Province with the sea. Strategically, economically, and politically, the Red River Delta was the key to control of Tonkin.

Feeling that the time was now ripe, in January 1951 Giap launched his regular forces on a major thrust to penetrate the French defenses. His first target was Vinh Yen, strategically located at an important road junction in the fringes of the delta, about forty miles northwest of Hanoi. The Viet Minh troops achieved surprise, but Giap had underestimated the French ability, aided by inland naval power, to react. General Jean de Lattre de Tassigny, who had taken command of French forces in Indochina on 17 December 1950, rushed reinforcements to the scene. One-third of the troops arrived in the vicinity of Vinh Yen in naval convoys which had steamed up the river past Hanoi. By the time the battle ended on 17 January, the French reportedly had killed 6,000 men in repulsing the Viet Minh assaults.

Two months later, on 23 March 1951, Giap tried again. This time the assault was aimed at Mao Khe, on the northern border of the delta, about twenty miles northwest of Haiphong and astride the coastal road from China. After three days of fighting, the Viet Minh had overwhelmed all but one of the French outposts guarding the city. At that crucial point, the massing Viet Minh were dispersed by gunfire from *Duguay-Trouin*, *Chevreuil*, *Savorgnan de Brazza*, and two landing support ships (LSSL–4 and LSSL–6) steaming on the Da Bach River just north of the city. Troops, including Navy commandos and a paratroop battalion, reinforced the 400 defenders of Mao Khe. Two days later the Viet Minh thrust was finally repulsed.[10]

Despite heavy losses at Vinh Yen and Mao Khe, Giap attempted once more to breach the delta defenses. This time he approached from the south. At least 40,000 Viet Minh regulars attacked French lines along the Day River. The battle began on the night of 28–29 May 1951 with an assault

---

[10] Mordal, *Navy in Indochina*, pp. 261–66; Fall, *Street Without Joy*, pp. 41–43; O'Ballance, *Indo-China War*, pp. 123–27, 130–33; NA Saigon, report, 37–C–51 of 13 Apr. 1951, JN 14557, box 22, FRC.

NH-79387

French LSSL goes into action.

NH-79371

French patrol boats pass a fortress near Ninh Binh on the Day River in northern Vietnam.

on Ninh Binh, where the determined resistance of a French Navy commando unit slowed the enemy advance. The next day *Dinassaut* 3 sailed for Ninh Binh from Nam Dinh with a convoy of 1 LCT, 4 LCMs, 3 LCVs (landing craft, vehicle), and several LCVPs, carrying reinforcements to the besieged town. Twelve kilometers from Ninh Binh, the Viet Minh sprang an ambush. After a brisk engagement, the *dinassaut* made its way to Ninh Binh. Some 20,000 reinforcements were rushed into the area by river, road, and air.

The French counterattacked on 30 May. *Dinassaut* 3, together with two temporary *dinassauts* organized for the emergency, provided mobility and naval gunfire support. The battle climaxed on 4 and 5 June with the fight for Yen Cu Ha, a few miles south of Ninh Binh. An LSSL arrived just as the enemy entered the town. After a round from the ship's 76-millimeter gun hit the watchtower where the enemy centered his defenses, Viet Minh resistance crumbled and the French attack carried the post. Fifty-five enemy soldiers trapped in the tower surrendered to the advancing French.

The key to victory in this campaign was control of the Day River by French naval forces. Deploying as many as forty-five boats in the operation, river patrols severed Viet Minh lines of communication. Fresh troops brought into the area then overwhelmed the isolated Viet Minh forces. By 18 June, the battles for the Red River Delta were over, as the shattered remnants of Giap's army retreated to limestone hills to the west.[11]

Led by General de Lattre, a resolute and inspirational commander, strengthened by American aid, and fighting in areas where naval forces could operate, the French had won the winter and spring campaigns of 1951 in Tonkin. Viet Minh regular forces had suffered serious losses and would need time to recuperate.

As Giap's main forces retired to rebuild their battered units, de Lattre carried out mopping-up operations within the Red River Delta and went ahead with plans to construct a series of forts, concrete bunkers, and pillboxes along the line enclosing the Red River Delta and the coastal region north to the Chinese border. It was the Navy's task to patrol the waterways in the area.[12]

Once again the United States evaluated the possibility of Chinese aggression. The appearance of a large number of Chinese troops on the battlefields

---

[11] NA Saigon, report. 63–C–51 of 13 June 1951. JN 14557, box 22, FRC; NA Saigon, report, 128–S–52 of 20 Oct. 1952, JN 15531. box 32, FRC; Mordal, *Navy in Indochina*, pp. 266–70; Fall, *Street Without Joy*, pp. 43–47; O'Ballance, *Indo-China War*, pp. 136–39.

[12] Fall, *Street Without Joy*, pp. 175–77.

of Korea in the fall of 1950 indicated the willingness of the People's Republic of China to fight in support of Communist struggles in neighboring states. A United States assessment of the threat in August 1951 concluded that, after a Korean armistice, the "Chinese would be capable of intervention in considerable strength. . . ." It was then believed that the Peking regime would be "inhibited from acting overtly by a number of factors, including the risk of American retaliation and the disadvantages attendant upon involvement in another protracted campaign." [13]

Naval Operations in the French 1951 Fall Offensives

Admiral Ortoli's ability to support operations ashore gained a new dimension when light aircraft carrier *Arromanches* and her forty-four air-craft (F6F and SB2C) arrived off Indochina on 24 September 1951 after a twenty-month absence. During a seven-month deployment she launched over 1,400 sorties in a wide variety of missions, including bombing runs against Viet Minh bases, close air support, convoy escort, and air recon-naissance. [14] With the carrier's ability to range along the coast, tactical naval air could be concentrated where needed. *Arromanches's* operations were all the more notable since the period of her cruise, coinciding with the north-east monsoon, was unfavorable for close support and visual bombing in the North, where the main Viet Minh army forces were located.

General de Lattre planned to launch his own offensive that fall. The objective of Operation *Lotus* was to gain control of the Black River between Hoa Binh and the point where its waters joined those of the Red River on the way to the sea. If successful, *Lotus* would cut supply routes from the north to the Viet Minh forces in the southern regions of Tonkin.

Success of the campaign would depend on riverine operations and the transportation of supplies, mainly by water, to sustain the French Army. The French naval officers participating in planning for the operation pointed out the vulnerability of river boats to ambush along the Black River near Hoa Binh, but their warnings went unheeded. [15]

---

[13] Quoted in *U.S.-V.N. Relations*, bk 1, pt. IIA.3, pp. A47–A48.

[14] ONI, "Operations of the French CVL *Arromanches* in Indochina," *The ONI Review*, VIII (Jan. 1953), pp. 23–26; ONI. "French Naval and Air Operations in Indochina," p. 437; NA Saigon, report, 40–S–52 of 18 Feb. 1952, JN 15531, box 32, FRC; NA Saigon, report, 86–53 of 10 Apr. 1953, JN–N–59488, box 25, FRC.

[15] NA Saigon, report, 88–S–52 of 3 June 1952, JN 15531, box 32, FRC.

In preparation for the operation, the French formed a temporary *dinassaut* of eight LCMs and four patrol craft and established a river command post at Trung Ha. Then, on 14 November 1951, three French paratroop battalions occupied Hoa Binh. Additional troops from the Red River Delta approached the city along Route 6. Others were transported in landing craft up the Black River, winding its way through the delta to Lang Tu Vu, at the base of the foothills of the Annamese mountain chain and then to Hoa Binh.

Giap focused his main attacks against the river line of communication at a point where the highlands on either side provided ideal cover for the Viet Minh, just as naval officers had feared. After Lang Tu Vu fell to the Communists, the French continued to push river convoys through to Hoa Binh in the face of ever-mounting casualties from river ambushes. Then, on 12 January 1952, the Viet Minh ambushed a convoy south of Notre Dame Rock. In the face of murderous fire, the escorts raked the banks with their machine guns. In former engagements, their fire had enabled convoys to make their way through ambushes, but this time intense Viet Minh firepower forced the units to turn back. An LSSL and four patrol boats were sunk. Further efforts to force convoys up the river were abandoned.

As more and more ambushes intercepted supplies coming by land from the delta along Route 6, General Raoül Salan, who had relieved the cancer-stricken de Lattre of his duties as Commander of the French Expeditionary Force in January 1952,[16] became convinced that the value of controlling Hoa Binh was not worth the cost. By 24 February he had withdrawn his forces. Two LCMs, trapped upriver by low water, were sunk during the withdrawal, one by Viet Minh fire and the other by its own crew to keep it from falling into enemy hands.[17]

Planning for the Defense of Southeast Asia

During Tripartite talks on Southeast Asia, held in January 1951 in the Pentagon, the United States, France, and Britain discussed the possibility of issuing a warning to Communist China that aggression would result in certain retaliation, "not necessarily limited to the area of aggression."

---

[16] The Minister of the Associated States, Jean Letourneau, assumed de Lattre's duties as French High Commissioner.

[17] *Ibid.;* Fall, *Street Without Joy.* pp. 47–60; O'Ballance, *Indo-China War,* pp. 159–68.

Before issuing the warning, it was decided to review the measures each nation might take should the Chinese disregard the warning. For this purpose a five power, *ad hoc* committee, composed of the United States, France, Britain, Australia, and New Zealand, was appointed to study the matter.[18] The Five Power Conference, convened in Washington in February, agreed that the combination of a sea blockade and air action against China offered the best prospects for halting aggression.

Five months later the National Security Council suggested possible courses of action in case of large-scale Chinese intervention, including use of air and naval forces to interdict lines of communication and blockade of the Chinese coast. If this failed, air and naval actions might have to be taken "against all suitable military targets in China," preferably in coordination with British and French forces.[19]

The matter of international coordination came up that fall at another Five Power Military Conference on Southeast Asia. Vice Admiral Ralph A. Ofstie, Commander First Fleet, was the senior United States officer present, although Major General Joseph S. Bradley, USA, from the Strategic Plans Division of the Joint Staff, headed the delegation. At the conference, which lasted from 6 to 17 October 1952, the French and British pleaded for better liaison in planning the defense of Southeast Asia. The American delegation expressed the opinion that the Commander in Chief, Pacific had the necessary machinery for carrying out coordination.[20]

As the JCS Executive Agent for the Pacific Command, Chief of Naval Operations Admiral William M. Fechteler had already directed Admiral Radford to develop procedures for effective liaison in the event that American aircraft carrier support was ordered for Indochina. Radford dispatched a team to Indochina to confer with French military officials. The five-man team, headed by Captain Earl R. Eastwold of Admiral Radford's staff, visited Indochina from 10 to 18 November 1952 to study the French air control system. They looked at French communication procedures particularly, and concluded that the French system was highly effective in applying air power in support of ground troops. Therefore, they recommended that, while United States carriers would operate independently at sea, the aircraft should pass into the French air control system once they flew inland. If

---

[18] Msg, SECSTATE, of 15 Jan. 1952 in *U.S.-V.N. Relations,* bk 8, pp. 465–67.
[19] Quoted in *Ibid.,* bk 1, pt. IIA.3, pp. A48–A49.
[20] Memo, OP–004 to CNO, ser 1295–52 of 28 Oct. 1952.

such support was ordered, an eight-man United States Navy group within the French tactical air force headquarters would provide liaison between the two forces.[21]

The Communist 1952 Fall Offensives

As fall approached, Giap launched his regular forces on another offensive. The Viet Minh took the French by surprise and gained the initiative. An offensive had been expected, but not until later. Also the direction of the offensive and its objective surprised the French, as operations commenced in the T'ai Highlands of northwest Tonkin, an area remote from the sea. The Viet Minh objective was the string of forts in the mountains between the Red and Black Rivers. Giap concentrated his forces against Nghia Lo. After its fall, on 17 October 1952, the small outposts on the flanks were either abandoned or overrun.[22]

As in the case of the Communist attacks in the Viet Bac the previous year, the French Army was not able to defend its positions in jungled and mountainous regions remote from the sea, where it could not receive effective support from riverine forces. As a result of these victories and the failure of Operation *Lotus,* the Viet Minh now controlled the inland lines of communication from Kwangsi and Yunnan Provinces in China.

Light carrier *Arromanches* returned to Indochinese waters that month for her third deployment. Through 18 February 1953, her aircraft flew 1,561 sorties, about one-third of the total number of French Air Force flights in North Vietnam. With the exception of a short period at the end of January and early February, when her aircraft hit targets in the Central Highlands of Vietnam, *Arromanches* operated in the Gulf of Tonkin off Haiphong. After the carrier returned to France, her air group remained behind to operate from Cat Bi Airfield.[23]

In order to disrupt the flow of supplies from China and the Viet Minh base area in the Viet Bac, and at the same time relieve the pressure on the T'ai region, General Salan decided to strike north of the Red River. For the operation, code-named *Lorraine,* Salan deployed 30,000 troops, the

---

[21] Senior Member, CINCPACFLT Planning Team, report, of 24 Nov. 1952.

[22] O'Ballance, *Indo-China War,* pp. 176–77; Giap, *People's War, People's Army,* p. 23.

[23] NA Saigon, report, 86–53 of 10 Apr. 1953, JN–N–59488, box 25, FRC.

NH–79376

French river patrol boats ready for action.

largest French force yet assembled in the war. Planning to use the Red, Clear, and Chay Rivers as lines of communication, General Salan initially employed 2 LCIs, 4 monitors, 5 LCMs, and 7 French river patrol boats from *Dinassauts* 3 and 12.[24]

For several days prior to the operation, boats ferried a steady stream of supplies north from Hanoi to staging areas at Trung Ha on the Red River and Viet Tri on the Clear River. On 29 October, naval units assisted in bridging the Red River, as the task force moved out from Trung Ha heading for Phu Tho farther up the river. Just north of Phu Tho, at Ngoc Thap, on 7 November, the force linked up with a second column moving up from Viet Tri. The two columns continued northward to Phu Doan

---

[24] NA Saigon, report, 219–52 of 25 Nov. 1952, JN 15531, box 33, FRC; O'Ballance, *Indo-China War*, pp. 179–80.

(Doan Hung), a major Communist supply base at the junction of the Clear and Chay Rivers. As the forces marched overland toward Phu Doan, river units advanced up the rivers.

In typical *dinassaut*-type actions, embarked Moroccan infantrymen and naval commandos landed at times on the river banks to pursue the enemy. A French paratroop unit captured Phu Doan with little resistance. From there, patrols pushed to Phu Yen Binh on the Chay River, a point two-thirds of the way to Yunnan Province from the mouth of the Red River.

The French-Vietnamese forces had temporarily cut routes to Chinese supply sources and had overrun substantial forward supply dumps. However, having failed to draw Giap's forces from the T'ai region and faced with the danger of overextension, General Salan ordered a withdrawal of his forces on 14 November.

The French then turned back a Viet Minh attack on Laos. For four months neither opponent mounted large-scale operations, although the countless small engagements throughout the country resulted in continuing casualties on both sides.[25]

Naval Operations along the Coast

By far, the easiest way for the Viet Minh to deliver supplies to depots or base areas in the middle and southern sections of Vietnam was by sea. To effect such deliveries from China and northern Vietnam, they relied on stealth. Hiding in the numerous inlets and bays along the coast or mingling with the myriad fishing junks or sampans, the Viet Minh were difficult to detect. Even with the ships and craft received from the United States the French Navy lacked the necessary ships and crews to patrol fully the entire coast or to inspect all the traffic.

The Communists used a number of tactics to avoid French patrols. Sometimes Communist junks would put out from Hainan Island and head south. Often timing their arrival for a moonless night, the junks would move in to the coast at a point near a Viet Minh base and unload their critical cargo. At other times, the Viet Minh transported supplies from point to point along the coast. Moving only at night, and close inshore, the tiny flotillas often sent out a reconnaissance junk disguised as a fishing

---

[25] *Ibid.,* pp. 182–93; Fall, *Street Without Joy,* pp. 77–106.

boat. If this boat spotted a French patrol the others beached until the danger had passed.[26]

In attempting to choke off the supplies coming in by sea, the French used an average of fifteen to twenty ships, plus reconnaissance aircraft of the naval air arm, to search for suspicious contacts. Lacking modern radar on their patrol ships, the French often used ambush tactics, whereby they anchored near heavily traveled infiltration routes in hopes of catching Viet Minh craft moving at night.

In addition to their patrol efforts, the French raided such Viet Minh coastal bases as they could uncover. In one amphibious raid, Operation *Pirate,* on 30 August 1951, they assaulted a Communist base which had been established on Cu Lao Re, an island off the coast north of Quang Ngai. Escort *La Capricieuse* and two ex-German seaplane tenders, *Commandant Robert Giraud* and *Marcel Le Bihan,* carried LCVP landing craft in spaces normally assigned to aircraft. Supported by gunfire from the two ships, two naval commando companies landed over the beach. Together with Army paratroopers, who arrived an hour later, the commandos cleared the island. Supplies for a permanent outpost were delivered by an LCT the next day. Henceforth, rather than serve as a transshipment point for war materials to Communists on the coast, Cu Lao Re would function as a base to cut off the flow of such supplies along the coast.[27]

As they had in 1946, the French also resorted to the mobility, surprise, and concentrated power of amphibious operations to counter enemy build-ups near the ancient city of Hue. Here, during the dry summer season in the north, the Communists had deployed the Viet Minh 101st Regiment. Operation *Sauterelle* began on the night of 24 August 1952 along the coast north of the Perfume River. While landing forces from *Marcel Le Bihan* carried out two diversionary raids, 3 LSTs and 3 LCUs (landing craft, utility) along with LCMs and LCVPs, landed 4 Army battalions and 2 Navy commando companies. From his flagship, gunboat *Savorgnan de Brazza,* Rear Admiral G.L.J. Rebuffel, commander of the coastal forces, directed the operation. Four escorts provided gunfire support.

The landings caught the Viet Minh by surprise and four French Army battalions, approaching from north and south, completed the encirclement.

---

[26] COMNAVFORV, "The Naval War in Vietnam," 1 May 1970, pp. 8–9.
[27] NA Saigon, report, 141–53 of 15 June 1953, JN–N–59488, box 25, FRC; NA Saigon, report, 110–51 of 21 Sept. 1951, JN 14557, box 23, FRC; ONI, "French Naval and Air Operations in Indochina," p. 435.

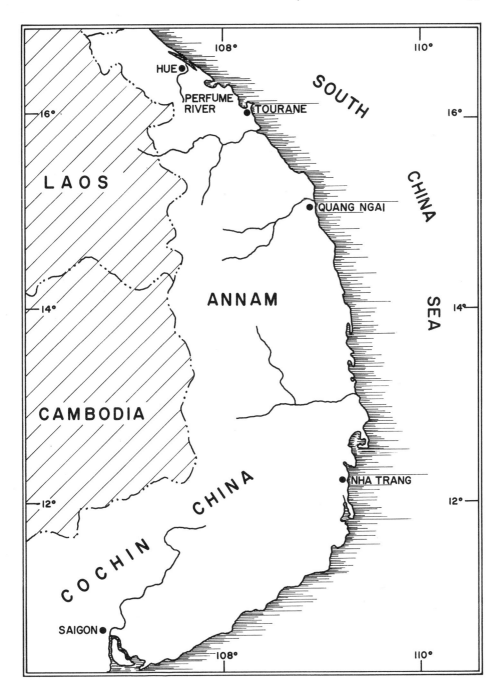

Central Coast of Vietnam.

The troops met stiff resistance, but the firepower of the ships offshore helped carry the day. On the afternoon of the 25th *Savorgnan de Brazza,* with the help of an airborne spotter, leveled several rebel-held villages. During most of the night the gunboat fired star shells for illumination and conducted harassing fire. Escort *Commandant Duboc* also carried out nightime missions in support of Navy commandos, while *Chevreuil* evacuated fifteen dead and twenty-three wounded Army troopers to Tourane. Naval gunfire continued on the 26th and two Navy Privateers, based at Tourane, flew six bombing missions in support of the operation.

A typhoon delayed the reembarkation for two days, but on 29 August, three LSTs beached and took on troops, as escorts *Commandant Dominé* and *La Capricieuse* covered the withdrawal. Against a loss of 25 dead and 37 wounded, the French reported killing 107 and capturing 1,061 Viet Minh.[28]

In a followup operation, code-named *Caiman,* the surprise possible in an amphibious landing again was achieved. The target in this landing was the remnant of the same Viet Minh 101st Regiment that earlier threatened Hue. The amphibious forces were essentially the same as those used in *Sauterelle,* but for *Caiman* the French Army deployed ten battalions instead of four. The Navy landed the troops at dawn on 4 September 1952, as ships lay offshore providing gunfire support throughout the day and night.

At 0030 on the 5th, the Viet Minh mounted a desperate counterattack, attempting to break through French troops toward the northwest. French North African troops and the naval commandos vigorously resisted and inflicted heavy losses on the enemy. The operation continued until the morning of 7 September when, despite unfavorable weather caused by another typhoon, the amphibious force again backloaded the landing force. *Caiman* realized results even more impressive than *Sauterelle.* The French reported 640 enemy killed, 1,400 captured, and large quantities of arms and ammunition seized.[29]

Although the French had met reverses in remote regions of Tonkin near the Chinese border, they had, with the assistance of their navy, achieved notable military successes in the Red River Delta and coastal regions since 1950. As a result, they had increased their control over the main centers of population, food, and industry. However, in view of the vast extent of

---

[28] NA Saigon, report, 170–52 of 13 Sept. 1952, JN 15531, box 33, FRC.

[29] NA Saigon, report, 195–52 of 14 Oct. 1952, JN 15531, box 33, FRC.

Indochina's waterways and the lengthy coastline of Vietnam, the size of the French Navy's seagoing and riverine forces was marginal at best.

The Beginnings of a Vietnamese Navy

Initial steps in the development of armed forces for the State of Vietnam had begun at the end of 1949. Problems encountered in efforts to develop a Vietnamese navy were similar to those that would be faced when the United States assumed military advisory responsibilities within Vietnam following the French-Viet Minh War.

The French-Vietnamese Military Agreement of 30 December 1949 called for the French to provide the cadre for the navy and to furnish its basic training and instruction. Only a river navy was proposed in Admiral Ortoli's preliminary plan of April 1950. Another plan, drafted concurrently by the Naval Ministry in Paris, recognized that the most pressing problem was the establishment of the nucleus of an officer corps. To that end, the Paris plan provided for the training of a small number of Vietnamese at the French Naval Academy at Brest. But the three students selected for the schooling did not last the year.[30]

Except for these plans, no progress was made in 1950. Some reports said the lag in developing Vietnamese naval forces was caused by personnel and budgetary limitations. Admiral Ortoli blamed the Permanent Military Committee in Saigon, to which the High Commissioner, General de Lattre, had assigned the task of making preliminary studies for the Vietnamese Navy.[31] Concerned over the delays, the Naval Ministry in Paris insisted on action.

Ortoli submitted a new development plan in April 1951. It included provisions for two naval assault divisions in 1951, a recruit training center in 1952, several river flotillas in 1953, four motor minesweepers in 1954, and a seaplane squadron in 1955. Paris accepted Ortoli's proposal, but added a requirement for seagoing ships. In the proposal of the French naval secretary, 1 corvette (*Chamois* class, 647 tons) would be transferred in 1952 and, through new construction in France, 2 escort ships (*Le Corse* class, 1,290 tons) and 4 minesweepers (*Sirius* class, 365 tons) would be

---

[30] Navy Division, TRIM, Study, "Naval Forces of Vietnam," 10 Dec. 1955, p. 1.

[31] NA Saigon, reports, 9–52 of 15 Jan. 1952 and 67–52 of 24 Apr. 1952, JN 15531, boxes 32 and 33, FRC; Victor J. Croizat, "Vietnamese Naval Forces: Origin of the Species," *United States Naval Institute Proceedings*, IC (Feb. 1973), pp. 49–58.

added. Ortoli was asked to propose a budget for the construction of a recruit training center, for the recruiting of cadres for the Navy, and for shipbuilding.[32]

Due to a desire to create a single armed service, General de Lattre did not agree initially with the concept of a separate navy. Ortoli had his own reservations. He was afraid that the manning of a Vietnamese navy would interfere with recruitment of Vietnamese for the French Navy in Indochina. As a result, the French naval secretary modified his proposals for a seagoing navy and agreed to the original plan providing for a limited river navy. In November 1951, construction of the Recruit Training Center at Nha Trang began and an officer's training course for deck and engineering officers was established on board a French ship. Early in 1952, the French High Commissioner in Indochina and Commander French Naval Forces, Far East, proposed opening the training center that year; organizing two *dinassauts;* transferring three YMSs to the Vietnamese in 1953; and creating a naval staff, an administrative and technical service, and a coast guard in 1954.[33]

On 6 March 1952, Chief of State Bao Dai signed Imperial Ordinance Number Two. This ordinance, the first since 1949, provided for the establishment of a Vietnamese navy.[34] The French took a tangible step toward such a navy when, in reorganizing their military mission in May, they included a department charged with "commanding, administering, and managing the units of the Vietnamese Navy and directing its development."

Although over two years had gone by since the decision to establish a navy, little progress had been made with the foremost problem—that of providing and training the personnel to man the force. To fill the complements of the Far Eastern fleet, then limited to a 10,000-man French ceiling because of a ban on draftees and demands elsewhere, 400 Vietnamese had been recruited. Although these Vietnamese received some training, they were assigned only to auxiliary units, small landing craft attached to Army units, and non-rated duties with the French river forces.[35]

The training problems were formidable. Although many Vietnamese

---

[32] "Naval Forces of Vietnam," pp. 1–2.

[33] *Ibid.;* Croizat, "Vietnamese Naval Forces," pp. 50–51.

[34] Ordinance Number One, signed by Bao Dai on 1 July 1949, was the basic constitutional document of the Bao Dai regime and remained the legal basis for the State of Vietnam until passage of the constitution of the Republic of Vietnam; Fall, *Two Viet-Nams,* p. 215.

[35] ONI, "Development of and Plans for the Vietnamese Navy," *The ONI Review,* VIII (Mar. 1953), p. 123; Croizat," Vietnamese Naval Forces," p. 52.

NH-79402

Inspection at the Naval Training School, Nha Trang.

populated the coastal and inland waterway regions, and earned their living from fishing or operating small craft, those with a technical education were few and illiteracy was common. Faced with heavy commitments to their own operations, the French were hesitant in diverting their limited resources to the supply of instructors for the lengthy process of creating a Vietnamese navy.

Two programs were initiated to acquire the necessary officers. Those needed immediately would be obtained by providing accelerated training to selected university graduates. The longer-range policy would be to train cadets in the established French naval schools. The first Vietnamese naval officer aspirants chosen after the short-lived group selected in 1949 were 9 former officers in the merchant marine (6 line and 3 engineering) who received a six-month course of instruction on board French ships. After graduation on 1 October 1952, they were assigned to French combat units for practical experience prior to the commissioning of the first Vietnamese ships and craft. A second shipboard class of 12 line and 4 engineering officer candidates began another course on 1 November 1952; 5 more officer candidates left for the French Naval Academy in Brest. By the end of January 1953, 25 officer candidates would be enrolled in courses of two or more years at naval schools in France; 16 at the Naval School and 5 at the Engineering School, both located in Brest, and 4 at the Paymaster School in Toulon.

Before an adequate enlisted training program could begin, a recruit training center had to be constructed. The site chosen was the deep-water bay at Nha Trang. While the center was under construction, French personnel were selected to form the first faculty and began to study Vietnamese. Since it would take some time before they became proficient in the language, the ability to speak some French was a prerequisite for the first recruits. The French instructors (five officers and twenty-five petty officers) arrived in May 1952. The initial class (150 apprentice seamen and 25 petty officer candidates including many who had served in the French Union forces) was admitted in June. The Nha Trang Naval School opened officially on 12 July.[36]

Although developments in 1952 were encouraging, the Vietnamese still had no navy of their own, despite the French-Vietnamese Military Agreement of 1949. It would not be until the spring of 1953 that the Vietnamese Navy finally would have its modest beginning.

---

[36] ONI, "Development of and Plans for the Vietnamese Navy," pp. 123–25.

CHAPTER IX

The Tangled Events Of 1953

The Effects of the Protracted War on France

By 1953, the French-Viet Minh War had entered its seventh year. The Communist strategy of a "long-term resistance war" was beginning to have its effects.

Giap later claimed that the Communists undertook a prolonged conflict because the French, after World War II, were considered to be weary of war, beset by internal political dissension, capable of democratically expressing their impatience, and lacking the "psychological and political means to fight a long-drawn-out war. . . ." [1] A decade and a half later, the United States—engaged in the seemingly endless Vietnam War, in a remote area, and constrained by limited objectives and the controlled application of force—would experience a similar erosion of national resolve.

Within Vietnam, the Communists had emphasized propaganda from the start as a key element in their struggle to gain control. This psychological offensive was orchestrated with military, cultural, and economic measures. Its importance in overall strategy was reflected by the statement of General Giap, with regard to the early phases of the war, that "the most essential and important task was to make propaganda among the masses and organize them. . . ." In stressing "armed propaganda," Giap stated that "political activities were more important than military activities, and fighting less important than propaganda. . . ."

French impatience increased as many reports were received of scattered guerrilla-type actions by individuals and small groups. These reports presented a cumulative image of far greater enemy successes than were actually being achieved. Discontent and divisiveness were fueled by persistent propaganda on the part of the Viet Minh and the world Communist movement, and by others voicing opposition to continuing the war. The eventual impact

---

[1] Quoted in Fall, *Two Viet-Nams*, p. 113; see also Giap, *People's War, People's Army*, pp. 98–100.

was highlighted by Giap's subsequent claim that the enemy had a "weak point" because he was "internally divided, not supported by the people of his own country and did not enjoy the sympathy of world opinion." The General cited, as one of the reasons for victory in the French-Viet Minh War, the support of "progressive peoples" throughout the world, "among whom are the French people under the leadership of their Communist Party. . . ." The French Communist Party had, throughout the war, retained links with the Viet Minh, and done its best to hinder the French efforts, even to the extent of sabotaging military equipment consigned to Indochina.[2]

In Giap's assessment, the fighting spirit of the French had been deteriorating as a result of their reduced manpower and wealth after World War II. The morale of the French Expeditionary Force in Indochina was indeed being depressed by the realization that their government and people were not fully behind their efforts, the knowledge that an unrestrained press was providing intelligence to the enemy, and the leaks of operational plans and security measures. Articles and reports which seemed deliberately written to hit at morale appeared in French newspapers and periodicals.[3]

The French "New Strategic Plan"

Although war weariness had not reached crisis proportions by the start of 1953, United States policy-makers were seeking an early conclusion to the war and urged more aggressive French military action. The situation in Indochina had been discussed at the North Atlantic Treaty Organization minister's meeting in Paris in December 1952. At this meeting, the delegates passed a special resolution which linked the efforts of the armed forces for France and the Associated States of Indochina against Communists to the common security of the "Free World."[4]

On 19 January 1953, in view of what he assessed as a "continued stalemate" in the military situation in Indochina, Deputy Secretary of Defense William C. Foster requested that the Joint Chiefs reexamine America's

---

[2] *Ibid.*, pp. 36, 78–79, 99, 101, 102, 126, 127; O'Ballance, *Indo-China War,* p. 198; Henri Navarre, *Agony of Indochina,* trans. by Naval Intelligence Command (Paris: Plon, 1957), pp. 189–90.

[3] CIA, "Probable Developments in Indochina through Mid-1954," 4 June 1953 in *U.S.-V.N. Relations,* bk 9, p. 48; O'Ballance, *Indo-China War,* p. 198.

[4] "Results of Meeting of North Atlantic Council, Paris, December 15–18," *The Department of State Bulletin,* XXVIII (5 Jan. 1953), p. 4.

role in the war, paying particular attention to the training of indigenous forces. In their response of 13 March 1953, the Joint Chiefs of Staff advised against active combat participation because of the extent of other world-wide United States commitments and their belief that France and the Associated States had the capability to provide the military strength required. They again recommended that the French be encouraged to augment the Vietnamese Armed Forces, suggesting that United States military aid pay for the additional troops.[5]

In reevaluating the situation in the spring of 1953, General Salan proposed to reassign thousands of French troops who had been tied down in static positions to mobile units. He planned to train Vietnamese soldiers to take over garrison duties. These proposals would require substantial American aid, estimated at about $1.5 billion for fiscal years 1954 and 1955.[6]

Since the initial decision in May 1950 to send aid to Indochina, the United States had continually urged the French to prepare an overall military plan upon which America could base its assistance program. The French had resisted justifying their aid requirements in this fashion. Now, faced with a hugh new aid request, the American government insisted that no further aid would be "considered without full knowledge of French political and military plans. . . ."[7]

French Prime Minister René Mayer and Foreign Minister Georges Bidault, accompanied by the Minister of Finance and the Minister of the Associated States, visited Washington from 25 to 28 March 1953 to present their case for increased aid. The French High Commissioner for the Associated States, Jean Letourneau, and the French Armed Forces Chief of Staff, Jacques Allard, presented "a new strategic plan" to the Assistant Secretary of Defense for International Security Affairs, Frank Nash, who was now responsible within the department for aid. The presentation was also attended by Brigadier General Thomas J. H. Trapnell, USA, Chief, MAAG Indochina, and the United States Ambassador to Indochina, Donald R. Heath. The objectives of the plan were the ultimate destruction of the Viet Minh forces and general pacification of Indochina through a series of operations

---

[5] Memo, DEPSECDEF to JCS, of 19 Jan. 1953 in *U.S.-V.N. Relations*, bk 9, pp. 4, 11–14.

[6] Philippe Devillers and Jean Lacouture, *End of a War: Indochina, 1954* (New York: Frederick A. Praeger, 1969), p. 33; memo, OP–30 to CNO, No. 135–53 of 13 Apr. 1953.

[7] Msgs, SECSTATE, of 26 Mar. 1953 and 19 Mar. 1953 in *U.S.-V.N. Relations*, bk 9, pp. 15–18.

generally extending from the south to the north; occupation of pacified territory by newly formed commando-type units; and the massing of forces in the Red River Delta for a final offensive against the Viet Minh regulars in Tonkin.

The Secretary of Defense sought advice from the Joint Chiefs of Staff. In preparation for the JCS meeting on the plan, Captain Arleigh A. Burke, head of the Strategic Plans Division, Office of the Chief of Naval Operations, provided a briefing memorandum to Admiral Fechteler, Chief of Naval Operations. In addition to outlining the objectives of the plan, the memorandum noted that in the past the French had been highly conservative in their operations. The plan was considered good in that it proposed to reduce the Viet Minh within a reasonable time. The Burke memorandum pointed out two possible objections to the plan; namely, that it was too costly and that its effectiveness was questionable. With regard to the latter Burke offered the following counter arguments:

(1) Extended offensive can be conducted only in dry season. It is doubtful that sufficient regular forces can be concentrated for successful Tonkin offensive during dry season 53–54. They must wait for the next dry season 54–55; (2) Regular forces should not be concentrated in north until south and central areas pacified and VN forces ready to take over.[8]

Three days later, another Burke memorandum to the Chief of Naval Operations highlighted the insufficiency of French forces and the need for indigenous forces, stating:

1. The war in Indochina is much like the old Indian Wars in the United States. The French tried at one time to cut off supplies coming down from China by occupying posts along the China border. The VM filtered around these posts. The French suffered perhaps their major defeat of the war so far in withdrawing from one of these posts. The French do not have sufficient forces to establish a continuous front with the enemy on one side and a secure rear area on the other. As M. Letourneau expressed it, "this war is in fact everywhere."

2. When the French win a battle, it doesn't stay won. The enemy disperses and builds up for another attack.

3. One object of the plan is to remedy this situation by raising sufficient indigenous forces to occupy areas as battles are won, thus gradually depriving the VM of their sources of recruitment, food, and supplies. Small indigenous

---

[8] Memo, OP–30 to CNO, No. 135–53 of 13 Apr. 1953.

units, as opposed to divisions, are adequate for this type duty. As the VM are dispersed, the villages from which they draw support will be occupied.

4. Another object of the plan is to place responsibility in the hands of the Vietnamese by:

a. Increasing size of regular VN forces so VN can take increasing part in campaign against regular VM units.

b. Creating new type VN commando units to take over control of large slices of territory.[9]

Submitting their views to the Secretary of Defense on 21 April 1953, the Joint Chiefs of Staff pointed out that the Letourneau plan had not been presented in writing, and that their knowledge of it was limited largely to minutes of an oral presentation. Reserving further opinions on the merits of the proposal, their collective judgement was that it did not appear to be sufficiently aggressive; that it directed excessive efforts to the cleaning up of the Viet Minh pockets without adequate consideration given to cutting enemy supply lines, particularly in northern Indochina; and that it placed insufficient emphasis on transfer of responsibilities to the Vietnamese and on the training of their leaders.[10]

One of the matters being considered at this time was the nature and extent of support to the Viet Minh from the U.S.S.R. and the People's Republic of China. Stalin had died on 5 March 1953 and a troubled time lay ahead in the Soviet Union. Violent disagreement between Soviet leaders had been in evidence since the Nineteenth Party Congress in October 1952; purges and arrests were carried out on a gigantic scale. After Stalin died, purging of the purgers commenced. Russian direction and support of the global Cold War eased as the Communist Party of the U.S.S.R. concentrated on internal problems. Until these problems were resolved the Viet Minh could expect little help from the Soviet Union. On the other hand, the Korean War was in its final phase and Chinese support of the Viet Minh was likely to increase.

Meeting from 6 to 10 April 1953 in Pearl Harbor, representatives of Australia, New Zealand, Great Britain, the United States, and France recommended the establishment of a body to coordinate their planning as it related to Southeast Asia. The Joint Chiefs of Staff, in late May, authorized American participation in the proposed machinery and appointed Admiral Radford as the United States representative.[11] Staff planners met from 15 June to

---

[9] Memo, OP–30 to CNO, of 16 Apr. 1953.

[10] Memo, JCS to SECDEF, of 21 Apr. 1953 in *U.S.-V.N. Relations,* bk 9, pp. 24–26.

[11] Memo, OP–30 to CNO, No. 159–53 of 5 May 1953.

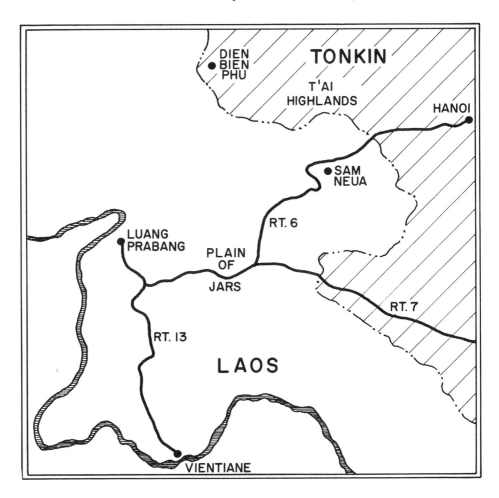

Area of the Laos Campaign, 1952.

1 July to discuss joint planning in connection with the Chinese threat to Southeast Asia and Hong Kong. They noted that, should the Chinese intervene in Indochina, the French planned to withdraw to the defensive perimeter of the Tonkin delta, in which case air and naval support would be needed. The American policy at the time was to let France and England furnish troops while the United States provided naval and air forces.

Thus, when the likelihood of future Chinese intervention increased at the end of the Korean War in late July, planning for possible military actions in such a contingency situation was well advanced. Clearly, if such actions were required, the United States Navy would have a major part to play.

The Viet Minh Thrust into Laos

Giap's forces followed their 1952 offensive into the mountainous T'ai country of northwestern Tonkin with a three-division thrust into Laos in the spring of 1953. The French reacted by withdrawing the bulk of the Army's offensive power from the Red River Delta and dispersing it at isolated strong points where the forces were largely dependent on air transport for logistic support. By the middle of April, twenty French battalions were either encamped on the Laotian Plain of Jars or were located near the capital, Luang Prabang. Local guerrilla forces and three regular Viet Minh divisions occupied the attention of the French Union forces which remained in the delta region. On 7 May 1953, Giap pulled back two of his divisions from Laos into Tonkin, leaving a third to harass the French and subvert the Laotians. That summer the Laotian Communist Pathet Lao forces, combined with "Vietnam People's volunteers," launched an attack against Sam Neua and captured territory in northern Laos. According to Giap this created "a new threat to the enemy."[12]

The Navarre Plan

General Henri Navarre had relieved Salan in April 1953. The new Commander of French Armed Forces, Far East was hand-picked by Prime Minister Mayer on the recommendation of Marshal Alphonse Juin. Included in Navarre's experiences between two world wars were operations against Syrian guerrillas and in the pacification campaigns in Morocco. In World War II he had served in the underground during the German occupation of France.[13]

Soon thereafter, a United States Joint Military Mission, headed by Lieutenant General John W. O'Daniel, USA, Commander in Chief, U.S. Army Pacific, was sent to "discuss with General Navarre . . . requirements for and utilization of U.S. military aid. . . ." Although O'Daniel normally

---

[12] O'Ballance, *Indo-China War.* pp. 189–92; Giap, *People's War, People's Army,* p. 192; CIA, "Probable Developments in Indochina through mid-1954," 4 June 1953 in *U.S.-V.N. Relations,* bk 9, pp. 47–49, states that four Viet Minh divisions thrust into Laos while two remained in the delta.

[13] Bernard B. Fall, *Hell in a Very Small Place: The Siege of Dien Bien Phu* (New York: J. B. Lippincott Co., 1967), pp. 28–29.

reported to his unified commander, Commander in Chief, Pacific, he was sent in this instance as a representative of the JCS, "under the over-all supervision of the Commander in Chief, Pacific. . . ." One of O'Daniel's tasks was to "expedite revision and aggressive implementation of French military plans for successfully concluding the war in Indochina, including the early initiation of aggressive guerrilla warfare, aimed at knocking the enemy off balance, disrupting enemy supply lines, and gaining the initiative for anticommunist forces." Early aggressive military action against the Viet Minh was deemed essential.[14]

During General O'Daniel's visit to Indochina, he was briefed by Navarre on the new aggressive concept of operations for the conduct of the war. According to the plan, the French would take the initiative that summer in local offensives and commando and guerrilla actions. They would attack the flanks and rear of the enemy in the north during the fall and winter, progressively pacifying regions not directly involved in the battle. The plan promised a maximum of cooperation with the Air Force and Navy, and a continuance of "the effort of instructing and organizing the Army of the Associated States so as to give them more and more participation as well as more autonomy in the conduct of operations."[15]

The outline of the plan, as reported by General O'Daniel in the summer of 1953, differed in one significant respect from the plan as recounted in General Navarre's memoirs—in the timing of the French offensive. In his book, *Agony of Indochina,* Navarre stated that the basis of his plan was similar to that of General Salan, namely:

> 1. During 1953–1954 campaign, maintain a strategically defensive attitude north of the 18th Parallel, and seek to avoid a general battle. On the other hand, take, whenever possible, the offensive south of the 18th Parallel, in order to clean up South and Central Indochina and recover our forces there. In particular, to seek to liquidate the L.K.5 [Vietnam from Tourane to just north of Saigon].
> 2. Having obtained the superiority in mobile forces, i.e., starting in autumn 1954, take the offensive north of the Porte d'Annam, with the goal of creating a military situation permitting a political solution to the conflict.[16]

During O'Daniel's trip to Indochina, he and other members of the mission also discussed naval operations with Vice Admiral Auboyneau, who had

---

[14] Memo, JCS to SECDEF, of 10 June 1953 in *U.S.-V.N. Relations,* bk 9, pp. 59–67.

[15] Memo, JCS to SECDEF, of 11 Aug. 1953 in *Ibid.,* pp. 134–37.

[16] See Navarre, *Agony of Indochina,* pp.135–36.

replaced Vice Admiral Ortoli in April 1952 as Commander of French Naval Forces, Far East.[17] Admiral Auboyneau agreed to reorganize his forces to include a joint amphibious command, with the purpose of "attaining increased amphibious effectiveness," and to delegate "increased responsibility to Vietnamese leaders and units."[18]

As the Navarre plan was being assessed in Washington, American policy-makers were concerned that the situation might worsen. A United States Central Intelligence Agency assessment of 4 June 1953 stated that, "if present trends in the Indochinese situation continue through mid-1954, the French Union political and military position may subsequently deteriorate very rapidly." Secretary of Defense Wilson summarized the situation as follows: "Communist aggression in Indochina presents, except for Korea, the most immediate threat to the free world. For more than 6 years communist forces, supplied with weapons and equipment from Communist China and Soviet Russia, have been waging open warfare."[19]

Admiral Felix B. Stump, the new Commander in Chief, Pacific, endorsed, with some reservation, the Navarre concept forwarded by O'Daniel, as it was relayed by O'Daniel to the JCS. The views of the Joint Chiefs of Staff on the plan were set forth in a memorandum of 11 August 1953 signed by their chairman, General Bradley. The Joint Chiefs of Staff hesitated to predict actual results, but felt the plan offered "a promise of success sufficient to warrant . . . additional U.S. aid. . . ."[20]

Admiral Radford succeeded General Bradley as Chairman of the Joint Chiefs of Staff on 15 August 1953. Having just completed his tour as Commander in Chief, Pacific and Commander in Chief, United States Pacific Fleet, a tour lasting from April 1949 until June 1953, Admiral Radford had a current understanding of the situation in Southeast Asia and the Far East. He had visited the friendly countries in the area and conferred with their military and civilian leaders. His tour had included all except the last month of the Korean War. Having been responsible for the performance

---

[17] Naval officers on the mission were Captain Stephen Jurika, Jr., and Ensign Pence, USNR, of the Pacific Fleet staff.

[18] Ltr, Chief, Joint Military Mission to Indochina to JCS, of 14 July 1953 in *U.S.-V.N. Relations*, bk 9, pp. 69–72.

[19] U.S., Defense Department, *Semianual Report of the Secretary of Defense*, Jan.–June 1953 (Washington: GPO, 1953), p. 61; CIA, "Probable Developments in Indochina through Mid-1954," 4 June 1953 in *U.S.-V.N. Relations*, bk 9, p. 47.

[20] Memo, JCS to SECDEF, of 11 Aug. 1953 in *U.S.-V.N. Relations*, bk 9, pp. 134–35; memo, OP–35 to CNO (no date, *ca.* Aug. 1953).

of units of the Fleet, under operational control of the Supreme Allied Commander when in the Korean area, he was familiar with the problems of that limited war. Impressed with Radford's capabilities, experiences, duties, and personality, key naval aviators recognized and respected him as their leader. A strong proponent of carrier air power, he had served three tours in the Bureau of Aeronautics and as Deputy Chief of Naval Operations for Air. His combat experience included command of carrier divisions and carrier task groups in World War II and participation in the intense naval actions during the last ten months of the war. Secretary of the Navy Forrestal had brought him to Washington in 1945 to head the "Secretary's Committee of Research on Reorganization" in connection with the question of unification. He had served as Vice Chief of Naval Operations from January 1948 to April 1949.

On 28 August 1953, in one of his early actions as Chairman of the Joint Chiefs of Staff, Admiral Radford signed a memorandum to the Secretary of Defense commenting on the Navarre plan. In it the Joint Chiefs of Staff considered the previous wording to have been "overly optimistic with respect to the 'promise of success' offered by the Navarre concept." The JCS noted that the actual success would *"be dependent upon the aggressiveness and skill with which the French and Vietnamese forces conduct their future operations."* [21]

Reorganization Plan No. 6

When Dwight D. Eisenhower became President of the United States in January 1953, he developed the "New Look" for his administration. One of the areas in which he sought changes concerned the responsibilities of those charged with providing for the common defense.

Some further steps toward functional centralization had already been taken. The Defense Supply Management Agency was established in July 1952 under the Office of the Secretary of Defense, although with limited responsibilities for the time being. In August, the office of Director of Installations was established whereby "direct surveillance over the planning and construction of all public works by the military departments was centralized in the Office of the Secretary of Defense." [22] The National Security

---

[21] Memo, JCS to SECDEF, of 28 Aug. 1953 in *U.S.-V.N. Relations*, bk 9, pp. 138–39.

[22] U.S., Defense Department, *Semiannual Report of the Secretary of Defense,* July–Dec. 1952 (Washington: GPO, 1953), p. 5.

Agency was formed in November to work on cryptography and communications security.

During his campaign for the Presidency, Eisenhower called for the creation of a commission to study the operations, functions, and acts of the Department of Defense. After the election, Truman suggested that Secretary of Defense Lovette place his recommendations on the record.

Lovette, who had been Assistant Secretary of War for Air at the time of the 1944 hearings on defense reorganization, expressed his views in a letter dated 18 November 1952. He wrote that certain areas had been identified in which the organization of the Department of Defense and the statutory agencies—the Joint Chiefs of Staff, the Munitions Board, and the Research and Development Board—should be improved and their authorities and responsibilities clarified. The changes, he concluded, appeared to require legislative action. Lovette outlined two alternate plans for reorganization. The one he considered the less radical would confine the Joint Chiefs of Staff to planning functions and reviewing war plans. It would relieve them of operating responsibilities in their services, and give the chairman a vote. The balance of the military staff functions would be transferred to the Office of the Secretary of Defense. Military officers in that office would have responsibilities to the secretary, similar to the Army General Staff Corps. They would aid him on such matters as resolving conflicts between the services and "matters involving policies regarding budgets, procurement, logistics, manpower, personnel, intelligence, etc." The JCS would not "operate" or "command." The secretary would be the President's Deputy Commander in Chief. Unified commands would report directly to the secretary and receive orders by his direction. He would establish these unified commands and assign them to the military departments as Secretary of Defense agents.[23]

The incoming President appointed a committee consisting of Secretary of Defense Robert A. Lovette, Nelson A. Rockefeller, General Omar N. Bradley, USA, Vannevar Bush, Milton S. Eisenhower, Arthur S. Flemming, and David Sarnoff to study defense reorganization. In its 11 April 1953 report the committee noted opinions which held that the original act, in requiring that the military departments be "separately administered," limited the Secretary of Defense's authority, especially with respect to functions

---

[23] SECDEF, *Semiannual Report,* Jan–June 1953, pp. 10, 65–66; Ltr, Lovette to Truman, of 18 Nov. 1952 in *Army, Navy, Air Force Journal,* XC (10 Jan. 1953), pp. 541–43.

assigned directly to the military departments by statute. Disagreeing with these opinions, the report recommended decisive administrative action or a statutory amendment to confirm "the direction, authority, and control of the Secretary over all the agencies of the Department, including the three military departments. . . ."[24]

The committee considered it unfortunate that the Secretary of Defense had delegated certain command functions to the Joint Chiefs of Staff. While recommending increased authority for the JCS chairman, it advised removal of the JCS command functions. Rather than military chiefs acting as executive agents of the Joint Chiefs, the committee recommended that a military department be designated as the executive agent of the Secretary of Defense for each unified command. Except in an emergency, the President and the Secretary of Defense were expected to give orders to military officers through their civilian secretaries. More assistant secretaries and other staff assistants were recommended for the Secretary of Defense, and a need was stressed for highly qualified military officers in the Office of the Secretary of Defense.

The committee believed it "essential to have a single channel of command or line of administrative responsibility" not only within the Department of Defense but also within each of the military departments. It opposed administrative division of responsibility between military affairs and civilian affairs. Whatever the intent, this opposition could be interpreted as critical of the "bilinear" system that had evolved in the Navy Department, particularly since the report considered it vital that "the organization of the military departments be thoroughly reviewed and adjusted in the light of the recommendations of the Committee."[25]

In a message to Congress on 30 April 1953, President Eisenhower announced his intention to bring about changes through executive actions, and stated that, "as a former soldier who has experienced modern war at first hand, and now, as President and Commander in Chief of the armed forces of the United States, I believe that our defense establishment is in need of immediate improvement." The main purpose of the message was to trans-

---

[24] U.S., Congress, Senate, Committee on Department of Defense Organization, *Report of the Rockefeller Committee on Department of Defense Organization* (83rd Cong., 1st sess.) (Washington: GPO, 1953), p. 2.

[25] *Ibid.*, pp. 3–4.

mit his Reorganization Plan No. 6 of 1953 to the Congress and to set forth the rationale.[26]

As a result of his plan, which went into effect on 30 June 1953, the number of Assistant Secretaries of Defense was increased by six and the Secretary of Defense was given the power of authorizing others to carry out any of his functions. The jointly manned Munitions Board, the Research and Development Board, and the Defense Supply Management Agency were abolished. In the name of efficiency and the elimination of unnecessary delays, their functions were transferred to the Office of the Secretary of Defense. Authority over these areas would now be exercised by three of the Assistant Secretaries of Defense.

Emphasizing "civilian control," the President ordered that "no function in any part of the Department of Defense, or in any of its component agencies, should be performed independent of the direction, authority, and control of the Secretary of Defense." Under the President, as Commander in Chief of the Armed Forces, the chain of command was now through the Secretary of Defense. The latter would issue orders to the unified commands through military departments designated as his agents; service chiefs would no longer function as executive agents for the JCS. The secretaries of the military departments could authorize the service chief of the designated military department to "act for that department" in strategic direction, operational control, and conduct of combat, but this authority was optional. "Civilian experts" would now be included in the process of strategic planning.[27]

The incoming secretary, Charles E. Wilson, reorganized his office to include a Deputy Secretary of Defense, a General Counsel, raised to the level of an assistant secretary, an Assistant to the Secretary for Atomic Energy, and nine assistant secretaries—manpower and personnel (later to become manpower and reserve affairs), comptroller, international security affairs, legislative and public affairs, research and development, applications engineering, supply and logistics, properties and installations, and health and medicine. An Assistant for Guided Missiles was added later. Authority over twelve major "fields of responsibility" was centered in the Assistant

---

[26] "Special Message to the Congress Transmitting Reorganization Plan 6 of 1953 Concerning the Department of Defense," 30 Apr. 1953 in *Dwight D. Eisenhower: 1953* in series *Public Papers of the Presidents of the United States* (Washington: GPO, 1960), pp. 225–38.

[27] *Ibid.*, p. 229; SECDEF, *Semiannual Report*, Jan.–June 1953, pp. 17–18; U.S. Congress, House, Subcommittee of the Committee on Government Operations, *Hearings on Military Supply Management Program* (83rd Cong., 1st sess.) (Washington: GPO, 1953), pp. 1–8.

Secretaries of Defense, the General Counsel, the Assistant for Atomic Energy, and the Joint Chiefs of Staff—although the authority of the latter was in fact reduced. Extensive powers over functional areas were thus transferred to staff members of the Office of the Secretary of Defense. Consequently, lines of authority had proliferated and at times conflicted one with another. As assessed by one observer, "in practice the assistant secretaries inevitably create supplementary lines of authority between themselves and the functional offices in the services whose duties fall within their assigned fields." One by-product was the involvement of the Office of the Chief of Naval Operations and the Navy Secretariat in more details, accompanied by reduction of delegation of authority within the Navy Department. While it may have looked simpler at the top, the decision and action process, as viewed from below, was becoming more involved and more time-consuming[28]

Impact on the Navy

The National Defense Act of 1947 had spawned added complexities in the Navy's external relationships. Nevertheless, the Navy Department was able to adjust to this without basic alterations of the internal organization or the principles of policy direction, administration, management, and command that had been in practice in World War II.

The 1949 amendments, however, had far greater impact. They called for downgrading the Department of the Navy from an executive department to a subdivision of the new Department of Defense, superimposing additional controls over functions performed within the military departments, and initiating fundamental changes in the direction of the defense effort and its management. After 1949, more extensive adjustments were necessary within the Navy Department, but once again these had been accomplished without major realignments of responsibilities and authority or basic organizational changes.

Now in 1953, as a result of the report by a committee whose members lacked an intimate knowledge of the internal functioning of the Navy, and as a result of executive actions, far-reaching changes at the level of the

---

[28] SECDEF, *Semiannual Report,* Jan.–June 1953, pp. 9–18; Stanley, *American Defense and National Security,* p. 126; Ries, *Management of Defense,* pp. 150–66.

Office of the Secretary of Defense and the Joint Chiefs of Staff were accompanied by a questioning of how the Navy Department was structured and managed. Following the guidance of the President in his Reorganization Plan, the Secretary of Defense directed the secretaries of the military departments to study their internal organizations. On 14 October 1953, Secretary of the Navy Robert B. Anderson, referring to the "Rockefeller Committee" report and the President's plan, established "the Committee on Organization of the Department of the Navy," chaired by Under Secretary of the Navy Thomas S. Gates, Jr.

The committee weighed the effect on the Navy Department of the newly established Assistant Secretaries of Defense and the abolition of boards and agencies. It considered the principle enunciated by the President concerning "civilian control" of all functions of the departments under the direction, authority, and control of the Secretary of Defense. After an extensive study, the "Gates Committee" concluded that the existing organization of the Department of the Navy was basically sound and had proved its ability to respond to changing demands of great magnitude. However, to comply with the principles held by the President and Secretary of Defense, to provide interfaces with subdivisions of the expanded Office of the Secretary of Defense, to ensure that actions in functional areas would not adversely effect the fulfillment of missions and roles of the operating forces, and to provide complete compatibility with the Office of the Secretary of Defense, a forced-fit of the bilinear system to the overall Department of Defense system would be required.

One result was doubling of the number of the Navy assistant secretaries required in World War II. The two new officials were an Assistant Secretary of the Navy for Financial Management (Comptroller) and an Assistant Secretary of the Navy (Personnel and Reserve Forces). The current assistant secretary was designated Assistant Secretary of the Navy (Material). An Assistant Secretary of the Navy (Air) was retained. The Under Secretary of the Navy was assigned supervision over the offices of the Judge Advocate General, the General Counsel, Analysis and Review, and Naval Petroleum and Oil Shale Reserves. A Naval Inspector General was established. For coordination between military and civilian officials, executive, material, facilities, personnel, reserve forces, and research and development advisory committees were formed. Other changes were recommended by the Gates Committee for the improvement of internal administration within the established principles of organization.[29]

Whether or not the changes in the Department of Defense and the Department of the Navy would achieve the Secretary of Defense's goals of greater effectiveness and economy, some long-term results were clear. There would be more management and more layers of review, coordination, and direction, and there would be added overhead. Casualties would include reduction in the delegation of mission-oriented authority within the Navy, and reduction in flexibility and responsiveness to changing service needs.

Policies and Strategy

As a part of his "new look at defense policies" and his avowed goal of "security with solvency," Eisenhower initiated, immediately after his election on 3 November 1952, a review of strategic concepts and implementation plans, roles and mission, composition and readiness of forces, development of new weapons, and military assistance programs. In the words of Secretary of Defense Wilson, the review "sought a military strategy that would deter both a major war and local aggression and, at the same time, could be implemented and maintained without undermining the social and economic foundations of the Nation." [30]

The month of Eisenhower's election witnessed a successful test of a thermonuclear device; the development of hydrogen bomb capabilities was well underway. Nuclear warfare readiness would take increasingly bigger shares of the budget, and in addition to the role of nuclear weapons capabilities to deter general war, the applicability of such capabilities to limited conflict situations would be considered.

Impact of the Korean War on the United States Navy

At the time of the signing of the uncertain Korean Armistice on 27 July 1953, the Navy, and the Seventh Fleet in particular, were in a high state

---

[29] U.S., Department of the Navy, *Report of the Committee on Organization of the Department of the Navy* (Washington: GPO, 1954).

[30] U.S., Defense Department, *Semiannual Report of the Secretary of Defense*, July–Dec. 1953, (Washington: GPO, 1954), pp. 1–2; Ries, *Management of Defense*, p. 167.

of readiness for deterrent or combat actions. The experiences of the Korean War had emphasized the importance of maintaining a balanced Navy of sufficient strength to react to emergency situations. The United Nations' response to North Korean aggression was dependent on seapower. Emergency sea transportation was required, together with escorts, to evacuate Americans from South Korea. Ground forces and supplies had to be brought in promptly by sea. Other naval operations, supplementing and supporting actions ashore, were also needed to stop the Communist thrust and force a retreat to the north. Carriers had proven their worth in attacks from the Yellow Sea against airfields beyond the effective range of tactical aircraft operating from Japanese fields, in strikes to retard the advance of the invading forces and against their lines of communication, and in close support of troops ashore, landings, and withdrawals. As a consequence, additional carriers would be maintained after the Korean War. Along with improvements in the conventional warfare readiness of the Fleet, carrier-based nuclear strike capabilities were greatly enhanced by the development of smaller and lighter nuclear bombs which could be delivered by tactical aircraft.[31]

Destroyers, cruisers, and battleships provided bombardment and gunfire support and blockaded the North Korean coast. The bold amphibious assault at Inchon reversed the North Korean offensive. As this flanking movement threatened the enemy's rear and lines of communication, the Communists hastily retreated. The operation provided a partial answer to those in the United States who had questioned the value of amphibious warfare in the post-World War II era and as a result this form of naval warfare received renewed emphasis. Helicopters, developed after World War II for the ship-to-shore movement of men and supplies, were first used in this role in the Korean conflict. During the war years, the Navy obtained authorization for four faster LSDs, fifteen faster LSTs, and an inshore fire support ship (IFS). The amphibious construction and conversion program which sought APAs and AKAs of higher speeds would continue after the war.

One of the areas of decreasing readiness in the months before the Korean War had been mine warfare. The time of reckoning came when Russian contact and pressure mines were encountered in the approaches to Wonsan

---

[31] For the naval aspects of the Korean War, see Field, *History of United States Naval Operations: Korea.*

and elsewhere. As a result, the United States Navy placed renewed emphasis, for a time, on readiness for offensive and defensive mine warfare.

Another deficiency at the start of the war concerned Service Force ships. In particular, there were no ammunition ships in Western Pacific waters and no supply ship equipped for underway replenishment remained in the Pacific Fleet. Having to return more frequently to Sasebo, Japan, the combatant ships could not be used initially with maximum efficiency in sustained operations. One result of this experience was that there would be no such gaps in underway replenishment capabilities when the need later arose in Southeast Asian waters.

Insofar as the United States Pacific Fleet was concerned, the period following the signing of the armistice in Korea was one of transition from wartime to a period of suspended hostilities. The Fleet had to maintain a state of readiness for the immediate resumption of combat operations in Northeast Asia, if necessary, while carrying out other widespread commitments in response to threats and crises throughout the entire Western Pacific area. Task Force 95 conducted patrols to help maintain the Korean armistice. Under Commander Seventh Fleet, Task Force 77 maintained two carriers at sea in the area of Japan and Korea, and conducted occasional maneuvers off Formosa. Task Force 72 continued patrol operations related to the defense of Formosa and the Pescadores.[32]

Plans called for a major reduction of ships in the Western Pacific, including the withdrawal of two carriers in January 1954. This reduction would later be revised in the light of events in Southeast Asia and concern over possible actions by the People's Republic of China.

Once again the United States Navy faced a difficult time in maintaining a balanced Fleet of adequate strength to meet future challenges. The ceasefire in Korea meant reductions to a peacetime budget. Over the preceding seven years, the size of the American nuclear weapon stockpile had been rapidly increasing and Air Force strategic forces greatly expanded. Further expansion would be stimulated by another of the momentous events of 1953. On 20 August, the Soviet Union announced the explosion of a hydrogen bomb. The United States Atomic Energy Commission confirmed the explosion, disclosing that a test involving both fission and thermonuclear reactions had occurred.

The postwar military budget of fiscal year 1954 was higher than that

---

[32] CINCPACFLT, "Annual Report," FY 1954, pp. 1–3.

at the start of the Korean War. However, with the emphasis on strategic warfare readiness, the Navy's share of funds was considerably smaller than in any of the prewar years. Modernization of the Fleet would have to be achieved in addition to meeting the continuing demands for readiness and worldwide deployments. Among the expanding requirements were nuclear propulsion, the equipping of ships with guided missile systems, the enhancement of antisubmarine warfare capabilities to meet the challenge of fast, deep-diving submarines, and the further development of the capabilities for carriers and their aircraft to deliver nuclear weapons. Replacement of ships built in World War II would continue to be deferred.

Increased Aid

An increase in military aid to the French in Indochina was approved in September 1953. One requirement not covered by the plan concerned aircraft carriers. *La Fayette* was scheduled for relief by *Arromanches* in mid-June 1953 and to enter drydock about mid-September for a six-month overhaul. The French needed an additional carrier which could be used for training French pilots in the use of the newly delivered Corsairs and then would be available to relieve *Arromanches* in the spring of 1954. Defense Minister Pleven had already initiated negotiations for a light carrier during his visit to Washington in March 1953. Accordingly, the President, with congressional approval, ordered the loan of *Belleau Wood* (CVL–24). *La Fayette* (transferred to France in 1951 under the Mutual Defense Assistance Program) and *Belleau Wood* were of the light carrier types built on cruiser hulls for service in World War II. Faster than the escort types, they were better able to land and recover fighter-type aircraft. Their aircraft capacity, however, was limited to a normal load of twenty-six.

Owing to the time taken to provide a qualified French crew, *Belleau Wood* (rechristened *Bois Belleau*) did not reach France until December 1953, two and a half months later than originally scheduled. The poor condition of her boilers at the time of reactivation and the need for further repairs caused some delay, as did French use of the ship to deliver planes to India.[33] The French Army would be badly in need of air support that

---

[33] Pierre Barjot, *Histoire de la Guerre Aeronavale* (Paris: Flammarion, 1961), pp. 402–05; memo, OP–30 to OP–03, ser 00025 of 25 July 1953; the authorization act, Public Law 188, is contained in U.S., Congress, *United States Statutes at Large: 1953* (83rd Cong., 1st sess.) (Washington: GPO, 1953), Vol. 67, p. 363; memo, Defense Member, NSC Planning Board to Presidential Assistant, of 10 Apr. 1954 in *U.S.-V.N. Relations,* bk 9, pp. 380–81.

French aircraft carrier La Fayette (ex USS Langley) operating in Along Bay.

winter and spring, but the carrier was not to arrive off Indochina until 30 April 1954.

One of the functional areas affected by the series of changes in defense responsibilities was that of planning and implementing military aid. During the Korean War years, the Department of Defense's military assistance organization had grown in size, and staff authority had increased. The proposals by the Army and Air Force, that operating functions be delegated to the military services and that the Office of the Secretary of Defense not undertake extensive operating functions, was rejected.[34] When the Assistant to the Secretary of Defense for International Security Affairs became one of the new assistant secretaries created in 1953, Department of Defense coordinating boards and committees involved with aid were dissolved.

The aid program had now developed separate lines of reporting and a separate budget. A typical pattern evolved whereby military assistance advisory groups in the various countries submitted requirements to be endorsed by the military departments and the Joint Chiefs of Staff. Invariably, the total worldwide program exceeded what was considered warranted for the President's budget. Then, last-minute decisions in the Department of Defense cut the programs to fit the President's budget. In the opinion of one writer, this pattern resulted "in all critical decisions being made without benefit of military advice and in ignorance of the recommendations of the military assistance advisory groups on which programs should be given greatest priority. . . . Military authorities had *de facto* transferred the power to make important decisions to the Office of the Secretary of Defense, in consultation with the State Department."[35]

A related problem concerning support of the conflict in Indochina was the review of military aid programs for the French and Associated States. Before being relieved as Commander in Chief, Pacific, Admiral Radford had felt that, since he had been assigned responsibility for planning in connection with the defense of Southeast Asia, he should have the authority to comment on assistance programs recommended by MAAG Indochina and MAAG Thailand. He requested such authority in January 1953. Under the split responsibilities that existed at the time, the Department of the Army continued as executive agent, now under the Secretary

---

[34] Stanley, *American Defense and National Security*, p. 52.
[35] Hovey, *United States Military Assistance*, p. 140.

of Defense, for military assistance matters in Thailand, the Philippines, Taiwan, and Indochina. Yet these countries were within the area of CINCPAC's unified command responsibility, for which the executive agent was the Navy. In March, the MAAGs were directed to submit information copies of their request to CINCPAC for comment. Six months later, MAAG Indochina and MAAG Thailand were told to forward recommended programs through CINCPAC, as was already the case in regard to Joint United States Military Assistance Advisory Group (JUSMAAG) Philippines and MAAG Formosa. Later, on 30 December 1953, Admiral Stump, who became CINCPAC in July 1953, requested military command over the MAAGs and JUSMAAGs in Southeast Asia. He would be given this authority when, on 1 May 1954, the executive agent responsibilities for these groups were transferred to the Department of the Navy.

The Coupling of Negotiations with Military Actions

The signing of the Korean Armistice was the culmination of two years of discussion between the Communists and United Nations representatives while the war continued. Admiral C. Turner Joy, of the United Nations truce delegation in Korea, later observed that "the measure of expansion achieved by Communism through negotiations is impossible to disassociate from what they have achieved by force, for the Communists never completely separate the two methods." [36] The comment was equally applicable to the conflict in Indochina, as was evident a few days after conclusion of the Korean Armistice when the Soviet Union and Communist China called for a settlement of the French-Viet Minh War.

That fall, Premier Joseph Laniel came under increasing parliamentary pressure to negotiate a settlement in Indochina. He won an important vote of confidence on 28 October 1953, but only after agreeing that everything should be done to achieve peace in Southeast Asia by means of negotiation.

Shortly thereafter, the Viet Minh feigned an attack on Phu Tho, along the Red River northwest of Hanoi, in order to lure General Navarre's forces away from Phu Ly on the Day River. When the Viet Minh tactic became apparent, General Navarre, in operation *Mouette,* moved six mobile groups against Phu Ly, which had recently been occupied by the Viet Minh 320th

---

[36] C. Turner Joy, *How Communists Negotiate* (New York: The Macmillan Co., 1955), p. xi.

Division. Several of the mobile groups moved to the battle in boats of
Dinassauts 3 and 12. Another part of the French force made for Phu Nho
Quan, the supply base for the Viet Minh 320th Division fifteen miles
west of the Day River on Route 12. Two Viet Minh regiments blocked
their advance until the supplies were removed. Everywhere the French
encountered stiffer opposition than they had expected. By the 7th of November, the fighting had reached a stalemate and the French withdrew rather
than commit more reserves to the battle. Despite the failure of *Mouette*
to achieve its full objective, the operation inflicted heavy casualties on the
Viet Minh 320th Division, putting it out of action for at least two months.[37]

On 20 November 1953, two French paratroop battalions captured the
post at the little valley town of Dien Bien Phu and established a defensive
position on the Laotian border to block the Viet Minh invasion of that
country. There is some disagreement as to whether the defense of Laos
was General Navarre's idea or based on directions from Paris.[38] Nevertheless,
the decision proved a fateful one.

On that same day, Ho Chi Minh, replying to a series of questions posed
by the Swedish newspaper *Expressen,* stated that, "if, having drawn the
lessons of these years of war, the French Government wishes to conclude
an armistice and solve the question of Vietnam by means of negotiations,
the people and government of the Democratic Republic of Vietnam
(D.R.V.) are ready to examine the French proposals. . . ."[39] Giap later
claimed that the French were "compelled to combine their plan of attacking
swiftly and win[ning] swiftly with that of invading step-by-step, and even
of negotiating with us . . . ."[40] One might infer that it was the Viet Minh
who sought the negotiations. Possible reasons were the recent casualties
sustained by the 320th Division plus evidence of a more aggressive French
campaign. A statement in *Khrushchev Remembers,* purported to be the

---

[37] O'Ballance, *Indo-China War,* pp. 205–06; Lancaster, *Emancipation of French Indochina,*
p. 285; NA Saigon, reports, 205–53 of 13 Nov. 1953, 208–53 of 27 Nov. 1953, 211–53 of
2 Dec. 1953, JN–N–59–488, box 25, FRC.

[38] Premier Joseph Laniel stated that at a meeting on 24 July 1953 Navarre was instructed that
the safety of the French forces was to be paramount. On the other hand, General Navarre claims
that at the July meeting Laniel gave no answer to his question about defending Laos. Furthermore,
Navarre continues, Maurice Dejean, the French Commissioner General in Indochina and Navarre's
superior, declared to him in November 1953 that there was "no question of not defending Laos."
Joseph Laniel, *Le Drame Indochinois de Dien-Bien-Phu au pari de Geneve* (Paris: Plon, 1957),
pp. 20–22; Navarre, *Agony of Indochina,* pp. 302–03.

[39] Quoted in Devillers and Lacouture, *End of War,* p. 45.

[40] Giap, *People's War, People's Army,* pp. 99–100.

memoirs of Nikita S. Khrushchev, tends to confirm this possibility. According to Khrushchev, Chou En-lai advised him that:

> Comrade Ho Chi Minh has told me that the situation in Vietnam is hopeless and that if we don't attain a cease-fire soon, the Vietnamese won't be able to hold out against the French. Therefore they've decided to retreat to the Chinese border if necessary, and they want China to be ready to move troops into Vietnam as we did in North Korea. In other words, the Vietnamese want us to help them drive out the French. We simply can't grant Comrade Ho Chi Minh's request. We've already lost too many men in Korea—that war cost us dearly. We're in no condition to get involved in another war at this time.[41]

The statement was reputedly made at a preparatory meeting in Moscow for the forthcoming Geneva conference. Ho and Pham represented the Democratic Republic of Vietnam and Chou the People's Republic of China.

On 27 November 1953, Russia agreed to a long-standing Western proposal for a Four Power Conference, ostensibly to discuss German unification. When representatives of the powers convened in Berlin on 25 January 1954, Russia's Foreign Minister, Vyacheslav Molotov, proposed an international meeting to ease world tensions, particularly in Korea and Indochina. On 18 February, the delegates agreed to discuss the Russian proposals in Geneva on 26 April.

General Navarre later stated that he opposed the conference because he believed the Viet Minh would not have risked a major commitment without the alternative of a settlement at Geneva. He also thought that China would not have sent substantial support to the Viet Minh without the prospect of negotiations alleviating the risk of United States intervention. He concluded bluntly, "that the fate of Dien Bien Phu was sealed" when it was decided to hold the Geneva conference.[42]

A Reassessment of the French Situation

Responding to an invitation from the French, the Joint Chiefs of Staff had ordered Lieutenant General O'Daniel back to Indochina on 6 November

---

[41] Quoted in Nikita S. Khrushchev, *Khrushchev Remembers,* Strobe Talbot, ed. (Boston: Little, Brown and Co., 1970), pp. 481–82.

[42] Devillers and Lacouture, *End of a War,* pp. 48, 54–59; Navarre, *Agony of Indochina,* pp. 410–11; see Laniel, *Le Drame Indochinois de Dien-Bien-Phu,* p. 32 for an opposing view.

1953 to survey progress made since his first visit there in June and July. Admiral Stump, after O'Daniel's first visit in the summer, had urged that the general return to Indochina as a representative of CINCPAC, rather than as Chief of Mission reporting directly to the JCS. Stump felt strongly that "he, as unified commander, [was] directly responsible for implementation" of many of the O'Daniel recommendations. Nevertheless, O'Daniel was once again ordered to Indochina as Chief of a Joint Military Mission, with primary responsibility directly to the JCS and not through CINCPAC as Stump had recommended.[43]

General O'Daniel submitted to the JCS, via CINCPAC, a report on the military situation. His report concluded that real military progress in the implementation of the Navarre Plan was evident and that the situation was far more favorable than it had been a year earlier. O'Daniel's views were somewhat more optimistic than those of either Stump or the Joint Chiefs of Staff. One reason for Stump's skepticism was O'Daniel's report of unsatisfactory progress by the French in training the Vietnamese. Stump also sensed a lack of determination in Indochina and declared that the U.S. and France should reaffirm their intent to prosecute the conflict to a satisfactory conclusion.[44]

After his trip, General O'Daniel reported increased French interest in amphibious operations. He noted that General Navarre had approved the creation of a Joint Amphibious Command, although development of the organization had lagged. To augment their amphibious capability for landing division-size forces, the French repeated their requests for acceleration in the effort to deliver naval craft, particularly LSMs (landing ships, medium), LSSLs, and LCUs (landing craft, utility). But recognizing that they could not be delivered in time to be used in planned amphibious operations, the French requested the loan until December 1954 of several large landing craft to carry out the landings programmed in the Navarre plan. As a result of the JCS approval of O'Daniel's recommendations on 31 December 1953, the Navy expedited delivery of 1954 MDAP naval craft, including 5 LSMs, 2 LSSLs, 3 LCUs, 40 LCMs, 45 LCVPs, and 70 armored river craft of French design procured in Japan. After receiving the assurance that the French could man the additional LSMs without jeopardizing the readiness of other ships, the Chief of Naval Operations proposed the loan of

---

[43] Memo, OP–35 to CNO (no date, *ca.* Aug. 1953).
[44] Memo, OP–35 to CNO, No. 85–53 of 23 Dec. 1953.

four additional LSMs to France until the end of 1954. The Office of the Secretary of Defense concurred.[45]

American naval equipment delivered to the French had already significantly enhanced the French Navy's ability to perform its mission in Indochina. The 550 craft programmed for, or delivered to, the French under the Mutual Defense Assistance Programs between 1950 and 1953 represented one-third of all naval craft in Indochina. Through the aid program, the French had been able to repair much broken-down equipment and to replace most obsolete ships, craft, and airplanes. Once the initial hardware was provided, the problem became that of ensuring optimum use of these items. As a consequence, the naval aid programs for fiscal years 1952 and 1953 placed primary emphasis on improvement of repair and maintenance facilities and on the provision of logistic support. These programs included major assistance to the French Naval Shipyard in Saigon, equipment for the repair facility at the Haiphong Naval Amphibious Base, the transfer of an LST-type repair ship and such specialized yard craft as tugs, water barges, and floating cranes.

At the end of 1953, the Navy Section of the Military Assistance Advisory Group, Indochina assessed the French naval capabilities as follows:

> The French Union naval forces in Indo China are very effective in the present type of warfare, which is on rivers and inshore areas. They have had much experience in river landings, combatting river ambushes and intercepting junk and small boat traffic on both the ocean and inland waterways. Also, logistic support by water to all services is a constant and heavy undertaking which they accomplish with facility. For guerilla warfare along the water ways in the Red River and Mekong River deltas, they are uniquely qualified and equipped.

Rather than a lack of proficiency on the part of individual personnel or shortage of equipment, the major shortcomings, as seen by the MAAG, were the scarcity of qualified personnel and the long-overdue need for a strong Vietnamese Navy. With French laws prohibiting conscripts from serving in Vietnam, a strong Vietnamese Navy could alleviate the chronic personnel shortage in the French Far Eastern fleet.[46]

---

[45] Memo, OP–41 to OP–004, No. 135 of 21 Jan. 1954; Navy Section, MAAG Indochina. Monthly Activity Reports, Nos. 13 and 14 for Dec. 1953 and Jan. 1954.

[46] Navy Section, MAAG Indochina, "Indo-China Country Statement for Presentation of the 1955 MDA Program," 26 Jan. 1954; Memo, OP–002 to OP–09 of 23 Nov. 1953, encl. 5, "The Military Assistance Advisory Group in Indochina."

The need for a Vietnamese navy would prove to be far greater than the American advisors could then foresee. The French-Viet Minh War was approaching its final phase and soon the State of Vietnam would have to rely on its own military capabilities.

The First Vietnamese Naval Units

Progress toward realization of the goal of a Vietnamese navy continued at a slow pace. At the time of a French-Vietnamese decision in February 1953 to increase the Vietnamese Army to fifty-seven battalions, the Permanent Military Committee had recommended a supplemental naval program to include 3 additional river flotillas (each composed of LCTs, LCMs, LCVPs, sampans, and river patrol boats), 1 LST, and 4 LSSLs. The supplemental program was forwarded to the Franco-Vietnamese High Committee, where it remained under discussion for the rest of 1953.

At this time, Vice Admiral Auboyneau, the new Commander French Naval Forces, Far East, proposed development of a complete riverine amphibious capability in the Vietnamese Navy by organizing naval infantry units, the French counterpart of the United States Marine Corps.[47] The Vietnamese Marine Corps subsequently was established by Diem on 13 October 1954.

At long last, the first Vietnamese naval unit was activated, on 10 April 1953. The unit, a *dinassaut,* consisted of only five landing craft,[48] armed and equipped with 50-caliber and 20-millimeter machine guns and organized for operations in the Mekong Delta. Although partly manned by French cadres and under French command, the craft flew the Vietnamese flag. The unit was based at Can Tho, a center of the Hoa Hao sect, strategically located at the junction of the Bassac and Can Tho Rivers. The second Vietnamese *dinassaut* was formed in the summer and based at Vinh Long, where the Mekong fans out into several outlets to the sea.[49]

Encouraging as these faltering steps were, the Vietnamese had much to do before they could develop an effective Navy. At every stage, the

---

[47] Croizat, "Vietnamese Naval Forces," pp. 53, 55.

[48] Three LCMs and two LCVPs.

[49] Croizat, "Vietnamese Naval Forces," p. 53; NA Saigon, report, 127–52 of 29 July 1952, JN 15531, box 33, FRC; NA Saigon, report, 79–S–53 of 28 Sept. 1953, JN–N–59–488, Box 24, FRC.

infant Navy, seeking recognition and resources, tended to be overwhelmed by the vastly larger Army and its extensive demands. Difficulties were multiplied by the fact that the Navy was placed under the predominately Army-manned Joint General Staff, established in June 1953. The staff controlled a single budget for all the military services. Naval personnel were but a tiny portion of the total armed forces, representing only about one-half of one percent. Furthermore, the French naval staff and the Vietnamese Armed Forces General Staff had differing programs. Little wonder that the tiny Navy had to struggle so hard for its very existence.

In 1953, there was yet another, and unexpected, cause for delay, when a dispute emerged over flags. The question of what flag the Vietnamese Navy units would fly became a matter of debate so heated that the French suspended further transfer of non-river ships and craft until the disagreement could be resolved. Some French officers wanted the tricolor jack; others favored a Vietnamese commission pennant which would include the national colors of both France and Vietnam; still others desired a unique flag for the French Union. The Vietnamese wanted to fly their own national flag and commission pennants. The issue was finally resolved in early 1954 by allowing the Vietnamese to fly their own flags. The French then resumed the transfer of ships, turning over three motor minesweepers to the Vietnamese in ceremonies at Saigon on 11 February 1954. A third *dinassaut* was soon established in March and a fourth in August.[50]

Throughout this period, the French Navy had continued to conduct operations in the Red River Delta against infiltrating guerrilla units. The enemy responded with mining and ambushes, but river mining incidents only averaged about one a month until the end of 1953, when the guerrillas stepped up their efforts. A landing ship, infantry, large (LSIL–9030) was sunk south of Haiphong in January 1954 and mining incidents involving smaller craft occurred every few days. Minesweeping of the larger waterways by small tugs and the shallower rivers and canals by LCMs brought the threat under control.[51]

---

[50] Croizat, "Vietnamese Naval Forces," pp. 53–54.

[51] Navy Section, MAAG Indochina, Monthly Activity Report, No. 14 (Jan.) of 19 Feb. 1954, p. 28; Comprehensive data on Viet Minh mining, based on field investigations, is contained in OinC, EOD Unit 1, ser 011 of 3 Feb. 1954; other sources include COMNAVFORFE, "Special Intelligence Study Indochina," ser 00895 of 12 July 1954; ltr, CINCPACFLT to COM1STFLT. ser 00035 of 25 Feb. 1952; Mordal, *Navy in Indochina,* pp. 181–82.

NH–79372

Riverine patrol.

NH–79373

Two LCVPs during a lull in operations.

NH–74117

USS Caperton *at Saigon, 1953.*

Prelude to Southeast Asian Deployments

On 2 September 1953, Secretary of State John Foster Dulles had warned the Chinese of the consequences of aggression in Indochina. During the next month, the visit of an American destroyer division gave visible evidence of American interest and support of France and the State of Vietnam. Commander Destroyer Squadron 30, Captain Willard Saunders, embarked in destroyer *Caperton* in company with *Dashiell, Dortch,* and *Gatling,* docked at the Catinat Wharf in Saigon for a two-day visit starting 20 October 1953. During his visit Captain Saunders met with Ambassador Heath and local French naval officers, including Vice Admiral Auboyneau. A few days later, *General W. M. Black* (APB–5) of the Navy's Military Sea Transportation Service, arrived at Saigon from Korea with a French infantry

NH–74137

French Korea Battalion debarking from USNS General W.M. Black.

battalion. The French unit had won an outstanding reputation fighting with the United States 2nd Division in Korea. Saigon newspapers reported that French naval and military authorities in Indochina were favorably impressed with continuing American efforts to aid their cause.[52]

---

[52] NA Saigon, reports, 216–53 of 21 Dec. 1953, JN–N–59–488, box 25, FRC and 10–54 of 23 Jan. 1954, JN–N–59–2184, box 44, FRC; *U.S.-V.N. Relations,* bk 1, pt. IIA.3, p. A50.

NH–74115

Left to right are General of Division Gardet, Commander in Chief Ground Forces South Vietnam; Vice Admiral D'Escadre Philippe Auboyneau, Commander in Chief French Naval Forces, Far East; Admiral Felix Stump, Commander in Chief, Pacific; His Excellency Le Van Hoach, Vice President of the Council, Government of Vietnam; and General Nguyen Van Hinh, head of Vietnamese Armed Forces, in Saigon, November 1953.

Vietnam was one of the first concerns of the new Chief of Naval Operations, Admiral Robert B. Carney, who had assumed his post in August 1953. He had previously served as Deputy Chief of Naval Operations for Logistics and as Commander in Chief, Allied Forces, Southern Europe. During World War II, he had served as Chief of Staff to Admiral Halsey, when the latter was Commander South Pacific Force and later as Commander Third Fleet.

On a trip to the Pacific in the fall of 1953, Admiral Carney met with Admiral Stump, the Commander in Chief, Pacific, who had recently been directed by the Joint Chiefs of Staff to prepare plans in case the Chinese intervened militarily in Indochina. Admiral Stump reported increasing U.S.

involvement in coordination and preparations should a worsening situation in Indochina occur. Possible tasks of the Pacific Fleet in the Western Pacific, in case of a Chinese intervention in Indochina, included blockade of the China coast and action against the Chinese mainland "to destroy or neutralize the Communist air, to interdict lines of logistic support and, generally, to reduce the military potential of Communist China." In case air strikes were ordered, Stump's concept was to employ naval aircraft operating from a carrier task force. If he was ordered to assist the French, he would use naval air and ship gunfire in direct support, accompanied by supporting air strikes against selected targets in Indochina. In the opinion of Admiral Stump, Chinese Communist ground forces then in position north of the border and air forces either within combat range or capable of rapid deployment could drive French forces out of Tonkin in a few weeks. He felt a Southeast Asia force should be organized under Commander First Fleet and based at Subic Bay, and believed the "existence of such a force would at least be a deterrent to further Chinese Communist aggression and might be a controlling factor in preventing such aggression." [53]

---

[53] Memo, OP–002 to OP–09, of 23 Nov. 1953, encl. For a discussion of deterrence of Chinese aggression, see Alexander L. George and Richard Smoke, *Deterrence in American Foreign Policy: Theory and Practice* (New York: Columbia University Press, 1974), pp. 235–65.

CHAPTER X

Southeast Asian Deployments And A Growing Crisis In Indochina, 1954

During the latter part of 1953, the United States had maintained a high degree of readiness to respond in case of renewed fighting in Korea. As the situation there stabilized, a major reduction in deployed naval forces was planned to take place in January 1954. Conditions elsewhere in the Far East, however, led to reconsideration. Now that the Chinese were no longer engaged in combat in Korea, the threat against Taiwan intensified and the possibility of the People's Republic of China intervening in Indochina increased. As a consequence, the planned cutback in naval forces in the Western Pacific was cancelled, except for the return of a battleship and a destroyer division to the Atlantic.[1]

Secretary of State Dulles repeated a warning given the previous September, when, in a major address on 12 January, he stated that open Chinese Army aggression in Indochina would result in "grave consequences which might not be confined to Indochina." Expressing concern over the total cost of national defense, Dulles announced that President Eisenhower and his advisors on the National Security Council had made a basic policy decision. The decision was "to depend primarily upon a great capacity to retaliate, instantly, by means and at places of our own choosing." The intention was to make allies and collective security "more effective, [and] less costly . . . by placing more reliance on deterrent power and less dependence on local defensive power." With regard to the Far East, Dulles referred to the President's 26 December 1953 statement which had announced the progressive reduction of the United States ground forces in Korea. Accord-

---

[1] CINCPACFLT, "Annual Report," FY 1954, p. 1.

234

ing to the President, American military forces in the Far East would now feature "highly mobile naval, air and amphibious units. . . ." [2]

"Fair Weather Training"

On 6 February 1954, Admiral Carney advised Admiral Stump that he was considering recommending to the Joint Chiefs of Staff that two carriers and about six destroyers be deployed in the Subic area for a period of approximately six weeks. He said that, "the ostensible and announced purpose would be fair weather training." Admiral Stump concurred, recommending eight destroyers and the inclusion of mobile logistic support units capable of underway replenishment of the combat ships with oil, provisions, and ammunition.[3] The training mission was logical. In more normal times of peace, units of the Fleet had usually operated mainly in northern Asiatic waters during the summer months, going south in the winter for training.

Nine days later the operational control of two attack carriers and a squadron of destroyers was transferred from Commander in Chief, Far East to Commander in Chief, Pacific. Carney informed Stump that the purpose was "to conduct training exercises as a cover for possible operations to assist French in Indochina if such operations become necessary. . . ." The task force, he said, "should be ready to render prompt assistance during the time they are in South China Sea." As Commander in Chief, Pacific Fleet, Admiral Stump ordered the carriers and destroyers south to be followed by a logistic support group. The latter consisted of 2 fleet oilers, 1 ammunition ship, 1 attack cargo ship, and 1 provisions store ship. An antisubmarine submarine (SSK) also joined the force. Two carriers remained in the Japan-Korean area under Commander in Chief, Far East's operational control.[4]

The assignment of command of the southern force to a senior flag

---

[2] Address, John Foster Dulles, "The Evolution of Foreign Policy," *The Department of State Bulletin*, XXX (25 Jan. 1954), pp. 107–10. Later in the year, growing concern in the United States and elsewhere over the implications of a policy of "massive retaliation" and the possible use of nuclear weapons led the secretary to make statements in clarification of the administration's policy. See Louis L. Gerson, *John Foster Dulles*, Vol. XVII of *The American Secretaries of State and their Diplomacy*, Robert H. Ferrell, ed. (New York: Cooper Square Publishers, 1967), pp. 144–51.

[3] Msgs, CINCPACFLT 090102Z Feb. 1954 and CNO 061717Z Feb. 1954.

[4] Msgs, CINCPACFLT 190016Z Feb. 1954 and CNO 152307Z Feb. 1954.

officer other than Commander Seventh Fleet (Vice Admiral Alfred M. Pride) was deemed desirable by Admiral Carney because of the continuing threat to Taiwan from mainland China, the need of a carrier strike force in that area to deter or counter an invasion attempt, the possibility of simultaneous crises there and in Indochina, uncertaintly as to the permanence of the Korean Armistice, and the different chains of command for the Japan-Taiwan area and for other portions of the Western Pacific. In a letter in which the CNO summarized his concept of using Commander First Fleet as a deployed task force commander under CINCPAC and CINCPAC-FLT, Carney stated that "the realism of the threat in the Pacific lends added importance to any thinking which involves the utilization of the Commander First Fleet as the tactical commander for special operations." [5]

Complying with Carney's desires, Stump ordered the commander of the First Fleet, Vice Admiral William K. Phillips, and a small operational staff, west to assume command. Phillips was well acquainted with the situation in the Western Pacific and the plans for action, if ordered. He had served as Chief of Staff to Commander in Chief, United States Pacific Fleet from September 1952 to October 1953, under both Admirals Radford and Stump.

The usual function of Commander First Fleet, normally operating off the West Coast of the United States, was fleet training. At Carney's instigation, the First Fleet commander already had been assigned responsibilities for coordinating and evaluating fleet readiness in the Western Pacific as well as off the West Coast of the United States. Carney envisaged occasional visits to the Far East to confer with Commander Seventh Fleet and Commander Naval Forces, Far East on training and readiness matters. [6]

Admiral Phillips's mission, while in command of the "Fair Weather Traning Force," was to conduct training in the South China Sea, to determine the state of readiness of forces assigned to him, and to evaluate the feasibility of future utilization of the Subic Bay-Sangley area as an operating base. He also had the classified mission of maintaining readiness for combat operations in case of a decision to employ his force against China or in support of French Union forces.

Phillips organized his ships into two task groups. One was an Attack Carrier Striking Group (TG 70.2), commanded by Rear Admiral Robert E. Blick, Jr. (also Commander Carrier Division 3), to which a carrier unit

---

[5] Ltr, Carney to Stump, of 8 Mar. 1954.
[6] *Ibid.*

of *Wasp* (CVA–18) and *Essex* (CVA–9), a screen unit of eight destroyers, and a submarine unit were assigned. The other was a Logistic Support Group (TG 92.2), commanded by Captain George H. Browne and consisting of the underway replenishment ships.[7]

While maintaining a high state of readiness for contingencies, the force conducted a wide variety of training, including air-strike exercises, antisubmarine and air-defense operations, and day and night replenishment. One of the carriers that later joined the force, *Boxer,* reported that its lack of the new and more powerful catapults being installed in the Fleet, combined with low-wind conditions, led to a number of cancellations of planned jet fighter sorties. But this was an isolated problem. The overall offensive capabilities of the force were considered excellent.[8]

In the spring of 1954, the force would be expanded to three carriers, twelve destroyers, and a larger logistic support group. Its deployment would be extended as a result of the deteriorating situation at Dien Bien Phu and training operations would be interrupted twice when the force was placed in readiness for possible combat action.

In the light of future events, one of Admiral Phillips's recommendations of particular interest was that the Subic-Cubi-Sangley area facilities in the Philippines should be completed to serve as a fleet base, especially in view of its proximity to the Southeast Asian trouble spot.[9] The validity of this recommendation would later be confirmed, when these facilities had to be expanded on an urgent basis in the 1960s to meet the needs of the Fleet and to support the programs of military assistance.

Navarre's Offensive

On 12 December 1953 General Navarre had notified his subordinate commanders of his decision to launch the promised offensive. His target was one of the six inter-zones into which the Communists had subdivided Vietnam for the administration and organization of their infrastructure. The Fifth Inter-Zone (Lien Khu V) in south-central Vietnam stretched along the coast from south of Tourane to north of Nha Trang and westward to the mountains along the Laotian and Cambodian borders. In addi-

---

[7] COM1STFLT, OP–ORDER 10–54, ser 01A of 28 Feb. 1954.
[8] COM1STFLT, report, ser 010A of 29 Apr. 1954; CAG 12, report, ser 031 of 4 Oct. 1954.
[9] COM1STFLT, report, ser 010A of 29 Apr. 1954.

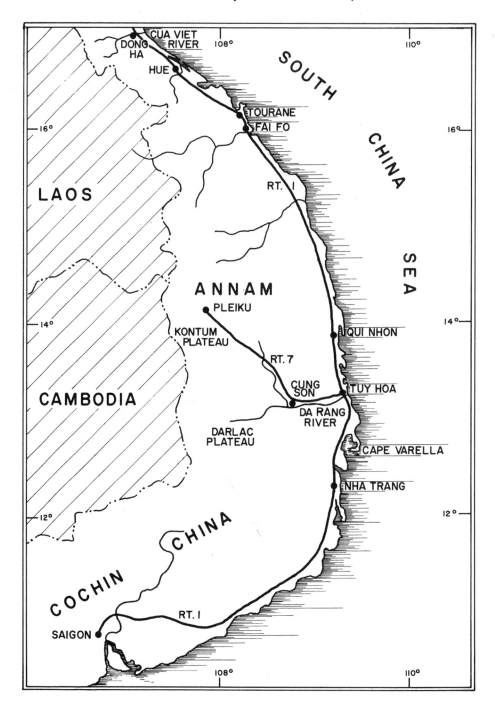

Area of Operation Atlante.

tion to their political apparatus extending down the pyramid of zones, provinces, districts, inter-villages, and villages, the Viet Minh now had an estimated 30,000 troops in the Fifth Inter-Zone.

Prior French operations in this area had been of the hit and run variety and had not established continuous control. In *Atlante,* as his campaign was called, Navarre planned to move up the coast, establishing bases in three or four successive operations. Tasks would involve finding and destroying the enemy, detecting and eliminating traps and mines, installing a military police and administrative system, repairing roads and bridges, and carrying out general public reconstruction. By this means he intended to establish firm control over the populated narrow lowland region along the coast from Cape Varella to Fai Fo. In addition to the political value of the region, this was the main channel for supplies and personnel, either along Route 1 and the railroad, or waterborne off the coast.

Despite signs of an imminent major action in the T'ai highlands of Tonkin and his 5 December 1953 decision to accept battle there, Navarre assigned top priority to *Atlante,* stating to his subordinates:

> In view of the considerable strategic and political results which one is entitled to expect from the complete execution of that operation, I have decided to *subordinate* to it the conduct of the whole Indochina campaign during the first semester of 1954.[10]

Called *Arethuse,* the first phase of this offensive consisted of the seizure of Tuy Hoa by an amphibious assault and subsequent operations from a base area to be established there. The amphibious force, including LSTs and merchant ships from Tourane, was asssembled at Nha Trang under the command of the captain of landing ship dock *Foudre.* The transport group consisted of LSD *Foudre,* LSTs *Rance* and *Chéliff,* and the merchant ships. A landing force of two parachute battalions, two Navy commando units (*Jaubert* and *Montfort*), an Army commando unit, a 75-millimeter recoilless rifle battalion, a 105-millimeter artillery battery, an airfield engineer company, artillerymen, and pioneers was embarked. *Dumont D'Urville,* two patrol craft, *Commandant Duboc* and *L'Inconstant,* a seaplane tender, *Commandant Robert Giraud,* and a naval air detachment of Grumman Goose aircraft formed a naval support group.[11]

---

[10] Quoted in Fall, *Hell in a Very Small Place,* pp. 45–46.
[11] NA Saigon, report, 40–54 of 25 Mar. 1954, JN–N–59–2184, box 44, FRC.

French amphibious force, Operation Arethuse.

On 19 January 1954 part of this force conducted an amphibious demonstration off Qui Nhon to fix Viet Minh troops stationed in the area, and then headed south during the night to rejoin the rest. The next day—as Army forces from Nha Trang advanced along Route 1 and troops from the mountain plateau headed east to open Route 7—the amphibious landing commenced. Weather conditions were favorable except for a low cloud ceiling. As spotters in two Grumman Goose aircraft guided preparatory gunfire from the Navy ships, the first wave of landing craft entered the lagoon and landed commandos and engineers on the northern bank of the Da Rang River. In the afternoon another landing was conducted, this time on the south bank.

No serious opposition was encountered, although mine clearance operations ashore slowed the advance. Two hours after the initial landing on the dried-mud flats, Commando *Montfort,* with air support by a Grumman Goose, seized the bridge approaches at Cung Son on Route 7 to the west of Tuy Hoa. By evening, the beachhead was well established; Tuy Hoa and its bridge were under French control. That night the ships furnished star-shell illumination. Although beach conditions frustrated the landing of field artillery on the 21st, the guns were landed successfully the next day. Commandos continued to guard the bridge and its approaches until the force coming down from the plateau arrived on 24 January. With the amphibious phase of *Arethuse* completed, Tuy Hoa would serve as a logistics base area for operations along the coast and into the highlands.[12]

An American Assessment of the Progress

It was probably no coincidence that General O'Daniel arrived on 23 January 1954 to make another assessment for the Joint Chiefs of Staff. As a result of the trip, which lasted until 5 February, he was generally optimistic about the military situation. After a visit to the garrison at Dien Bien Phu, O'Daniel stated: "I feel that it can withstand any kind of an attack that the Viet Minh are capable of launching. However, a force with two or three battalions of medium artillery and with air observation could make the area untenable. The enemy does not seem to have this capability at

---

[12] *Ibid.;* NA Saigon, report, 11–S–54 of 18 May 1954, JN–N–59–2184, box 44, FRC; Fall, *Hell in a Very Small Place,* pp. 46–47; *Lessons of the War in Indochina,* Vol. II, p. 189; for an account of the fighting in the highlands, see Fall, *Street Without Joy,* pp. 185–250.

present." In his report, O'Daniel added prophetically: "I believe that if I were charged with the defense of the area, I would have been tempted to have utilized the high ground surrounding the area. . . ." [13]

In addition to assessing the military situation, O'Daniel had been instructed to explore—in view of the ever growing United States involvement —the possibilities of his being stationed permanently in Vietnam for liaison with General Navarre, to expedite Mutual Defense Assistance Program deliveries, and to inject American thinking on strategy and training at the highest French command levels. General O'Daniel found Navarre flatly opposed to the liaison idea, since he viewed it as an attempt to undermine his control. However, he did agree to periodic visits by the American general. [14]

One of the major topics of discussion between O'Daniel and Navarre was the assistance program. General Navarre complained that he was not getting essential equipment fast enough. In addition to the inevitable time involved in providing items to a foreign government and delivering them to a remote area, added delays stemmed from the administrative processes of the Mutual Defense Assistance Program and staffing in the Office of the Secretary of Defense and the State Department. In commenting on a proposal that military assistance for Indochina be administered and financed separately from MDAP, Rear Admiral David M. Tyree, Assistant Chief of Naval Operations (Material), agreed that MDAP procedures were not well suited to support of combat operations. He stated:

> The most significant reason for this is the usual delay of several months from the time funds are appropriated by Congress until supply action can be initiated, even though items may already be in Navy stocks. This delay is caused by the many echelons of approval required both for the items in a program and for the release of funds to the responsible department.

He contrasted the procedures with the streamlined ones of the Korean War, when immediate action could be taken to provide material from Navy stocks—"limited only by availability of materiel and status of naval appropriations." While Vice Admiral Roscoe E. Good, Deputy Chief of

---

[13] Chief, U.S. Special Mission to Indochina, report, of 5 Feb. 1954 in *U.S.-V.N. Relations,* bk 9, pp. 246–52. His reservations contradict most accounts which assert that U.S. military observers found the Dien Bien Phu defenses satisfactory; Navarre, *Agony of Indochina,* pp. 316–17; Giap, *People's War, People's Army,* pp. 207–08; Fall, *Hell in a Very Small Place,* pp. 108, 296.

[14] Navarre, *Agony of Indochina.* p. 229.

Naval Operations (Logistics), agreed that logistic support for Indochina should be separately administered and financed, he was concerned over budgetary implications and opposed a solution which would charge Indochina expenditures to the Navy budget. His opposition was understandable in view of the cuts then being applied to the funding of the military departments.[15]

While some success was being achieved along the coast in *Atlante* during the winter and spring of 1954, the French were hard-pressed on the mountain plateau near the Laotian border. Nevertheless, to provide troops for Dien Bien Phu and prepare for subsequent action expected in the region of the Red River Delta, Navarre redeployed the bulk of the mobile forces from the plateau. Only one Vietnamese mountain division, one Vietnamese mobile group of limited offensive value, and small commando units remained. As a consequence, the main burden of defending the area fell upon a regimental task force, the *Groupement Mobile* 100. Activated in November 1953, the hard corps of the task force consisted of the French battalion which had been transported from Korea by the United States Navy in October. In a series of actions and ambushes lasting from February to July 1954, the French 1st Korea Battalion fought valiantly but was almost completely annihilated.[16]

Dien Bien Phu

Located in a valley of the T'ai highlands in the remote northwestern part of Tonkin, eight miles from the Laotian border, Dien Bien Phu was the site of a small airfield built in the late 1920s. For two months after the Japanese coup in the spring of 1945, it had been the headquarters for a remnant of French forces, before they withdrew to China. Dien Bien Phu was next occupied by the Chinese after World War II. The French moved back in during the spring of 1946. They pulled out when the Viet Minh attacked posts in the mountains in the fall of 1952.[17]

When French forces returned to Dien Bien Phu in November 1953, Giap lost no time in starting a buildup of Viet Minh troops in the area,

---

[15] Memo, ACNO (Material) to DCNO (Logistics), ser 000231P41 of 12 Feb. 1954; memo, DCNO (Logistics) to DCNO (Operations), ser 000232P41 of 13 Feb. 1954.

[16] Fall, *Street Without Joy*, pp. 185–250.

[17] For a detailed account of the Dien Bien Phu campaign, see Fall, *Hell in a Very Small Place*.

committing the bulk of his regulars as he prepared to lay siege. Whether or not the deployment of naval strike forces to the South China Sea deterrred the Chinese from intervening militarily in Vietnam, it did not stem the flow from China of weapons, equipment, and other military supplies to the besieging forces. Before Viet Minh forces and Chinese-supplied artillery had been built-up for the assault, General Navarre considered a fighting withdrawal from Dien Bien Phu. On 29 December, he ordered initiation of planning for such a withdrawal, but in January, after receiving from the commander of the French forces in the northern portion of Vietnam (General René Cogny), advice "that Dien Bien Phu be held at all costs," General Navarre decided to retain the position.[18]

A series of actions were launched from the base, but French reconnaissance forces failed to prevent the Viet Minh from establishing positions on high ground around the base and its outposts. The frequent adverse cloud conditions of the northeast monsoon hampered air operations, and heavy rains in the spring complicated the situation on the ground. Although three-fourths of the French combat aircraft available were committed to the suport of Dien Bien Phu, they had little more than marginal success against Viet Minh troops and their hidden artillery, and were unable to cut off the flow of supplies over the jungle-shrouded roads and trails from China.

As these events were taking place in Indochina, Washington officials wrestled with the problem of establishing a policy with regard to the impending Geneva talks. United States naval officers, with the Korean experience of the Panmunjom negotiations fresh in their minds, were particularly concerned about negotiating from a position of weakness. In a memorandum to the Chief of Naval Operations concerning the development of American policy with regard to Geneva, Captain William R. Smedberg, III, head of Naval Operations' International Affairs Division, feared that the French might abandon the aggressive concept of the Navarre plan prior to achieving a position of strength in Indochina. He felt that a good basis for recommendations would be conditions set down by Premier Laniel on 5 March, calling upon the Viet Minh to evacuate Laos, the Tonkin delta, and South Vietnam. Vigorous implementation of the Navarre plan would, it was hoped, result in military victories during the fall offensive and force the Viet Minh to sue for an armistice on terms favorable to the

---

[18] Quoted in *Ibid.*, p. 48.

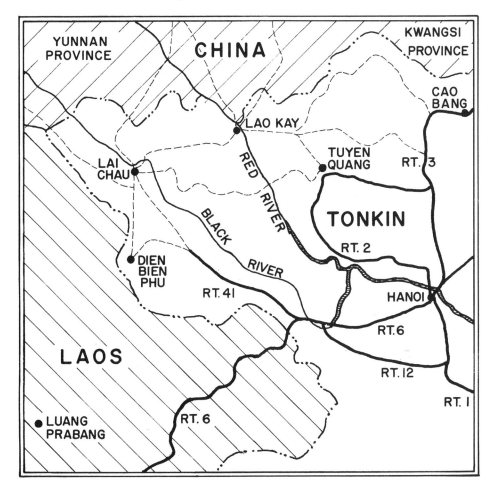

Theater of operations, Dien Bien Phu.

French. Therefore, these anticipated victories should be awaited before the French entered into serious negotiation with the Viet Minh.[19]

Recommendations by the Joint Chiefs of Staff to the Secretary of Defense on 12 March 1954 were consistent with these views. They felt that, "in the absence of a very substantial improvement in the French Union military situation . . . it is highly improbable that Communist agreement could be obtained to a negotiated settlement which would be consistent

---

[19] Memo, OP–35 to CNO, ser 00051 of 9 Mar. 1954, p. 35.

with basic United States objectives in Southeast Asia." They were concerned that a settlement involving substantial concessions would lead to the loss of Indochina and undermine the national will to oppose communism of other countries in the Far East. In case of a negotiated settlement which would fail to provide reasonably adequate assurance of the future political and territorial integrity of Indochina, they felt that the United States "should decline to associate itself with such a settlement, thereby preserving freedom of action to pursue directly with the governments of the Associated States and with other allies . . . ways and means of continuing the struggle against the Viet Minh in Indochina without participation of the French." [20]

That same day, 13 March east longitude time, the battle for Dien Bien Phu began in earnest when, after five months of preparation, the Viet Minh launched their first major assaults on the French garrison of about 13,000 men. The Communists, 50,000 strong, opened their attack with a furious artillery barrage from about 100 artillery pieces, heavy mortars, recoilless rifles and flak guns, which had been dragged through the jungles and emplaced in the hills overlooking the stronghold in the valley. The earth, sandbag, and log fortifications of the French simply could not withstand the concentrated fire; nor could French artillery or air strikes silence the Viet Minh guns which were cleverly camouflaged and deeply dug into the mountainsides.

Rain clouds the next day prevented air reconnaissance and the delivery of supplies to the air strip. French paratroops were dropped on the 16th but the weather again closed in.

After three days of bloody fighting, the outnumbered French had lost three major strongpoints situated on high ground to the north of the airfield. Colonel Christian B. F. de Castries, commander of the French garrison, ordered a counterattack to retake these positions, but his troops succeeded only in recapturing part of one. The Viet Minh immediately placed their own artillery on the former French positions overlooking the airfield, and zeroed in. Colonel de Castries could no longer count on the vital landing strip for local air support, evacuation of wounded, or resupply. The fate of Dien Bien Phu hung in the balance. [21]

---

[20] Memos, JCS to SECDEF, of 12 Mar. and 7 May 1954 in *U.S.-V.N. Relations*, bk 9, pp. 266–70, 430–34.

[21] Fall, *Hell in a Very Small Place*, pp. 125–90.

Operations in the Tonkin Gulf

On 19 March 1954, as fighting raged at Dien Bien Phu, Admiral Carney ordered Vice Admiral Phillips to maintain a twelve-hour alert and prepare to steam near the entrance to the Gulf of Tonkin, ready to begin operations in support of the French on about three-hours notice. By now *Boxer* had replaced *Wasp*. Admiral Carney emphasized:

> Although there is no approved plan nor even any tentative plan for inter-vention in Indochina, authorities here including Secretary Dulles, are aware of the potential critical military situation in Indochina and the possible impli-cations of serious French reversals. There is an approved expression of national policy recognizing the grave consequences that could result from loss of Indochina to the Communists.

As Chairman of the JCS, Admiral Radford notified Secretary of State Dulles regarding the task force's condition of readiness. Complete informa-tion on the capabilities of the carriers was presented to President Eisenhower on the 20th.[22]

Admiral Carney followed his alert order by stating that the force was to be placed in a position to support the defenders of Dien Bien Phu. He emphasized that no decision had been made for American offensive operations. Admiral Phillips was to proceed to sea on 22 March and, once beyond the sight of land, make full preparations for rendering prompt support if ordered. Not even the French were to be informed of the possible availability of the force, but Admiral Stump was authorized to initiate with French authorities technical preparations necessary to assure effective air support. Carney directed the issuance through CINCPACFLT of other alert-ing orders, including those for logistic support.[23]

The Attack Carrier Striking Group put to sea on the designated date, ostensibly for routine training, and proceeded at flank speed to an operating area about 100 miles south of Hainan Island. Under the command of Rear Admiral Blick, the task group's composition on 22 March was:

---

[22] Msg, CNO 192323Z Mar. 1954.
[23] Msg, CNO 202023Z Mar. 1954.

TASK GROUP 70.2

TG 70.2 Attack Carrier Striking Group	RADM R. E. Blick
TU 70.2.2 Screen Unit	CAPT G. R. Donaho
DESDIV 171	CAPT G. R. Donaho
Marshall (DD–676)	CDR H. V. Bird
Porterfield (DD–682)	CDR W. S. Bradway
Halsey Powell (DD–686)	CDR A. S. Freedman
Gregory (DD–802) F	CDR J. P. Wier
DESDIV 172	CDR R. E. Freeman
Twining (DD–540) F	CDR G. W. Miller
Shields (DD–596)	CDR L. C. Winters
Erben (DD–631)	CDR W. A. Keefe
Colahan (DD–658)	CDR W. K. Brooks
TU 70.2.3. Carrier Unit	RADM R. E. Blick (COMCARDIV 3)
Wasp (CVA–18)	CAPT P. Henry
	VADM W. K. Phillips (COM1STFLT) embarked
Essex (CVA–9)	CAPT F. Turner
TU 70.2.9 Submarine Unit	LCDR M. G. Grazda
Bluegill (SSK–242)	LCDR M. G. Grazda[24]

Fleet oiler *Cacapon* (AO–52) also was sent to the area.

Admiral Carney stressed the importance of secrecy to avoid leaks or dangerous speculation. The carriers were supplied with ultra-high-frequency radio equipment which had previously been stored at Subic to receive ground control communications from the French. Commander Robert M. Hinckley, Jr., of CINCPACFLT's staff, was directed to discuss secretly with Major General Trapnell technical preparations and other arrangements for effective air support of French forces, should it become necessary. A visit to Saigon to discuss MAAG matters had been planned even before the crisis, so that Hinckley's arrival on 26 March aroused no speculation. A liaison support group from the staff of Commander Carrier Division 1 (Rear Admiral Stanhope C. Ring) also was sent to the operating area.[25]

The carriers and destroyers had been scheduled to return to the operational control of Commander in Chief, Far East, on 3 April, which would

---

[24] USS *Essex* and USS *Wasp*, Deck Logs, Mar. and Apr. 1954; COM1STFLT, OP–ORDER, 10–54, ser O1A of 28 Feb. 1954.

[25] Msgs, CINCPACFLT 222141Z, 221944Z, and 231936Z Mar. 1954.

have required redeployment from the South China Sea on 29 March. Admiral Stump's request for a two-week delay was granted.[26]

The Question of American Air Support

General Paul Ély, Chief of Staff of the French Armed Forces, had arrived for talks with American officials in Washington on 20 March 1954. A sense of urgency was imparted to his mission when, on the eve of his departure from Paris, a message from General Navarre arrived. Ély was asked to "intercede directly with the Pentagon, as soon as [he] arrived, to obtain aviation and air-drop material which was urgently needed since the ring of fire surrounding Dien Bien Phu had tightened."

Ély's objectives were to inform Admiral Radford of the deteriorating military situation, determine if combat action by American aircraft could be expected in response to Chinese air intervention, learn how such actions would take place, and request increased American aid in equipping a Vietnamese national army. In addition to conversations with Radford, Ély conferred with the President, the Secretary of State, the Secretary of Defense, the Joint Chiefs of Staff, the Director of the Central Intelligence Agency, and the United States Military Representative to the North Atlantic Treaty Organization. Ély stressed the great importance of the Dien Bien Phu battle from the political and psychological standpoint, and evaluated the outcome as "50–50." He sought urgent action on various items previously requested through MAAG Indochina. The requests for military aid were granted with the exception of fourteen C–47s, twenty helicopters, and additional U.S. maintenance personnel.[27]

Accompanied by Admiral Radford during his call on Secretary of State Dulles, Ély asked whether the United States would respond with air power if China sent aircraft into Indochina. Dulles replied that, "if the United States sent its flag and its own military establishment—land, sea or air—into the Indo-china war, then the prestige of the United States would be engaged to a point where we would want to have a success." A precondition

---

[26] Msgs, CINCPACFLT 250121Z, 302105Z Mar., and CNO 252253Z Mar. 1954.

[27] Paul Ély, *Indo-China in Turmoil,* trans. by ACOS (Intelligence), Department of the Army (Paris: Plon, 1964), pp. 25–27; memo, JCS to President, of 24 Mar. 1954 in *U.S.-V.N. Relations,* bk 9, pp. 288–90.

NH–84166

President Eisenhower, General Ély, and Admiral Radford, March 1954.

would be greater partnership, particularly with regard to independence for the Associated States and the training of indigenous forces.[28]

During discussions between General Ély and Admiral Radford, a separate question also was raised—the possibility of American air support for French forces at Dien Bien Phu in the absence of Chinese Communist aerial intervention. Admiral Radford noted that this decision, as well as American reaction to overt Chinese participation, could be determined only at the highest political levels of the United States. Further, such a decision would depend upon a review of the overall situation in the Far East, including the danger of Chinese Communist counteractions. Nevertheless, the American admiral noted that, assuming France requested such aid and the United

---

[28] Quoted in Gerson, *John Foster Dulles,* p. 157.

States Government agreed to take action, as many as 350 carrier aircraft could be employed in a period of two days. Discussions also covered the possibility of committing American medium bombers. However, Admiral Radford noted that their employment probably would require more time to arrange.[29]

On 24 March 1954, Radford advised the President:

> I am gravely fearful that the measures being taken by the French will prove to be inadequate and initiated too late to prevent a progressive deterioration of the situation. The consequences can well lead to the loss of all of S.E. Asia to Communist domination. If this is to be avoided, I consider that the U.S. must be prepared to act promptly and in force possibly to a frantic and belated request by the French for U.S. intervention.[30]

Subsequent to his last meeting with Ély, Radford discussed with the service chiefs the question of assistance by United States Navy and Air Force aircraft to the French in the defense of Dien Bien Phu. One major consideration was uncertainty as to the effectiveness of air strikes against the Communist forces deployed in the screening jungles of the highlands around the French base. Another was the dilemma which would result if combat action by American air forces did not produce decisive results. None of the service chiefs endorsed the used of combat forces in the absence of Chinese air intervention. Admiral Carney felt that the commitment of air forces, both Navy and Air Force, would improve somewhat the French tactical situation, but did not believe that such a contribution would be decisive. He felt that any tactical advantage must be weighed against the potential military and political consequences of this United States involvement in the Indochina war.[31]

---

[29] Based on conversations between Admiral Radford and Vice Admiral Hooper in 1973. For Ély's differing concept of the nature of possible American air support at Dien Bien Phu, see Ély, *Indo-China in Turmoil*, pp. 34–35. About this time the French apparently began to apply the code name of *Vulture* to such an operation. However, as noted in Melvin Gurtov, *The First Vietnam Crisis: Chinese Communist Strategy and United States Involvement, 1953–1954* (New York: Columbia University Press, 1967), p. 188, Admiral Radford stated that from an American point of view "no operation *Vulture* existed, since the plan to save Dienbienphu by an air strike never reached the operational stage."

[30] Memo, JCS to President, of 24 Mar. 1954 in *U.S.-V.N. Relations,* bk 9, p. 290.

[31] Carney comments on Hooper ltr of 5 Sept. 1974.

Prior to General Ély's departure on 29 March, he and Admiral Radford agreed that:

> It was advisable that military authorities push their planning work as far as possible so that there would be no time wasted when and if our governments decided to oppose enemy air intervention over Indo-China if it took place; and to check all planning arrangements already made under previous agreements between CINCPAC and CINC Indo-China and send instructions to those authorities to this effect.

To the President's Special Committee on Indo-China, Radford noted that in the event of Dien Bien Phu's loss, deterioration of the French position could occur very rapidly. He stated: "In such a situation only prompt and forceful intervention by the United States could avert the loss of all of South East Aasia to Communist domination. I am convinced that the United States must be prepared to take such action." [32]

On 29 March, in a speech to the Overseas Press Club, Secretary Dulles alerted the public to the possibility of an American combat role. He began by detailing the increase in Chinese Communist aid to the Viet Minh—vast supplies of artillery and ammunition and military and technical guidance by an estimated 2,000 Chinese Communists. He reasserted the importance of Indochina "astride the most direct and best-developed sea and air routes between the Pacific and South Asia." He then stated:

> Under the conditions of today, the imposition on Southeast Asia of the political system of Communist Russia and its Chinese Communist ally, by whatever means, would be a grave threat to the whole free community. The United States feels that that possibility should not be passively accepted but should be met by united action. [33]

That same day, the Chief of Naval Operations concurred with Admiral Stump's recommendation made four days earlier that carrier aircraft conduct reconnaissance of nearby Chinese airfields, assembly points for shipment of supplies, critical roads and trails over which artillery and other military items had been flowing for the Dien Bien Phu siege during the previous three or four months, and of Lang Son and Cao Bang across from Kwangsi

---

[32] Memo, JCS to President's Special Committee on Indo-China, of 29 Mar. 1954 in *U.S.-V.N. Relations,* bk 9, pp. 281, 285.

[33] Address, John F. Dulles, "The Threat of a Red Asia," of 29 Mar. 1954 in U.S.-V.N. *Relations,* bk 7, pp. B6–B9.

Province and Lao Kay south of Yunnan Province. The carriers launched the reconnaissance aircraft approximately sixty miles off Cape Ron (18°N— 107°35'E) in order to avoid detection. Because of the distance to some of the points designated in the reconnaissance plan, Admiral Phillips obtained permission to move his force deeper into the Gulf of Tonkin to a position about 125 miles off Haiphong.[34] On 31 March, Admiral Carney informed Admiral Stump of the discussions with Ély. Carney directed that a review of plans and arrangements with Commander in Chief, Indochina and discussions with General Navarre be conducted, as necessary, to remedy any deficiencies. He emphasized the importance of good communications, target information, and timely intelligence. Carney said no commitment had been made, but that the general discussion had included the possibility of carrier aircraft strikes against airfields, deployment of American Air Force planes to Indochina for air defense, and support of French Union ground forces by carrier aircraft and Air Force bombers. On 1 April, Carney abandoned plans for a visit to the mid-Pacific, telling Stump, "time is in short supply." [35]

In Paris meanwhile, on 29 March, a thirteen-man committee, including Premier Laniel, Deputy Premier Paul Reynard, Foreign Minister Bidault, and General Ély had met to consider the recent discussions in Washington. They decided that no decision regarding possible American air support should be made until General Navarre was consulted. Therefore, Colonel Raymond Brohon of Ély's staff was dispatched to Indochina to obtain Navarre's views. On 2 April, Colonel Brohon met with the general and described the possibility of an American air strike at Dien Bien Phu. Navarre did not completely favor the concept, especially since he feared the consequences of Chinese intervention. However, the situation had become so desperate at Dien Bien Phu that Navarre finally agreed that an American air strike could destroy the Viet Minh artillery and antiaircraft guns and thus help stabilize the situation. American air operations could "have a decisive effect" if executed before 11 April, he conceded.[36]

On 4 April, the United States Ambassador in Paris, Douglas Dillon, reported that Laniel and Bidault had requested "immediate armed interven-

---

[34] Msgs, CINCPACFLT 250116Z Mar., 022108Z, Apr., CNO 292337Z Mar., and 031703Z Apr. 1954.

[35] Msgs, CNO 312313Z Mar. and 011307Z Apr. 1954.

[36] Quoted in Ély, *Indo-China in Turmoil*, pp. 38–40; Devillers and Lacouture, *End of a War*, pp. 75–77; Navarre, *Agony of Indochina*, pp. 388–93.

tion by US carrier aircraft at Dien Bien Phu . . . to save the situation." According to Dillon, the French stated that the extensive presence of Chinese Communist personnel and supplies in the area of the besieged garrison "fully established" the fact of Chinese intervention. They acknowledged that such action by the United States might lead to Chinese air attacks in the Red River Delta. Nevertheless, since Bidault considered the fate of Southeast Asia dependent on the outcome at Dien Bien Phu, he did not hesitate to request immediate United States action.[37]

Prior to receipt of this request and in compliance with President Eisenhower's desires, Secretary Dulles and Admiral Radford discussed the possibility of the use of American combat aircraft with eight members of Congress. The congressmen were told that the operation was not supported by the other four service chiefs and that the plan had not been discussed with friendly nations. As a consequence, the congressmen advised Dulles first to seek allies.[38]

President Eisenhower wrote a letter on 4 April 1954 to British Prime Minister Winston Churchill suggesting an "*ad hoc* grouping or coalition" of nations concerned with checking Communist expansion in Southeast Asia. In addition to the United States and Great Britain he suggested including France, the Associated States of Indochina, Australia, New Zealand, Thailand, and the Philippines. On 5 April the French were told that American combat action was "impossible except on a coalition basis with active British Commonwealth participation." The French reaction was expressed by George Bidault who felt that the time for formulating coalitions had passed and said that the fate of Indochina would be solved in the next ten days at Dien Bien Phu.[39]

Meanwhile, during an 8 April meeting with Rear Admiral Herbert G. Hopwood, Stump's Chief of Staff, General Navarre reported that his radar had picked up several flights of jets over the Tonkin delta during the last few days which he suspected were United States aircraft. He told Hopwood that he had no objections to American planes overflying the area, but that he would appreciate advance information on the flights. The primary pur-

---

[37] Msg, U.S. Embassy Paris, of 5 Apr. 1954 in *U.S.-V.N. Relations,* bk 9, pp. 296–97.

[38] Chalmers M. Roberts, "The United States Twice Proposed Indochina Air Strike," *Washington Post,* 9 July 1954 in *The Congressional Record—Senate* (83rd Cong., 2nd sess.), Vol. 100, pp. 10137–39. The article was based both on the scanty public record and private information.

[39] Msgs, SECSTATE, of 5 Apr. and 6 May 1954 in *U.S.-V.N. Relations,* bk 9, pp. 359–60; Dwight D. Eisenhower, *Mandate for Change, 1953–1954* (Garden City, NY: Harper and Brothers, 1956), pp. 346–49.

pose of Hopwood's visit had been to ensure the adequacy and suitability of plans previously formulated with Commander in Chief, Indochina. The general agreed with Admiral Hopwood that the Eastwold Plan, drawn up in November 1952, and previously established liaison procedures between United States and French military authorities, were adequate for the present.[40]

That same day (7 April 1954 in Washington), Carney informed Stump of the decision that there would be no unilateral military action then. Admiral Stump was told to complete the reconnaissance along the border by 12 April. Requirements were added for reconnaissance over the Dien Bien Phu battlefield and the Viet Minh supply routes to the north of the French positions. Carney reminded Stump that the flights were to be undertaken covertly, without even the French being notified. At this time, other American planes also flew over the Dien Bien Phu battlefield. In order to view the situation first hand, General Joseph Caldara, USAF, Chief of the Far Eastern Air Force Bomber Command participated in three reconnaissance flights over the valley during a visit to Indochina in early April. Caldara would command the Air Force bombers should their participation be ordered. In addition to reconnaissance, American civilian pilots flying C-119 "Flying Boxcars" made numerous flights over the valley to augment French efforts to parachute vital supplies of food and ammunition into the base.[41]

In the second week of April, as the possibility of direct American participation in the Indochina conflict faded, Task Group 70.2 returned to the Philippines. By mid-month, *Boxer* had relieved *Wasp* which headed for Yokosuka, Japan, enroute to San Diego.

---

[40] Msgs, CINCPACFLT 081941Z Apr. and 090115Z Apr. 1954.
[41] Fall, *Hell in a Very Small Place.* pp. 305, 327–28, 373–74; msgs, CNO 072241Z and 082159Z Apr. 1954.

CHAPTER XI

The End Of
The French-Viet Minh War

The United States responded to the worsening situation in April 1954 by agreeing to send more military aid to the French and Associated States. Added evidence of American support was given when Lieutenant General O'Daniel replaced Major General Trapnell as head of the U.S. MAAG on 11 April. Because of American concern over a rank predating that of Lieutenant General Navarre, O'Daniel was assigned to Indochina as a major general.[1]

The French continued to call for more and more American equipment, particularly aircraft. Vice Admiral Auboyneau, Commander of French Naval Forces, Far East, had suggested to General Navarre the use of twenty-four idle pilots from the carrier *La Fayette,* now drydocked in France, to fly Corsair aircraft that might be provided by the United States Navy from stocks in the Western Pacific. Navarre requested the pilots because the French Navy was conducting the majority of the sorties in support of Dien Bien Phu. He felt that the higher instrument qualifications of naval aviators and the better instrument capabilities of their aircraft made them better suited for support missions in the poor weather which so often enveloped the valley at Dien Bien Phu in the spring.

The French request for naval aircraft was approved on 13 April 1954, and *Saipan* (CVL–48) set sail from Yokosuka, Japan, with twenty-five AU–1 Corsair aircraft (formerly designated F4Us), maintenance material, and spare parts. Also on board were one officer and five enlisted men with temporary duty orders to Indochina to help the French with maintenance problems. On 18 April at 0830 *Saipan,* in company with destroyer *Colahan*

---

[1] Admiral Carney agreed with General Ridgway, Army Chief of Staff, that it was unfortunate the Joint Chiefs of Staff were not consulted on the appointment of General O'Daniel, and that the latter's rank was being reduced. Memo, OP–004 to CNO, of 26 Feb. 1954.

NH–84043

USS Saipan *prior to launch of Corsairs off Vietnam.*

(DD–658), rendezvoused with the French patrol craft *L'Inconstant* off Tourane harbor. Two French liaison officers came on board and shortly thereafter the Corsairs were flown off by Marine Corps pilots attached to *Saipan's* air group. The original plan had been to fly the aircraft to Cat Bi airfield near Haiphong, but because that airfield was so overcrowded, the planes were order to Tourane. When the aircraft touched down on the steel Marston-matting of the airfield, the American aviators were greeted by French pilots, many of whom had trained with the Americans at the Pensacola Naval Air Station in Florida. Soon thereafter, *Saipan* sailed into the harbor and anchored near the French carrier *Arromanches*. The United States pilots returned to their carrier by helicopter while deck crews unloaded the spare parts for the aircraft into French LCUs and LCMs. The entire operation was completed without incident by 1600 that afternoon, when the carrier and its escort put to sea for the Philippines.[2]

---

[2] *Saipan,* reports, ser 060 of 28 Apr. 1954 and 21 Apr. 1954.

NH–84042

Lieutenant Colonel Julius W. Ireland, USMC, Commanding Officer VMA–324 delivering Corsairs to French at Tourane Airfield.

Within a week of their arrival, French naval pilots began flying the Corsairs in support of Dien Bien Phu. They went into battle just in time to bolster the badly depleted squadrons of *Arromanches,* which were down to two-thirds of their original strength. On 30 April, carrier *Bois Belleau* finally arrived on station to augment the air effort. In praise of the naval air arm. General Navarre later declared that it was the only military service which met and surpassed its obligations at Dien Bien Phu.[3]

Other aid also continued to flow to Indochina. In May, the French obtained a second squadron of ten Privateer patrol planes.[4] Although their

---

[3] Barjot, *Histoire de la Guerre Aeronavale,* pp. 402–05; Navarre, *Agony of Indochina,* p. 84.

[4] By July 1954, the United States had delivered aid to Indochina at a cost of $2.6 billion. The items included 2 light aircraft carriers, 438 other naval ships and craft, and approximately 500 aircraft. NA Saigon, report, 14–S–54 of 24 June 1954, JN–N–59–2184, box 44, FRC; *U.S.–V.N. Relations,* bk 1, pt. IVA.2, p. 15.

primary mission was to augment the coastal patrol against Viet Minh infiltration, most of the Privateers were diverted to flying bombing missions in support of the garrison of Dien Bien Phu.

The battle at Dien Bien Phu was now raging on the valley floor. Outposts to the west of the field had been evacuated. Major Viet Minh assaults on defensive positions just north of the airstrip on 3 to 5 April were repulsed, but the situation was ominous. By now, Soviet 75-millimeter antiaircraft guns were interfering with the dropping of supplies and reinforcements, and with air strikes.[5]

In the light of America's refusal to fly combat missions, Navarre suggested sorties by unmarked aircraft. Admiral Radford rejected the proposal on 11 April. Then the French Secretary of State for Air, Louis Christianens, on a visit to the United States, discussed the loan of American B–29 bombers, only to discover that there were no French pilots trained to fly the planes. General Navarre proposed that the United States carry out night raids on Viet Minh supply lines leading to Dien Bien Phu, but this suggestion also was rejected.

The United States continued to explore the possibility of united action with its allies in Southeast Asia. However, not even Dulles's personal trip to Europe, during 11–15 April, could persuade the British to agree to such a course. On 20 April, upon the secretary's return, he informed congressional leaders that, under these circumstances, American action in Indochina was neither imminent nor under consideration.[6]

On the night of the 13th, a Communist commando force infiltrated the airfield at Dien Bien Phu and blasted a trench across it. With the help of such trenches and underground passageways, the Viet Minh steadily closed their lines. Defensive positions to the west and north were almost cut off from the rest of Dien Bien Phu. Fortification *Huguette* 6 just north of the airfield was evacuated on the 18th.

At that point, the military situation at Dien Bien Phu took another turn for the worse. The loss on 23 April of the key outpost of *Huguette* 1, located on the western side of the strip, made parachuting of reinforcements virtually impossible. Compounding the disaster was the loss of an elite parachute battalion in a desperate attempt to retake the position. It was

---

[5] Fall, *Hell in a Very Small Place.* pp. 210–24.

[6] Devillers and Lacouture, *End of a War,* pp. 89, 91–92; Ély, *Indo-China in Turmoil,* p. 42; Gurtov, *The First Vietnam Crisis,* pp. 101–102.

the garrison's last operational reserve. The Viet Minh trench system grew tighter around the fortress, which had shrunk to only one and a half kilometers in diameter. French leaders estimated, even before the battle for *Huguette* 1, that Dien Bien Phu would fall by asphyxiation within ten days and after that the Viet Minh would break through to the Tonkin delta.[7]

That same day in Washington, Admiral Donald B. Duncan—the Vice Chief of Naval Operations, who was acting for Admiral Carney during the latter's temporary absence—studied an alarming dispatch from Secretary of State Dulles, who had returned to Europe, reporting conversations with French Foreign Minister Bidault. Bidault had taken Dulles aside during a North Atlantic Treaty Organization meeting in Paris to show him a message in which General Navarre again declared that only massive air support could save Dien Bien Phu. Bidault asked Dulles point-blank if the United States would reconsider the 5 April rejection of air support. Only American military intervention could save the fortress. Its loss, said Bidault, would result in public revulsion against the war and an irresistable demand for the French to withdraw. Bidault was not interested in Dulles's proposal of a Far Eastern collective security treaty to defend Indochina, which he felt would do nothing to save Dien Bien Phu. When Dulles stated that he would like to get Britain into the picture, Bidault countered that the British contribution would be small at best.

Admiral Duncan immediately ordered that Phillips's attack carrier striking force be placed on "twelve hours notice for possible resumption of operations previously conducted in western South China Sea."[8]

In anticipation of a scheduled meeting with the President on the morning of the 23rd, Radford consulted with Duncan about the deployment of Seventh Fleet carriers. Duncan informed Radford that *Boxer* and *Philippine Sea* (CV–47) were in Subic on a twelve-hour steaming notice. Radford urged that *Essex* (CV–9) be returned to the force. *Essex* was then midway in a passage from the Philippines to Japan, but Duncan withheld action, pending the White House meeting. The consensus at the conference on 23 April, at which the Navy was represented by Secretary of the Navy

---

[7] Fall, *Hell in a Very Small Place*, pp. 243, 258, 271, 276; Devillers and Lacouture, *End of a War*, p. 90; Navarre, *Agony of Indochina*. pp. 378–79.

[8] Memo, VCNO to CNO, of 23 Apr. 1954; Devillers and Lacouture, *End of a War*, p. 93; msg, CNO 222323Z Apr. 1954.

80G637793

USS Boxer *and* Colahan *refueling from* Platte *in the South China Sea, April 1954.*

Anderson, was that Bidault's alarming report would need to be evaluated before any action was taken. The Navy was to retain its high state of readiness and "Fair Weather Training" operations were extended another two weeks. But no decision to enter the fray was made.[9]

On the 24th, Admiral Radford arrived in Paris to join Dulles in the deliberations with the French. So desperate was the French situation that Premier Laniel instructed Bidault to make still another plea for American assistance. In a letter to Dulles on the 24th, Bidault declared anew that French military experts firmly believed that a massive United States air raid could indeed save the garrison. Again the State Department replied that such action depended on British cooperation, which the British refused

---

[9] Memo, VCNO to CNO, of 23 Apr. 1954; msg, CNO 271611Z Apr. 1954.

to give. Then, on the 25th, René Massigli, the French Ambassador in London, hurried to the British Foreign Office with a report on conversations between Under Secretary of State Walter Bedell Smith and Henri Bonnet, the French Ambassador in Washington. Massigli pled for British intervention. Citing Admiral Radford's statement to that effect the day before, British Foreign Minister Anthony Eden told Massigli that the proposed operation could not save Dien Bien Phu. British military officers did not believe that attacks on the Viet Minh rear lines of communication would have much effect on the battle. Instead, Eden continued to place his hopes in the Geneva Conference, then in session, which he felt would surely be doomed to failure by a decision to intervene.[10]

In one final attempt to get British agreement, Laniel instructed Massigli to meet with Prime Minister Churchill on the 26th. The old statesman expressed his admiration for the defenders at Dien Bien Phu, but declared that he could do nothing to save them. He reiterated the previous British arguments against intervention. After the meeting, Churchill appeared before the House of Commons to announce the final British decisions: "Her Majesty's Government are not prepared to give any undertaking about United Kingdom military action in Indochina in advance of the results of Geneva. We have not entered into any new political or military commitment."[11]

News of the British position had been reported to Washington by Admiral Radford on the morning of the 26th but Under Secretary of State Smith tried one final move. He suggested that Australia and New Zealand join in the intervention, thus bypassing Britain. Some congressional leaders contacted on the matter were favorably disposed to the idea, but no action was taken.[12]

On 28 April, Admiral Carney informed Vice Admiral Phillips that he would be designated Commander Southeast Asia Defense Command, as a subordinate unified commander under Commander in Chief, Pacific. It was contemplated that he would establish headquarters in Saigon, but the command was never activated.[13]

---

[10] Victor Bator, *Vietnam: A Diplomatic Tragedy: The Origins of United States Involvement* (Dobbs Ferry, N.Y.: Oceana Publications, 1965), pp. 67–73; Devillers and Lacouture, *End of a War*, pp. 96–99; Gurtov, *First Vietnam Crisis*, pp. 105–10.

[11] Quoted in Devillers and Lacouture, *End of a War*, pp. 97–98.

[12] *Ibid.*, p. 98.

[13] Msg, CINCPACFLT 280532Z Apr. 1954.

On 29 April, President Eisenhower discussed the possibility of an air strike with the Joint Chiefs of Staff. He later wrote: "Although the three service chiefs—Army, Navy, Air Force—had recommended against this course, there was some merit in the argument that the psychological effect of an air strike would raise French and Vietnamese morale and improve, at least temporarily, the entire situation." No such strike was ordered. However, carrier *Essex* was directed south from the area of Commander Naval Forces, Far East, on 5 May, in order to augment Admiral Phillips's force.[14]

Dien Bien Phu fell on 7 May 1954 when at 1730 Viet Minh troops swarmed over the command post and captured recently promoted General de Castries and his staff. After a feeble breakout attempt failed, the last French outpost of the main camp fell. Later that night, a French naval Privateer was shot down while bombing Viet Minh communication lines. The plane commander, Ensign Monguillon, and the eight-man crew were the last Frenchman killed in action at Dien Bien Phu.[15]

Geneva

The day after the fall of Dien Bien Phu the delegates at the Geneva Conference took up the problem of Indochina. The only important bargaining chip possessed by the French to forestall a breakdown of negotiations at Geneva was the threat of American intervention. To give credibility to the French position, Laniel once again inquired as to the circumstances in which the United States would intervene in the Indochina war. In the reply which Douglas Dillon handed Maurice Shumann, the French Deputy Minister for Foreign Affairs, on 15 May, the United States set down a number of conditions which would have to be met before this course would even be contemplated. This time the United States stipulated that only British consent, not participation, was necessary. There was the familiar call for the French to reaffirm the complete independence of the Associated States. The United States also insisted that the French promise not to withdraw their troops since any American forces committed would be intended to supplement rather than to replace French troops. The decision for intervention would also be conditioned upon agreements as to the

---

[14] Msg, CNO 061031Z May 1954; Eisenhower, *Mandate for Change,* p. 354; Fall, *Hell in a Very Small Place,* pp. 310–11.

[15] *Ibid.,* pp. 410–15.

Meeting to discuss Southeast Asian security, June 1954, from left to right, are Major General W. G. Gentry, New Zealand; Field Marshal Sir John Harding, United Kingdom; Lieutenant General Sir Sidney F. Rowell, Australia; General J. E. Valluy, France; and Admiral Robert B. Carney, Chief of Naval Operations, United States.

United States taking over the training of native troops and upon a suitable command structure with a United States deputy to the French General Navarre.[16]

Between 3 and 10 June 1954, Admiral Carney represented the United States at a Five Power Conference held in the Pentagon to discuss the Southeast Asian situation. The conference convened as the French withdrew to the Red River Delta. The French, represented by Lieutenant General J. E. Valluy, used the meeting to stress the obvious gravity of the situation

---

[16] Devillers and Lacouture, *End of a War*, pp. 189–96; msgs, SECSTATE, of 11 and 15 May 1954 in *U.S.-V.N. Relations*, bk 9, pp. 451–55, 465–68.

and to discuss the aid needed to save the country from Communist domination. However, the question of combat support became academic when on 30 June Pierre Mendèz-France replaced Laniel as prime minister and pledged to bring peace to Indochina within thirty days.

On 20 July 1954, the French and Viet Minh concluded at Geneva three agreements on the cessation of hostilities—one for Vietnam, one for Laos, and one for Cambodia. In the case of Vietnam, the Vice Minister of National Defense of the Democratic Republic of Vietnam signed for "the Commander-in-Chief of the People's Army of Viet Nam." A French officer signed for the French Union Forces. The same Vice Minister of the Democratic Republic signed the Cambodian agreement for "the Units of the Khmer Resistance Forces and for the Commander-in-Chief of the Vietnamese Military Units." A Cambodian officer signed for the Khmer National Armed Forces. The Laos agreement, involving the People's Army of Viet Nam and the Pathet Lao on one side and the French Union Forces on the other, was signed by the same officials who signed the Vietnam agreement.[17]

The first agreement provided for the division of Vietnam into regrouping zones on either side of a provisional military demarcation line at the Ben Hai River (17th parallel), and a narrow demilitarized zone on either side of the line. Within 80 days of the signing date, the agreements would become effective and the French Union Forces would withdraw from the Hanoi perimeter; within 100 days from the Haiduong perimeter; and within 300 days from the Haiphong perimeter. The forces of the People's Army of Vietnam had a similar withdrawal schedule from the south, although the bulk of their forces were already concentrated in the north.[18]

One provision eventually resulted in a major operation by the United States Navy. Until the movement of troops was completed, any civilians residing in one zone who wished to migrate to the other zone would be permitted and helped to do so by the authorities in their original district. Naval craft were authorized to provide transportation between regrouping zones.

Other provisions had implications with regard to future military assistance. One prohibited "the introduction into Viet Nam of any reinforce-

---

[17] Anita Lauve Nutt, "Troika on Trial: Control or Compromise?," Sept. 1967, Rand Corp., Vol. III, App. II.
[18] Indochina Armistice Agreements in U.S., State Department, *American Foreign Policy, 1950–1955: Basic Documents* (Washington: Department of State, GPO, 1957), Vol. I, pp. 750–67.

ments in the form of all types of arms, munitions and other war material, such as combat aircraft, naval craft, pieces of ordnance, jet engines and jet weapons [*sic.*] and armoured vehicles," although "war materials, arms and munitions which have been destroyed, damaged, worn out or used up after the cessation of hostilities" could be replaced. The establishment of new military bases was prohibited and none was to be established under the control of a foreign state. No additional military personnel could be introduced into Vietnam.

The Agreement on the Cessation of Hostilities was primarily a military settlement of the war. A political settlement was only alluded to in Article 14, which stated that, "pending the general elections which will bring about the unification of Viet Nam" each party to the agreement would administer its own regroupment zone.[19]

Such a settlement was spelled out more clearly in a Final Declaration. The declaration emphasized "that the military demarcation line is provisional and should not in any way be interpreted as constituting a political or territorial boundary." It further called for elections in July 1956 on establishing "democratic institutions" in Vietnam.[20] The declaration also specifically noted that the French-Democratic Republic of Vietnam agreement forbade the introduction of foreign military personnel, the establishment of military bases under foreign control, and the use of the zones as part of any military alliance or "for the resumption of hostilities or in the service of an aggressive policy." It was also stipulated that the military demarcation line was provisional and not in any way to be interpreted as constituting a political or territorial boundary.

At the Geneva Conference the United States had been "an interested nation which, however, is neither a belligerent nor a principal in the negotiations." At the conclusion of the conference on 21 July, Under Secretary of State Smith issued a unilateral declaration setting forth the United States' position. He stated that the United States was not prepared to concur in the conference's "Final Declaration," but took note of the agreements concluded on the 20th and 21st of July. Referring to the United Nations' Charter, Smith declared that the United States would refrain "from the threat or use of force" to disturb the agreements, and "would view any renewal of the aggression in violation of the . . . agreements with grave

---

[19] "Agreement on the Cessation of Hostilities in Vietnam (1954)" in Nutt, "Troika on Trial," Vol. III, App. II, pp. 27–43.
[20] "Final Declaration of the Geneva Conference, July 21, 1954" in *Ibid.*, App. V, pp. 48–50.

concern and as seriously threatening international peace and security." He then restated a Washington declaration of 29 June 1954 as follows: "In the case of nations now divided against their will, we shall continue to seek to achieve unity through free elections supervised by the United Nations to insure that they are conducted fairly." On the other hand, Smith reiterated the traditional American position that "peoples are entitled to determine their own future" and declared that the United States would not "join in any arrangement which would hinder this" policy.[21]

The South Vietnamese had presented their own plan "designed to obtain an armistice, without even the temporary partitioning of Vietnam. . . ." In a statement issued on 21 July, they protested the fact that their proposal was rejected without even having been considered. Furthermore, the South Vietnamese "solemnly" protested the fact that the French "arrogated [to themselves] the right to set the date for future elections. . . ."[22]

Because the United States and South Vietnam refused to sign the Final Declaration, the other nations at Geneva did not sign either. The French-Viet Minh War was over, but a complete political settlement had not been achieved.

Shortly after the fall of Dien Bien Phu, increased Chinese Communist activity was noted in the coastal areas near Taiwan, particularly by air and naval units close to Chinese Nationalist offshore islands. In particular, the Tachen Islands appeared to be threatened. Under the operational control of Commander in Chief, United States Pacific Fleet, Commander Seventh Fleet deployed forces, including carriers *Tarawa* (CV–40) and *Boxer,* to the area and increased the reconnaissance efforts of Task Force 72. On 7 July 1954, a P2V patrol plane on a reconnaissance flight in the Formosa Strait was attacked by Chinese Communist aircraft, but was not damaged.[23]

On 22 July, Chinese fighters twenty miles southeast of Hainan Island shot down a British Air Cathay Skymaster enroute from Bangkok to Hong Kong with eighteen passengers on board. Vice Admiral Phillips, embarked in *Hornet* (CVA–12) on training exercises in the South China Sea, in company with *Philippine Sea* and a screen group of twelve destroyers, reacted immediately upon hearing the British distress call. He ordered Rear Admiral

---

[21] Msg, SECSTATE, of 12 May 1954 in *U.S.-V.N. Relations,* bk 9, pp. 457–59; Statement, Under Secretary of State at the concluding plenary session of the Geneva Conference of 21 July 1954 in *The Department of State Bulletin.* XXXI (2 Aug. 1954), pp. 162–63.

[22] Statement by the Government of Vietnam, July 21, 1954 in Nutt, "Troika on Trial," Vol. III, App. VI. pp. 51–52.

[23] COM7THFLT, report, FY 1955. p. 11; msg, CINCPACFLT 260006Z May 1954.

Harry D. Felt, then Commander Carrier Group (TG 70.2) and embarked in *Philippine Sea,* to aid British and United States Air Force units searching for survivors. Nine survivors, one of whom subsequently died, were rescued without incident.

Then on the 26th, three search planes from *Philippine Sea,* led by Commmander G. C. Duncan, Commander Carrier Air Group 5, were attacked by two LA–7 Chinese Communist fighters. The "bogies" made a low-side run on Lieutenant R. M. Tatham in an AD Skyraider and opened fire at about 3,000 feet. After failing to score hits, the Chinese pilots broke off and made a head-on firing run against Commander Duncan's Skyraider. Commander Duncan alerted the rest of the flight to join the action. In the meantime, Lieutenant Tatham made firing runs on the lead LA–7. Hits were observed. Another AD made a firing run on the LA–7 as it slowly rolled on its back and spun into the water. Taken under fire by eight Skyraiders the second LA–7 crashed into the water near a fishing junk. As the pilots regrouped, a small gunboat, escorting two Polish merchantmen in the vicinity of the air action, began firing on the Navy pilots. On orders from Admiral Felt the aircraft withheld their fire and returned to the carrier.[24]

Although a reduction of the overall force levels of the United States Navy had been underway since the Korean armistice, extensive demands for deployed naval forces had continued. The withdrawal of two carriers from the Western Pacific, planned for January 1954, had been continually deferred. Forces were no longer sufficient to maintain the required level of peacetime deployments without adverse effects on readiness in other areas and on morale. This situation led the Navy to seek a reduction of the requirement for carriers in the Western Pacific from four to three, as of 1 July. In the words of Admiral Duncan, acting Chief of Naval Operations:

> The deployment of 4 CVA to the Far Eastern Command is the most difficult commitment to maintain. It has now been extended for over two years. To continue it: ships have been switched from ocean to ocean, sometimes temporarily, at other times permanently; carrier Air Groups from one Fleet have been married to carriers of the other Fleet and the entire unit pressed through an abbreviated training period which has proved unsuitable to prepare the ship for its intended duty.[25]

The request was denied.

---

[24] Memo, OP–33 to OP–03, ser 0072 of 29 July 1954; CARDIV 3, reports, ser 0059 of 7 Aug. and ser 0193 of 23 Aug. 1954; CAG 5, report, of 26 July 1954.
[25] Memo, Duncan to Radford, ser 00034P33 of 26 May 1954.

Meanwhile, the United States was groping for means of ensuring the security of South Vietnam and other Southeast Asian countries. As the Seventh Fleet continued operations to protect American interests throughout the Far East, it was ordered to assist in the transportation of refugees from North Vietnam.

CHAPTER XII

Passage To Freedom, 1954-1955

One of the immediate results of the French-Viet Minh Agreement on the Cessation of Hostilities in Vietnam was the involvement of the United States Navy in the humanitarian task of helping provide passage south for those who desired and were able to flee Communist rule in the North. Throughout its history and in many scattered areas of the globe, the Navy had often been called upon to rescue people from areas of natural disasters, political turmoil, warfare, or oppression. The task was thus a familiar one, but each case had its own set of problems. Difficulties encountered in the Vietnam operations were in many respects unique.

In addition to requiring that each party regroup military forces, equipment, and supplies to its own zone (the Viet Minh forces to the north of the demarcation line and French Union Forces to the south), the agreement also stipulated that "until the movement of troops is completed, any civilians residing in a district controlled by one party who wish to go and live in the zone assigned to the other party shall be permitted and helped to do so by the authorities in that district." The United States had urged such a provision during the negotiations. Experience in Eastern Europe and Korea had emphasized the importance of timely provisions to assist those who wished to escape a Communist dictatorship. Wherever the Communists had gained control, they had taken extraordinary steps to restrict communications across the borders and to prevent the inhabitants from leaving; in each case, the "iron curtain" had descended. Those remaining behind who actively sought freedom had often been subjected to coercion, imprisonment, torture, or even death. France sought the provision concerning movement of civilians so that it could withdraw not only military dependents and French citizens but also Vietnamese who would be in danger because of close affiliations with the French.

United States assistance would be requested because of the large number of people who desired to leave North Vietnam and the importance of civilian movements in the initial phases of regroupment. Although 300

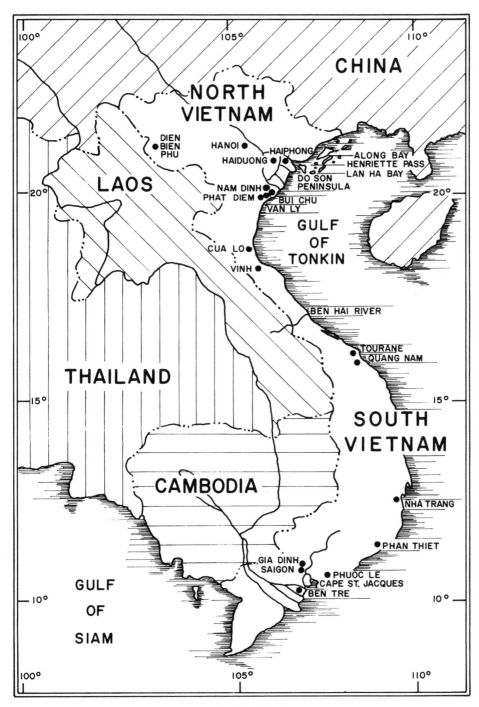

Indochina, 1954

days were allowed for final withdrawal of troops, they were to be moved into provisional assembly areas within 15 days after the cease-fire date. Departure from the "Hanoi perimeter" was to be completed in 80 days and from the "Haiduong perimeter" in 100 days. Fear that once they gained control over an area the Communists would interfere with Vietnamese departures later proved justified.

On 23 July 1954, two days after the Geneva Conference ended, France offered to assist South Vietnam in evacuating civilian as well as military personnel from North Vietnam. The French agreed to build refugee camps in both the North and the South and to help resettle the refugees once they reached their destination. Doubting that the French could handle the task alone, Diem advised the United States Ambassador, Donald Heath, in Saigon that South Vietnam would need help in transporting Catholics and other anti-Communists from the North to the free zone of Vietnam.[1]

The cease-fire went into effect in northern Vietnam on 27 July, and by the end of the month, French troops had withdrawn into the Hanoi-Haiduong-Haiphong area. Along with the French military personnel, numbering some 80,000, thousands of refugees from the cities of Bui Chu and Phat Diem had already poured into the reduced area of French control.[2]

To help evacuate their equipment, much of which had been funded by the Mutual Defense Assistance Program, the French requested the services of twenty American LSTs and one LSD. Concerned over the scarcity of such units in the Pacific Fleet, Admiral Carney proposed the use of ships of the Navy's Military Sea Transportation Service.[3] However, the French request soon was overtaken by a much larger commitment.

On 5 August 1954 the French started a major effort by sea and air to transport troops, military equipment, and refugees from the Hanoi-Haiphong area to the South. They commandeered all available civilian and military passenger aircraft and began an intensive airlift, first from Hanoi, and then after 20 September, from Haiphong. Efficient as their efforts were, they could not handle all of those who wished to leave.

Also on the fifth, President Diem dispatched a personal message to President Eisenhower asking for American help in moving a million refugees from North Vietnam to South Vietnam. When France made an urgent plea

---

[1] Richard W. Lindholm, ed., *Viet-Nam: The First Five Years* (East Lansing, Mich.: Michigan State University Press, 1959), pp. 48–60.

[2] *Ibid.*, p. 55; O'Ballance. *Indo-China War*, p. 245.

[3] Memo, OP–63 to CNO, ser 00033 P63C of 11 Aug. 1954.

for the United States to transport 100,000 refugees a month to the South, Ambassador Heath urged acceptance of the request. Anticipating a favorable response, Admiral Carney alerted Admiral Stump to the probability of American participation in the large-scale evacuation from Haiphong and informed him of a Secretary of Defense authorization to employ elements of the Amphibious Force, Western Pacific together with such Military Sea Transportation Service units as were required to do the job.[4]

The possibility of assisting with an airlift as well as sealift was explored. However, it soon became clear that the French were making maximum use of the air terminals available in North Vietnam in transporting 3,000 refugees a day to the South.[5]

On 7 August 1954, Admiral Carney directed Admiral Stump to implement the evacuation plan, in an operation which became known as the "Passage to Freedom." The Commander in Chief, United States Pacific Fleet was responsible for the sea evacuation and for providing overall support. Under CINCPACFLT, Rear Admiral Lorenzo S. Sabin, Commander Amphibious Force, Western Pacific (Task Force 90) and also Commander Amphibious Group 1, was assigned command of the sea operation. He was authorized to "use elements of PHIBFORWESTPAC [Amphibious Force, Western Pacific] and MSTS WESTPAC in proportions at your discretion as required to accomplish the task expeditiously." Stump directed Sabin to confer with Commander Naval Forces, Philippines (Rear Admiral Hugh Goodwin) concerning logistic support. The Chief of the Military Assistance Advisory Group, Indochina (Major General O'Daniel) was designated the "over-all military co-ordinator ashore," responsible for refugee affairs. General O'Daniel designated Captain James Collett, head of the Navy Section of the MAAG, as his deputy.[6]

The Vietnamese Foreign Ministry was advised on 8 August that:

The United States Government desires to extend to the Government of Viet-Nam all reasonable assistance to evacuate from areas defined in the cease-fire agreement its nationals who understandably are unwilling to face

[4] Msg, CNO 062207Z Aug. 1954; Lancaster, *Emancipation of French Indochina*, pp. 341–45; CTF 90, report, ser 0252 of 8 Nov. 1954.

[5] "Exodus: Report on a Voluntary Mass Flight to Freedom: Viet-Nam, 1954," *The Department of State Bulletin*, XXXII (7 Feb. 1955), pp. 223–26.

[6] Lindholm, *Viet-Nam: The First Five Years*, p. 63; msgs, CNO 071633Z and CINCPACFLT 080259Z Aug. 1954.

the grim certainties of life under the Communists. . . . The United States is also prepared to provide as far as possible material help needed to enable refugees from Viet Minh domination to resume existence under their chosen government with maximum opportunity to add to the strength of that government through their own efforts.[7]

Before ships of the amphibious group could be deployed to Southeast Asian waters and begin the evacuation, operational control had to be transferred from Commander in Chief, Far East to Commander in Chief, Pacific. Despite the termination of the occupation of Japan in 1951 and the signing of the Korean Armistice in 1953, command over operations of units of the Pacific Fleet was still divided between two unified commands, which in turn came under two executive agents. Under the Department of the Army, Commander in Chief, Far East, was responsible for an ocean area encompassing Japan, Korea, North China, and the Ryukyus. Under the Department of the Navy CINCPAC was responsible for the rest of the Pacific area and the Indian Ocean. In this instance the decision had already been made in Washington, and the transfer of operational control took place on 8 August. Commander Naval Forces, Far East (Vice Admiral William M. Callaghan) was advised that the last amphibious units would leave for Indochina on or about 19 August. The first ships were on their way by the 10th.[8]

On 10 August 1954 Rear Admiral Sabin flew to Haiphong to confer with General O'Daniel; Vice Admiral Auboyneau, the senior French naval officer in Indochina; Rear Admiral Jean Querville, Commander of the naval facilities at Haiphong; Jerry Strauss, head of the United States Special Technical Economic Mission in Hanoi; and the Vietnamese Mayor of Haiphong. Admiral Sabin promised to provide 4 LSTs and 4 AKAs immediately, to be augmented by as many as 4 LSDs, 8 APAs, 18 LSTs, and 4 AKAs, if necessary. Except for screening the refugees for diseases or the presence of Communist agents, the French Army would handle the details of the embarkation. The French Navy agreed to supply all the port services, including pilots for the LSTs entering Haiphong and the landing craft making the four and a half hour trip to the Along Bay anchorage. French

---

[7] U.S., State Department, *American Foreign Policy 1950–1955,* Vol. II, p. 2398.
[8] CTF 90, reports, ser 0252 of 8 Nov. 1954 and ser 04 of 3 Jan. 1955, encl. 1; ltr, Sabin to Settle, of 14 Mar. 1955.

and Vietnamese liaison teams would be embarked in each ship to control the refugees.[9]

Admiral Sabin organized his forces as follow:

TF 90—Amphibious Task Force, Western Pacific, RADM L. S. Sabin
  TG 90.8—Embarkation Group, CAPT W. C. Winn, Commander Transport Division 13
    TU90.8.1—Transport Unit, CAPT W. C. Winn (2 APDs, 8 APAs, 4 AKAs, 4 LSDs)
    TU90.8.2—MSTS Transport Unit, CAPT P. W. Mothersill, Commander LSD Squadron 1
    TU90.8.3—Landing Ship Unit, CDR F. W. Logsdon, Commander LST Squadron 3
    TU 90.8.4—Embarkation Control Unit
    TU90.8.5—Control Unit, CDR A. E. Teal, Commander Amphibious Control Division 12 (1 APD, 1 Underwater Demolition Team)
  TG 90.9—Debarkation Group, CAPT B. N. Rittenhouse, Commander Transport Division 14 (1 APD).

A MSTS advisor was assigned to Admiral Sabin's staff and the MSTS office in Saigon was expanded.[10]

Over the years, one of the lessons of amphibious and emergency sealift operations has been that the bottlenecks are invariably at loading and unloading sites. Anticipating problems in embarkation, Admiral Sabin, in his operation order of 11 August, provided for the use of Navy shore parties to build the camps, process the refugees, control the over-the-beach operation, and direct the loading of landing craft and lighters. Captain Clarence Coffin and the 200 men of Naval Beach Group 1 were enroute to Southeast Asia at the time, embarked in the flagship *Estes* (AGC–12). However, the planned United States Navy operations at embarkation sites were prevented by French concern about giving any appearance of violating the Geneva agreement provision concerning foreign troops. The French would allow no more than fifteen to twenty Americans on the beach to handle communications, liaison, beach supervision, and medical problems. This resulted in delays in processing the refugees and, at times, less than

---

[9] "Memo on Haiphong Conference," 10 Aug. 1954.
[10] "MSTS Historical Diary: 1 January–31 December 1954," Sept.; CTF 90, report, ser 04 of 3 Jan. 1955, encl. 2.

full use of available ships. The few Americans who were allowed ashore performed invaluable service.[11]

The Passage Starts

The first amphibious ship to arrive in Indochina was *Menard* (APA–201), from Hong Kong. Admiral Sabin thought it best to keep her offshore and out of visual range until other ships arrived. Since many ships had been promised the Vietnamese, it was feared that the arrival of but one might feed Communist propaganda. The transports and cargo ships coming from Korean waters were delayed by a typhoon. Nevertheless, on 14 August, five days after the President's announcement, *Montague* (AKA–98) anchored in Along Bay, followed the next day by *Montrose* (APA–212), *Algol* (AKA–54), *Montrail* (APA–213), and *Telfair* (APA–210).

In anticipation of over-the-beach operations, Commander Teall and detachments of Underwater Demolition Team 12 surveyed possible beach sites, particularly on the Do Son Peninsula, which juts into the Tonkin Gulf twenty-five miles below Haiphong. On 16 August, attack transport *Menard* began loading refugees off Do Son, where in 1945 other United States naval units had embarked Chinese occupation troops being redeployed from North Vietnam. As in the earlier operation, the American ship loaded off the coast rather than at the city docks in order to avoid grounding on the bar east of Haiphong and because of the possibility of ambushes along the tortuous thirteen-mile-long channel.

A French LCT beached near Do Son and embarked refugees designated for evacuation in *Menard*. The 150-foot landing craft usually carried four or five tanks and a few dozen men, but on this day her valuable cargo consisted of frightened and seasick refugees crowding its hot, open well. After loading its human cargo, *Menard* weighed anchor and set sail for Saigon on the 17th with more than 1,900 passengers. Three days later, on the 20th, she docked at Saigon and unloaded her passengers according to plans formulated by Captain Rittenhouse, who commanded the Debarkation Group. Bands, honor guards, and French and American officials welcomed the first load of refugees. Priests assisted in carrying out the debarka-

---

[11] *Ibid.*, encl. 1; CTF 90, report, ser 02 of 5 Jan. 1955; CTF 90, report, ser 0252 of 8 Nov. 1954.

tion, while ship's cranes hoisted baggage over the side. As the Vietnamese walked down the gang-plank, the Red Cross handed out packets of food before trucks took them off to the refugee camps surrounding the city.[12]

Other ships—APAs, AKAs, LSDs, and LSTs—followed. After the first day, embarkation at Do Son was suspended because of the heavy swells which crashed the landing craft against the ships and made the transfer too dangerous. Instead, the French landing craft picked up the refugees at the Haiphong docks and sailed the forty miles to the ship at Henriette Pass in Along Bay.

Preparing for the lift was a routine matter for the transports. However, for the cargo ships it meant working around the clock for several days. With five large holds and three levels each for carrying tanks and trucks, installing accommodations for 2,000 individuals per AKA—building ladders, providing some means of ventilation, making provisions for drinking water, washing, and sanitary facilities, and obtaining special supplies to accommodate the oriental refugees—presented an unusual challenge.

On the 21st, it was attack cargo ship *Montague's* turn. An LCT came alongside and *Montague's* sailors lowered a gangway to its deck. The Vietnamese hesitated. Finally, a wizened, hunched elder took the lead. With one hand clutching a bamboo pipe and the other a framed picture of the Blessed Virgin, he started up the steps. A sailor clattered down the gangway to help, but the gesture frightened the man. He froze. Only the press of people behind forced him up the ladder. After a few others mounted the ladder, sailors installed a canvas cover over and under it so that the waves crashing in the trough between the LCT and *Montague* could not be seen. The Vietnamese carried balance poles with large shallow baskets on either end in which they carried all their belongings—clothes, a rice bowl, chopsticks, and often a Catholic icon. Most were children or old men. In the confusion, the Vietnamese brought on board a huge barrel of the odorous *Nuoc Mam* fish sauce. The ship's doctor spotted it and ordered the pungent cargo heaved overboard. Too late, he learned that it contained a condiment considered indispensable to Vietnamese cookery.

During the passage of *Montague* to the south, three babies were born—the first of ninety Vietnamese births that would be recorded in United States Navy ships through mid-November 1954. Since many of the embarkees

---

[12] CTF 90, report, ser 0252 of 8 Nov. 1954; UDT 12, command history, 21 May 1946–31 Dec. 1958.

80G644449

Vietnamese refugees in French LSIL about to embark in USS Montague, *August 1954.*

suffered from smallpox, malaria, and other diseases, Navy doctors and corpsmen were kept busy with almost continuous sick calls. Navy cooks learned how to prepare rice and other dishes in a Vietnamese style.

In this, as in subsequent ships, valuable assistance was rendered by a

80G652327

Vietnamese embark in LSM, Haiphong area.

French Army liaison officer and a control team which translated from Vietnamese into French and sometimes into English. Along with the priests and elders, the control teams explained Navy procedures to the refugees. So important were the control teams that the ships retained them on board during each succeeding trip to supplement the crews.

As the third day dawned, *Montague* sighted the mouth of the Saigon ship channel. At Saigon the Vietnamese Youth Organization greeted the ship and helped with the unloading, carrying children and baggage and assisting the elderly. Milk was distributed to the children by the American Women's Association of Saigon. Just before the refugees departed for their new homes, Bishop Pietro Martino Ngo Dinh Thuc, the brother of Ngo Dinh Diem, visited the ship to bless the refugees and thank the officers and crew for their undertaking.

For the crew of *Montague,* the voyage had had its trying aspects, but there was a deep sense of satisfaction for the services provided to the refugees. And the lessons learned on this and other early trips would be put to good use.[13]

While the majority of the refugees carried by American ships were Vietnamese, some 13,000 individuals of Chinese ancestry also fled the Viet Minh takeover in the North. *Montrose* embarked the first 2,340 Chinese on 2 September 1954.[14]

Security

In mid-August a U.S. intelligence report concluded that: "In view of the Indo-China cease-fire agreement, it is unlikely that the Viet Minh will create any incidents to deter the peaceful evacuation of civilian and military personnel from the Hanoi area."[15] General O'Daniel also believed that the Viet Minh would not interfere. But the Navy had long before learned the danger of basing actions solely on assumptions of enemy intentions. Precautions were taken against sneak attacks by swimmers, small boats, or mines. In addition to posting extra deck watches, ship captains organized nighttime harbor security patrols in Along Bay and at debarkation points in the South.

Ship's crews patrolled refugee spaces to forestall sabotage, but they rarely searched belongings and then only with a Vietnamese interpreter present. The crew of *Magoffin* (APA–199) discovered two grenades hidden

---

[13] CTF 90, reports, ser 0252 of 8 Nov. 1954 and ser 04 of 3 Jan. 1955; Thomas A. Dooley, *Deliver Us From Evil: The Story of Viet Nam's Flight to Freedom* (New York: Farrar, Strauss and Cudahy, 1956), pp. 29–42.

[14] CTF 90, report, 0252 of 8 Nov. 1954; Lindholm, *Viet-Nam: The First Five Years,* p. 49.

[15] COMPHIBGRU1, operation order, 2–54 of 11 Aug. 1954.

80G644528

A Vietnamese volunteer helping to chip paint on board USS Bayfield.

in a lower hold on 4 September. After receiving word from the French high command, citing intelligence reports indicating that the Viet Minh intended to sabotage American ships during September, Admiral Sabin warned his men to be especially watchful. As overall insurance, Admiral Stump deployed antisubmarine warfare forces to the South China Sea where they conducted exercises, ready to take protective action if required.[16]

---

[16] Ltr, Sabin to Stump, of 24 Aug. 1954; CTF 90, report, ser 0252 of 8 Nov. 1954; COMPHIBGRU1, operation order, 2–54 of 11 Aug. 1954.

The only potentially serious incident occurred in mid-September 1954 in LST–1148. Enroute to Tourane with Vietnamese troops and dependents, the ship faced a riot incited by a Communist agent armed with grenades. Admiral Sabin ordered *Begor* (APD–127) and LST–845, the latter with French Foreign Legionnaires embarked, to rendezvous with the LST. Meanwhile, the ship's crew had disarmed and arrested the Communist.[17]

Special Lifts

The question of lifting Vietnamese and French troops had arisen early in the operation. Admiral Stump left the decision to Admiral Sabin and General O'Daniel, as long as it did not interfere with the lift of refugees and MDAP equipment.

The Vietnamese 18th Infantry Battalion, twice decorated for gallantry during three years of fighting, was the first combat unit carried by American ships during the evacuation. Its 700 soldiers, 1,500 dependents, 33 vehicles, and baggage departed on 27 August from Haiphong in two LSDs bound for Nha Trang, where the Vietnamese Army gave them a hearty welcome. By 15 November, 13,657 troops had been evacuated from the North by United States Navy ships.[18]

The United States Navy also assisted the French in repatriating sick and wounded French soldiers recently released by the Viet Minh. Hospital ship *Haven* (AH–12) was sent south from Korea. Moored to the Catinat Wharf in Saigon for three days beginning on 8 September, she loaded 721 French troops, most of whom were repatriated prisoners of war. The ship sailed via Suez for Oran and Marseilles, where she disembarked the soldiers before steaming for her homeport, Long Beach, California.[19]

Medical Team

After the 10 August Haiphong conference, Admiral Sabin had toured a

---

[17] CTF 90, report, ser 0252 of 8 Nov. 1954; NA Saigon, report, 138–54 of 23 Sept. 1954, JN–N–59–2184, box 44, FRC.

[18] CTF 90, report, ser 0252 of 8 Nov. 1954; COMPHIBGRU1, report, ser 055 of 15 June 1955, encl. 1.

[19] USS *Haven,* "Operation Repatriation;" Withers Moore, "Navy Chaplains in Vietnam, 1954–1964," 1968, Navy Department Library, pp. 27–29.

refugee camp. He described the experience as "one of the most awful sights I have ever seen." A recent rain had turned the camp, located near a rice paddy, into a sea of mud. The only existing refugee shelters were a few tents of tattered cloth hung on bamboo sticks. Conditions were amazingly squalid and unsanitary. Raw sewage was all about, attracting swarms of flies and insects which then bedeviled the half-clothed adults and the children. Pungent odors permeated the steamy air. Despite the sickening aspects of their condition, Sabin found the spirit of the refugees inspiring:

> Old and young alike gathered about us holding up the "V" for victory sign, bowing low and even falling prostrate before us as they shouted in French: "Pour la Liberté. Vives les Americains." [20]

A United States Navy medical team arrived off Haiphong on 18 August in *Estes* and soon afterward went ashore to confer with French medical authorities. Commander Julius Amberson, Preventive Medicine Officer then attached to the 3rd Marine Division, headed the unit. Also in the unit were Lieutenant Edmund Gleason, an expert in hygiene and sanitation, and Lieutenant David Davis and Lieutenant (jg) Thomas Dooley, who initially served as interpreters. Deeply moved by the suffering of the Indochinese and their need for competent medical attention, Dr. Dooley later achieved worldwide fame when he established a jungle hospital in Laos. There, he dedicated the rest of his life to easing the suffering of the people. [21]

Commandant Guiguen at the French Army Hospital in Haiphong showed the Americans the hundreds of French and Vietnamese casualties, most of them from Dien Bien Phu, who had arrived in an almost continuous stream from the field. His overtaxed facilities could barely handle military casualties, much less a flood of refugees. Representatives of the *Bureau Mixte du Transport,* the French organization responsible for all aspects of the civilian evacuation, eagerly welcomed Dr. Amberson's offers of medical assistance in the refugee camps to help French and Vietnamese doctors and technicians. [22]

The first task was to advise the French Army on designing and locating

---

[20] Lorenzo S. Sabin, "South Vietnam—An Exercise in Tragedy," *Shipmate,* XXVIII (Apr. 1965), pp. 12–16.

[21] BUMED, "The History of the Medical Department of the United States Navy, 1945–1955," NAVMED Pub. P–5057, pp. 197–205. For a colorful story of problems encountered afloat as well as ashore, see Dooley, *Deliver Us From Evil.*

[22] Memo, Grindell to Sabin, of 24 Aug. 1954.

80G647050

Dr. Thomas A. Dooley, PHC A. B. Cory, Dr. J. M. Amberson, and Dr. E. G. Gleason work on a water pump at a refugee camp in the North.

the refugee camps to insure proper sanitation. Lieutenant Dooley drew the job, and for the first camp he selected the site of an old village, approximately four miles from Haiphong on the dirt road leading to Hanoi. The United States Foreign Operations Administration furnished 400 tents purchased from the United States Army. Moroccan soldiers, plus a few hundred Vietnamese laborers put them up within a few days, and the site was christened Camp de la Pagode.

An elaborate system of drainage ditches kept the tents reasonably dry. Several rice paddies bordering the camp became latrines. The doctors constantly warned the people against bathing in such areas, and used strong germicides to kill the bacteria. Hundreds of Vietnamese owed their good health to these precautions and to a water purification unit, which sometimes pumped as much as 12,000 gallons daily of filtered and chlorinated water from the chocolate-colored rice paddy nearby.

One day the rice paddy water was black. An investigation revealed that a Vietnamese woman had dumped black vegetable dye into it after she had dyed her clothes. On several occasions the doctors found young boys sailing wooden boats or swimming in the 3,000-gallon storage tanks for treated water. After the Viet Minh attempted to slash the rubber tanks, a barbed-wire fence was erected and Senegalese guards mounted a twenty-four hour watch.[23]

Several tents were set aside for sick bays. There, Dr. Amberson and his staff assisted Vietnamese public health officials in treating the sick and vaccinating the people against smallpox and cholera. Much of the soap, vitamin pills, antibiotics, dressings, and aspirin dispensed to the refugees was obtained as a result of pleas by the doctors during visits to ships. Difficult as conditions were, these teams did their job well. The threatened plagues never materialized.

Once the refugees were provided sanitary camps, medical care, and pure water, the Navy medical team turned its attention to building delousing and first aid stations at the embarkation point. A team of six corpsmen, operating two machines to dust all refugees with DDT before they were embarked, processed an average of 1,000 refugees an hour. As the Vietnamese passed through the stations, Dr. Amberson and his crew scrutinized the people for evidence of contagious diseases and transferred the sick to a first aid tent for treatment. Eventually these patients resumed emigration as their health improved.[24]

Captain Caldwell J. Stuart, surgeon of the Far East command, and Commander James A. Grindell, Medical Officer on Admiral Sabin's staff, had accompanied the medical team when it arrived in August. Concerned over the possibility of a widespread epidemic which might decimate the large refugee population encamped around Haiphong and sweep through the crews of the ships, they recommended the establishment of a Preventive Medicine and Sanitation Unit in Haiphong.

---

[23] Dooley, *Deliver Us From Evil*, pp. 66–73.
[24] "History of the Medical Department," pp. 202–04.

Commander Amberson was relieved by Commander Sidney Britten in September. As a result of the latter's request, Fleet Epidemic Disease Control Unit 2, with Lieutenant (jg) Richard Kaufman in command, was assigned to Vietnam from the fleet hospital at Yokosuka, Japan. Arriving in Vietnam in *Haven* during the first week in September, the unit set up its laboratory in an empty warehouse at the French Naval Base in Haiphong and undertook an extensive study of the disease potential in the refugee camps and in the city of Haiphong itself.[25]

Logistics

Sabin had stopped in the Philippines on 9 August 1954, while enroute to Vietnam in a special mission aircraft. Since obtaining logistic support from the Philippines would require long diversions of the evacuation ships across the South China Sea, Rear Admiral Roy A. Gano (Commander Service Squadron 3) proposed the more efficient concept of employing a mobile force. After obtaining the concurrence of Sabin, Gano gained Stump's approval.[26]

The most efficient location for a mobile support force would have been off Haiphong where the receipt of fuel and supplies and repairs could be dovetailed into the schedule of receiving passengers. Admiral Sabin, concerned about concentrating too many ships in a potentially hostile environment, instead selected Tourane. Midway between Haiphong and Saigon, it was a good location until the onset of the northeast monsoon in the fall caused such heavy seas in the roadstead that the force was moved to the better protected anchorage at Along Bay.

Carrying out his responsibilities for logistic support and services in the Western Pacific, Rear Admiral Gano ordered ships south from the Japan-Korea area. He proceeded to the scene in his flagship, repair ship *Ajax* (AR–6).

On 23 August 1954, Rear Admiral Gano reported to Rear Admiral Sabin:

---

[25] *Ibid.,* pp. 201–02; CTF 90, report, ser 0252 of 8 Nov. 1954.

[26] Commander Service Squadron 3 was a subordinate of Commander Service Force, United States Pacific Fleet (Rear Admiral Barton Biggs), who was responsible under CINCPACFLT for providing logistic support to naval forces in the Pacific. Operating as a part of Naval Forces, Western Pacific, Admiral Gano was also Commander Logistic Support Force, Western Pacific (CTF 92); ltr, Sabin to Hooper, of 18 Dec. 1973.

Ganos garage general store gas station now going X Grocery annex opens twenty fifth X Movies and mail on demand X Your patronage solicited.

Ships ordered supplies as they passed on their way south and picked them up on their return trip. Support at this time was provided by *Ajax* and fleet oiler *Caliente* (AO–53), anchored nearby. The first mail, 1,700 pounds, was carried in an R4D aircraft, which landed at Tourane on 24 August. *Montrose* loaded the first supplies that same day when it took on mail and fuel.[27]

Provisions ship *Karin* (AF–33) and cargo ship *Sussex* (AK–213) arrived on the 25th, joined the next day by salvage ships *Grapple* (ARS–7) and *Reclaimer* (ARS–42), and by a water barge. Arriving from Japan on 28 August, attack cargo ship *Uvalde* (AKA–88) brought epidemic control material, rice, and other goods for distribution to the evacuation ships. Hospital ship *Consolation* (AH–15) got there on 4 September directly from the United States. Fuel barge *Derrick* (YO–59) reached Tourane on 9 September and *Piscataque* (TAOG–80) arrived on 10 September with 900,000 gallons of fresh water.

The large number of refugees being transported and the unusual demands for certain types of supplies produced extraordinary requirements. Store ship *Castor* (AKS–1) replenished Task Force 90 ships from 9 to 19 September and filled orders for a time, but the Seventh Fleet depended on her underway replenishment capabilities and specially tailored load of repair parts. Weekly shuttle runs from Subic by small cargo ships *Sharps* (AKL–10) and *Estero* (AKL–5) eased the problem.

Admiral Gano stationed two landing craft repair ships, *Atlas* (ARL–7) and *Sphinx* (ARL–24), at Henriette Pass near Haiphong. There was little need for the major repair capabilities of *Ajax* at Tourane. More pressing need in northern waters resulted in her release on 20 September. *Sphinx* replaced her but returned to the Haiphong area when *Atlas* sailed for Japan on 27 September. In turn, *Sphinx* was relieved by *Askari* (ARL–30).[28]

MSTS Lifts

Whereas amphibious ships had been deployed promptly to Vietnam, delays had been encountered in obtaining MSTS ships. Upon receiving

---

[27] CTF 90, reports, ser 0252 of 8 Nov. 1954 and ser 04 of 3 Jan. 1955, encl. 4.
[28] *Ibid.*

Admiral Sabin's request for sixteen MSTS transports with a capacity of 2,000 passengers each and fifteen MSTS deep-draft cargo ships, Commander Naval Forces, Far East advised that, although the cargo ships could be spared, it would be preferable to delay the deployment of all MSTS troop ships in the Pacific until others were sent out to the Far East. Admiral Callaghan withdrew his objections when he learned that additional MSTS passenger ships were being sent across the Pacific. Meanwhile, four cargo ships were converted to carry passengers.[29]

The first MSTS ship, *USNS Beauregard* arrived on 2 September. Problems initially encountered by MSTS ships were largely the result of the small size of the merchant marine crews and inadequate supervision of the refugees. Corrective steps were taken and by 19 September Captain Rittenhouse in Saigon was able to report that the MSTS transports were "maintaining high standards already set by PACFLT ships in the operation."[30]

The treatment of the refugees in the MSTS ships was similar to the compassionate care they received in those of the Pacific Fleet. After his trip south in the MSTS ship *General W. M. Black,* Vong Phu Dan wrote the captain:

> All names of my people, I beg to send Mr. Master of the ship and all naval officers my gratefulness. There are three days in your ship, you are nursery my people with vigilance, and Mr. Doctor is for-ever my benefactor. I never to forget together on this ship, because you are very goodness.[31]

Military Cargo

In addition to passengers, Task Force 90 lifted thousands of tons of military cargo, mostly Mutual Defense Assistance Program items. The primary concern was to evacuate the MDAP supplies; but since they were largely indistinguishable from other French equipment, Admiral Sabin had decided to lift whatever cargo General O'Daniel approved. Early in the operation, Vietnamese officials asked Admiral Sabin to transport industrial material. He refused, noting that this was a French responsibility and that American participation would lead to Communist charges that the

---

[29] CTF 90, report, ser 04 of 3 Jan. 1955, encl. 1; "MSTS Historical Diary," Sept.; msg, COMNAVFE 130804Z Aug. 1954.

[30] Memo, Sabin to Stump, of 10 Nov. 1954; CTF 90, report, ser 0252 of 8 Nov. 1954.

[31] *Ibid;* ltr, Vong Phu Dan to Master *General W. M. Black,* of 21 Sept. 1954.

80G652355

Arrival of 100,000th refugee at Saigon, September 1954. Rear Admiral Aaron P. Storrs, Lieutenant General W. O'Daniel, Rear Admiral Lorenzo S. Sabin, and Ambassador Donald Heath during the Passage to Freedom operation, 1954.

Passage to Freedom was a commercial rather than a humanitarian operation. Only special exceptions to this policy occurred, such as the transport of fifty tons of equipment from a girl's school moving from Haiphong to Tourane.[32]

Delays in the loading of military cargo at Haiphong were so serious that action was taken in Washington. At a meeting there from 27 to 29 September between Admiral Carney, Secretary of State Dulles, Guy la Chambre, Minister for the Associated States, and General Ély, Commissioner General and Commander in Chief of the French Union Forces in Indochina, Carney stressed the necessity for improved port operations. Ély assured him

---

[32] CTF 90, report, ser 0252 of 8 Nov. 1954.

that his country would take all necessary steps to evacuate U.S. funded material before the Communists took over in the North. The French kept their promise. When Vietnamese cargo handlers protested working conditions and staged a slowdown, perhaps encouraged by the Viet Minh, the French assigned their own Foreign Legionnaires to work the docks and impressed Chinese as stevedores. Several weeks after the Washington meeting, Sabin reported, "I still had difficulties and troubles but the cooperation and coordination was much better from that time on."[33]

To help remove the large number of vehicles, the French at the end of September asked for the retention until 15 November of all fourteen Navy LSTs in Indochina. The LSTs would permit the French to move units intact with their vehicles and to offload them easily at Tourane which had no piers to accommodate deep draft ships. The number of LSTs retained in use in October varied from seven to ten. Admiral Sabin phased out the remainder in November, but assured the French that he would order them back in time for final withdrawal of French vehicles.[34]

The Saigon Bottleneck

In September, the flow of refugees soon began to be restricted by the limited capacity of the terminal in the South. As previously noted, there were some delays at the embarkation sites, but these were nowhere near as serious as the bottleneck that soon developed in the Saigon area.

With the United States Navy landing about 3,000 refugees a day and the French air and sea lift discharging many more, the facilities in Saigon quickly became overcrowded. It had been planned that refugees would stay in the Saigon camps only one or two days for processing and then would be transported to their permanent homes. A reluctance to leave the camps was heightened by Communist propaganda, which claimed that those who departed the North would become slaves on French rubber plantations As a result, at times as many as 100,000 refugees huddled in camps designed for less than half that number.[35]

---

[33] Ltr, Sabin to Will, of 15 Nov. 1954; ltr, CNO to SECNAV, ser 00170P61 of 23 Oct. 1954; James D. Collett, transcript of interview, of 15 Dec. 1970.

[34] CTF 90, report, ser 0252 of 8 Nov. 1954; COMPHIBGRU1, report, ser 055 of 15 June 1955, encl. 1.

[35] "Exodus: Report on a Voluntary Mass Flight to Freedom: Viet-Nam, 1954," pp. 222–29.

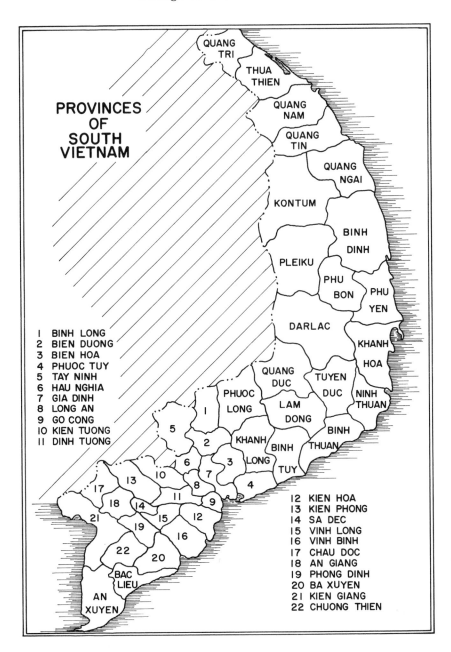

PROVINCES
OF
SOUTH
VIETNAM

QUANG TRI
THUA THIEN
QUANG NAM
QUANG TIN
QUANG NGAI
KONTUM
BINH DINH
PLEIKU
PHU BON
PHU YEN
DARLAC
KHANH HOA
QUANG DUC
TUYEN DUC
NINH THUAN
PHUOC LONG
LAM DONG
BINH THUAN
KHANH LONG
BINH TUY
BAC LIEU
AN XUYEN

1 BINH LONG
2 BIEN DUONG
3 BIEN HOA
4 PHUOC TUY
5 TAY NINH
6 HAU NGHIA
7 GIA DINH
8 LONG AN
9 GO CONG
10 KIEN TUONG
11 DINH TUONG

12 KIEN HOA
13 KIEN PHONG
14 SA DEC
15 VINH LONG
16 VINH BINH
17 CHAU DOC
18 AN GIANG
19 PHONG DINH
20 BA XUYEN
21 KIEN GIANG
22 CHUONG THIEN

When the Phu Tho debarkation camp in Saigon could absorb no more immigrants, Vietnamese, MAAG, and American Embassy representatives selected a new site at Cape St. Jacques, on the peninsula near the entrance to the Saigon ship channel. The United States mission brought in technicians and grading equipment from an irrigation project in Cambodia to build the new camp.

Making an exception to their rule against allowing American military personnel ashore, the French permitted the Naval Beach Group to help lay out tent sites, dig latrines, and clear the jungle. A Vietnamese Army battalion erected 436 tents to house a refugee population as high as 17,000. The camp, which opened on 29 August, soon brimmed with occupants. On the 28th, *Epping Forest* (LSD–4) anchored offshore to serve as a station ship. Its LCUs delivered the passengers ashore from the refugee ships, until French LCMs took over the job in the middle of September. By 14 September, the camp was full and 142 more tents were erected to increase the camp's capacity to 20,000 people.

As of 2 September, only 5,000 refugees had moved from Saigon to temporary camps in Bien Hoa, Tay Ninh, and Binh Duong Provinces, but by the middle of the month new camps had been established near Phuoc Le, Ben Tre, Gia Dinh, Quang Nam, and Phan Thiet. Each one housed between 1,000 and 3,000 settlers in French Army tents or temporary buildings funded by American aid.[36]

By this time General O'Daniel, at the request of the French and Vietnamese, had asked Admiral Sabin to slow the arrival of refugees. He asked that for two weeks, beginning on 11 September, only one ship with less than 2,500 passengers unload in Saigon daily. The request came just when the number of refugees streaming into the French perimeter took a momentary upswing.[37]

Nevertheless, when the first month's operation came to a close, American ships had carried 85,000 refugees to the South. At the start of the month, Admiral Sabin had estimated the figure would be 100,000. The 70,000 northerners transported by amphibious ships exceeded the number provided for in the plan, but as a result of the delay in the arrival of MSTS ships, the latter were able to transport only 15,000 of the 40,000 planned.[38]

By the end of September, there was evidence of a tapering off of the flow to the embarkation point. It is impossible to say how much of this

---

[36] *Ibid.;* Lindholm, *Viet-Nam: The First Five Years,* pp. 50, 77–94; John W. O'Daniel, *The Nation That Refused to Starve: The Challenge of the New Vietnam* (New York: Coward-McCann, Inc., 1960), pp. 37–55; CTF 90, report, ser 0252 of 8 Nov. 1954; U.S., MAAG, Indochina, "Coordinator's Report," 1954, pp. 23–25.

[37] CTF 90, report, ser 0252 of 8 Nov. 1954.

[38] *Ibid.;* Lindholm, *Viet-Nam: The First Five Years,* p. 49.

was caused by word of the Saigon bottleneck and the resettlement difficulties, for there were other causes as well. Some of those who planned to leave decided to wait until after the rice harvest or until they could get their affairs in order following the Chinese New Year. The most significant restraints were the travel distances involved for many individuals and the efforts of the Communists to discourage or prevent movement to the embarkation area. These efforts included vicious propaganda, travel restrictions, high transportation charges, short-term exit visas, delays, and hideous torture. Once the French had withdrawn their troops to the provisional assembly area, the "bamboo curtain" had descended.[39]

Representatives of the United States Information Service in Haiphong and Hanoi worked with the French to counter the propaganda campaign, but whatever the impact in these two cities, their leaflets and radio broadcasts had little or no success in penetrating territory controlled by the Communists.[40]

The Viet Minh imposed many obstacles to discourage all but the most determined. The refugee first had to sell his house and belongings to raise money for costly passport and land transportation fees. Restrictions on group travel forced families to split up. Viet Minh soldiers harassed and harangued travelers and forced many to turn back.[41]

One group of refugees from Thanh Hoa Province, led by an old patriarch, arrived in Haiphong after a two and a half month trek. They had suffered from Communist reprisals and loss of their belongings. Starvation and disease had wiped out half their number but the remainder kept on going. Other refugees bore the physical marks of Communist cruelty. Doctor Dooley reported performing a series of single and double amputations of feet and legs of a group of young men who had been clubbed with rifle butts when they insisted on the right to leave their village. One day a Catholic priest staggered into the Haiphong camp with chop sticks jammed into his ears and his body badly beaten.[42]

Despite such deterrents, many persisted in their efforts to gain freedom. In one case, more than a thousand refugees sailed the 200 miles from Cua Lo, near Vinh, to Along Bay in small fishing craft. Thousands of

[39] Dooley, *Deliver Us From Evil.* pp. 125–27, 147–48, 174–87.
[40] COMPHIBGRU1, report, ser 055 of 15 June 1955; *U.S.-V.N. Relations,* bk 2, pt. IV. 5, tab 1, p. 11; CTF 90, report, ser 0252 of 8 Nov. 1954.
[41] *Ibid.;* ltr, Sabin to Stump, of 15 Sept. 1954; CTF 90, report, ser 04 of 3 Jan. 1955.
[42] Sabin, "South Vietnam," pp. 12–16.

others sailed from Bui Chu, about fifty miles south of Haiphong, where the bishop had encouraged his people to flee. Some made Haiphong on their own, but most were picked up by French patrol boats. The refugees put to sea in hopes of finding the French craft, no mean task in the dark of night on storm-tossed waters. In several instances French boats beached in Viet-Minh controlled territory to save the refugees.[43]

The coast near the fishing village of Van Ly, south of Nam Dinh, was a favorite pickup point. There the French for a time anchored escort *Commandant de Pimodan* offshore to take on the refugees from the smaller patrol boats. After the French requested United States Navy assistance, Admiral Sabin ordered USNS *General A. W. Brewster* to the scene, telling the French that the navigators could pilot their ships to within inches of the three-mile limit. The MSTS passenger ship embarked 1,209 fishermen and peasants off Van Ly before sailing for Haiphong on 30 October. By 10 November, 20,000 Vietnamese had reached freedom via the sea from the Bui Chu area.[44]

The Flow Diminishes

During the first three months of the Passage to Freedom, 80 United States Navy and MSTS ships had carried 28,102 tons of cargo, 5,791 vehicles, and 173,311 passengers to South Vietnam. By November, due to French withdrawal into the Haiphong perimeter, the need for American shipping had declined. Admiral Sabin designated Captain Nicholas J. Frank, Jr., as on-scene commander and sailed for Hong Kong on 15 November 1954. All amphibious ships were withdrawn except *Balduck* (APD–132), which served as the flagship. Since the operation now employed largely MSTS ships, Sabin recommended that a naval captain of that organization relieve Captain Frank. Even though it meant the loss of one amphibious squadron commander from the Seventh Fleet, Admiral Stump disagreed. He believed that the task group should be kept in being under Commander in Chief, Pacific Fleet's operational control, ready to respond promptly in

[43] Dooley, *Deliver Us From Evil*. pp. 131–38; B.S.N. Murti, *Vietnam Divided: The Unfinished Struggle* (New York: Asia Publishing Co., 1964), pp. 73–75; Devillers and Lacouture, *End of a War*, pp. 335–36.

[44] CTF 90, report, ser 04 of 3 Jan. 1955; COMPHIBGRU1, report, ser 055 of 15 June 1955; ltr, Sabin to Hooper, of 18 Dec. 1973; Dooley, *Deliver Us From Evil*, pp. 149–55.

NH–79401

Vietnamese refugees from the Bui Chu region fleeing North Vietnam.

case more ships of the Amphibious Force were later required for the regroupment effort.[45]

When the evacuation rate declined in October, only Lieutenant (jg) Dooley and three corpsmen remained ashore. As sanitation improved, Dooley spent more and more time treating various ills of the unfortunate refugees. When a few cases of smallpox appeared in February 1955, he

[45] CTF 90, report, ser 04 of 3 Jan. 1955, encl. 8; ltr, Sabin to Settle, of 22 Nov. 1954. Admiral Sabin continued as overall commander of the operation into February 1955.

took aggressive steps to prevent an epidemic. Then, during the mosquito breeding season, he supervised an intensive spraying program to keep malaria under control. When the decreasing number of Fleet ships reduced his usual source of medicine, Dooley wrote to the Charles Pfizer Company in the United States, explaining his work and asking for a "small contribution—of say, 25,000 capsules—of terramycin." The company responded with double that amount and later sent penicillin, streptomycin, and magnamycin as well. The Meade-Johnson Company shipped gallons of liquid vitamins; Pan American Airways sent 10,000 bars of soap; and other companies made additional contributions. President Diem recognized Dooley's work by personnally decorating him with the *Officier de L' Ordre National de Viet Nam* at a ceremony on 12 May 1955.

Through the end of 1954, several unexpected throngs of people streamed into the Haiphong camps. The first major influx came from the Catholic parishes around Phat Diem south of Haiphong, where in mid-November the International Control Commission worked out arrangements with the Viet Minh allowing their departure. By December, over 10,000 refugees had fled Phat Diem.[46]

About 20 November, local Catholics in Vinh discussed with French naval officers possible coastal pickups similar to those off Bui Chu. Hoping to rescue as many as 6,000 refugees, the French scheduled the operations for 30 November. The rough weather of the northeast monsoon delayed the operation for a time, but on 19 December the French picked up 525 wet and tired souls representing the first refugees from Vinh. On the 23rd French ships transported about 2,400 more people to Haiphong for the trip south. French ships then swept the coast off Vinh several more times during the next two weeks but no other refugees appeared.

A third group of refugees, many of whom were Chinese, comprised permanent residents within the Haiphong perimeter. Before 1 December, few inhabitants of the city were counted among the refugees. On that date, however, Jacques Compaign, who headed the French civilian government in North Vietnam, relinquished his power to General Cogny in order to centralize authority for possible emergency action. General Cogny immediately announced that he would not guarantee the security of the residents of the city after 1 February. Conservative French estimates of the

---

[46] Lindholm, *Viet-Nam: The First Five Years,* pp. 63–72; COMPHIBGRU1, report, ser 055 of 15 June 1955, encl. 1; Dooley, *Deliver Us From Evil,* pp. 70–71, 83, 119, 144–48.

number planning to leave the city ran to 100,000. Added to the steady stream of refugees coming from the interior of the country, these estimates led to the assignment of an additional transport to the Passage to Freedom in January 1955.[47]

Despite such demands, the emphasis after mid-November 1954 had shifted from passengers to cargo. Long-range planning called for the evacuation of 1,500 long tons of cargo per day during November, 2,000 during December, and 1,000 in January. The goal for November was exceeded, thus reducing the amount of material available for lift in December. On 22 November 1954, the French decided to retain only 2,000 vehicles and 18,000 troops in the North. Starting on 14 December, four MSTS LSTs were made available in response to a French request for sealift in evacuating the 1,500 vehicles now excess to their needs in the North. By the end of January, all military cargo, other than that required to support the dwindling French garrison in Haiphong, had been evacuated.[48]

As the backlog of military cargo decreased, the pressure to move civilian cargo correspondingly increased. The French largely abandoned the industrial capacity of Hanoi and Nam Dinh, partly because of a lack of time and partly because Vietnamese businessmen staying behind hoped to maintain a business-as-usual attitude even after the Communists came to power. On 30 November, Admiral Stump clarified his policy on civilian cargo by stating that none was to be accepted unless the French specifically declared it beyond their capacity to carry. Thirty-six barges fell into this category. Charging the commercial French rate, *Gunston Hall* (LSD–5) hauled the barges south in five trips between 10 January and 28 February 1955. A request from Chinese fishermen in the Along Bay region to transport their 100 fishing boats to Tourane was turned down when the French offered to transport the smaller ones and to provide escorts for the larger boats in April, normally the end of the monsoon, when the weather was expected to turn favorable for the proposed voyage south.[49]

The Final Phase

Commander Amphibious Squadron 1, Captain Augustus R. St. Angelo,

---

[47] COMPHIBGRU1, report, ser 055 of 15 June, encl. 1; Lindholm, *Viet-Nam: The First Five Years*, pp. 69–72.

[48] CTF 90, report, ser 0252 of 8 Nov. 1954; COMPHIBGRU1, report, ser 055 of 15 June 1955, encl. 1.

[49] *Ibid.;* Lindholm, *Viet-Nam: The First Five Years*, pp. 69–71.

had relieved Captain Frank as Commander Task Group 90.8 on 23 January 1955, during the slowdown in operations accompanying the Chinese New Year. At the end of the month, USNS *General R. L. Howze* departed Haiphong on her final trip, with 4,253 passengers. She had carried more than 50,000 refugees during her four and a half month tour in Indochina.

On 18 February, the Vietnamese Refugee Committee officially suspended registration for the evacuation by sea until 1 March. The Committee's president gave two reasons; he hoped to induce more registration later and he felt the camps needed a respite to process the 17,256 refugees who had already registered. Gradually, the backlog declined, the tent camps were closed, and the remaining refugees moved into vacant public buildings in downtown Haiphong. By 20 March, only Camp Lach Tray remained open with a population of 2,165.

In April, USNS *Marine Adder* (AP–193) and *Marine Serpent* (AP–202) sailed on an eight-day cycle. *General A. W. Brewster* (AP–155), arriving to take care of any last-minute influx of refugees, joined the group on 22 April and kept the same schedule. Late in the month four MSTS LSTs joined the force to evacuate the remaining French security troops and their equipment. By the first of May, the camps sheltered only 1,300 people and less than 10,000 others were registered for future transportation.

Captain Winn (now designated Commander Task Group 50.1) had been ordered by Admiral Stump to proceed to Indochina at the beginning of May to supervise the final days of the evacuation. On 6 May, Winn hoisted his pennant in *Cook* (APD–130) at Sangley Point and set sail for Haiphong. Then, on the 13th, the last American ships departed Along Bay and operations shifted to Do Son Peninsula, the final zone to be turned over to the Viet Minh. The next day Captain Winn arrived off the Do Son beaches to observe the final loading. During the embarkation of French troops, ten refugees, among them Nguyen Van Lang, carrying his infant daughter, arrived at the beach and asked to be evacuated. Mr. Lang had chosen freedom for himself and his daughter at the last possible moment, despite the decision of his wife to remain in the North. They boarded *General A. W. Brewster* for the trip south, the last official refugees of the Passage to Freedom.

The French planned to give the Vietnamese one last chance to flee the North. Captain Winn ordered his remaining ships—*Cook, Diachenko* (APD–123), and *Marine Adder*—to join the French Fleet rendezvousing in Lan Ha Bay just south of Henriette Pass. The next day, 16 May, all ships took station in international waters off the coast to rescue any refugees who could reach them. But General Ély had delayed the decision on the rescue operation until too late, and agents had no chance to alert potential refugees to the presence of the rescue ships offshore. As a result, none appeared.

According to the Geneva agreement, the movement of civilians between the North and South was scheduled to cease on 19 May 1955. At the last moment, on the morning of 18 May, all United States ships departed Indochinese waters. Captain Winn sailed for Sangley Point in the Philippines, where on the 20th the Passage to Freedom task force was disestablished.[50]

Since the preceding August, 74 United States Navy and 39 MSTS ships had evacuated 310,848 passengers from North Vietnam, all but 17,846 of them civilians. In addition, the United States Navy and MSTS saved 68,757 tons of cargo and 8,135 vehicles from the Viet Minh. The performance was particularly notable since most of this was accomplished on short notice over the initial three-month period. In combination with the effective ten-month operations of the French, about 800,000 people had been carried to freedom.[51]

In addition to humanitarian considerations, the decision to transport refugees to South Vietnam had economic, political, and security implications. Many of the refugees were settled on fallow fields to grow rice for domestic consumption and export. Their presence, and the realization that they had left their homes for an uncertain future in their search for freedom from Communist dictatorship, represented a potential element of strength in the emerging state of Vietnam.

---

[50] COMPHIBGRU1, report, ser 055 of 15 June, encl. 1: ltr, Winn to Sabin, of 19 May 1955.

[51] COMPHIBGRU1, report, ser 055 of 15 June 1955, encl. 1; Fall, *Two Viet-Nams,* pp. 153–54; SECNAV, "Semiannual Report," Jan.–June 1955 in U.S., Defense Department, *Semiannual Report of the Secretary of Defense,* Jan.–June 1955 (Washington: GPO, 1955), p. 146; Lindholm, *Viet-Nam: The First Five Years,* pp. 49, 56, 60. The figures on the total number of refugees fleeing the North conflict. Bui Van Luong, General Director of the Refugee Committee of the Government of Vietnam, explains that the records of the refugees were destroyed by fire in 1955. He claims that the figure 888,503 is the most reliable. Viet Minh relocations from the South to the North consisted of 90,000 troops but only 40,000 non-active military, including dependents. *U.S.-V.N. Relations,* bk 2, pt. IVA.5, tab 1, pp. 16–17.

CHAPTER XIII

The Changing Role Of The United States In Southeast Asian Security

As the United States Navy helped the French and the State of Vietnam carry out the resettlement provisions of the 20 July 1954 Vietnam agreement, Washington grappled with the more fundamental problem of the security of Southeast Asian states against external and internal threats. The Communists had gained control of China and northern Korea. Now they had been accorded the right to rule northern Vietnam down to the provisional demarkation line along the 17th parallel, halfway between the northern boundary earlier claimed by the Kingdom of Champa and the southern limits of China's zone of occupation after World War II. The future role of the French with regard to the security of South Vietnam was uncertain. Lacking the organization, support, and means of providing for its own defense, the survival of the South Vietnamese government was in doubt.

Ho Chi Minh had characterized the Geneva Conference as "a great victory for our diplomacy," but he and his comrades had much to do before they would be in a position to launch a military offensive or until North Vietnam could act as an effective base for operations in the South. Giap would describe the months that followed as the time when "the north entered the socialist revolutionary phase." First of all, the Viet Minh would consolidate their rule over areas they already occupied and gain control of the "neutral zones" and those areas from which the French were withdrawing. Secondly, they would eliminate opposition and create "an independent and socialist state with a complete national administrative structure." [1]

This would give South Vietnam some time, but it had a long way to go

---
[1] Giap, *Banner of People's War*, p. 45.

before it could become a nation. In the scattered villages and hamlets, and in the delta, lowlands, and mountains, the local populace had, in many cases, lived in relative isolation from other communities and the central government. Ethnic backgrounds, customs, and religions varied. Key areas in the South were largely controlled by three armed, semi-autonomous groups, the so-called Sects. After the majority of the Viet Minh regular forces had been withdrawn to the North, the Communists no longer posed an immediate military threat within South Vietnam. However, they would, through their infrastructure, create and exploit dissension, take political actions, and exert coercion in opposition to Diem and his government. The Viet Minh units which had remained in the South provided nuclei for the formation of guerrilla and organized military units. The long-range danger was particularly great in three areas that had been centers of Viet Minh armed strength—the central highlands of Annam, the region along the Cambodian border west of Saigon, and the Camau Peninsula in the extreme south.[2]

The United States would adopt a twofold approach to the problems of military defense within Southeast Asia. Through collective actions, it would attempt to provide for regional security and strengthen the resolve of peoples within the area. Through unilateral military aid, advice, and training, it would try to enhance the self-defense capabilities of individual states. The United States Navy would be involved in both approaches.

One of the early American actions was to increase its aid to Thailand as the Geneva Convention drew to a close in July 1954.[3]

Southeast Asia Treaty Organization

Assessing the implication of Geneva on 20 August 1954, the National Security Council recommended negotiation of "a Southeast Asia security treaty with the UK [United Kingdom], Australia, New Zealand, France, the Philippines, Thailand and, as appropriate, other free South and Southeast Asian countries willing to participate. . . ." The council identified the following significant consequences which it felt would jeopardize the security interests of the United States in the Far East and increase Communist strength there:

---

[2] *U.S.-V.N. Relations,* bk 2, pt. IVA.5, pp. 8–9.
[3] *U.S.-V.N. Relations,* bk 2, pt. IVA.5, tab 1, p. Q.

a. Regardless of the fate of South Vietnam, Laos and Cambodia, the Communists have secured possession of an advance salient in Vietnam from which military and non-military pressures can be mounted against adjacent and more remote non-Communist areas.

b. The loss of prestige in Asia suffered by the U.S. as a backer of the French and the Bao Dai Government will raise further doubts in Asia concerning U.S. leadership and the ability of the U.S. to check the further expansion of Communism in Asia. Furthermore, U.S. prestige will inescapably be associated with subsequent developments in Southeast Asia.

c. By adopting an appearance of moderation at Geneva and taking credit for the cessation of hostilities in Indochina, the Communists will be in a better position to exploit their political strategy of imputing to the United States motives of extremism, belligerency, and opposition to co-existence seeking thereby to alienate the United States from its allies. The Communists thus have a basis for sharply accentuating their "peace propaganda" and "peace program" in Asia in an attempt to allay fears of Communist expansionist policy and to establish closer relations with the nations of free Asia.

d. The Communists have increased their military and political prestige in Asia and their capacity for expanding Communist influence by exploiting political and economic weakness and instability in the countries of free Asia without resort to armed attack.

e. The loss of Southeast Asia would imperil retention of Japan as a key element in the off-shore island chain.[4]

Discussions between the United States, France, Thailand, and the Philippines during the French-Viet Minh War had already laid much of the groundwork for a regional defense organization. The United States position was that its military actions would be confined to the application of sea and air power in support of the ground forces of other countries. Participation by both European and Asian nations would be a precondition to American military involvement.[5]

Representatives of Pakistan, Thailand, the Philippines, Australia, New Zealand, France, the United Kingdom, and the United States met in Manila in September 1954. The conference adopted a Pacific Charter strongly affirming the right of self-determination and expressing the intent of the signatories to prevent, or counter by appropriate means, any attempt in the treaty area to subvert freedom or to destroy sovereignty or territorial integrity. Another result of the meeting was the drafting of a Southeast Asia Collective Defense Treaty, the basis for the subsequent Southeast Asia

---

[4] NSC, Policy Statement, 5429/2 of 20 Aug. 1954 in *Ibid.*, bk 10, pp. 731–37.

[5] *Ibid.*, bk 1, pt. IVA. 1, pp. A10–A13.

Treaty Organization (SEATO). Each party to the agreement recognized that:

> Aggression by means of armed attack in the treaty area against any of the Parties or against any State or territory which the Parties by unanimous agreement may hereafter designate, would endanger its peace and safety, and agrees that it will in that event act to meet the common danger in accordance with its constitutional processes.

In case of threats by other than armed attacks, which one of the parties considered might endanger the peace of the area or threaten the territory, sovereignty, or political independence of those protected by the treaty, the parties would consult to reach agreement on the measures to be taken for the common defense.[6]

Vice Admiral Arthur C. Davis, Deputy Assistant Secretary of Defense for International Security Affairs and chief Defense Department representative with the delegation at Manila, observed in his report that:

> The Manila Conference convened following communist military achievements in Indochina and political and psychological successes at Geneva. Against this background the effort of the Manila Conference to construct a collective defense arrangement for Southeast Asia and the Southwest Pacific was directed in large measure to recovering from the psychological blow thus administered to the Free World. Much of what was said at the Conference bore witness to the preeminence of psychological objectives in the thinking of participating States. In a real sense, the Treaty that emerged at Manila is a response to the Geneva Agreements.[7]

SEATO, it was hoped, would strengthen the resolve of countries threatened, encourage a combined approach to threats of mutual concern, and help deter aggression.

The Security of South Vietnam

Ho made it clear from the outset that the struggle for control of all Vietnam would continue. Forecasting that "the peaceable and democratic

---

[6] "Southeast Asia Collective Defense Treaty" and "Pacific Charter," of 8 Sept. 1954 in Department of State, *United States Treaties and other International Agreements* (Washington: GPO, 1956), Vol. VI, pt. 1, pp. 81–85, 91–92.

[7] Quoted in *U.S.-V.N. Relations,* bk 1, pt. IVA.1, p. A13.

forces in the world will win," he called on "compatriots, armymen, and cadres" in the South as well as the North "to follow strictly the lines and policies laid down by the [Communist] Party and Government. . . ." Then, describing the situation in Vietnam as shifting "from a state of war to a state of peace," he issued an appeal that "in order to secure all-out and lasting peace, we must fight with might and main." [8]

As France withdrew its forces from the North, the Viet Minh transferred most of their units from the South in accordance with the regroupment provisions of the Geneva agreement. The troops withdrawn could be prepared for reentry into areas in which they had previously operated. About 5,000 Viet Minh troops stayed in the South and provided a nucleus upon which the Communists could later build. An estimated 3,000 members of the Communist political apparatus also remained to provide an infrastructure and spearhead a renewed struggle for power. [9]

Questions remained to be resolved concerning the nature and extent of American assistance to enhance the stability of South Vietnam and aid its efforts to provide security against a Communist take-over. As noted in the Final Declaration of the Geneva Conference, France had declared its readiness "to withdraw its troops from the territory of Cambodia, Laos, and Viet Nam, at the requests of the Governments concerned. . . ." The situation was further complicated by the uncertain status of the government of South Vietnam. France and the State of Vietnam had concluded treaties of independence and association on 4 June 1954. The former treaty recognized the state as fully independent and sovereign, and provided that France would "transfer to the Vietnamese Government all jurisdictions and public services still held by her on Vietnamese territory." The other treaty affirmed the state's association within the French Union. Both treaties were to come into effect when signed, but the signing had never taken place. [10]

Upon conclusion of the treaty negotiations in June, Prince Buu Loc had resigned as South Vietnam's Prime Minister. In France, where he had remained since April, and with the concurrence of the French, Chief of State Bao Dai once again sought the services of the staunch anti-Communist

---

[8] Ho, *On Revolution,* pp. 271–78; "Agreement on the Cessation of Hostilities in Viet-Nam, July 20, 1954" in Allan W. Cameron, ed., *Viet-Nam Crisis: A Documentary History: 1940–1956* (Ithaca, N.Y.: Cornell University Press, 1971), Vol. I, pp. 288–304.

[9] *U.S.-V.N. Relations,* bk 2, pt. IVA.5, tab 1, pp. 16–17.

[10] "Treaty of Independence of the State of Viet-Nam," 4 June 1954, "Treaty of Association between France and Viet-Nam," 4 June 1954, and "Final Declaration of the Geneva Conference," 21 July 1954 in Cameron, *Viet-Nam Crisis,* pp. 268–71, 305–07.

leader Ngo Dinh Diem. This time Diem accepted. On 19 June, Bao Dai appointed him Prime Minister and asked him to form a new government. Coming to the premiership of South Vietnam while the war was still being fought, Diem was given extensive powers. Emperor Bao Dai granted him extensive civilian and military authority.[11]

Ngo Dinh Diem

In view of the predominant part Diem would play in the events to follow, we pause to summarize his background. Jean-Baptiste Ngo Dinh Diem was born on 3 January 1901. The son of a mandarin who had served as both head of the Ministry of Rites (the same agency in which Ho's father once had been employed) and as the Grand Chamberlain to the king, Diem was born into the elite. The Ngo family was deeply attached to Catholicism and counted among its forebearers seventeenth century Catholic converts, some of whom had suffered martyrdom. So strong was Diem's spirtual side that as a young man he took a vow of chastity and never married.[12]

In addition to its ardent Christianity, the family was fiercely nationalistic, a sentiment traceable in part to the service of Diem's father with the Vietnamese monarch. When King Thanh Thai was deposed by the French in 1907, Diem's father retired to his farmlands, while his son attended school at Hue. Meanwhile, Diem had absorbed his father's counsel that he should work for reform from within the system and not by revolution. At Hue, Diem attended the same *Lycée* where Ho had studied ten years before. In 1921, Diem completed the course at the School for Law and Administration at Hanoi, where Indochinese students qualified to enter the government's civil service. As a young man in his twenties, Ngo Dinh Diem became a district chief who administered nearly 300 villages in central Vietnam. His responsibilities included those of a sheriff, judge, tax collector, and director of public works. In 1925, Diem uncovered a Communist underground organization operating in the vicinity of Hue. This discovery led him to the study of communism. According to Diem, his advice was ignored when he informed his French superiors of these subversive activities and advised the

---

[11] Fall, *Two Viet-Nams*, pp. 235–44.
[12] *Ibid.*, p. 40; Fall, *Two Viet-Nams*, p. 235; Joseph Buttinger, *Vietnam at War*, Vol. II of *Vietnam: A Dragon Embattled* (New York: Frederick A. Praeger, 1967), p. 846.

French that, if they were to combat the Communist underground success-fully, they should adopt certain progressive programs in the villages.[13]

By 1929, Diem had become a provincial governor, and had earned the reputation of being a fair judge who refused bribes. He was known for his opposition to the revolutionary rhetoric of many of the young students trained in Canton, Hong Kong, and Saigon.[14]

When Emperor Bao Dai ascended the throne of Annam in 1932, some moderates believed that the young monarch would press for political change. It was apparent to some that Bao Dai's objective was to demonstrate that the Vietnamese could work successfully with the French to effect reforms and advance self-government. When this goal had been accomplished, Bao Dai hoped to secure for Vietnam a greater degree of autonomy. To assist in carrying out this plan, he named Diem Minister of the Interior and head of a reform commission.[15]

In 1933, after Diem had tried unsuccessfully to achieve reforms, he resigned his post, for it seemed clear to him that the French showed no disposition to grant real power to the Vietnamese. Ostensibly, Diem then retired and lived quietly for ten years. In fact, he actively corresponded with other non-Communist Vietnamese nationalists who shared his goal of independence from France.[16]

At the time he assumed office in 1954, Diem's actual military control was confined essentially to a few blocks of Saigon. Moreover, the French controlled the South Vietnamese Armed Forces. The Chief of Staff of the Vietnamese Armed Forces, General Nguyen Van Hinh, was a French ap-pointee, a citizen of France with an air force commission, and a political rival of Diem. Thus, in the summer and fall of 1954, the chances of Diem overcoming the difficulties that his infant government faced seemed slight. In Washington, those responsible for national intelligence estimates judged the prospects for building a strong regime in South Vietnam poor. Further-

---

[13] Robert Shaplen, "The Cult of Diem," *New York Times Magazine* (14 May 1972), p. 42.

[14] Fall, *Two Viet-Nams*, pp. 235, 238–39; Shaplen, "Cult of Diem," p. 40.

[15] Buttinger, *Vietnam: A Political History*, p. 180; Richard Allen, *A Short Introduction to the History and Politics of Southeast Asia* (New York: Oxford University Press, 1968), p. 124; Fall, *Two Viet-Nams*, p. 239.

[16] *Ibid.*

more, they considered it likely that the situation would continue to deteriorate during the next year.[17]

Vietnamese military units created during the French-Viet Minh War were in reality part of the French Union Forces. A sizeable Vietnamese Army was in existence at the time of the Geneva Conference, but it was still largely controlled by the French and lacked the means of independent logistic support. Comparable progress had not been realized in the development of the Vietnamese Navy, which in 1954 consisted of only 1 LSIL, 3 AMSs (high-speed minesweepers), 18 LCMs and LCVPs, and 2 LCUs. Even these few units had French cadres. This force was but a small complement to the French Navy in Indochina, which consisted of 2 small aircraft carriers, 2 cruisers, 75 patrol vessels and minesweepers, almost 300 amphibious ships and craft, and a squadron of PB4Y patrol aircraft.[18]

The Franco-Vietnamese High Committee had proposed a five-year naval development plan, but by the time the plan was sent to the Vietnamese and French governments for approval, it was far too late for any action prior to conclusion of the Geneva agreement. Following this, the High Committee produced yet another plan. It included a shore establishment consisting of a headquarters and receiving station in Saigon; the naval schools at Nha Trang; bases at My Tho, Can Tho, Vinh Long, Hoi An, Tam Ky, and Quang Ngai; and boat repair facilities at Hue, My Tho, and Can Tho. Recognizing the importance of amphibious operations, the committee's plan also included a force of marines, to consist of a headquarters unit, four river companies for duty with *dinassauts,* and one battalion landing force. The Chief of the Vietnamese Joint General Staff, General Hinh, recommended additional ships, a Navy communication station, and the addition of three commando and six light support companies to the marine contingent.[19]

The United States Assumes Added Responsibilities

Thus, Washington faced a number of uncertainties as it sought to arrive

---

[17] *U.S.-V.N. Relations,* bk 2, pt. IVA.5, tab 2, pp. 5–10, 32, 42–43, Q–R; McAlister, *Viet Nam: The Origins of Revolution,* pp. 197–99; Wesley R. Fishel, "Vietnam's Democratic One-Man Rule" in *Viet Nam: History, Documents, and Opinions on a Major World Crisis,* Marvin E. Gettleman, ed. (New York: Fawcett Publications, 1965), pp. 354–55.

[18] Memo, OP–60 to CNO, No. 301–54 of 21 Sept. 1954, App. to encl. A.

[19] Croizat, "Vietnamese Naval Forces," pp. 53–55; NA Saigon, report, 75–S–53 of 19 Sept. 1953, JN–N–59–488, box 24, FRC and 27–54 of 24 Feb. 1954, JN–N–59–2184, box 44, FRC.

at decisions concerning the nature and level of military assistance. Several interrelated questions had to be resolved, including whether or not the United States would carry out training and advisory functions, the nature of relationships with the French, the missions of Vietnamese forces, and the subsequent composition and strength of the Vietnamese armed services.

The question of training had arisen earlier when, in June 1954 after the collapse of Dien Bien Phu, General Ély had requested that the United States take over the training of Vietnamese divisions. On that occasion Washington declined. A week after the Geneva agreement was formalized, General O'Daniel recommended that the United States assume complete control of training the Vietnamese Army in order to develop Vietnam as an "effective barrier [to] continued Communist expansion. . . ." In O'Daniel's view, the following conditions had to be met to achieve this goal: "Financial material and personnel support by US as required; successful execution this program and open cooperation French Government; Vietnamese acceptance US assistance; and active support US program within Free Vietnam means." [20]

In considering General O'Daniel's proposal and a subsequent Army study, the JCS concluded that before the United States undertook the training of Vietnamese armed forces, four preconditions should be met. First, they considered it "absolutely essential that there be a reasonably strong, stable civil government in control." Second, a formal request should be made by the government of each of the Associated States. Third, "arrangements should be made with the French granting full independence to the Associated States and providing for the phased, orderly withdrawal of French forces. . . ." Lastly, "the size and composition of the forces of each of the Associated States should be dictated by the local military requirements and the over-all U.S. interests." Secretary Wilson forwarded these views, with his concurrence, to the Department of State on 12 August.

The State Department did not agree to insistence on preconditions. On 18 August, Dulles wrote to Wilson that reorganization and training of the Vietnamese forces was "one of the most efficient means of enabling the Vietnamese Government to become strong. . . ." Noting that "there is no obstacle whatever to the setting up of a U.S. training mission" in Cambodia, Secretary Dulles recommended that the JCS "give their consent to the establishment of a MAAG/Phnom Penh." In addition, he asked that they give

---

[20] *U.S.-V.N. Relations,* bk 2, pt. IVA.4, pp. P, 3, bk 1, pt. IVA.3, pp. 7–8; msg, CHMAAG, of 8 Aug. 1954 in *Ibid.,* bk 10, pp. 703–04.

their "sympathetic consideration" to the establishment of a training mission within MAAG Indochina. Two days later the National Security Council concluded that the United States "would continue to provide limited military assistance and training missions, wherever possible, to the states of Southeast Asia. . . ." Military and economic assistance should be given to Indochina "working through the French only insofar as necessary." [21]

Another matter to be resolved, upon which the size of the military assistance program would hinge, was determining the objectives of the armed forces of the Associated States. In the judgement of the Joint Chiefs, these objectives were:

> VIETNAM—To attain and maintain internal security and to deter Viet Minh aggression by a limited defense of the Geneva Armistice demarcation line.
> CAMBODIA—To maintain internal security and provide for a limited defense of the country.
> LAOS—To maintain insofar as possible internal security. (It is recognized that LAOS does not have the capability to defend against overt aggression.)

The Joint Chiefs noted that the Vietnamese government's request for withdrawal of French forces would create a power vacuum. Although the Vietnamese Armed Forces would not be capable of stemming or repelling aggression, they could sustain a limited defense and complement collective action. The JCS pointed out that the Geneva agreement had been interpreted as restricting the number of American military advisors in Vietnam to 342—a number which "would permit only limited participation in the over-all training program" with "limited beneficial effect. . . ." For this reason, the Joint Chiefs concluded that from a military point of view the United States should not train the Vietnamese Armed Forces. They added, however, that "if it is considered that political considerations are overriding, the Joint Chiefs of Staff would agree to the assignment of a training mission to MAAG, Saigon. . . ." [22]

The resultant United States policy, as defined by the State and Defense Departments on 21 October 1954, essentially followed the former's views. The policy statement defined the American goal as giving support to Diem's

---

[21] Memo, JCS to SECDEF, of 4 Aug. 1954, ltrs, SECDEF to SECSTATE, of 12 Aug. 1954 and SECSTATE to SECDEF, of 18 Aug. 1954, and NSC, Policy Statement, 5429/2 of 20 Aug. 1954 in *Ibid.*, pp. 717–18, 728–41.

[22] Memo, JCS to SECDEF, of 19 Oct. 1954 in *Ibid.*, pp. 771–74.

government and assisting that government initially "(a) to promote internal security and political stability in Free Vietnam, (b) to establish and maintain control by that Government throughout the territory of Free Vietnam, and (c) effectively to counteract Viet Minh infiltration and paramilitary activities south of the 17th parallel." [23]

A joint message from the State and Defense Departments authorized the American Ambassador and the Chief of the MAAG in Saigon to initiate a "crash" program for training. President Eisenhower notified Diem of his desire to provide more effective aid to Vietnam, the purpose being to assist in "developing and maintaining a strong, viable state, capable of resisting attempted subversion or aggression through military means."

The die was cast. By making commitments for both direct aid and military training, the United States was in effect relieving the French of some of their responsibilities for the future security of the new state of South Vietnam. However, before the aid was furnished, the President required assurances from the State of Vietnam concerning standards of performance and expectations of reform on the part of Diem's government. The assurances were given. [24]

Force Levels

In their recommendation of 4 August 1954, the Joint Chiefs of Staff had proposed a South Vietnamese Army of 234,000 men and an Air Force of 5,000 men and five aircraft squadrons. The Office of the Chief of Naval Operations concluded that the Vietnamese Navy's needs were far too great to be satisfied practically in the near future. Based on the limited number of trained officers and men available, the goals recommended were 152 small ships and craft for fiscal year 1955, increasing to 162 the next year. These goals were endorsed by the Joint Chiefs. The recommendation of forces was based on two assumptions: first, that the French would leave behind MDAP supplied craft; and second, that the Vietnamese Navy would expand gradually to take over these craft, beginning with the current personnel level of 1,400 and increasing to 3,000. [25]

---

[23] Msg, Joint State-Defense, of 21 Oct. 1954 in *Ibid.*, pp. 784–88.

[24] *Ibid.;* "Aid to the State of Viet-Nam: Message from the President of the United States to the President of the Council of Ministers of Viet-Nam, October 23, 1954" in *The Department of State Bulletin,* XXXI (15 Nov. 1954), pp. 735–36.

[25] Memo, OP–60 to CNO, No. 301–54 of 21 Sept. 1954.

The JCS submitted no force levels for Laos because the Geneva Armistice restrictions on Laos permitted training, assistance, and supervision by French instructors only. For Cambodia, ground forces of some 57,000 men were recommended. Two decades later the fate of Cambodia would hinge on the ability to transport munitions and supplies up the Mekong. However, despite the importance of this great river, its tributaries, and other waterways, the Joint Chiefs of Staff provided for no naval forces in the plan. Their reason was the absence of a trained Cambodian nucleus for this service. For the same reason the JCS did not include a recommendation for an air force.[26]

The State Department disagreed with the force levels proposed for Indochina. In a lengthy letter to Secretary of Defense Wilson, which also dealt with the Joint Chiefs' reservations concerning support and training, Dulles set forth "important political and policy" considerations. In his evaluation, he stated that the JCS-proposed force levels "seem to be excessive" and he considered it "imperative that the United States Government prepare a firm position on the size of the forces we consider a minimum level to assure the internal security of Indochina." The President then requested that the Joint Chiefs of Staff submit, as soon as possible, a "long-range program for the reorganization and training of the minimum number of Free Vietnamese forces necessary for internal security." [27]

Attempted Coup

While these matters were being debated, Diem faced a crisis in Saigon. In September 1954, after learning of a coup being planned by Chief of Staff Hinh, he reorganized his cabinet to win the cooperation of some leaders of the Hoa Hao, Cao Dai, and Binh Xuyen Sects in the coming confrontation. General Hinh made his move on 26 October, when an attack on the palace was repulsed. Three weeks later, at Bao Dai's request, Hinh left for France. Not until 12 December was Diem able to obtain French assent to the appointment of General Le Van Ty as Hinh's replacement. Ty was considered by Diem to be loyal to his government. Yet, in gaining French concurrence, Diem was forced to agree to appoint General

---

[26] Memo, JCS to SECDEF, of 22 Sept. 1954 in *U.S.-V.N. Relations,* bk 10, pp. 756–58, bk 1, pt. IVA.3, p. 9; memo, OP–60 to CNO, No. 301–54 of 21 Sept. 1954.

[27] Ltr, SECSTATE to SECDEF, of 11 Oct. 1954 in *U.S.-V.N. Relations,* bk 10, pp. 768–69, bk. 2, pt. IVA.4, p. 5.

Nguyen Van Vy as the inspector general of the Vietnamese Armed Forces. In contrast to General Ty, General Vy was reportedly pro-French and pro-Bao Dai.[28]

Ordered to Vietnam as Special United States Representative with the rank of Ambassador, General J. Lawton Collins, former Army Chief of Staff, was directed to confer with Ambassador Heath, soon to return from a four and a half year tour in Indochina; and to explore with Prime Minister Diem and his government how a program of direct aid could best assist them in resolving "their present critical problems." Collins also was instructed to maintain close liaison with General Paul Ély, the French Commissioner General and Commander in Chief of the French Union Forces, "for the purpose of exchanging views on how best, under existing circumstances, the freedom and welfare of Viet-Nam can be safeguarded." To carry out his mission, Collins was given the authority to coordinate the operations of all American agencies in Vietnam.[29]

In early November, the Joint Chiefs of Staff, as directed by the President, prepared revised force levels based on the assumption that the sole military objective would be the maintenance of internal security. Secretary Dulles now had his own source of military as well as political advice. Before the JCS views were received, Ambassador Collins submitted his recommendations to the secretary. The number of military personnel he recommended, an army of 77,685 and a small navy and air force, was about half the current strength. Although Collins felt Diem's initial reaction to his presentation of the broad concepts and the program outlined was favorable, he thought it would be very difficult to obtain Diem's acceptance of the proposed reduction in Vietnamese forces from the current level of about 170,000 men to less than 90,000.[30]

Diem hardly could have been expected to react otherwise. British experiences in Malaya were furnishing some indication of the numbers required to defeat Communist guerrillas in the Southeast Asian environment. The 5 to 1 security forces to guerrilla ratio at the beginning of the Malayan

---

[28] *Ibid.,* pt. IVA.4, pp. S–W, pt. IVA.5, tab 2, p. 43; Buttinger, *Vietnam: A Political History,* p. 398.

[29] "Mission of the Special United States Representative in Viet-Nam: Statement issued by the White House," 3 Nov. 1954 in U.S., Congress, Senate, Committee on Foreign Relations, *Background Information Relating to Southeast Asia and Vietnam,* 4th Rev. Ed. (90th Cong., 2nd sess.) (Washington: GPO, 1968), p. 107.

[30] Memo, SECSTATE to President, of 17 Nov. 1953 in *U.S.-V.N. Relations,* bk 10, pp. 800–01, bk 2, pt. IVA.4, p. 18.

emergency was insufficient; during the critical pacification phase, a ratio of 12 to 1 was needed to defeat the insurgents; and in the final phase a ratio of at least 25 to 1 was employed. Moreover, the job to be done was far more than countering guerrilla actions. South Vietnam had not yet been forged into a nation. Before this could be done there were armed forces other than the Communists with which to contend. These were the established armed forces of the three, semi-autonomous regional Sects, equipped by the French during the French-Viet Minh War and numbering 30,000 to 40,000 troops. Also, the Communist threat was more than a purely internal one. North Vietnam would provide a main base for the provision of military supplies and personnel. In addition to the Viet Minh cadre who remained in the South and the Communist cells, many southerners—one estimate was 50,000—were in training in the North to prepare for infiltration below the 17th parallel.[31] And there was always the possibility of a North Vietnamese Army offensive against the State of Vietnam.

Concurring in Collins's recommendations, the Secretary of State requested that the Department of Defense reconsider its position with respect to Vietnamese force levels. The Joint Chiefs of Staff submitted a revised proposal for a total of 88,000 personnel. By 20 January 1955, the United States agreed to train and support a Vietnamese force of 100,000 men. The increase from the earlier figure was accepted, in deference to continuing Vietnamese arguments for a larger force.[32]

With this compromise, the United States reached its basic decisions on military aid and training of Vietnamese forces. The succeeding months would reveal the inadequacy of the reduced force levels which the United States deemed sufficient for the internal security of South Vietnam. Step by step, these levels would have to be increased.

The effectiveness of American military assistance would hinge on the relationships established with the French as well as with the Vietnamese. On 16 November 1954, Ambassador Collins presented General Ély with his proposed arrangements for the development and training of autonomous Vietnamese armed forces. The draft of a minute of understanding specified that:

---

[31] Robert Thompson, *Revolutionary War in World Strategy 1945–1969* (New York: Taplinger, 1970), p. 122; Robert Thompson, *Defeating Communist Insurgency* (New York: Frederick A. Praeger, 1966), p. 48.

[32] *U.S.-V.N. Relations,* bk 2, p. Y, pt. IVA.4, pp. 17–19, bk 1, pt. IVA.3, pp. 11–12.

a. The U.S. agrees to support and maintain for one year (to 1 July 1956), a program of direct aid to Vietnam designed to develop military forces. . . .

b. "Full autonomy" (command by Vietnamese personnel) will be granted to the Armed Forces of Vietnam not later than 1 July 1955.

c. Full responsibility, to be exercised by US Chief MAAG Indochina, for assisting Vietnam in the organization and training of its forces to be assumed by the US on 1 January 1955.

d. French personnel to assist in the training of Vietnamese forces under direction of the US chief of MAAG.

e. Once the full US MAAG capability has been attained French training and advisory personnel will be gradually phased out.[33]

General Ély agreed to every stipulation set forth in Ambassador Collins's proposal except one. He could not accept the provision that all French personnel be removed from advisory positions with Vietnam's Armed Forces. General Ély explained that no French government or assembly would allow American personnel completely to replace the French in training Vietnamese and that he intended to notify Mendès-France of their fundamental difference on this basic point. During his visit to Washington, Mendès-France made it clear to Secretary Dulles that the French were strongly opposed to the United States assuming complete charge of training the Vietnamese and replacing French personnel and influence.[34]

Interim Solution

Faced with the possibility of further delay in obtaining a formal, written Franco-American agreement, American and French leaders in Saigon demonstrated an understanding of the urgency of the local situation by arriving at an interim compromise. The nucleus of a Franco-American Mission to the Armed Forces of Vietnam, designated the Training Relations Instruction Mission (TRIM), was established on 3 December 1954.

Lieutenant General O'Daniel[35] directed the *ad hoc* mission "to set in motion at once appropriate measures to assist the Armed Forces of Vietnam in preparing and carrying out a comprehensive . . . (pacification) program."

---

[33] Memo, OP–61 to SECNAV, ser 00190P61 of 19 Nov. 1954.

[34] *U.S.-V.N. Relations,* bk 1, pt. IVA.3, p. 18, bk 2, pt. IVA.4, pp. 13–18; memo, OP–61 to SECNAV, ser 000240 of 22 Nov. 1954; "Mission of the Special United States Representative" in *Background Information Relating to Southeast Asia and Vietnam,* p. 107.

[35] The rank of lieutenant general had been restored on 30 Aug. 1954.

Reorganization and training of the armed forces were to be accomplished concurrently, but military operations to establish governmental authority in South Vietnam clearly had priority. Operating procedures, yet to be established, were designed to exploit every opportunity to influence the Vietnamese to "do it themselves." Under no circumstances was the mission to put itself in the position of directing the activities of the Vietnamese forces or their commanders.[36]

Within the next five days, the mission installed its nucleus of 5 French and 5 American officers (in each instance 3 Army, 1 Navy, 1 Air Force) within the Vietnamese headquarters.[37] Although the assigned strength of the mission had increased to a total of 109 men (33 U.S. and 76 French) by the end of February 1955, and the number continued to grow, the United States Navy's representation consisted of only one officer. This small group reviewed Vietnamese Joint General Staff directives regarding pacification, surveyed all Vietnamese military training facilities, analyzed the Vietnamese force level requirements, and prepared for the establishment of a full-scale advisory mission in anticipation of formal agreements at the governmental level concerning American participation in training the Vietnamese.

Diem's position during this period remained precarious. Ambassador Collins expressed uncertainty that Diem was capable of managing the country. By mid-December, he was no longer "uncertain" but "convinced" that Diem did not have the ability to unify the divided factions in Vietnam. The general reported that, based on what he had observed in Saigon to that time, the only sound solution, though the "least desirable," might be for the United States gradually to withdraw from Vietnam altogether.[38]

North Vietnam

During this period, the Communists in North Vietnam had been encountering their own problems, but were making progress. One of the sources of opposition was in the mountainous regions of the northwest, where tribes

---

[36] Ltr, O'Daniel to Carbonel and Rosson, of 3 Dec. 1954.

[37] The naval officer was Commander Alan R. Josephson from the MAAG. He was relieved by Commander James E. Ross in March 1955.

[38] Memo, Heath to Robertson, of 17 Dec. 1954 in *U.S.-V.N. Relations,* bk 10, pp. 824–25, bk 1, pt. IVA.3, pp. 19–21, bk 9, p. XXXVIII.

of ethnically non-Vietnamese people resisted domination by the Vietnamese Communists. These tribes created such difficulties that, in May 1955, the party would announce the establishment of the Thai-Meo Autonomous Zone, for the purpose of eliminating dissension and providing a mechanism for control. More serious were the difficulties arising from widespread opposition to the land collectivization program, particularly in Thanh Hoa and Nghe An Provinces in central North Vietnam between the Red River Delta and Vinh. This region would later become the scene of anti-Communist revolts. To carry out this Maoist-style land reform program, which was initiated before Geneva, Ho's apparatus resorted to punitive taxes, terror, arrests, and public condemnation, trials, and executions. Determined to eliminate landlord and rich peasant classes basically opposed to communism and to gain the mass support of the poor majority, the Viet Minh stepped up their campaign of land expropriation and redistribution in the months following Geneva. This was accomplished by public denunciations of landowners, public trials before special People's Courts, sentencing of the "guilty" to penalties ranging from forced labor to death, and the immediate redistribution of the land and goods of those convicted. One Hanoi magazine divulged that, "people were arrested, jailed, interrogated, and cruelly tortured; people were executed or shot out of hand and their property confiscated. Innocent children of parents wrongly classified as landlords were starved to death." [39]

Once such sources of opposition were brought under control, the Communist Party and the government sought to establish a "stable and powerful revolutionary base" for the struggle to gain control over the rest of Indochina. They prepared for future combat by taking steps "to consolidate the national defense system of all the people" throughout Vietnam. The army in the North, increased by five divisions during the five months following Geneva, was employed as "the tool of the proletarian dictatorship. . . ." South of the 17th parallel, they sought to build solid bases "in cities, and to associate the local rear base area . . . with the common rear base of the entire country." [40]

---

[39] Quoted in J. Price Gittinger, "Communist Land Policy in North Viet Nam," *Far Eastern Survey,* XXVIII (Aug. 1959), p. 118.

[40] Giap, *Banner of People's War,* pp. 32–45; Giap, *People's War, People's Army,* p. 37; Ho, *On Revolution,* pp. 276–78, 301–03; *U.S.-V.N. Relations,* bk 2, pt. IVA.4, pp. 8–9.

A "Small, Highly Efficient Navy"

The naval objective of the combined French-American mission stemmed from recommendations made by United States advisors on 15 January 1955. These called for assistance in the development of a "small, highly efficient navy," capable of conducting operations which might involve any of the following tasks:

a. Limited amphibious operations.
b. River and coastal patrol.
c. Minesweeping.
d. Direct fire support.
e. Logistic support for military forces.[41]

The American objective was ambitious, but the need for such a navy was real. In the vast region of the Mekong Delta most of the transportation was by water. In some parts, inland waterways were the only means of surface transportation. The success of the State of Vietnam depended on the waterborne movement of rice and goods, on naval actions against enemy riverine lines of communication, on amphibious-type operations, on gunfire support of troops ashore, and on logistical resupply by water. Along the lengthy, indented coast, inshore and offshore naval units also could play important roles by intercepting enemy movements along the coast and preventing infiltration of supplies by sea.

Initially the French agreed to train deck, engineering, and supply officers and to carry out training exercises for all Vietnamese Navy units while under French operational control. The Americans would maintain a small detachment of officer and enlisted personnel at the Naval Training Center, Nha Trang. The detachment would assist with training aids, school equipment, and the material requirements of the center. United States personnel would conduct classroom instruction only in the event of a shortage of French or Vietnamese instructors. Additionally, the Americans were responsible for establishing and operating a small unit at Saigon to carry out afloat training of Vietnamese naval units (refresher training, lasting three weeks or less for each ship), and to provide short courses on the maintenance and operation of equipment in these units. The American element of the combined mission was also charged with arranging for certain out-of-country training

---

[41] Navy Section, TRIM, Monthly Report, No. 1 of 21 Mar. 1955.

of Vietnamese naval personnel. Vietnamese trainees would be required to have a working knowledge of English or be provided with qualified English-Vietnamese or English-French interpreters.[42]

Separate from the French Training Mission, the combined mission was at best a compromise arrangement for the transitional period. For the time being, American influence on the Vietnamese Navy would be minimal, since *de facto* control of operations and training was centered in one individual—French Captain Jean Récher. He served in three positions: Commander in Chief of the Vietnamese Navy, Senior French Naval Representative on the French Training Mission Staff, and head of the Navy Division of the combined mission. The American naval personnel assigned were thus, in essence, advisors to the French personnel who commanded the Vietnamese Navy, trained its personnel, and through the Navy Yard at Saigon, repaired its ships and craft.[43]

Although obviously in its infancy, this Navy soon would be called upon to do its part to eliminate armed opposition to the government within South Vietnam.

---

[42] Navy Section, MAAG, "Directive of Chief MAAG Indochina Establishing the Training Relations and Instruction Mission to the Armed Forces of Vietnam," of 27 Feb. 1955. Also, this directive made the Vietnamese Navy responsible (with advice and assistance from TRIM) for all training of personnel and units not specifically allocated to the French and U.S. elements of TRIM.

[43] Navy Section, MAAG Vietnam, "Naval Forces of Vietnam," p. 6.

CHAPTER XIV

The Republic Of Vietnam And A National Navy, 1955-1956

During the next three years, the South Vietnamese would gain operational control over their riverine naval units, and replace French personnel in the Vietnamese Navy Headquarters with their own officers and men. The operation of the small river force would play crucial roles in the action to put down dissident military forces, thus helping pave the way for the establishment of the Republic of Vietnam. First jointly with the French, and then alone, United States training, advisory, and maintenance assistance would help the Vietnamese in this period to build their navy and establish a Sea Force and a Marine Force to complement the River Force. The Sea Force would "show the flag" in visits to nearby countries and conduct limited coastal patrol and landings on strategically located islands. But, this would be a period of low-level activity in the conflict between the Communists and South Vietnam, as North Vietnam consolidated its control and prepared for a period of increased violence in its continuing efforts to gain control of the South.

The foremost problem facing Diem's government in 1955 was that of overcoming the opposition of the three Sects. Both political and military actions would be required. The strongholds of these semi-autonomous states were in the area formerly known as Cochin China, peopled in earlier times by Malays and Khmers and later by Vietnamese who had migrated south from Annam. Waterways were the key to control of the regions where the Sects were located and riverine operations would be required.

Each of the Sects had military forces, with arms, munitions, and equipment supplied to them by the French to aid in the war against the Viet Minh. Although this aid had been formally withdrawn, the Sects continued to receive French funds and advice. The Cao Dai religious Sect was centered at Tay Ninh, northwest of Saigon next to the "Parrot's Beak" section of the Cambodian border. Its armed followers totalled 15,000 to 20,000 men.

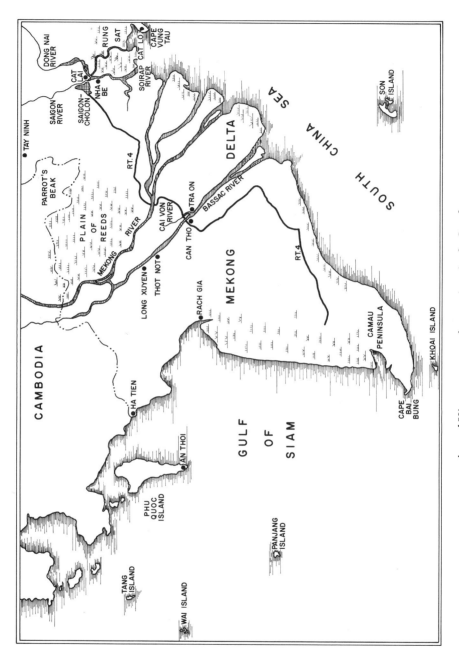

Area of Vietnamese naval operations in the South.

Further south were the Phat Giao Hoa Hao, believers in a Vietnamese development of Therevada Buddhism with a history of religious, political, and military organization and activity. Mainly occupying a belt across the Mekong Delta (centered at Can Tho on the Bassac River, one of the two main branches of the Mekong system), the Hoa Hao maintained 10,000 to 15,000 men under arms. The third so-called Sect was the Binh Xuyen which, through its army of 2,500 soldiers, its control of the police apparatus, and the support of 5,000 to 8,000 other followers, dominated prostitution, narcotics, and gambling in Saigon-Cholon.[1]

Before the State of Vietnam could cope with the threat posed by these dissident forces, the government would have to gain control of its own armed forces. A breakthrough was realized in January 1955, when the United States reaffirmed its backing of Diem, when American military aid was placed under the control of the State of Vietnam, and when General Ély announced that the French would withdraw as soon as there was a secure government. The Franco-American military mission achieved official status and a new name in February as General O'Daniel was given the additional assignment as Chief of the Training Relations and Instruction Mission to the Armed Forces of Vietnam.[2]

On 11 February, France announced transfer of command of the Vietnamese Armed Forces to Diem.[3] The full transfer would not be completed until several months later, but Diem could now conduct his own military actions to promote internal security.

Civil War

Shortly thereafter, Diem initiated actions against the Binh Xuyen by shutting down vice concessions in Saigon and Cholon. Then, on 4 March,

---

[1] *U.S.-V.N. Relations,* bk 2, pt. IVA.5, tab 2, pp. 5–8, 18; Ann C. Crawford, *Customs and Culture of Vietnam* (Rutland, Vt.: Charles E. Tuttle Co., 1966), pp. 70–73, 80–83.

[2] Navy Section, MAAG Vietnam, "Naval Forces of Vietnam," p. 6; Navy Section, TRIM, Monthly Report, No. 1 of 21 Mar. 1955; *U.S.-V.N. Relations,* bk 1, pt. IVA.3, pp. 25–26. Initially the Franco-American mission was designated Advisory Training and Organization Mission (ATOM), later briefly changed to Military Support Mission (MSM); see NA Saigon, report, 5–S–55 of 22 Feb. 1955, JN 60A–2142, box 62, FRC.

[3] *U.S.-V.N. Relations,* bk 2, pt. IVA.4, pp. X, Y, Z.

with an announcement by the Cao Dai pope of the formation of a United Front of Nationalist Forces, the Cao Dai, Hoa Hao, and Binh Xuyen began a civil war. Four days later rebel forces staged uprisings in towns northwest of Saigon and on the Camau Peninsula at the southern tip of Vietnam. Diem, ordering that the rebel bands be destroyed, sent forty infantry battalions into action. On 21 March, the United Front released a declaration opposing Diem. Attached to the declaration was a thinly veiled ultimatum requesting that Diem form a government of national union within five days. Diem refused.[4]

National Army troops took over the Central Police Headquarters in Saigon a week later. Diem announced his intention to replace the Binh Xuyen police commissioner and to occupy the *Sureté* headquarters in central Saigon, but the French dissuaded him.

On the night of 29–30 March 1955, the Binh Xuyen attacked the National Army headquarters and the central police compound. They fired into the palace grounds. As Diem prepared to retaliate, General Ély—concerned over the security of European nationals in Saigon, possibly influenced by the anti-Diem feelings of many French officials, and supported by Ambassador Collins—pressured Diem into calling off a major assault. While French and Binh Xuyen troops took up fortified positions in Saigon, some sectors were declared off limits to the National Army. The French, still controlling supplies for the Vietnamese Army, withheld ammunition and fuel.[5]

Tensions mounted daily in Saigon. Both Ély and Collins reached the conclusion that Diem should be replaced. Then, on 26 April, Diem dismissed the Binh Xuyen police chief and ordered members of the police force to report to his successor by 28 April. When the Binh Xuyen moved against the government that morning, Diem promptly ordered his troops to attack. Bao Dai directed that Diem proceed to Paris and turn command of the Army over to French-sponsored General Vy. Diem again refused.

By 10 May 1955, Diem had established effective control over Saigon. To further strengthen his position, the cabinet was reformed by adding many of his own followers. On the 15th, Diem dissolved the Imperial Guard of

---

[4] *Ibid.,* p. AA, pt. IVA.5, tab 2, p. 18; Lancaster, *Emancipation of French Indochina*, pp. 334–85.

[5] *U.S.-V.N. Relations,* bk 2, pt. IVA.4, pp. AA–BB; Lancaster, *Emancipation of French Indochina*, pp. 385–86; Buttinger, *Vietnam: A Political History*, pp. 401–04.

the Emperor and merged it with the Army. Bao Dai was deposed as Emperor six days later.[6]

That same month the Vietnamese Ministry of Defense approved a development plan for an eventual 3,000-man Vietnamese Navy and Marine Corps as proposed by the Chief of TRIM. Americans in the mission on 31 May totalled 155. However, there were only two U.S. Navy and one Marine officers.[7] Several months later when the total force level for the Vietnamese armed services was raised to 150,000, their Navy and Marine Corps were authorized 4,000 men.

Operations in the Delta

In May 1955, when the French transferred command of the four Vietnamese *dinassauts* to the senior officer of the new navy, Lieutenant Commander Le Quang My, the State of Vietnam was ready for limited riverine operations. Then, on 5 June, little more than a month after the victory in Saigon, Diem launched an offensive against the Hoa Hao in the Mekong Delta. Under My's command, the Vietnamese River Force patrolled the waterways and transported Army troops and supplies in areas where travel by boat was the major, and often only, means of travel.[8]

On the first day of the operation, the Vietnamese Navy landed two Army regiments on the Cai Von River near Can Tho. General O'Daniel had forbidden American Army or Navy observers to participate. However, reports reached the Naval Attache that, although communication problems delayed maneuvering and beaching, the Vietnamese Navy displayed "enthusiasm and pride in conducting their own show," carried out their mission, and "made a fine impression." The first day's operation resulted in the capture of the insurgent headquarters of Tran Van Soai, one of the Hoa Hao leaders, and the surrender of two of his battalions. Two nights later, *Dinassauts* 22, 23, and 25 (commanded by My from flagship LSSL *No Than*) landed 2,000 Army troops near Tra On, on the Bassac River

---

[6] *U.S.-V.N. Relations,* bk 2, pt. IVA.4, p. BB, pt. IVA.5, tab 2, p. 18; NA Saigon, reports, 55–55 of 18 July 1955 and 66–55 of 30 Aug. 1955, JN–60A–2142, box 62, FRC; Lancaster, *Emancipation of French Indochina,* p. 390.

[7] Navy Section, TRIM. Monthly Report, No. 4 of 1 June 1955; MAAG Indochina, "Personnel Roster as of 31 May 1955;" Navy Section, MAAG Vietnam, "Naval Forces of Vietnam," pp. 6–9.

[8] NA Saigon, reports, 12–S–55 of 8 July 1955 and 49–55 of 23 June 1955, JN 60A–2142, box 62, FRC.

twenty miles below Can Tho. During this operation naval units captured six Hoa Hao patrol boats and two LCMs.[9]

In a third major operation during the week of 12 June, two *dinassauts* transported Army units through a difficult marsh area in the vicinity of Thot Not thirty miles upriver from Can Tho. Almost the entire Vietnamese Navy continued to participate in other operations against the Hoa Hao. Organized resistance in the Can Tho area ended on 19 June after Ba Cut, a dissident Hoa Hao leader, was forced to withdraw his 3,500-man force.[10]

The Anti-Communist Denunciation Campaign

The Final Declaration of the Geneva Conference—approved in a voice vote by all participants except the United States—had provided for general elections to be held in Vietnam in July 1956, "effected on the basis of respect for the principles of independence, unity, and territorial integrity. . . ." The declaration specified that consultations would be held on this subject between representatives of the two zones from 20 July 1955 onward. The United States favored elections in Vietnam as a means of unifying the country, "provided they are held under conditions of genuine freedom which the Geneva armistice agreement calls for." As the time for the 1955 consultations approached, Diem concluded that these conditions could not be met in the North. He declared that "South Viet Nam, not having signed the Geneva Agreement, would not take part in general elections unless they were guaranteed to be free in the North as well as in the South." Consequently the State of Vietnam refused to participate in the scheduled consultations on the grounds that the people in the more populous North would not be able to express their will freely and that their falsified votes could overwhelm the votes in South Vietnam.[11]

The Communists continued to be occupied by their own problems in the North and hoped that their ambitions in the South would be furthered by internal disintegration of the State of Vietnam. Their efforts in the South focused primarily on fostering opposition to the government of Diem and

---

[9] *Ibid.;* NA Saigon, report 47–55 of 17 June 1955, JN 60A–2142, box 62, FRC.

[10] *Ibid.;* NA Section, Joint Weekly Analyses, 23 of 12 June 1955, 24 of 19 June 1955, and 25 of 26 June 1955.

[11] *U.S.-V.N. Relations,* bk 2, pt. IVA.4, p. EE; John F. Dulles, Press Conference of 20 June 1955 in *The Department of State Bulletin,* XXXIII (11 July 1955), p. 50.

creating conditions that would favor the Democratic Republic of Vietnam in a general election. They also took preparatory measures for a possible future uprising, in case political success was not achieved, by recruiting in the villages, constructing base areas, and expanding an increasingly intricate administrative, intelligence, and propaganda network. Diem answered with anti-Communist denunciation campaigns in the summer of 1955 and the establishment of centers for political re-education of the Communists and their active supporters.[12]

Command of the Vietnamese Navy

On 1 July 1955, the French finally relinquished their overall command of the Vietnamese Navy, which had been exercised through Captain Rechér. Diem assigned Brigadier General Tran Van Don, the Army's Deputy Chief of Staff (Operations), additional duties as Deputy Chief of Staff (Navy) and as Commander in Chief of the Vietnamese Navy. This unusual development arose from differences between French and Vietnamese authorities over the proposed appointment of Lieutenant Commander My as Captain Rechér's relief. Vice Admiral Edouard Jozan, Commander in Chief French Naval Forces, Far East and Acting Commander in Chief, Indochina, threatened to withdraw all French naval personnel and logistical support assigned to the Vietnamese Navy if My assumed the command. His objections stemmed from allegations against My of misappropriation of funds and other questionable behavior. A routine TRIM report, attributable to Captain Rechér, stated that "the shift in command was apparently for political considerations only, as the entire administrative section of the Navy at *FAVN* [Vietnamese Armed Forces] Headquarters is staffed with French personnel."[13]

General Don's tour as head of the Navy was soon terminated. By Presidential Order, on 20 August 1955, Diem appointed Lieutenant Commander My Deputy Chief of Staff (Navy) and Commander in Chief of the Vietnamese Navy. Four days later My declared that all French naval personnel "would be available for reassignment to duties other than with the FAVN

---

[12] *U.S.-V.N. Relations*, bk 2, pt. IVA.5, tab 2, pp. 27, 50.

[13] NA Saigon, report, 12–S–55 of 8 July 1955, JN 60A–2142, box 62, FRC; Navy Division, TRIM, Monthly Report, No. 6 of 1 Aug. 1955.

staff as of 1 September." Admiral Jozan promptly directed French head-quarters personnel to report to TRIM.[14]

Operations in the Rung Sat

Driven out of Saigon, the hard core of the Binh Xuyen fled to the Rung Sat swamp, south of Saigon. During the summer, they used the area as a base for acts of terrorism, such as the employment of plastic explosives against American vehicles and buildings in Saigon and mortar attacks against the Vietnamese base at Nha Be, about seven miles downriver from Saigon. Nha Be later would be the site of a major base for United States Navy operations on inland waters.

As Americans would learn later, rooting guerrillas out of the Rung Sat, the "Forest of Assassins," posed extraordinarily difficult problems. Covering about 300 square miles, the area consisted almost entirely of waterways and mangrove-covered swamp land. The western boundary of this strategi-cally located swamp was the Soirap River, one of the two major branches that diverged from the Saigon River at Nha Be. The other branch was the main shipping channel to Saigon (the Long Tau River) which wound its way through the the eastern fringe of the Rung Sat to the South China Sea off Cape Vung Tau. The Rung Sat was crisscrossed by many waterways with tidal ranges between five and eight feet, and the only road was a short secondary one which traversed the southern tip of the area.

In addition to using the Rung Sat as a base for guerrilla actions, Binh Xuyen forces attacked shipping on the Long Tau. On one occasion, seven Vietnamese and French sailors were wounded and one Frenchman was killed in minesweeper *Chuong Duong* as the ship undertook trials after an overhaul in the Saigon shipyard. In response to such attacks, the South Vietnamese government announced on 5 September 1955 that shipping on the Long Tau and Soirap would henceforth be escorted by LCMs.[15]

Diem launched a major offensive against these entrenched forces in the same month. In a joint Army-Navy operation, South Vietnamese units

---

[14] Navy Division, TRIM, Monthly Report, No. 7 of 1 Sept. 1955. According to a Naval Attache report, Admiral Jozan tried to deny Lieutenant Commander My his assignment. In a conference with Diem, Jozan criticized My as an officer and attacked his professional capability. Diem reportedly observed that, "the French Navy trained him;" see NA Saigon, report, 14–S–55 of 4 Oct. 1955, JN 60A–2142, box 62, FRC.

[15] NA Section, Joint Weekly Analyses, 28 of 17 July, 30 of 31 July, and 35 of 10 Sept. 1955.

Vietnamese forces in the Rung Sat await President Ngo Dinh Diem's review.

entered the Rung Sat, bombarded the Binh Xuyen command post and supply areas, and occupied the site where supplies had been delivered from Cape Vung Tau. All four Vietnamese Navy *dinassauts* participated in the offensive. Their first objective was to cut off the supply of water, food, and ammunition from outside the area. Although losses in Saigon and defection of supporters to the national government had reduced the Binh Xuyen to between 1,200 and 1,500 armed men, those remaining were well equipped with mortars, rockets, projectors, machine guns, automatic rifles, recoilless guns, and bazookas. The U.S. Naval Attache reported that some of these arms had been recently supplied by the French.

On 21 September 1955, the Vietnamese Armed Forces attacked the main Binh Xuyen force. The young Vietnamese Navy blocked the movement of Binh Xuyen forces and landed Army and Marine units. Encircled within a closing perimeter, the remaining Binh Xuyen surrendered. Diem then visited the area and was given a naval review.

American naval officers from Saigon reported that this was their first opportunity to see the Vietnamese Navy in action. They observed:

> The results were quite gratifying in that all small boats appeared in running condition and satisfactorily handled. Although there was no great resistance . . . the Vietnamese Navy showed itself capable of coordinated planning and operation in the completion of its assigned mission of (1) logistical support of the forces in the field, and (2) securing the sea and river approaches to the RUNG SAT, and (3) transportation of Vietnamese Army troops.[16]

The Republic of Vietnam

Diem now took a major step on the political front by scheduling a referendum whereby the Vietnamese could choose between Bao Dai and himself as Chief of State. Although Bao Dai protested that the election was illegal, the referendum was held on 23 October 1955. The lopsided count (5,721,735 votes for Diem, 63,017 for Bao Dai) raised obvious questions. Nevertheless, it seemed clear that the overwhelming majority of the people favored the resolute nationalist Diem over the weaker and absent Bao Dai. Interpreting the results as clearly indicating the will of the Vietnamese people to the establishment of his regime, Diem proclaimed the State of Vietnam a republic on the 26th, declared himself President, and charged a committee with drafting a constitution.[17]

American naval officers in the combined mission (TRIM) explored ways in which they could best help their hosts to fill, at least partially, the gaps that soon would be left by departing French naval power. These officers drafted a plan, that was submitted to the Vietnamese on 1 November 1955. It proposed organization of the Vietnamese Navy into a Coastal Patrol

---

[16] NA Saigon, report, 75–55 of 29 Oct. 1955, JN 60A–2142, Box 62, FRC; see also Buttinger, *Vietnam: A Political History*, pp. 412–13.

[17] *U.S.-V.N. Relations*, bk 2, pt. IVA.4, pp. GG, HH; "Provisional Constitutional Act Establishing the State of Viet-Nam," of 26 Oct. 1955 in Cameron, *Viet-Nam Crisis*, pp. 404–05.

Force, a River Force, a Transport Force, a Corps of Marines, and a naval command headquarters. The need for a navy to prevent Communist infiltration and resupply was recognized by General Le Van Ty, Chief of Staff of the Vietnamese Armed Forces. He emphasized the requirement for coastal patrol and surveillance, stating: "If the Vietnamese Navy were well equipped, it would be able to closely supervise the southeast coast of Vietnam and also the area between HUE and BEN HAI. . . ."[18] The TRIM plan was approved by Ty on 7 December.

Force levels recommended by the plan were modest and confined to those judged to be reasonably attainable. As before, the numbers and types of ships and craft were limited by the number of personnel who could be adequately trained to man them. The plan assumed that the "Naval Schools at Nha Trang could under an accelerated program, turn out 300 trained recruits quarterly, 300 specialist ratings semi-annually, and 60 reserve ensigns every nine months." The need for such a program was acute. At the end of the year, Vietnamese Navy personnel strength stood at 1,735, an increase of only 219 over the 1 September 1954 figure.[19]

Although the French had passed command of the Naval Schools at Nha Trang to the Vietnamese on 7 November 1955, seven French naval officers and thirty-seven enlisted men stayed on as instructors. The training center now conducted a basic recruit school, petty officer schools, a specialist course, and a six-month officer training program. A special three-month accelerated officer course began on 8 November to satisfy the increased need for river operations. Three motor minesweepers at Nha Trang served as training ships. The center could now graduate 1,200 men a year, but the training was still far too slow to meet the demands of the Vietnamese Navy, and the courses were weak in maintenance, tactics, and supply procedures.[20] Furthermore, the qualifications required to man, operate, and maintain seagoing ships were much more demanding than those for amphibious craft on inland waters.

In the fall of 1955 President Diem emphasized his independence by announcing that no more Vietnamese military personnel would be sent

---

[18] Ltr, Ty to Naval Attache in NA Saigon. report, 79–55 of 17 Nov. 1955, JN 60A–2142, box 62, FRC; Navy Section, MAAG Vietnam, "Naval Forces of Vietnam," pp. 12–18.

[19] Navy Section, MAAG Vietnam, "Country Statement," of 15 Jan. 1956; Navy Section, MAAG Vietnam, "Naval Forces of Vietnam," pp. 12–17.

[20] *Ibid.*, p. 10; NA Saigon, report, ser 7–57 of 22 Jan. 1957, JN 62A–2681, box 69, FRC; Navy Section, MAAG Vietnam, "Country Statement," of 15 Jan. 1956.

to France for training. By mid-1956, American advisors were offering courses in the English language to prepare twenty-two Vietnamese prior to their attendance at naval schools in the United States.[21]

Continuing Operations against the Sects

Many in the Cao Dai military arm had by now joined forces with Diem, and the Binh Xuyen had surrendered. In October 1955, defecting Cao Dai generals disarmed their pope's palace guard. However, the civil war was not yet over.

Some elements of the Hoa Hao continued to resist the Republic of Vietnam. On 17 November, a joint Army-Navy campaign was launched against the Ba Cut faction, now in the area of Rach Gia on the Gulf of Siam. Two Vietnamese Navy *dinassauts* participated in the operation.[22]

Activities against the government also continued along the Mekong River, and took on a new dimension when the French reported that there were 100 Viet Minh advisors with the Hoa Hao. In December 1955, the Navy was assigned the mission of patrolling the Mekong River from the Cambodian border to the sea and the coastal waters from Cape Vung Tau to Ha Tien. The Vietnamese minesweeper *Bach Dang* started patrols between Saigon and Cape Bai Bung and LSSL *No Than* cruised between the cape and Rach Gia. Minesweeper *Chi Lang* was sent south from Danang to assist. Two other ships on temporary loan from the Vietnamese customs office were stationed at the Vietnamese-Cambodian border.[23]

In January 1956, South Vietnamese Army units occupied Tay Ninh, the Cao Dai stronghold. After their pope fled to Cambodia in February, the Cao Dai leaders signed an agreement with the government. Under its terms, the Cao Dai religion was legalized, but members of the sect were forbidden to engage in political activity.[24]

---

[21] Navy Section, MAAG Vietnam, "Naval Forces of Vietnam;" Navy Section, MAAG, "Country Statement," of 20 July 1956.

[22] Buttinger, *Vietnam: A Political History,* p. 412; NA Section, Joint Weekly Analyses, 47 of 30 Nov. 1955, 50 of 17 Dec. 1955, and 16 of 20 Apr. 1956.

[23] NA Section, Joint Weekly Analyses, 49 of 11 Dec., 50 of 17 Dec., 51 of 23 Dec. 1955; NA Saigon, report, 14–56 of 7 Feb. 1956, JN 62–A–2199, box 80, FRC.

[24] Buttinger, *Vietnam: A Political History,* p. 412; *U.S.-V.N. Relations,* bk 2, pt. IVA.4, pp. GG, HH.

By the end of the month, the Vietnamese had opened a second front against the Hoa Hao in the Plain of Reeds region, a stronghold of the Soai faction along the Cambodian border. Four *dinassauts* operated on the Mekong and waterways southwest of Saigon. When the Soai faction rallied to the government on 12 February, the *dinassauts* redeployed and then proceeded to the Rach Gia area to press the illusive Ba Cut in operation *Nguyen Hue*. Ba Cut was finally trapped and captured in April 1956 and the Hoa Hao resistance collapsed.[25]

At the height of the campaign against the Hoa Hao, General Ty praised the role of the Vietnamese Navy, saying:

> The most remarkable feats . . . are no doubt those realized during the operations against the rebels. South Vietnam is a country watered by numerous rivers and streams, thus forming isolated regions. This is why during operations Dinh Tien Hoang [against the Hoa Hao], Hoang Dieu [against the Binh Xuyen], and Nguyen Hue, the . . . [Vietnamese Navy units] have played a preponderant and decisive role for the success of the Army. The daring assaults of the marines have increased the value of the Vietnamese Navy.[26]

Successes in the Sect Civil War released an increasing percentage of the republic's armed forces for participation in the efforts to reduce Communist strength and influence. Evidence of Diem's resoluteness, progress in the Anti-Communist Denunciation Campaign, and the extension of governmental controls produced highly favorable results in the State of Vietnam. That spring a government official claimed that "94,041 former communist cadres had rallied to the . . . [South Vietnamese government], 5,613 other cadres had surrendered . . . 119,954 weapons had been captured . . . and 707 underground arms caches had been discovered." The claim may have been exaggerated and the declaration that the campaign had "entirely destroyed the predominant communist influence of the previous nine years" was certainly an overstatement, but there could be no doubt that substantial progress had been realized. By 1956, according to the authors of the Department of Defense study, *United States-Vietnam Relations,* "Diem's success in the South had been far greater than anyone could have fore-

---

[25] NA Section, Joint Weekly Analyses, 49 of 11 Dec., 50 of 17 Dec. 1955, 4 of 27 Jan., 7 of 17 Feb., and 9 of 3 Mar. 1956; Buttinger, *Vietnam: A Political History,* p. 413; *U.S.-V.N. Relations,* bk 2, pt. IVA.4, p. JJ.

[26] NA Saigon, report, 14–56 of 7 Feb. 1956, JN 62–A–2199, box 80, FRC.

seen. . . ." The North Vietnamese Politburo member Le Duan confirmed Diem's progress when, after visiting the South in 1955 and 1956, he concluded that, unless the Democratic Republic of Vietnam reinforced the supporters in the South, the Communist movement there would be stamped out.[27]

Military Assistance Problems

Training was but one of many obstacles to be overcome in the development of a navy adequate to South Vietnam's needs for self-defense against the Communist threat. Strong French feelings against My made it difficult for TRIM to assist the Vietnamese Navy in overcoming its general lack of experience and leadership—no officers over thirty years of age were in the Navy. Although Captain Rechér no longer headed the Vietnamese Navy, he remained Chief of the Navy Division of TRIM. Another factor reducing the effectiveness of TRIM's assistance efforts was the virtually constant commitment of the bulk of Vietnamese Navy and Marine forces to pacification operations.

Further development of the Vietnamese Navy was impeded also by its subordinate status within the Vietnamese Armed Forces General Staff. Although the Navy commander was a Deputy Chief of Staff, his rank was only that of lieutenant commander, junior even to the lieutenant colonel who headed the Marines, a part of the naval establishment. Other members of the general staff were, except for the Air Force deputy, from the Army. Under the Chief of Staff of the Vietnamese Armed Forces, the Navy and Air Force were at the level of the Army Quartermaster and Chief of Engineers. The Navy had no control over its funds. With the Army managing common-type supplies, the Navy encountered difficulties in competing with the extensive demands of the far larger ground forces.[28]

A continuing problem during this transitional period was that of providing urgently needed aid in a timely fashion. As in the French-Viet Minh War, administrative delays were encountered. In the assessment of the American Chief of Naval Operations, Admiral Burke, "of course one

---

[27] *U.S.-V.N. Relations,* bk 2, pt. IVA.4, pp. EE, pt. IVA.5, pp. 6, 28, tab 2, pp. 27–28, 50.

[28] NA Saigon, report, 5–56 of 16 Jan. 1956, JN 62A–2199, box 80, FRC; Navy Section, MAAG Vietnam, "Naval Forces of Vietnam," p. 11.

difficulty in the MDAP field is that there are many interested parties with consequent diffusion of responsibility and complexity of administration." His views were shared by other Americans, and the troubles were not confined to Vietnam. Subsequently, an official of the Office of the Secretary of Defense would announce to Congress that the administrative lead-time for the aid program had been reduced from six to three months between 1956 and 1957. But a three-month administrative lag in addition to the time required to obtain the items and deliver them to Southeast Asia was still undesirably long for actions in response to rapidly changing situations.[29]

Two years later, in the light of growing criticism concerning administration of the Military Assistance Program, President Eisenhower would appoint a committee to study this effort and help in its justification to the Congress. The committee, chaired by William H. Draper, Jr., submitted its preliminary conclusions on 17 March 1959. While strongly supporting the program, the committee acknowledged that many criticisms had been made by the public, by the Congress, and by persons within the Executive Branch. It reported evidence of "long delays from the initiation of proposals to the development of a firm program and of an excessive number of reviews and over-coordination during the programming process." Among various other shortcomings, the committee cited "faulty or uneconomic programming" and criticized deficiencies in the promptness and effectiveness of policy coordination.[30] Actions were then taken to improve the situation.

Having been largely dependent on the French for logistic support, the Vietnamese Armed Forces needed additional training and assistance before they could be self-sufficient. United States help to them would be limited by the number of American military personnel permitted in-country. Although not a party to the Geneva accord, Washington continued the self-imposed 342-man ceiling which was consistent with the cease-fire agreement's prohibition of "the introduction into Viet Nam of any troop reinforcements and additional military personnel. . . ."[31]

Admiral Stump had recommended, with the concurrence of Admiral Burke, that additional manpower be authorized to fill TRIM spaces vacated

---

[29] Ltr, CNO to OP–63, ser 0101P60 of 6 Apr. 1956; U.S., Congress, House, Subcommittee of the Committee on Appropriations, *Hearings on Security Appropriations for 1958* (85th Cong., 1st sess.) (Washington: GPO, 1957), p. 357.

[30] The President's Committee to Study the United States Military Assistance Program, "Composite Report" of 17 Aug. 1959, Vols. I, VII, pp. 3–15.

[31] Article 16 of "Agreement on Cessation of Hostilities in Viet-Nam" in *American Foreign Policy, 1950–1955: Basic Documents* (Washington: GPO, 1957), Vol. I, p. 757.

by the French. Two and one-half months of protracted discussion between the State and Defense Departments followed a request to this effect from the Joint Chiefs on 9 December 1955 to the Secretary of Defense. Once the State Department agreed to a manpower increase in principle in February 1956, discussions shifted to determining the exact number of personnel to be authorized.[32]

A team headed by Major General William Lawton, sent to Vietnam to study military finances and the logistic situation, found that:

> Since the recent heavy phasedown in French forces, an adequate logistic capability in Free Viet-Nam no longer exists. . . . From the standpoint of preservation of U.S. assets, the situation is also most unsatisfactory. Adequate control of MOAP [*sic.*] spares and supplies has, in large part, been lost.

Although this was largely a problem concerning ground forces, the small Vietnamese Navy experienced similar deficiencies, as highlighted by an assessment made later in the year by Navy members of the MAAG, who reported: "The Vietnamese Navy did not know what equipment was on hand or what was required; and they lacked the experience and training to know how to find out."[33]

On 6 January 1956, the Vietnamese urgently requested American assistance, taking the position that replacing Frenchmen with Americans "would not violate either the spirit nor the letter of the Geneva Accords." The JCS and the Secretary of Defense agreed with the Vietnamese and concluded that at least $100 million worth of Mutual Defense Assistance Program material could be saved if 150 to 200 Americans skilled in supply management and logistics were sent to Vietnam. Both Admiral Stump and General O'Daniel requested that more U.S. personnel be assigned to Vietnam. The JCS concurred, stressing the gravity of the situation and recommending an increase in the manpower ceiling.[34]

The situation was becoming even more critical as French armed forces in Vietnam were being steadily reduced. Then, on 26 February 1956, the

---

[32] Memo, OP–62 to CNO, ser 00103P62 of 29 Nov. 1955; *U.S.-V.N. Relations,* bk 2, pt. IVA.4, p. 19, bk 10, pp. 1057–59.

[33] Ltr, SECDEF to SECSTATE, of 31 Jan. 1956 in *Ibid.,* bk 10, pp. 1046–47; Navy Division, MAAG Vietnam, "Summary of MAAG-TERM Activities," of 21 Nov. 1956.

[34] Ltr, SECDEF to SECSTATE, of 31 Jan. 1956 in *U.S.-V.N. Relations,* bk 10, pp. 1046–47, bk 2, pt. IVA.4, pp. II, 19; Navy Division, MAAG Vietnam, "Summary of MAAG-TERM Activities," of 21 Nov. 1956; Memo, OP–61 to SECNAV, ser 0050P61 of 2 Mar. 1956.

Republic of Vietnam asked France to withdraw its military forces completely. That same day the United States Departments of State and Defense announced a plan to send 350 additional military logistic experts to Vietnam. They would advise and assist the Vietnamese with the huge amounts of American-supplied material left by the French. Augmented by experienced Japanese or Filipino technicians, these experts "would provide for the continued maintenance of an estimated 100 million of U.S. military equipment . . . threatened with . . . abandonment." This group, known as the Temporary Equipment Recovery Mission (TERM), would be separate from the MAAG because of the Geneva Agreement restrictions.[35] Negotiations began immediately to obtain the approval of France, Britain, and the nations of the International Control Commission (ICC)—India, Canada, and Poland—for the introduction of these men.

The ICC's reaction to the American proposal to introduce equipment recovery personnel had been cool initially, but finally the member governments acquiesced to the TERM program after receiving United States assurances that this would reduce the military equipment in South Vietnam. In view of this understanding, the State Department emphasized that, while the "TERM personnel will perform functions of training which are inseparable from their tasks of recovering and maintaining . . . [American] equipment in Viet-Nam, such functions should in no case . . . become the . . . primary duty of TERM." The Chief of the MAAG was authorized to transfer men between the MAAG and the TERM as needed.[36]

Then, at the last minute, India, which had previously expressed no objections to TERM, raised the question of the International Control Commission's authority to approve or disapprove such a mission. At this point Admiral Burke, who was charged with implementing the TERM program as executive agent for the JCS, declared that "the TERM project has, since its inception, been plagued by time-consuming delays." He recommended that TERM be dispatched with or without ICC approval. Finally, on 1 June, the Temporary Equipment Recovery Mission was activated. It would complete its initial mission in 1957 when it merged with the MAAG.[37]

---

[35] *Ibid.; U.S.-V.N. Relations,* bk 2, pt. IVA.5, tab 1, p. 4.

[36] Ltr, Deputy Under SECSTATE to SECDEF, of 1 May 1956 in *U.S.-V.N. Relations,* bk 10, pp. 1057–59.

[37] Navy Division, MAAG Vietnam, "Summary of MAAG-TERM Activities," of 21 Nov. 1956; *U.S.-V.N. Relations,* bk 2, pt. IVA.4, p. LL; memo, OP–61 to SECNAV, ser 00186P61 of 8 May 1956; memo, CNO to ASD(ISA), ser 0085P62 of 9 May 1956.

The Sea Force

The Vietnamese had organized a Sea Force in January 1956. Shortly thereafter several American advisors were assigned to the Vietnamese naval base in Saigon to assist the French with on-the-job training of ship crews.

Five Sea Zones were established, stretching from the 17th parallel to the Cambodian border and with units operating from Danang, Nha Trang, Vung Tau, Son Island, and later Qui Nhon. Under their Sea Zone commanders, two naval posts were established "at tactical points . . . to control [coastal] traffic or to guard the naval territory. . . ." One post was located at the mouth of the Cua Viet River just south of the 17th parallel and the other at Khoai Island off the southern tip of Vietnam. Ships and craft of the Sea Force were administratively organized into eight flotillas, which were in essence tiny type commands. But however sound this concept may have been, the Vietnamese Navy lacked the full capability to deny Communist use of the coastal waters.

The physical difficulties of patrolling the long coastline effectively, as well as Vietnamese limitations, were well known by American naval officers in the MAAG. In the spring of 1956, they examined a Vietnamese plan to organize fifty civilian-manned, fourteen-ton motorized junks in a force which would patrol inshore waters along the coast and act as an auxiliary to the Sea Force. Four years would pass before the concept was implemented.[38]

The Vietnamese Navy now began to test its sea legs during a month-long goodwill cruise of two PCs (submarine chasers) and an LSM. The squadron, under the personal command of Commander My, was well received in its ports of call—Manila, Singapore, and Bangkok.[39]

Disestablishment of French Naval Forces, Far East

On 26 April 1956, French Naval Forces, Far East was disestablished. In an emotional "Last Order of the Day of the French Naval Forces, Far East," Vice Admiral Edouard Jozan said:

---

[38] NA Saigon, reports, 17–S–56 of 9 Apr. and 20–S–56 of 29 June 1956, JN 62A–2199, box 80, FRC.

[39] NA Saigon, reports, 48–56 of 15 May and 49–56 of 16 May 1956, JN 62A–2199, box 80, FRC, and 11–57 of 24 Jan. 1957, JN 62A–2681, box 69, FRC.

I am addressing you for the last time . . . to thank you for the ardor and abnegation with which you have written the last pages of the history of the Naval Forces of the Far East dissolved today.

*   *   *   *   *

Under my command, you have, in peacetime, continued to serve with the same ideal of your predecessors. Before we separate I ask you to think of their sacrifice; to the world, it has shown unselfishness, faith and courage of the Forces of the French Union, loyal to the word of their country.

Loyal to this word, the Expeditionary Corps has left Vietnam today and the French Naval Forces cease to exist.[40]

Two days later, the combined United States-French Training Relations Instruction Mission was deactivated and the MAAG assumed responsibility for advising the Vietnamese Army. But, in the case of the Vietnamese Navy and Air Force, training advisors remained French, reassigned to the truncated, although still active, French Training Mission.

In the days following the Geneva Conference, State and Defense Department planners debated whether the proper role of the new Vietnamese Armed Forces was to maintain internal security or also to defend against external aggression. The State Department's position—limiting South Vietnam's Armed Forces mission to maintenance of internal security—was accepted over the JCS view. With the withdrawal of the French, the South Vietnamese had no defense against external aggression unless the United States was prepared to fulfill this mission. Hoping to avoid this necessity, President Eisenhower, on 16 July 1956, deemed it desirable:

> (1) To encourage Vietnamese military planning for defense against external aggression along lines consistent with U.S. planning concepts based upon approved U.S. policy.
> (2) To discreetly manifest in other ways U.S. interest in assisting Free Vietnam, in accordance with the Manila Pact, to defend itself against external aggression.[41]

The scope of responsibilities assumed by the United States and its latest goals were reflected in objectives assigned the military assistance program, which were "to assist in organizing, training and equipping the

---

[40] NA Saigon, report, 46–56 of 14 May 1956, JN 62A–2199, box 80, FRC.
[41] Memo, SECDEF, of 16 July 1956 in *U.S.-V.N. Relations,* bk 10, p. 1064.

Armed Forces of Vietnam in order to insure the maintenance of internal security and provide limited initial resistance to attack by the Viet Minh." To form the basis of American assistance to the Vietnamese Navy, these defensive goals were translated into three missions, namely:

a. Maintain control and security of the inland waterways of South Vietnam.
b. Provide naval support to the other Vietnamese Armed Forces.
c. Maintain naval security of the coastal waters of South Vietnam, including the off shore islands within those waters.

Required tasks in order to fulfill these missions were identified as:

a. River and coastal patrol for reconnaissance, security and interdiction of enemy waterborne traffic.
b. Limited minewatching and minesweeping operations to keep lines of communication free of mines, with particular attention to the requirements for such operations in the inland waterways.
c. Minor inland/coastal waterborne operations including lightly opposed counter landings designed to envelope [*sic.*] dissident forces or enemy lodgements.
d. Shore bombardment operations including limited fire support, with emphasis on the requirement peculiar to such support in the inland waterways.
e. Transport of ground forces and their waterborne logistic support on inland waterways to facilitate combat deployment and support of deployed ground units.
f. Seizure, repulsion or destruction of small enemy surface forces.
g. Effective internal security of naval installations.
h. Maintenance of a naval logistic organization and facilities capable of providing maximum practical support to own naval forces.[42]

The job of the Navy Section of the American Military Assistance Advisory Group was to help the Vietnamese achieve the capabilities for fulfilling these tasks, within the limits of the approved force structure and aid programs.

This was a large order. Ships and craft of the Vietnamese Navy had seen hard use in combat during the French-Viet Minh War and in later operations against Sect forces. They were in dire need of major overhaul, and the French-controlled Saigon Naval Arsenal was the only facility in South Vietnam capable of performing the required work. In January 1956, the United States MAAG had attempted to negotiate a contract with the French

---

[42] Ltr, CINCPAC, ser 000138 of 27 July 1956, encl. 3 and app. B to encl. 3.

for overhaul and repair of Vietnamese Navy ships at the shipyard. The inordinately high estimated costs provided by the French resulted in a decision to send Vietnamese ships to the United States Ship Repair Facility at Subic Bay in the Philippines, where the first of fifteen scheduled overhauls began in June. After their overhaul period, many of the ships conducted three weeks of underway training with the Fleet Training Group, Subic.[43]

Incidents in the South China Sea

In 1956, the possibility of aggression by the People's Republic of China against the Paracel and Spratly Island groups drew the attention of the new South Vietnamese Navy and at the same time became a matter of concern to the United States and other members of SEATO. Although their land areas were small, both island groups lay along the important north-south shipping lanes through the South China Sea. The Paracels, some 200 miles east of Danang and southeast of Hainan, also lay astride air and sea routes between Luzon and the northern part of South Vietnam. The Spratlys were located midway between Vietnam and Borneo. As a prelude to their offensives in Southeast Asia, the Japanese had occupied both groups of islands in 1939.

At various times since August 1955, United States intelligence sources had received indications of a Chinese Communist presence on Woody Island in the Paracels. In the spring of 1956, information had been received that 200 Communist Chinese were occupying eleven new or rehabilitated buildings on the island. On 9 June, a French-Vietnamese meteorological team on Pattle Island reported 200 Chinese Communist troops landing on nearby Robert Island. The Vietnamese responded by dispatching a PC, an LSM, and two LSILs to the Paracels. A territorial company was landed there early in July. Part of the company joined the forces already on Pattle and the rest occupied the now deserted Robert Island. The Vietnamese Navy continued to support garrisons in the Paracels throughout the decade of the 1950s.[44]

---

[43] Navy Division, MAAG Vietnam, "Summary," of 31 Dec. 1957; Navy Section, MAAG Vietnam, "Monthly Activities Report," of 10 Mar. 1956; Navy Division, MAAG Vietnam, "Quarterly Activities Report," No. 4 of 7 Mar. 1957.

[44] Memo, OP–61 to OP–06, of 27 Feb. 1956; "Disputed Islands in the South China Sea: Part I," *The ONI Review* (May 1956), pp. 186–91; NA Section, Joint Weekly Analyses, 23 of 9 June and 27 of 7 July 1956.

Meanwhile, the Chief of Naval Operations, Admiral Burke, had directed Admiral Stump to reconnoiter the islands and be prepared to support the thirty-man Vietnamese garrison on Pattle Island, in case such action was directed. On 11 June, carrier *Yorktown* (CV–10) and attack cargo ship *Merrick* (AKA–97) were alerted for possible action, and destroyers *Stoddard* (DD–566) and *Mullany* (DD–528) were dispatched for an on-site inspection. Reconnaissance by Task Force 72's air unit stationed at Sangley Point revealed about seventy-five men gathering guano. *Stoddard* and *Mullany* arrived at Robert Island on the 13th and found no evidence of military activity.[45]

Shortly thereafter an incident in the Spratly area (over which sovereignty was claimed by Communist China, Nationalist China, Vietnam, and the Philippines) focused attention on that group of islands. To challenge the Philippine claim, a platoon of Nationalist Chinese marines, transported in two destroyer escorts, scouted the islands in June 1956. On 22 August, Vietnam's PC *Tuy Dong* stopped at Spratly Island enroute to Saigon after an overhaul at Subic. The Vietnamese hauled down a Chinese Nationalist flag and substituted their own, thus affecting the symbolic occupation of the Spratly group.[46]

Although the Spratly and Paracel Islands were deemed of little direct strategic importance to the United States, they had been of value to the Japanese in World War II and could serve another power in the future as weather, radar, radio, and observation sites, or possibly as advanced fuel and ammunition depots. Although possible actions by the United States were discussed, Washington preferred not to become involved.[47]

In the fall of 1956, one Vietnamese YMS and one LSSL patrolled out of Danang to stop Communist craft. Later that year the Vietnamese employed the Navy to establish positions on strategically located islands in the south. Under the command of Le Quang My, 7 ships (2 PCs, 2 LSMs, 2 LSILs, and 1 LSSL) departed Cape Vung Tau on 6 November 1956.

---

[45] Ltr, OP–61 to CNO, ser 00248P61 of 11 June; memos, DCNO (Fleet Operations and Readiness) to CNO, No. 0464–56 of 11 June, OP–61 to CNO, ser 000120P61 of 12 June, and OP–61 to CNO, ser 000122P61 of 13 June 1956.

[46] NA, Saigon, report, 11–57 of 24 Jan. 1957, JN 62A–2681, box 69, FRC; memo, OP–61 to SECNAV, ser 00237P61 of 5 June 1956; "Disputed Islands in the South China Sea: Part II," *The ONI Review* (June 1956), pp. 238–42; NA Section, Joint Weekly Analyses, 34 of 24 Aug. 1956.

[47] Memo, OP–60 to CNO, No. 241–56 of 3 Aug. 1956; ltr, OP–61 to OP–06, ser 00140P61 of 12 Mar. 1957.

For training purposes and in order to reassert Vietnamese sovereignty, the force then conducted amphibious landings on Son Island, east of the Camau Peninsula; on Khoai Island, south of the cape; and on Phu Quoc Island, Panjang Island, Wai Island, and Tang Island in the Gulf of Siam. In the 1960s, several of these islands would serve as U.S. bases in the effort to prevent the infiltration of men and supplies into South Vietnam. An Thoi, off the Cambodian border and on the southern tip of Phu Quoc Island, later also would serve as a base of operations for United States Navy ships and craft.[48]

United States Naval Assistance

The Saigon government requested United States Navy and Air Force participation in a first anniversary celebration of Vietnamese independence on 26 October 1956. Initially, the Saigon embassy and the Deputy Secretary of State for Far Eastern Affairs treated the proposal coolly. However, General Samuel Williams, Chief MAAG Vietnam, and Admiral Stump, CINCPAC, heartily endorsed the idea. With the backing of Admiral Radford, Chairman of the JCS, and Admiral Burke, the State Department was persuaded to accept the Vietnamese request insofar as the Navy was concerned. Because of possible operating difficulties and the likelihood of International Control Commission objections to use of Vietnamese airfields by American military aircraft, a fly-over by Navy planes from carrier *Essex* was substituted for Air Force participation.[49]

On 24 October, the cruiser *Los Angeles* (CA–135) (Captain Frederick C. Lucas, Jr.), with Commander Cruiser Division 5, Rear Admiral George C. Wright, embarked, steamed up the Saigon River to the Vietnamese capital for a four-day visit. The fledgling Vietnamese Navy had assumed French responsibility for making all the arrangements for the visit. As the first visit by an American man-of-war to the new Republic of Vietnam, the occasion provided evidence of United States armed strength and demonstrated United States interest in South Vietnam and its future. But the American Naval Attache, concerned over giving the impression that the

---

[48] NA Section, Joint Weekly Analyses, 45 of 10 Nov. and 49 of 8 Dec. 1956.
[49] Ltrs, OP–61 to CNO, of 15 Aug. and 8 Sept. 1956.

NH–84168

President Diem reviewing USS Los Angeles *on the first anniversary of the Republic of Vietnam.*

United States was moving in to replace the French, recommended that future visits not be made too frequently.[50]

Another form of American assistance was the continuing use of the naval shipyard in Subic to overhaul Vietnamese ships. At the same time, efforts were made to increase the capabilities of the shipyard in Saigon which, on 14 September 1956, was transferred from French control to the Vietnamese. Although the facility was the largest industrial plant in South Vietnam and capable of handling ships the size of light cruisers, the depar-

---

[50] Navy Section, MAAG Vietnam, "Country Statement," of 22 Jan. 1958; USS *Los Angeles,* report, ser 1734 of 9 Nov. 1956; NA Saigon, report, 105–56 of 19 Dec. 1956, JN 62A–2199, box 81, FRC.

ture of the French had left the installation with few trained and experienced supervisors. Several weeks before the turnover, an American team from Subic surveyed the yard to determine the size of the work force which the Vietnamese would need to run the yard. Taking into account differences in physique and in skill levels, the team determined that the yard would require about 1,350 civilians. Steps were taken to build a core of trained managers for the yard and to recruit a competent work force. At the end of 1956, fifty-two Vietnamese commissioned officers, petty officers, and civilians began training at the Subic Bay Ship Repair Facility. Nineteen highly skilled Japanese shipyard specialists were recruited to assist the Vietnamese. By the end of the next year, 800 civilians would be working at the yard in Saigon, but the Vietnamese experienced difficulty in increasing the complement to the 1,500-man level then deemed desirable. The low wage scales set by the Vietnamese Army officers in control discouraged many, and other potential workers were ruled out for security reasons.[51]

A National Navy

From the point of view of the Vietnamese Naval Staff, 1956 had been a momentous year. The extent of its pride in the transition that had taken place was reflected in a report that stated, "from the beginning of the year 1956 when the Vietnamese Navy liberated itself from the influence and authority of the French Navy, the whole Naval Force has completely changed in every respect." In regard to combat, the Vietnamese Navy claimed to have "participated in all operations. With a year-end strength of 4,807 men (3,371 Navy, 1,436 Marines), the Navy now was composed of the River Force, the Sea Force, and the Marine Force. The number of craft in the River Force had increased by 50 percent. Their *dinassauts* now numbered six—with units based at My Tho, Cat Lo, Vinh Long, Cat Lai, Can Tho, and Long Xuyen.

Great pride was derived from the Sea Force, particularly because it symbolized South Vietnam's status as a nation. In the Vietnamese Navy headquarters' view, "the year 1956 is the very year when the Vietnamese

---

[51] NA Saigon, report, ser 167–57 of 19 Dec. 1957, JN 62A–2681, box 69, FRC; Navy Division, MAAG Vietnam, "Summary," of 31 Dec. 1957; Navy Division, MAAG Vietnam, "Quarterly Activities Report," of 7 Mar. 1957; Navy Section, MAAG Vietnam, "Monthly Activities Report," of 10 Mar. 1956; ltr, CNO to ASD(ISA), ser 0261P60 of 27 Aug. 1957.

Navy became officially a member of the Navy family of the World and introduced itself to friendly nations by visits made during the month of April to these nations." Noting the extent of the coastal waters and river network, the Vietnamese Navy command identified deficiencies. They high- lighted the lack of repair personnel, weakness in technical matters of rapidly trained river force personnel, the need to send commissioned and noncommissioned officers to technical courses in foreign countries, and insufficient overall naval strength. They concluded that, "the present de- fense activities must be more active and permanent," and that this could only be obtained "when equipment and strength become more complete."

Their aspirations were high. Once the Vietnamese Navy was well equipped and carefully trained, its leaders hoped to be able to perform the following offensive actions:

1. blockade the enemy naval territory
2. make landings to occupy enemy territory
3. conduct operations for the destruction of enemy positions
4. destroy the enemy naval forces

These ambitions were beyond the Vietnamese missions as then envisaged by the United States.[52]

Nevertheless, during 1957 the Vietnamese Navy continued to make valuable contributions to the new nation. In February, twenty Vietnamese sailors from Danang established a base at Dong Ha, near the 17th parallel, from which 6 utility boats conducted inshore patrols along the northern border. Also in February, 1 LSIL, 2 LCMs, and 4 LCUs repatriated 2,400 Vietnamese recently expelled from Cambodia. During the last week in April, 4 LSMs and 3 LSILs transported 1,500 Vietnamese from Danang to Cat Lai on the Dong Nai River near Saigon for future resettlement in Phuoc Long Province next to the Cambodian border.[53]

Between 29 May and 5 June 1957, a Vietnamese LSSL and three LSILs conducted tactical maneuvers and gunnery exercises in the Gulf of Siam. A second purpose of the operation was to investigate alleged Cambodian seizures of Vietnamese fishing boats in the gulf. In the months that followed, the Vietnamese Navy continued to operate and support Army garrisons

---

[52] NA Saigon, reports, 48–56 of 15 May, 49–56 of 16 May 1956, JN 62A–2199, box 80, FRC, and 11–57 of 24 Jan. and 126–57 of 11 Sept. 1957, JN 62A–2681, box 69, FRC.

[53] NA Section, Joint Weekly Analyses, 6 of 9 Feb., 7 of 16 Feb., 17 of 26 Apr. 1957.

in the area. That summer the Navy transported a marine battalion from Nha Trang to Phu Quoc for a two-month occupation of the island.[54]

As evidence of continuing American support of the small Vietnamese Navy, Rear Admiral Paul D. Stroop, Commander of the Taiwan Patrol Force, paid a four-day visit to Nha Trang during July in his flagship, seaplane tender *Pine Island* (Captain William L. Dawson). A luncheon held at the Vietnamese Naval Training Center and hosted by Lieutenant Commander Chung Tan Cang, who would later serve as head of the Vietnamese Navy in the 1963–1965 period, highlighted the visit. In December, an American team of one officer and six petty officers began assisting in the instruction of Vietnamese officers at the training center.[55]

One of the concerns earlier that year had been the proposed diversion of the Saigon shipyard's limited capabilities into non-naval work, as when the Vietnamese discussed plans to use the facility's machine shops for the production of 60,000 bayonets and scabbards for the Vietanmese Army. The American naval advisors warned that the capacity of the yard was limited and that such projects might interfere with the yard's primary mission of support for the Navy. If the proposed projects resulted in the yard passing to civilian control, then it would lose United States military assistance support. The plans were abandoned and the shipyard commenced its first ship overhaul in August 1957.[56]

The Threat of North Vietnam

As Diem struggled with the problems of establishing a South Vietnamese nation and providing for its security, Ho had been facing the problems of consolidating his rule over North Vietnam. By August 1956, the situation had deteriorated to the point that Ho admitted errors and promised to redress incorrect classifications and misjudgments by Land Reform Committees. In a public statement at the Tenth Congress of the Communist Party Central Committee in October, Giap listed past excesses in the handling of minority problems and in the collectivization program. He said:

---

[54] NA Section, Joint Weekly Analyses, 23 of 8 June, 32 of 9 Aug., and 42 of 18 Oct. 1957.

[55] NA Saigon, report, 126–57 of 11 Sept. 1957, JN 62A–2681, box 69, FRC; USS *Pine Island*, report, ser 767 of 6 Aug. 1957.

[56] Navy Section, MAAG Vietnam, "Country Statement," of 22 Jan. 1958; NA Saigon, reports, 57–57 of 9 Apr. 1957, 14–57 of 12 Feb. 1957, JN 62A–2681, box 69, FRC; Navy Section, MAAG Vietnam, "Quarterly Activities Report," of 10 Sept. 1957.

In regions inhabited by minority tribes we have attacked tribal chiefs too
strongly, thus injuring, instead of respecting, local customs and manners. . . .
When reorganizing the party, we paid too much importance to the notion
of social class instead of adhering firmly to political qualifications alone.
Instead of recognizing education to be the first essential, we resorted exclusively to organizational measures such as disciplinary punishments, expulsion
from the party, executions, dissolution of party branches and cells. Worse
still, torture came to be regarded as a normal practice during party reorganization.[57]

Despite these statements and changes in top leadership, violence broke
out in Nghe An Province the next month. On 9 November 1956, several
hundred peasants gathered near Vinh to petition the International Control
Commission to sanction migration to the South and to bring about a return
of land that had been confiscated. A Communist propaganda team and
armed forces were sent to the scene of the disturbance. Efforts to make
arrests produced a riot which grew to the proportions of an uprising. On 13
November, troops stormed the town, dispersing the rebels and causing heavy
casualties. Two reinforced divisions of 20,000 men were committed to
suppress the rebellion.

Early in 1957 the Democratic Republic of Vietnam, again following
the Maoist example, invited criticism by sponsoring a "Hundred Flowers"
campaign. The party leaders expressed surprise over the strength of the
response. Critics were identified, arrested, and tried and much blood was
spilt. The exact number of persons killed is unknown, but estimates range
up to 500,000. Whatever the precise count, it was a costly period in terms
of human lives. In any case, the various steps taken after the Geneva agreement tightened Communist control over the North, strengthened the Communist leadership in the army, and accelerated the "advance to socialism."[58]
With the blunting of opposition and the consolidation of power, North
Vietnam would now be able to provide increased support to Communist
efforts in the South.

---

[57] Quoted in *U.S.-V.N. Relations,* bk 2, pt. IVA.5, p. 7, tab 3, pp. 11–12; Ho, *On Revolution,*
pp. 304–06.
[58] *U.S.-V.N. Relations,* bk 2, pt. IVA.5, p. 7, tab 3, p. 13; *Human Cost of Communism,* p. 7.

CHAPTER XV

A Transitional Period

Since 1953 the Vietnam conflict had gone from war through a time of consolidation of Communist control in the North, the establishment of the Republic of Vietnam in the South, and the phasing out of the French to a period of increasing violence. The period had been transitional also in other respects. Initially Cold War tensions eased after Stalin's death but, as a new regime resolved its problems within the Soviet Union, a more aggressive policy was resumed on the international scene. The Far East continued to be a troubled area in which the United States Navy was frequently required to respond to crisis situations, many of which involved the People's Republic of China. Meanwhile, technological achievements altered the capabilities of the United States Navy and the roles of its Fleet. The period also witnessed changes in strategic policy, the chain of command of the operating forces, and the administration of the national defense.

The Employment of United States Naval Forces

Vietnam had been brought to the forefront of United States attention by events during the final phase of the French-Viet Minh War and by Communist gains at the Geneva bargaining table. In the long term, Vietnam—at least insofar as the United States Navy and its operations were concerned—was but one feature of a much larger picture. Many of the problems of stability, self-determination, and security for the emerging Republic of Vietnam were intertwined with the overall security problems of Southeast Asia. These in turn were related to those of the Far East as a whole and, with regard to both the international Communist movement and the employment of naval operating forces, the instabilities, threats, and crises of the Western Pacific were linked to similar events elsewhere, such as in the Mediterranean and Middle East. Moreover, the influence of a naval presence in one area was bolstered by evidence of the willingness to act and effectiveness demonstrated in other areas.

347

After the Geneva accords the United States continued to maintain a Navy presence in Southeast Asian waters. Vice Admiral Phillips remained in command of the "Fair Weather Training" force until 21 August 1954 when operational control of Task Group 70.2 was transferred to Vice Admiral Pride (Commander Seventh Fleet). Phillips then returned to his First Fleet command in the Eastern Pacific.

Signs soon appeared of a potential crisis resulting from a Chinese Communist threat against the Tachens, a group of Nationalist-held islands off the mainland about 200 miles from the northern tip of Taiwan. Seventh Fleet destroyers visited the Tachens on 19 August and other major units of the Fleet were assembled nearby. Further south, the People's Republic of China tested Quemoy Island on 26 August with a small raid. This was followed by a heavy bombardment from the mainland on 3 September. Seventh Fleet units, including Task Group 70.2, were sent to the Taiwan area, where they remained until the crisis eased. The shelling continued sporadically during the months that followed, as the Chinese Communists increased their military forces on the mainland opposite the Taiwan Strait. Seventh Fleet task forces were sent to the area at critical periods, in readiness for action if required and to help deter offensive actions by the Chinese Communists.[1]

Shortly after midnight on 14 November 1954 the Chinese Nationalist destroyer escort *T'ai P'ing* was patrolling north-east of the Tachen Islands when two suspicious contacts appeared on the radar. Minutes after general quarters sounded, a torpedo from either a motor torpedo boat or a submarine slammed into the port side of the ship. Meanwhile, the ship opened fire on the attackers with 3-inch and 40-millimeter guns. The engagement was over in five minutes. Crippled *T'ai P'ing* radioed for held and by 0530 destroyer escort *T'ai Ho* had *T'ai P'ing* under tow. Less than two hours later the forward bulkhead, severely damaged by the torpedo, collapsed and the ship rolled over and sank. Washington considered, but rejected, a show of force in response to this incident.[2]

Starting on 10 January 1955, the Chinese Communists started a heavy aerial bombing of the Tachens. Not only did the Chinese Nationalist Air Force lack the capabilities of providing continuous air cover at that distance

---

[1] A discussion of this crisis from the deterrence point of view is in Alexander L. George and Richard Smoke, *Deterrence in American Foreign Policy: Theory and Practice*, pp. 266–94.

[2] NA Taipei, report, 158–54 of 1 Dec. 1954, JN 59A–2184, box 16, FRC.

from its fields, but the defensive needs of Taiwan prohibited the diversion of a significant portion of their fighter planes. The situation became critical when, on 20 January, the mainland Chinese seized Ichiang Island, which was within artillery range of the Tachens. Admiral Carney alerted the Pacific command and Commander Seventh Fleet to the possibility that carrier aircraft might be directed to cover an evacuation of the Nationalists, and that the American ships might be called upon to assist in the withdrawal.

Rear Admiral Hopwood, Acting CINCPACFLT during the temporary absence of Admiral Stump, issued a tentative operational plan on 23 January. Vice Admiral Pride deployed his striking force to the area. On the 28th, a joint congressional resolution authorized the President to employ the Armed Forces of the United States as he deemed necessary for the defense of Taiwan and the Pescadores, "this authority to include the securing and protection of such related positions and territories of that area now in friendly hands and the taking of such other measures as he judges to be required or appropriate in assuring the defense of Formosa and the Pescadores." Admiral Stump delayed the return to the United States of *York-town*, which was completing a tour in the Western Pacific. As a result, five attack carriers (*Kearsarge* (CVA–33), *Essex, Wasp, Midway,* and *York-town*) were available when the planned operations were ordered.[3]

On 6 February the Republic of China formally requested United States help in evacuating armed forces and civilians from the threatened islands. That morning the Seventh Fleet's Surface Action Force (TF 75) started patrols off the Tachen area, while aircraft from the Attack Carrier Striking Force (TF 77) flew overhead. By afternoon, all the ships of Rear Admiral Sabin's Amphibious Evacuation Force (TF 76) were enroute from Taiwan and Okinawa. Minesweeping and beach reconnaissance started the next morning. Two days later, ships of the Chinese Nationalist Navy and the United States Navy began to embark the evacuees. A Hunter-Killer Group (TG 70.4) provided antisubmarine protection, the Formosa Patrol Force (TF 72) conducted patrols, the Chinese and United States Air Forces furnished air cover within 100 miles of Taiwan, and the Logistic Support Force (TF 73) provided underway replenishment. Within 85 hours, 15,627 civilians, 11,120 military personnel, 8,630 tons of military equipment and

---

[3] "Congressional Authorization for the President to Employ the Armed Forces of the United States to Protect Formosa, the Pescadores, and Related Positions and Territories in that Area," in *American Foreign Policy, 1950–1955: Basic Documents,* Vol. II, pp. 2486–88; COM7THFLT, report, ser 0033 of 10 Apr. 1955.

supplies, 166 artillery pieces, and 128 vehicles had been brought out from the Tachens by Nationalist and American ships. On 9 February, the Nationalist Navy conducted similar evacuations from the Yu Shan and Pei Shan Islands again under the protection of the Seventh Fleet.[4]

The Twentieth Congress of the Communist Party of the Soviet Union met in February 1956, with delegates from fifty-five foreign Communist parties in attendance. The discussions focused mainly on internal Soviet policies. Khrushchev and others promoted the concept that there were different roads to socialism, and advanced the theory of "co-existence." Several of the Communist leaders from other nations, including China, were not in full agreement. The Chinese Communists reportedly still adhered to their belief in the inevitability of war along the path to socialism. Two months later the Cominform was dissolved.[5]

Soon thereafter, the United States Navy became involved in a complex crisis of the Middle East, where the Israeli-Arab struggle, Egyptian receipt of arms from the Communist bloc, and other events led to increased Sixth Fleet operations in the Eastern Mediterranean. In June 1956, Britain completed the withdrawal of troops who had been stationed in the Suez area. In response to threats against American oil interests in Saudi Arabia, two Sixth Fleet destroyers were ordered to the area. However, Egypt delayed their passage through the canal. Because of rising tensions in the Middle East, Admiral Burke alerted the Sixth Fleet on 7 July. The alert lasted four days.

On 26 July, one week after the United States had withdrawn its offer to assist in building the Aswan Dam, the Egyptian leader Gamal Abdel Nasser announced nationalization of the Suez Canal. Events were now in motion that would culminate three months later in what became known as the Suez War. The main employment of the Sixth Fleet during that crisis was what is often loosely labelled as "naval presence." The American position, as highlighted by Vice Admiral Charles R. Brown's query to the Chief of Naval Operations on 8 November, "whose side am I on?," was ambiguous.[6] Nevertheless, some measure of the Fleet's influence would be

---

    [4] *Ibid.*

    [5] Wolfgang Leonhard, *The Kremlin Since Stalin* (New York: Praeger Publishers, 1962), pp. 120–66.

    [6] Quoted in Hugh Thomas, *Suez* (New York: Harper and Row, 1966), pp. 141–42; see also "Proceedings, Naval History Symposium," Annapolis, Md. United States Naval Academy, 1973, p. 50.

provided by the requests from foreign nations for its assistance. These included an Egyptian request for Sixth Fleet intervention and later for its presence at Port Said to enforce the cease-fire resolution, a German request for escort of an evacuation ship, Greek and Turkish inquiries as to protection by the Fleet, and a French request for the external security of Port Lyautey. The most startling of all was a Soviet Union proposal to Eisenhower on 5 November that the Sixth Fleet and the Soviet Navy join in a cooperative effort to end the Suez War.

Exercising in the Ionian Sea, the Sixth Fleet again was placed on the alert by Admiral Burke, on 28 October 1956.[7] When, a day later, Israel launched an attack into Sinai against Egypt, Commander Sixth Fleet, Vice Admiral Brown, dispatched amphibious task groups to evacuate United States citizens from Haifa and Alexandria, and on a space-available basis also to transport "friendly nationals." A Seventh Fleet amphibious task group, with a Marine battalion embarked, steamed from the South China Sea through the Malacca Strait into the Indian Ocean, and an American Hunter-Killer antisubmarine force left northern Europe for the Mediterranean.

England and France, in the process of mounting a combined amphibious operation, issued an ultimatum on 30 October. They called for both sides to withdraw ten miles from the canal, ostensibly for the purpose of stopping the fighting. The British and French planned to seize "temporary control" of key locations within the area. An American resolution urging the nations involved to refrain from the use of force was vetoed by Britain and France in the United Nations Security Council. Hostilities commenced on 31 October when British planes from Cyprus attacked selected airfields, ports, railways, and communication centers in Egypt. A United States-sponsored cease-fire resolution, passed by the General Assembly on 2 November, was rejected by Britain and France.

On 5 November, landing of helicopter-borne British troops signified the start of an assault to capture Port Said. Troops were landed on the beaches the next day. The French provided combat support with Corsairs from aircraft carriers that previously had seen action in the French-Viet Minh War—*La Fayette* and *Arromanches.*

---

[7] The Sixth Fleet then included the carriers *Coral Sea* (CVA–43) and *Randolph* (CVA–15), the heavy cruisers *Salem* (CA–134) and *Macon* (CA–132), 18 destroyers, 16 amphibious ships, 13 Service Force ships, 4 minesweepers, and 2 submarines.

Under diplomatic pressure from the United States and with threats of Soviet intervention, Britain and France now agreed to a cease-fire. Although fighting would cease on 7 November, the possibilities of a Soviet-North Atlantic Treaty Organization confrontation intensified. The Russians started recruiting "volunteers" for service in the Middle East. Already on alert, the United States Atlantic Fleet took actions to maximize the preparedness of its forces against the possibility, however remote, of general war. Task Force 26, composed of carriers *Forrestal* (CVA–59) and *Franklin D. Roosevelt,* a cruiser, and two squadrons of destroyers left United States waters on 7 November and headed for the Eastern Atlantic. Shortly thereafter the danger of Soviet action eased.

With the Sixth Fleet providing logistic support, United Nations forces supervised the disengagement. British and French troops were withdrawn in December 1956. Israeli troops would pull out of Egypt five months later.

Added complications on the international scene were posed at this time by events in Eastern Europe where expectations for greater degrees of independence had been spawned by the Soviets' de-Stalinization policy. Signs of a change in this policy had already appeared when a strike started in Poland in July 1956 and took on the proportions of an uprising. Although the unrest was subdued, a reform movement of the party gained power in Poland in October. A far more extensive popular uprising started in Hungary on 23 October and the crisis deepened when the Soviet Army moved in on 4 November to suppress ruthlessly the dissent.[8]

Following the Suez crisis, the Sixth Fleet spent much of its time in the Eastern Mediterranean. In an address to Congress on 5 January 1957, Eisenhower expressed concern over Russia's desires to dominate the Middle East. Congress responded to the President by passing a joint resolution authorizing him "to undertake economic and military cooperation" with nations in that area "to assist in the strengthening and defense of their independence." [9]

Changing Capabilities of the United States Navy

Remarkable advances were being achieved in the capabilities of the Fleet and its weapon systems. These were the result of the rapid application

---

[8] Leonhard, *Kremlin Since Stalin,* pp. 209–30.

[9] "Special Message of the President to the Congress, January 5, 1957" and "Initial Text of the Middle East Resolution," in U.S., State Department, *American Foreign Policy: Current Documents, 1957* (Washington: State Department, GPO, 1961), pp. 784–92.

of technology and, through development, design, testing, and production, the equipping of the Fleet. In part this progress was due to the emphasis placed on research and development in the post-World War II period. Whereas the low funding levels prior to the Korean War had resulted in the deferment or cancellation of many projects, the technological stockpile had been accumulating. The higher peacetime budgets following the Korean armistice and the increasing realization that substantial capabilities were required for conventional as well as nuclear warfare provided new opportunities.

Another reason for the rapid progress achieved in the late 1950's was the simple and direct alignment of responsibility and authority within the Navy Department, a carry-over from World War II. The material bureaus were still product-oriented, responsible for all phases—development, production, introduction into the Fleet, and support within their assigned areas. They had authority over the means, including relatively flexible use of appropriated funds. Although staffs had become increasingly involved in the review and approval processes, particularly after the implementation of Reorganization Plan No. 6 in 1953, it was still possible, in many areas, to gain prompt approval of worthy developmental projects.

The most notable achievement during this time was in ship propulsion, the product of an effort which had been jointly sponsored by the Navy Bureau of Ships and the Atomic Energy Commission since 1948.[10] The submarine *Nautilus* (SSN–571) first got underway on nuclear power on 17 January 1955. Operational tests conclusively proved the tremendous military step forward of a submarine that, for the first time, could operate underwater for the length of a cruise, and at sustained high submerged speeds. New and expanded roles for the submarine would follow. Not only did the new type of propulsion plant add new dimensions to undersea warfare, but it represented potential advances for surface ships fully as significant in terms of Fleet operations as the shift from coal to oil.

Another major transitional achievement was the introduction of guided-missiles into the Fleet. This was an area which had received much attention in the post-World War II era, both for antiship and antiaircraft purposes. The absence of potential enemy surface fleets of consequence had led to the placing of emphasis on the latter. The world's first guided-missile

---

[10] For a history of the development of nuclear propulsion, see Richard G. Hewlett and Francis Duncan, *Nuclear Navy* (Chicago: University of Chicago Press, 1974).

ship, the modernized *Boston* (CAG–1), equipped with her Terrier anti-aircraft system, joined the Fleet in November 1956. To stay abreast of the modern air threat, many ships would have to be equipped with missiles and other advanced systems. The cost would not be minor. One beneficial by-product, insofar as future warfare was concerned, was that experience with the Navy's own antiaircraft missiles and their technology would aid in developing tactics and countermeasures whereby aircraft could survive and maintain effectiveness during strikes in the Soviet missile environment later established over North Vietnam.

Along with enhanced air defense capabilities, the new systems led to new problems. One was the competition with guns for shipboard weight and space. A compromise would have to be reached between offensive and defensive weapons in new and modernized ships. Naval guns would have important missions to perform during the Vietnam War—in amphibious assaults, gunfire support, shore bombardment, and actions against enemy craft.

Significant improvements in Fleet capabilities were also being achieved in a wide variety of other areas, including antisubmarine weapons and detection systems, air-to-air guided missiles, a new generation of air-to-ground weapons, and tactical nuclear weapons.

It was during this period that the development of the Fleet Ballistic Missile system was started. A February 1955 study entitled "Meeting the Threat of Surprise Attack," prepared by a group headed by Dr. James R. Killian of the Massachusetts Institute of Technology, recommended such missiles, including submarine-launched types. That fall, after approving the Navy's recommendations, Secretary of Defense Wilson authorized the development of this capability. Chief of Naval Operations Admiral Burke established the Special Project Office, administratively supported by the Bureau of Ordnance. Assigned top priority within the Navy, the office was given essentially overriding authority insofar as naval resources were concerned. The result would be Polaris and the Fleet Ballistic Missile Sub-marine, which became operational in 1960. Subsequently the Navy would fulfill the keystone role in nuclear deterrence.

The problems of "block obsolescence" of ships built in World War II had already become a matter of major concern to naval leaders. However, faced with the funding needs of programs to gain new or improved capabili-ties, the demands for maintaining deployed forces, and the readiness needs of the Fleet as a whole, little progress could be made in replacing ships built in World War II. Temporary relief had to be gained through the expedient of extensive overhauls and modernization programs.

Command Responsibilities

One of the changes occurring during this period was in the unified command structure in the Pacific. During World War II, Admiral Nimitz had commanded both the Pacific Fleet and the joint and combined forces in the Pacific Ocean Area. This alignment of responsibilities was remarkably efficient in the campaigns to gain control of the sea and advance westward across the vast mid-Pacific. When the unified Pacific Command was established in the post-World War II period, a similar dual command arrangement was adopted. As the time neared for disestablishing the Far East Command, some in the Army and Air Force sought the elimination of the "double-hatted" assignment. In April 1957, the Chief of Naval Operations reacted to the pressures by assigning command responsibility for the fleet, under Commander in Chief, Pacific, to the Deputy Commander in Chief, U.S. Pacific Fleet, Vice Admiral (later Admiral) Maurice E. Curts. Retaining the title of CINCPACFLT, Stump continued to carry out the Navy's responsibilities with regard to governing the Bonin and Volcano Islands and the Northern Marianas Trust Territory.

When the Far East Command was disestablished on 1 July 1957, the Pacific Command assumed the former organization's missions, tasks, and responsibilities. The advocates of complete separation of the unified and fleet commands finally succeeded in their efforts. On 13 January 1958, Admiral Stump was divested of his duties as Commander in Chief, United States Pacific Fleet, while retaining those of Commander in Chief, Pacific.[11] In effect a new echelon had been added to the chain of command under the JCS executive agent.

One of the more active trouble spots in the Far East early in 1958, was Indonesia, and when civil strife intensified and an active rebellion broke out in Sumatra and the Celebes, American ships were sent to the area. Commander Seventh Fleet (Vice Admiral Wallace M. Beakley) formed Task Force 75 on 9 March 1958 for the protection of American citizens and such other actions as might be required in the Philippines-Indonesia area. The

---

[11] CINCPACFLT, Annual Report, FY 1957, p. 4.

force was initially composed of carrier *Philippine Sea* (CVS–47), cruiser *Bremerton* (CA–130), escorting destroyers, and amphibious ships. Carrier *Hornet* (CVA–12) and other units of the Seventh Fleet were prepared to augment the task force if needed. Later that month, the situation eased and the ships reverted to their normal task forces.[12]

Tensions in the Mediterranean had continued to rise after the overthrow of the Syrian government in August 1957. During the spring of 1958, Admiral Burke initiated action to delay the scheduled departure from the Mediterranean of Amphibious Squadron 4 and a Marine battalion landing team, which were being relieved by Amphibious Squadron 6 and its landing force. Amphibious Squadron 2, with a third battalion landing team embarked, also was deployed from the United States.[13]

When the government of Iraq was overthrown on 14 July 1958, President Camille Chamoun of Lebanon requested United States armed assistance in forty-eight hours. Burke had already stationed the Sixth Fleet where it was in readiness nearby. In response to Eisenhower's order that evening, Marines were landed in Beirut the next day. Admiral James L. Holloway, Jr., Commander in Chief, Eastern Atlantic and Mediterranean (CINC-NELM), was designated Commander in Chief Specified Command, Middle East. The Joint Chiefs of Staff assigned executive agent responsibilities for the Specified Command to the Chief of Naval Operations. Holloway flew to Lebanon, where he broke his flag in a destroyer until *Taconic* (AGC–17) reached the area. United States Army troops started arriving by air on the 19th. As a result of diplomatic actions, the situation soon stabilized. American troops were withdrawn in October.

Later, in reference to these events, Admiral Burke observed:

> In those days the Chief of Naval Operations had command of the Fleets. He was in reality the Chief of Naval Operations. . . . The CNO had the naval unified commanders under him—that is, he was in command of Cincpac, Cinclant, and Cincnelm. In addition, the CNO was the principle naval advisor to the President. The Chiefs were members of the National Security Council and all of them sat in on every conference pertaining to national security matters.

---

[12] ACNO (General Planning), "Summary of Important and Unique Naval Accomplishments, 3rd Quarter, FY 1958," of 22 May 1958; CINCPACFLT, Annual Report, Feb.–June 1958.

[13] As the crisis reached a climax that summer, the Sixth Fleet also included carriers *Saratoga* (CVA–60), *Essex,* and *Wasp* (CVA–18); guided missile cruiser *Boston;* heavy cruiser *Des Moines* (CA–134); two squadrons of destroyers; and Service Force ships.

Since the CNO was in command of the Fleets, I was responsible to the JCS and to the President for the readiness and movement of the Fleets. I followed President Eisenhower's and the JCS directives but it was up to me to have the Fleets positioned and ready for action whenever and wherever they were needed.

So I moved the Sixth Fleet and made other necessary preparations including reinforcing for any emergency—or at least for some of them. Naturally everyone was informed, but I did not have to wait until the end of weeks of debate before getting ready. It was a very flexible command system in which action could be taken very fast. It was a decentralized system.

The effectiveness of the Lebanon operations was possible because of this command system.[14]

Yet, by the time of the Lebanon landings, a congressional act altering these responsibilities was in the final stages of passage.

Meanwhile, a concurrent crisis came to a head in the Far East in the form of a threat against Taiwan. Evidence accumulated of a Communist military buildup on the mainland nearby. A third Chinese Communist airfield in that area was placed in operation on 6 August 1958, and a fourth on the 18th. Five days later the Communists commenced a heavy shelling of Nationalist-held Quemoy, a strategically located island near Amoy across the strait from Taiwan and in the vicinity of the Pescadores. What followed was a classic example of the use of United States Navy and other elements of national power in a deterrence role.[15]

As soon as information was received of the intense bombardment, Admiral Burke ordered the Seventh Fleet to the Taiwan area, where it would be in readiness for whatever operations might be required. The Seventh Fleet was then composed of carriers *Hancock* (CVA–19) and *Lexington* (CVA–16), 2 cruisers, 36 destroyers, 4 submarines, and 20 amphibious and support ships. About half the fleet was in Southeast Asian waters when the order was received.

The crisis intensified when, on 27 August, Chinese Communist radio broadcasts spoke of the imminence of an invasion of Quemoy and expressed a determination to "liberate" Taiwan. At this point, additional American ships were dispatched to the Western Pacific. One task group, composed

---

[14] Arleigh Burke, "The Lebanon Crisis," in "Proceedings, Naval History Symposium," pp. 70–80.

[15] For a study of the Quemoy crisis in the broad context of military, political, economic, psychological, and international elements, see Jonathan Trumball Howe, *Multicrises, Sea Power and Global Politics in the Missile Age* (Cambridge, Mass.: The Massachusetts Institute of Technology Press, 1971), pp. 161–282.

of the carrier *Essex* and escorting destroyers, recently involved in the Lebanon operation, was ordered through the Suez Canal to join the Seventh Fleet. Other ships, including the carrier *Midway* (CVA–41), were deployed from the Eastern Pacific. An amphibious task group, with Marines embarked, proceeded north from Singapore. A future combined United States-Republic of China amphibious exercise was announced. At the same time, destroyer patrols in the Formosa Strait were increased and additional United States Air Force planes flew to Taiwan. American naval advisors were sent to instruct the Chinese Nationalists in the loading and offloading of LSTs, and additional LSTs were furnished them.

By 28 August, carrier task groups and a Hunter-Killer antisubmarine force were operating near Taiwan. Supersonic carrier aircraft conducted sweeps between Taiwan and the mainland. Starting on 4 September, American escorts added their protection to the Nationalist resupply missions, operating up to the three-mile limit of Quemoy, as carriers furnished air cover. Secretary of State Dulles made a statement indicating that securing and protecting Quemoy and Matsu Islands had become increasingly related to the defense of Taiwan.

One of the uncertainties at the start of the Quemoy crisis was the extent to which the Nationalists would be able to establish air control in combat against the higher-performance, Communist MIG fighters. Reacting to the concentration of aircraft on mainland fields opposite Taiwan, the United States transferred Sidewinder missiles and aircraft modification kits to the Nationalists in early September. The Sidewinder was a simple heat-seeking, rocket-powered weapon developed under the cognizance of the Bureau of Ordnance by the Naval Ordnance Test Station, China Lake, California. By 15 September 1958, twenty Chinese F–86Fs had been equipped for the use of Sidewinders by an American field advisory team and eight pilots had completed training. By the 22nd all twenty-four pilots of a squadron of aircraft had qualified in the use of the missile. Three days later, four Sidewinder-equipped Chinese F–86Fs engaged MIG–17s. Six missiles were fired, destroying four of the opposing fighters. This was the first time in the history of the world that "kills" were registered by air-launched guided missiles. With these and other weapons the Chinese Nationalist Air Force performed well during the crisis, shooting down thirty-three Communist jets while losing only four of their own aircraft.[16]

------

[16] NA Taiwan, reports, 27–S–58 of 9 Sept., 32–S–58 of 15 Sept., 38–S–58 of 22 Sept., and 45–S–58 of 26 Sept. 1958, JN 63A–2336, box 75, FRC.

As the Nationalists succeeded in their resupply missions, the Communists gradually eased their siege of Quemoy. By the time the crisis was over, six attack carriers were operating in the Seventh Fleet.

SEATO Operations

Since the Geneva Conference, the Seventh Fleet had been engaged also in operations to enhance the readiness of the Southeast Asia Treaty Organization, give assurance of United States support, increase the resolve of Southeast Asian states, and help them achieve improved military capabilities. The range of possible United States actions in support of SEATO broadened when, early in 1955, in response to a Secretary of Defense request the Joint Chiefs reexamined plans for the possible application of power in response to aggression in Southeast Asia. Three of the four military services favored the concept which had been in effect since the days of the Dien Bien Phu crisis, namely readiness to retaliate immediately with air and naval attacks. As a result of Army recommendations, the concept became "readiness to retaliate promptly with attacks by the most effective combination of U.S. armed forces." [17]

Admiral Stump proposed a demonstration in Thailand of American mobile striking power. After the idea won initial approval in Washington, the Assistant Secretary of Defense (ISA) delayed the issuance of invitations until the cost of the exercise over and above normal operating costs could be determined.

Firm Link, as the demonstration was called, was the first combined SEATO exercise to be scheduled in Southeast Asia. United States Navy forces, under the command of Rear Admiral Lester K. Rice, included carrier *Princeton* (CVS–37), destroyers *McDermut* (DD–677) and *Tingey* (DD–539), and seaplane tender *Salisbury Sound* (AV–13). In addition to American Army, Navy, Marine, and Air Force units, soldiers of Thailand and the Philippines participated. Britain contributed two destroyers and a light cruiser and Australia two destroyers. Vietnam, Burma, Laos, Cambodia, and Indonesia sent observers. The forces of the various countries were not formed into a combined command but operated on a basis of

---

[17] *U.S.-V.N. Relations,* bk 1, pp. 13–14, bk 2. pt. IVA.4, pp. 10–11; memo, JCS to SECDEF, of 16 Nov. 1956 in *Ibid.,* bk 10, pp. 1096–97.

mutual cooperation and coordination. Since the invitation to participate was sent out little more than a week before the scheduled date, Australia, New Zealand, and Pakistan complained that they did not have time to plan a greater role in the exercise.[18]

On 15 February 1956 helicopters flew an 850-man Marine assault force from *Princeton,* cruising off Bangkok, to Duan Muang Airport near the city. That same day *Salisbury Sound* offloaded Philippine troops at the Klong Toi docks. A day later, participating forces provided exhibitions for the populace. Tours were conducted through *Salisbury Sound, Princeton,* and *McDermut.* On the 17th, the exercise concluded with a military parade witnessed by a crowd of about 750,000 people. In evaluating the demonstration, the American Ambassador to Thailand, Max Bishop, stated that *Firm Link* was one of the few American actions that maintained the impetus behind the policy of containing Communist expansion in Asia.[19]

Taking another step to strengthen SEATO, the United States, at the Karachi SEATO Council meeting in March 1956, proposed that a permanent military planning staff replace the existing *ad hoc* one. The Joint Chiefs's position reflected that of Admiral Stump. He was satisfied with the old system but felt that, if it became a political necessity to demonstrate the American commitment to SEATO, the United States should take the initiative and propose a permanent organization. The permanent staff would consist of three American officers and representatives from each of the other SEATO signatories.[20]

In May 1956 the United States and the Philippines sponsored exercise *Sea Link* to instruct participating personnel in amphibious procedures and to develop proficiency in the delivery of naval gunfire support to ground operations in the SEATO area. Instruction of the representatives of member nations was provided by a team from the Pacific Fleet's Amphibious Training Command. This was followed by a naval gunfire support exercise conducted by a combined task group (Captain Reid P. Fiala, commanding), consisting of 2 American destroyers, 2 Australian destroyers, 3 Philippine ships, and an American shore-fire control unit.

---

[18] Memos, OP–60 to CNO, ser 0001532 of 12 Jan. 1956, OP–61 to SECNAV, ser 0036P61 of 10 Feb. 1956; CARDIV 17, report, ser 044 of 12 Mar. 1956.

[19] Memo, OP–61 to SECNAV, ser 00192 of 9 May 1956; CARDIV 17, report, ser 044 of 12 Mar. 1956.

[20] Memos, OP–60 to CNO, No. 54–56 of 20 Feb. 1956, ser 0019 of 17 Jan. 1956, and No. 398–56 of 26 Nov. 1956.

Later that year the Southeast Asian members of SEATO sought a definite commitment of American forces to add substance to the new organization. But conscious of its own security needs and other bilateral and multilateral commitments, the United States was not willing to assign forces permanently.[21]

In 1957, the United States Navy participated in four SEATO exercises. The first, *Astra*, a British-sponsored exercise held in April and May, simulated the escort of a convoy from Singapore to Bangkok against air and submarine opposition. The Seventh Fleet provided three destroyer escorts, a submarine, and antisubmarine warfare patrol aircraft. This was followed, in October, by an Australian-sponsored exercise, *Albatross,* to improve combined air-surface operations in the protection of maritime shipping in the South China Sea. Again, Seventh Fleet destroyer escorts, patrol aircraft, and a submarine participated. Another SEATO exercise that same month was *Teamwork,* co-sponsored by the United States and Thailand. During this exercise, United States naval forces conducted an amphibious demonstration by a Seventh Fleet amphibious task group and a Marine battalion landing team supported by Marine aircraft. Classroom instruction preceded the exercise. The final SEATO operation that year was a larger exercise, *Phiblink,* in November and December. Participating forces included the Seventh Fleet Amphibious Force, the Third Marine Division, a Hunter-Killer task group, and a Philippine Navy task group. Other SEATO nations sent observers.

Efforts to enhance the military preparedness of SEATO continued. Another exercise was *Ocean Link,* held in May 1958 to provide training on advanced operations by a combined task force. The force included carriers from the United States, Britain, and Australia. Other SEATO maritime and amphibious exercises were conducted in the following months. Whatever else the Southeast Asia Treaty Organization may or may not have accomplished, there could be no doubt of the advances made in understanding and in teamwork insofar as SEATO naval forces were concerned.

Changes in Responsibility

That summer, the Defense Reorganization Act of 1958 brought about fundamental changes in the chain of command and in departmental responsi-

---

[21] Memo, JCS to SECDEF, of 16 Nov. 1956 in *U.S.-V.N. Relations,* bk 10, pp. 1096–97, bk 1, pt. IVA.1, pp. A12, A14.

bilities. In his State of the Union Message at the start of the year, President Eisenhower had presented his views on the defense establishment and how it could be improved. After highlighting the development of intercontinental ballistic missiles and Polaris, and referring to "revolutionary new devices," he stated that some important new weapons did not fit into any existing categories. In his opinion, they not only cut across military services but also transcended all services, and in some cases defied classification by "branch of Service." [22] Eisenhower announced the initiation of an administration study of reorganization, the objectives of which were:

1. "Real unity" of the Defense Establishment in "all principal features of military activities."
2. Better integration of defensive resources, particularly newer weapons.
3. Single control of some advanced development projects.
4. Clear subordination of the military services to duly constituted civilian authority.
5. The elimination of excessive compartments.
6. Clear organization and decisive central direction to end interservice disputes.[23]

As he had in 1953, the President drew upon a study to bolster his stand, which this time was a report released by the Rockefeller Brothers Fund four days earlier. The report recommended removing the military departments from the chain of operational command; continuing the participation of the service chiefs on the Joint Chiefs of Staff, but only as advisors to the chairman and with particular responsibility for the areas of logistics, training, and procurement; making generals and admirals officers of the Armed Forces of the United States with their permanent promotions being issued by the Department of Defense instead of each service; and giving the Secretary of Defense authority over all research, development, and procurement, including the right to cancel or transfer programs.[24]

---

[22] One case of inter-service rivalry in 1957 was Army-Air Force competition for cognizance of land-based ballistic missiles. Another arose from the needs of continental air defense. On the one hand, the Army was developing a Nike system. On the other, the Air Force was developing a system which would use the Navy's Talos guided missile.

[23] "Annual Message to the Congress on the State of the Union," 9 Jan. 1958 in *Dwight D. Eisenhower* in series *Public Papers of the Presidents: 1958* (Washington: GPO, 1959), pp. 2–9.

[24] Rockefeller Brothers Fund, Special Studies Project, Panel II, *International Security: The Military Aspect* in series *America at Mid-Century* (Garden City, N.Y.: Doubleday and Co., 1959), p. 63. Military members of Panel II were Generals Frederick L. Anderson, USA, and James McCormack, USAF, and Colonel George A. Lincoln, USA.

In a later message to Congress on 3 April 1958, the President expressed his opinion that:

> First, separate ground, sea and air warfare is gone forever. If ever again we should be involved in war, we will fight it in all elements, with all services, and one single concentrated effort . . . strategical and tactical planning must be completely unified, combat forces organized into unified commands . . . singly led and prepared to fight as one, regardless of service. The accomplishment of this result is the basic function of the Secretary of Defense, advised and assisted by the Joint Chiefs of Staff and operated under the supervision of the Commander-in-Chief.[25]

The President's legislative proposal incorporated many of the recommendations of the Rockefeller report. Secretary of Defense McElroy supported the President's plan by stating that he felt it would eliminate one step in the line of command from the commander in chief to the unified commanders. He noted that "the military departments, their respective Secretaries and individual service chiefs will no longer be interposed between the Secretary of Defense and the unified commanders";[26] yet the insertion of the secretaries of the military departments into the chain had been not through law but by executive action in 1953.

Congress did not agree to all of the features recommended by the President, but it included many of them in the Defense Reorganization Act on 6 August 1958. In one radical revision of authority the Secretary of Defense was now permitted to make changes in the responsibilities of the military departments. The latter were now merely "separately organized" instead of "separately administered." Subject to overall policy with regard to the revised act and a thirty-day notification for possible congressional rejection, the Secretary of Defense was directed to "take appropriate steps (including the transfer, reassignment, abolition, and consolidation of functions . . .) to provide in the Department of Defense for more effective, efficient, and economical administration and operations and to eliminate duplication." The congressional act specified that this provision did not apply to "major combatant functions." A loop-hole, however, was provided by a statement that for this purpose, "any supply or service activity common

---

[25] *Dwight D. Eisenhower*, p. 274.

[26] U.S., Congress, House, Committee on Armed Services, *Hearings on Sundry Legislation Affecting the Military Establishment, 1958* (85th Cong., 2nd sess.) (Washington: GPO, 1959), bk 4, pp. 5975–76.

to more than one military department shall not be considered a 'major combatant function.' " This significant qualification resulted not from the deliberations of the Armed Services committees at the time of the hearings, but from an amendment proposed during a general session of the House of Representatives.[27]

Another provision of the act authorized the Secretary of Defense to "assign, or reassign, to one or more departments or services, the development and operational use of new weapons or weapon systems." A Director of Defense Research and Engineering with extraordinary statutory authority was established in the Office of the Secretary of Defense.

One of the most far-reaching changes was the elimination of executive agents, the culmination of a step-by-step process begun after World War II. During the fall of 1945, President Truman had disestablished the position of Commander in Chief, United States Fleet and transferred the responsibilities and authority to the Chief of Naval Operations. As a consequence, the Chief of Naval Operations then commanded the operating forces of the Navy and acted as the Joint Chiefs of Staff executive agent for certain unified commands, one of which was the Pacific Command. In 1953, President Eisenhower's executive actions altered the chain of unified command so that it went from the Secretary of Defense via the secretaries of the military departments, who acted as his executive agents. However, as a result of authority delegated by the Secretary of the Navy, the role of the Chief of Naval Operations continued much as before. Now, under the latest act, the unified and specified commands were made directly responsible to the President and the Secretary of Defense. They would establish, with the advice and assistance of the Joint Chiefs of Staff, unified or specified commands and determine their force structures. Military missions were to be assigned by the Secretary of Defense. He would assign responsibility for support of these commands to one or more of the military departments.

The act strengthened the authority of the Chairman of the Joint Chiefs of Staff over the Joint Staff. He was now permitted to vote on JCS decisions. The authorized ceiling for the Joint Staff was raised from 210 to 400.

The statutory responsibilities of the Chief of Naval Operations, which had been assigned in 1915, were revised. No longer was he charged by law "with the operations of the fleet and with the preparation and readiness of

---

[27] U.S., Congress, House, *Congressional Record* (85th Cong., 2nd sess.), 12 June 1958, Vol. 104, pt. 8, pp. 11031–33.

plans for its use in war." Now his responsibilities were similar to those of the Chief of Staff of the Army, namely, to "exercise supervision over such of the members and organizations of the Navy and Marine Corps as the Secretary of the Navy determines."

Questions had been raised in congressional hearings concerning the CNO's responsibilities and why they should differ from those of the Army's Chief of Staff, whose duties within the General Staff system under the Department of War were to supervise the members and organizations of the Army. Admiral Burke responded with a clear explanation of the function of command in the Navy.[28]

Command, at least as practiced in the Navy, meant many functions, not always including operational control. Naval ships, highly mobile and versatile, operated throughout the oceans of the world, sometimes singly, sometimes in groups. In war and in peace they often shifted on short notice from task group to task group, from task force to task force, and even from fleet to fleet—now under one operational commander, now another. The lessons of history, particularly in World War II, had demonstrated the importance of continuity of the chain of command for most functions under the CNO, the Fleet commanders in chief, and the type commanders, regardless of shifts of operational control. Moreover, all forces not assigned to unified commands or specified combatant commands remained for all purposes, according to the act, in their respective departments.

When Thomas S. Gates, Jr., then Secretary of the Navy, later became Secretary of Defense he clarified some of the unresolved questions of leaders within the Navy when he directed that "the chain of command for purposes other than the operational direction of unified and specified commands runs from the President to the Secretary of Defense to the Secretaries of the military departments." The Chief of Naval Operations continued to be responsible to the Secretary of the Navy for "the command, use, and administration of the Operating Forces of the Navy." He was to discharge this responsibility "in a manner consistent with the full opera-

---

[28] For a discussion of Navy principles of command, see Admiral Burke's testimony before the House Committee on the Armed Services in *Sundry Legislation Affecting the Naval Establishment,* bk 4, pp. 6359–64. Admiral Burke's statement on pages 6344–50 gives an excellent summary of his views with regard to the principles which should govern the organization of national defense.

tional command vested in their unified and specified combatant commanders." [29]

Other provisions of the Reorganization Act would influence or force the Navy Department to alter radically its principles of operation. Some of these were in continuation of gradual changes taking place since 1949, such as the creation of centers of authority within the Office of the Secretary of Defense. After the 1953 executive actions, the Secretary had added still more areas of functional authority across departmental and military service lines. In 1956, the secretary designated military departments as "single managers." One of the areas of single management was land transportation within the United States, and to that end the Military Traffic Management Agency was established under the Army. A single manager system was set up for supply management of certain categories of "common use items." Secretary of Defense Neil McElroy expanded the single manager system in fiscal year 1957, establishing the Medical, Clothing and Textile, and Military Petroleum Supply Agencies. The Navy and the other military services were becoming ever more dependent on others for some of the essentials upon which the readiness, effectiveness, and endurance of the operating forces depended.

The system of designating military departments as single managers would last only a short time. An Armed Forces Supply Support Center was established directly under the Office of the Secretary of Defense to "integrate supply channels" and to coordinate procurement efforts more closely. The center administered certain supply programs common to more than one service. [30] The Defense Advanced Research Project Agency was organized in February 1958. By creating new agencies directly under the Office of the Secretary of Defense, rather than fixing responsibilities on one of the three military departments, the number of "components" under the secretary was increasing and authority within the Department of Defense becoming more fragmented. In addition to their staffing and

[29] Defense Department, "Functions of the Armed Forces and the Joint Chiefs of Staff," DOD Directive 5100.1 of 16 Mar. 1958; Navy Department, "Assignment and Distribution of Authority and Responsibility for the Administration of the Department of the Navy," General Order No. 5 of 14 May 1959.

[30] U.S., Defense Department, *Semiannual Report of the Secretary of Defense,* Jan.–June 1956 (Washington: GPO, 1957), pp. 32–35; U.S., Defense Department, *Semiannual Report of the Secretary of Defense,* Jan.–June 1957 (Washington: GPO, 1958), pp. 35–36; U.S., Defense Department, *Semiannual Report of the Secretary of Defense,* Jan.–June 1958 (Washington: GPO, 1959), pp. 49–50.

coordinating functions, subordinates in the Office of the Secretary of Defense would now, in effect, exercise line authority in certain areas.

All in all the act was the culmination of a process leading away from result-oriented management principles. Increasingly the way in which responsibilities would be carried out focused on such objectives as "unified controls," "consolidation," "amalgamation," "common services," "single agencies," "common policies" to the extent that these tended to be treated as primary goals.

Impact on the Navy Department

The cummulative effects of the step-by-step process, that had been taking place since the passage of the 1947 National Defense bill, and of the changes that were in the offing as a result of the new Reorganization Act raised serious questions as to whether or not the Navy Department organization, division of responsibilities, and principles of management would be adequate to ensure full effectiveness of the naval operating forces. An increasing number of the defense-wide actions, in line with recommendations by individuals during the 1944 hearings, had an impact on a number of functional areas on which Fleet effectiveness, efficiency, and endurance depended. Now that the Navy Department was no longer "separately organized," others would be making decisions, issuing directives, directing procedures, conducting reviews, and exercising controls over areas crucial to Fleet readiness. Delegation of authority within the Navy Department would be more difficult. Increasingly it was found necessary for the Navy Secretariat and the Office of the Chief of Naval Operations to become involved in the areas for which the bureaus had been responsible. In the view of one analyst of defense management, provisions of the act resulted in the sharing of authority "not by those responsible for the operational performance of the armed services, but by an undetermined (if not unidentified) number of functional assistant secretaries and directors." [31]

In August 1958, Secretary of the Navy Gates appointed the Committee on Organization of the Department of the Navy, chaired by Under Secretary of the Navy William B. Franke. While making an overall review of the department's organization, the committee explored comparative forms

---

[31] Ries, *Management of Defense,* p. 185.

of organization. One form specifically examined was "the vertical-type organization, as exemplified by the general staff system in particular." This system was characterized as concentrating both military and non-military responsibilities in the person of a single military officer acting under a civilian political superior. After examining the pros and cons, the committee concluded that "a continuation of the present bilinear system, with its definite division of military and nonmilitary duties and responsibilities among uniformed and civilian officials, offers a greater prospect for the successful prosecution of future naval warfare. . . ." Some organizational changes were recommended in light of the Reorganization Act, and to carry out the Navy's current and future functions in the most effective, efficient, and economical manner.[32]

One example of the impact on the Navy Department of changes in the Office of the Secretary of Defense was the assignment of cognizance over research and development within the Office of the Chief of Naval Operations to a Deputy Chief of Naval Operations (Development). Another was the designation of an Assistant Secretary of the Navy (Research and Development), although the assistant secretaries had been reduced from four to three by the recent act.

Changes in organizational responsibilities beyond those recommended by the Franke committee would follow in later years. Many of these would be in response to Department of Defense actions authorized by the act. Others would be deemed necessary to meet the expanding demands of the growing staffs under the Secretary of Defense and the Joint Chiefs and to provide effective interfaces with defense agencies.[33] By June 1959, personnel attached to Office of Secretary of Defense activities had grown to 2,773 (1,704 civilians and 1,069 military).

Strategy

Organizational changes were accompanied by gradual adjustments in the strategic policy of the United States. These adjustments were reflected in

---

[32] *Report of the Committee on Organization of the Department of the Navy: 1959* (Washington: GPO, 1959), pp. 16–18.

[33] U.S., Defense Department, *Annual Report of the Secretary of Defense,* July 1958–June 1959 (Washington: GPO, 1959), pp. 38, 41, 45; SECNAV, "Annual Report," FY 1959 in *Ibid.,* p. 279.

programs and budgets after time-lags which had become longer as a result of the echelons added to the review processes.

As the Soviet Union built up its nuclear stockpile and delivery capabilities, continental defense increasingly became a claimant for limited peacetime funds. The Soviets tested an intercontinental ballistic missile and launched satellites into orbit around the earth. By 1956, a condition was reached which some described as a "balance of terror." Hints of continuance of a policy of "massive retaliation" continued, as evidenced by the President's statement in January 1958 that "the most powerful deterrent to war in the world today lies in the retaliatory power of our Strategic Air Command and the aircraft of our Navy." In the same address, he stressed the threat of Communist imperialism, observing that "the Soviets are, in short, waging total cold war."

Such statements were, however, accompanied by evidence of increased recognition of the need for conventional forces to cope with limited warfare situations. One sign of a shifting policy toward a more balanced strategy was the President's highlighting of the need to maintain freedom of the seas. In January 1960 Eisenhower would identify conventional forces required to meet "situations of less than general nuclear war." Among these forces were Navy carriers and the Marine Corps.[34] An eventful period lay ahead for these conventional forces.

The Struggles for Power Continue

The year of 1959 started with Fidel Castro's overthrow of Fulgencio Batista; Cuba soon would be under the rule of the Communists. During the Twenty-First Party Congress of the Soviet Union, which convened in Moscow on 27 January 1959 with seventy foreign Communist parties represented, Khrushchev highlighted the "national liberation" struggles in Asia, Africa, and South America, with lesser attention focused on Europe.

In March, the Chinese employed military force to crush Tibet. Thomas Gates, now Secretary of Defense, assessed the overall situation in the Far East later that year, when he observed: "During Fiscal Year 1959, Communist China stepped up the pace of its offensive against the independent

---

[34] "Annual Message to the Congress on the State of the Union," 9 Jan. 1958 in *Dwight D. Eisenhower*, pp. 3–4.

nations along its frontiers, again resorting to overt military action while continuing its policy of constant political and economic pressure." [35] Communist struggles for power were continuing.

---

[31] SECDEF, *Annual Report,* FY 1959, p. 90; Leonhard, *Kremlin Since Stalin,* p. 331.

CHAPTER XVI

The Stage Is Set, 1957-1959

In June 1957, the United States MAAG had reported a "slight but notable increase" in Communist violence within the Republic of Vietnam. Aggressive acts were particularly evident along the Mekong and its interconnecting Bassac River, which flowed from the Cambodian border to the sea. Chau Doc (Chau Phu), was the scene of a mass murder of seventeen citizens in July. In September a district chief and his family were gunned down in My Tho. In November 1957, Chau Doc, Sa Dec, Long Xuyen, Vinh Long, Can Tho, My Tho, and Truc Giang were scenes of killings, other acts of violence, and kidnappings of civilian officials, civil guardsmen, security agents, and others. December witnessed more spectacular assassinations. Then, major incidents occurred in An Giang and Phong Dinh Provinces downriver from Chau Doc Province, and at the village of Thanh My Tay (near Chau Doc). Attacks on shipping and against foreign nationals were reported.[1]

Vietnamese military operations against guerrilla units in these and other areas were largely dependent on supplies transported by water. The Danang area alone required 2,000 tons of military supplies a month. Although much of the cargo was shipped in merchant marine bottoms, the Vietnamese Navy now employed four LSMs, a small tanker (YOG), a small cargo ship (AKL), and LCUs to transport cargo along the coast.[2]

Despite the acts of violence, Diem continued to make remarkable progress in building a nation within South Vietnam. As assessed by one student of the period, "Diem alone carried Vietnam into statehood."[3] Communist sources confirmed the effectiveness of the campaign against their infrastructure. One South Vietnamese Communist observed that "from 1957 to 1960 the cadres who had remained in the South had almost all been arrested." Another stated that "the period from the Armistice of 1954 until 1958 was

---

[1] *U.S.-V.N. Relations,* bk 2, pt. IVA.5, tab 1, p. 30, tab 2, p. 56; NA Saigon, report, ser 2–S–58 of 10 Jan. 1958, JN 63A–2336, box 53, FRC.

[2] Navy Section, MAAG Vietnam, "Country Statement," of 22 Jan. 1958.

[3] Shaplen, "Cult of Diem."

the darkest time for the VC [Viet Cong] in South Vietnam," and that "the political agitation policy proposed by the Communist Party could not be carried out due to the arrest of a number of party members by RVN [Republic of Vietnam] authorities." Referring to the 1957–1958 period, a captured Viet Cong history stated:

> At this time, the political struggle movement of the masses, although not defeated, was encountering increasing difficulty and increasing weakness; the Party bases, although not completely destroyed, were significantly weakened, and in some areas, quite seriously; the prestige of the masses and of the revolution suffered.[4]

As Diem reacted to assassinations and other Communist activities, criticism began to mount against the priority he assigned to security, rather than to land reform and "rural revolution." In some cases, the criticism was Communist inspired, but negative comment also emanated from those who felt that the resolution to South Vietnam's problems lay primarily in peaceful reforms in the countryside rather than the use of force.[5]

By 1958 the Communists were in firm control of North Vietnam. Bolstered by the moral and material support of other "socialist" countries, the North Vietnamese were able to devote an increasing amount of their effort toward the longer-range goal of extending Communist control to South Vietnam. The aid they were receiving was substantial. According to a Communist source, "the socialist countries" through 1959 provided approximately two billion rubles worth of uncompensated aid and long-term credits to the Democratic Republic of Vietnam. Of this amount, 400 million rubles in uncompensated aid was given by the U.S.S.R. Also, for the period 1955–1958, 4,755 technical experts from "socialist countries" visited North Vietnam, 1,083 of whom were from the Soviet Union and 3,245 from the People's Republic of China.[6]

The Soviet Union by now had resolved the internal struggle which had been triggered by Stalin's death. When a Conference of Communist and Workers' Parties of Socialist Countries convened in November 1957, Ho and Le Duan went to Moscow. In the final declaration, concurred in by all

---

[4] Quoted in *U.S.-V.N. Relations,* bk 2, pt. IVA.5, tab 2, pp. 51, 52, 54.

[5] *Ibid.,* pp. 24–26.

[6] Bui Kong Chyng, "Pomoshch'stran sotsialisticheskogo lageria v vosstanovlenii i razvitii narodnogo khoziastra DRV," in *Demokraticheskara Respublika V'etnam, 1945–1960,* ed. A. A. Guber and Nguyen-khan'-Toan (Moscow: Publishing House of Eastern Literature, 1960).

the participants except Yugoslavia, note was made of the establishment of the Democratic Republic of Vietnam as an independent state, the intensification of struggle in colonial and dependent countries for "national liberation," the war in Indochina, the SEATO "aggressive bloc," "the possibility of nonpeaceful transition to socialism," the fostering of "solidarity between the Communist and Workers' parties of all countries . . . [as] the main guarantee of . . . victory," their "responsibility with regard to the destinies of the world Socialist system and the International Communist movement," and "the joint struggle for the common goals. . . ." After his return to Hanoi, Le Duan issued a statement in which he said that the North Vietnamese viewed the Moscow declaration as a signal from Peking and Moscow to pursue their objectives in the South by force.[7]

The Vietnamese Navy

Under these threatening circumstances, the task of strengthening the South Vietnamese Navy was becoming more urgent. The first group of Vietnamese had returned from the United States and its members were serving as instructors at the Vietnamese naval schools. Saigon MAAG officers concluded that, "judging by the performance of US trained Vietnamese Navy instructors, the US school training program has proved very effective." Further progress in the training within Vietnam was made possible by increases in the number of American naval officers and enlisted men assigned there. However, the total number of naval personnel, including Marines, assigned to MAAG and the Temporary Equipment Recovery Mission was still only seventy-eight, a marginal number considering the future problems anticipated. By the spring of 1958, the Saigon shipyard had gained the capabilities needed to take over the entire overhaul program for the Vietnamese Navy, in addition to providing routine upkeep for small craft and dry-docking services for merchant ships. Subic completed the last scheduled overhaul of a Vietnamese ship in April 1958.[8]

---

[7] "Declaration of Representatives of the Communist and Workers' Parties of the Socialist Countries," *Current History,* XXXIV (Jan. 1958), pp. 42–47; *U.S.-V.N. Relations,* bk 2, pt. IVA.5, p. 28.

[8] Navy Section, MAAG Vietnam, "Country Statement," of 22 Jan. 1958; NA Saigon, reports, 14–57 of 12 Feb. and 57–57 of 9 Apr. 1957, JN 62A–2681, box 69, FRC; Navy Section, MAAG Vietnam, "Quarterly Activities Report," of 10 Sept. 1957; Navy Division, MAAG Vietnam, "Summary," of 31 Dec. 1957.

Two factions competed for leadership of the Vietnamese Navy; one was led by the head of the Navy, Captain My, and the other by his rival Lieutenant Commander Ho Tan Quyen, who had political backing in the Defense Ministry and the Vietnamese Army's General Staff. One of the criticisms leveled against My was his advocacy of a "much bigger Navy than the U.S. or his own government considered necessary or would support." In November 1957, My was ordered to report for training at the Navy's Post Graduate School at Monterey, California.[9]

Prior to My's departure, the MAAG helped Quyen draft a new plan for the organization of the Vietnamese Navy, which Diem approved on 1 July 1958. As reported by the Navy Section of the U.S. MAAG:

> The new organization formalized for the first time a written organization for the VN Navy approved by the President and established missions and command channels. The Naval Deputy now has under his direct, exclusive command a prescribed Naval Staff, shore facilities command (Naval Stations and Schools Command), and three operating commands; viz, Sea Forces, River Forces, and Marine Corps. It places part of the Supply Depot functions under Navy control but leaves all other logistics functions, including the shipyard, under the Director of the Naval Technical Service, who in turn reports to the General Staff on logistical matters and to the Director of Administration, Budgeting and Accounting on finance matters.

The Navy Section viewed the reorganization as "a step in the right direction," but stated, "it is impossible to evaluate all the ramifications of the change at this early date."[10]

American naval officers who visited Saigon early in 1959 left with favorable opinions of the condition of the small South Vietnamese Navy, which then had a strength of about 3,600 men. Admiral Hopwood reported in March 1959 that, on a recent trip through Southeast Asia, he was "favorably impressed with the Vietnam Navy, its ships, craft and facilities." His Assistant Chief of Staff for Intelligence, Captain Rufus L. Taylor, had previously concluded, after a four-day visit to Saigon, "that the Vietnamese are really trying to achieve an effective naval force." These assessments were more favorable than those of the Naval Attache's office, which con-

---

[9] NA Saigon, reports, ser 14–58 of 18 Jan., 25–S–58 of 6 May, and 27–S–58 of 9 May 1958, JN 63A–2336, box 54, FRC.

[10] NA Saigon, reports, 25–S–58 of 6 May and 27–S–58 of 9 May 1958, JN 63A–2336, box 54, FRC; Navy Section, MAAG Vietnam, "Narrative Study," of 24 Aug. 1958.

sidered most of the Vietnamese ships to be in an unsatisfactory overall condition "by U.S. standards." [11]

Preliminaries to a New Phase

The period of low-level conflict between the Communists, following the 1954 Geneva Agreement, was drawing to a close. Although the implementing order would not be issued until four months later, North Vietnam's decision to resume the armed struggle apparently was made at the Fifteenth Central Committee Conference in January 1959.[12]

Early in 1959, Hanoi ordered the preparation of guerrilla bases in South Vietnam. By sea and by land the Viet Cong in the south were receiving increased military supplies from North Vietnam. When Admiral Felt, now Commander in Chief, Pacific, visited Saigon in February 1959, Diem informed him of infiltration from Laos and Cambodia and of his protest to the International Control Commission over Viet Minh incursions into the demilitarized zone.

From January 1957 to July 1959, the Republic of Vietnam reported 174 assassinations to the commission. In May 1959, the Fifteenth Plenum of the Communist Party's Central Committee in North Vietnam "called for a strong North Vietnam as a base for helping the South Vietnamese to overthrow Diem and eject the United States." On 13 May, one day after the conference communique. an editorial in *Nhan Dan* stated:

> Our compatriots in the south will struggle resolutely and persistently against the cruel U.S.-Diem regime, holding aloft the traditions of the (1941) South Vietnam uprising, the (1945) Ba To uprising, and the August (1945) general uprising . . . and other valuable traditions of the workers' movement and of countless legal and semilegal struggles. . . . Our people are determined to struggle with their traditional heroism and by all necessary forms and measures so as to achieve the goal of the revolution.

The Democratic Republic of Vietnam began to commit its armed forces

---

[11] Ltrs, CINCPACFLT to CNO, ser 2/00226 of 17 Mar. 1959 and CINCPACFLT to CINCPAC, ser 61/00257 of 26 Mar. 1959. For the views of the Naval Attache, see NA Saigon, report, 87–59 of 16 Apr. 1959, JN 63A–2990, box 46, FRC.

[12] King C. Chen, "Hanoi's Three Decisions and the Escalation of the Vietnam War," *Political Science Quarterly,* (Summer 1975), p. 246.

to the conflict in Laos the following month. Guerrilla actions in South Vietnam soon would approach a state of insurgency.[13]

Increased aid would be required by the Republic of Vietnam to counter the mounting Communist offensive, and the primary source of that aid would be the United States. The Vietnam conflict had undergone many changes since World War II. Step-by-step the United States had progressed from a period of non-involvement in the military aspects of the conflict, through a stage in which the Navy and other military services were indirectly or remotely involved, to the point where primary responsibility had been assumed by America for assisting South Vietnam in its defensive efforts.

The Prolonged Conflict

By 1959, the Vietnam conflict was completing its fourteenth year. The time was nearing when United States military forces would become more directly involved in the struggle. In many respects the experiences of the French and Vietnamese naval forces foreshadowed roles the United States Navy later would be required to fulfill.

The conflict had emerged at the end of World War II during the transitional period from hostilities to peace in the Far East, where the situation differed basically from that in Europe. At the time the Germans surrendered, the Allied armies occupied Germany and possessed the position and strength to force their enemy's disarmament and to carry out the duties of occupation. In the Pacific, when the war ended with unanticipated suddenness American forces were preparing for an assault on the Japanese home islands. The immediate military concerns of the United States involved projecting occupational forces by sea into Japan, where opposition was still possible, supporting the occupation, aiding the Chinese during surrender of the powerful Japanese forces on the mainland, and assisting in the Japanese evacuation from Asia.

In Vietnam, the four-month-old Bao Dai government, installed by the Japanese in March 1945 when they ousted the French, was tenuous at best and lacked military forces. By striking when signs of an impending Japanese surrender first appeared, Ho Chi Minh and his comrades were able to gain

---

[13] Quoted in *Ibid.; U.S.-V.N. Relations*, bk 2, pt. IVA.5, tab 1, p. 30, tab 2, pp. 23–31; "Speech Opening the Third National Congress of the Viet-Nam Workers' Party," in Ho, *On Revolution*, pp. 345–51.

footholds in key cities, force Bao Dai's departure, announce the establishment of a provisional government, and proclaim independence—all prior to the arrival of Allied occupational forces.

Advocating eventual independence for the states of Indochina, the United States refrained from supporting the French return. No alternate plan charted the way toward the ultimate goal of free and independent states. Occupational responsibilities, assigned essentially on the basis of the wartime Allied military situation, placed China in control of the area of Vietnam that it had ruled for so long in early history. Chinese use of Haiphong and the railroad into Kwangsi was the price paid by the French for the final withdrawal of the Chinese occupational forces. Meanwhile, the Viet Minh had extended their influence in Tonkin. Through negotiations, they achieved tacit French recognition of their government. Involvement of the United States Navy during this period was confined to the amphibious withdrawl of Chinese occupation forces in 1945–1946 and their transportation to North China.

In the South the British welcomed the French, to whom they transferred occupational responsibilities. Through riverine and amphibious operations, the French Navy gained control of critical points in the Mekong Delta and along the coast. An amphibious operation landed troops in Tonkin, where French naval forces assisted in the occupation of key cities.

The struggle for power between the Viet Minh and France erupted into war in December 1946. By now the United States Navy was extensively involved as a complement to diplomacy in the expanding Cold War. Torn between the goal of independent Indochinese states and the desire to stem Communist advances, American decision-makers denied the military aid requested by France for use in the French-Viet Minh War, pending substantial progress toward Vietnamese independence. Although France took some steps in this direction, the United States government considered them insufficient. Despite the lack of direct aid, French Union forces, making effective use of their limited naval capabilities in combination with their land and air forces, won or regained control of heavily populated and strategically important delta and coastal regions in the North as well as the South. Withdrawing to remote bases, the Viet Minh confined their armed activities to guerrilla-type actions.

The Communist victory in China in 1949 then led to a new phase of the French-Viet Minh War. Following the ratification by the French National Assembly in February 1950 of an agreement with the State of

Vietnam, the United States determined that the minimum prerequisites for economic and military aid had been met. Trained in China and supplied with increasing quantities of arms and munitions, Viet Minh regular forces seized key points along lines of communication south of the Chinese border. On 1 May 1950, President Truman approved funding for urgently needed military items. When war started in Korea, the President ordered expansion and acceleration of the aid for Indochina. Some American naval and other military aid to France and the Associated States arrived barely in time to help defeat Viet Minh offensives against the Red River Delta.

As 1952 drew to a close, the United States sought an early conclusion to the protracted French-Viet Minh War, urged more aggressive French military actions, and sought information on French strategy. Major increases in military aid were approved after France presented a new strategic plan.

The Korean armistice in July 1953 resulted in the release of more Chinese arms and munitions to support the Viet Minh. China's troops and aircraft could now deploy elsewhere and the United States became increasingly concerned with the possibility of Chinese intervention in the war in Indochina. A United States Navy task force was deployed to the South China Sea. It primary purpose was to deter such aggression.

Early in 1954 France launched a major offensive in central Vietnam, but this operation would have little effect on the outcome of the war. Reacting to Viet Minh incursions into Laos, French troops had already occupied a land-air base at Dien Bien Phu. This occupation and the subsequent siege by Chinese-equipped Viet Minh troops were preludes to the final engagement. Support by American carrier aircraft, requested by France, was considered but not approved. War weariness, dissension, and the defeat at Dien Bien Phu led to French compromises at the negotiating table whereby the Democratic Republic of Vietnam was accorded the right to rule Tonkin and northern Annam. In 1954–1955, United States ships would aid in the transportation of large numbers of refugees to the South.

The conclusion of the conference at Geneva in July 1954 was followed by a period of consolidation of Ho's rule in the North and the extension of Diem's authority in the South. The United States gradually assumed training and advisory responsibilities for South Vietnam's military forces, at first jointly with the French. Following establishment of the Republic of Vietnam and the departure of French forces in 1956, France no longer shared direct responsibility for the security of South Vietnam, and American naval advisors faced the challenge of helping to develop an infant Vietnamese Navy into an effective fighting force. Regional security through collective action was a major objective during this period. Under the Southeast Asia Treaty Organization, established in 1954, the United States Navy played a leading role in military demonstrations and combined exercises to bolster the determination of states in the area and to improve their military preparedness.

Piece by piece the stage was being set for more direct American military involvement in the Vietnam conflict. The remaining pieces would soon be in place, for in 1959, as this volume draws to a close, the Communists were increasingly resorting to acts of violence in their efforts to bring about the fall of the Republic of Vietnam. These actions would soon lead to yet another phase in the prolonged conflict, open warfare between North and South Vietnam. The United States would increase its military aid and expand its advisory and assistance actions in support of the Republic of Vietnam. And, it would not be long before the United States Navy and other military services would be engaged in combat in the Vietnam conflict.

Secretaries Of The Navy And Key United States Naval Officers, 1946-1959

SECRETARIES OF THE NAVY

James V. Forrestal	19 May 1944–17 Sep 1947
John L. Sullivan	18 Sep 1947–24 May 1949
Francis P. Matthews	25 May 1949–31 Jul 1951
Dan A. Kimball	31 Jul 1951–20 Jan 1953
Robert B. Anderson	4 Feb 1953–2 May 1954
Charles S. Thomas	3 May 1954–31 Mar 1957
Thomas S. Gates, Jr.	1 Apr 1957–7 Jun 1959
William B. Franke	8 Jun 1959–20 Jan 1961

CHIEFS OF NAVAL OPERATIONS

Fleet Admiral Chester W. Nimitz	15 Dec 1945–15 Dec 1947
Admiral Louis E. Denfeld	15 Dec 1947–2 Nov 1949
Admiral Forrest P. Sherman	2 Nov 1949–22 Jul 1951
Admiral Lynde D. McCormick, Acting	22 Jul 1951–16 Aug 1951
Admiral William M. Fechteler	16 Aug 1951–17 Aug 1953
Admiral Robert B. Carney	17 Aug 1953–17 Aug 1955
Admiral Arleigh A. Burke	17 Aug 1955–1 Aug 1961

COMMANDERS IN CHIEF, PACIFIC

Admiral John H. Towers	1 Jan 1947–28 Feb 1947
Admiral Louis E. Denfeld	28 Feb 1947–3 Dec 1947

Vice Admiral Harold B. Sallada, Acting   3 Dec 1947–12 Jan 1948
Admiral Dewitt C. Ramsey   12 Jan 1948–30 Apr 1949
Admiral Arthur W. Radford   30 Apr 1949–10 Jul 1953
Admiral Felix B. Stump   10 Jul 1953–31 Jul 1958
Admiral Harry D. Felt   31 Jul 1958–30 Jun 1964

COMMANDERS IN CHIEF, U.S. PACIFIC FLEET

Admiral Raymond A. Spruance   24 Nov 1945–1 Feb 1946
Admiral John H. Towers   1 Feb 1946–28 Feb 1947
Admiral Louis E. Denfeld   28 Feb 1947–3 Dec 1947
Vice Admiral Harold B. Sallada, Acting   3 Dec 1947–12 Jan 1948
Admiral Dewitt C. Ramsey   12 Jan 1948–30 Apr 1949
Admiral Arthur W. Radford   30 Apr 1949–10 Jul 1953
Admiral Felix B. Stump   10 Jul 1953–13 Jan 1958
Admiral Maurice E. Curts   13 Jan 1958–1 Feb 1958
Admiral Herbert G. Hopwood   1 Feb 1958–31 Aug 1960

COMMANDERS SEVENTH FLEET

Vice Admiral Daniel E. Barbey   19 Nov 1945–8 Jan 1946
Admiral Charles M. Cooke, Jr.*   8 Jan 1946–24 Feb 1948
Vice Admiral Oscar C. Badger**   24 Feb 1948–28 Aug 1949
Vice Admiral Russell S. Berkey   28 Aug 1949–4 Apr 1950
Rear Admiral Walter F. Boone, Acting   4 Apr 1950–19 May 1950
Vice Admiral Arthur D. Struble   19 May 1950–28 Mar 1951
Vice Admiral Harold M. Martin   28 Mar 1951–28 Mar 1952
Vice Admiral Robert Briscoe   28 Mar 1952–20 May 1952
Vice Admiral Joseph J. Clark   20 May 1952–1 Dec 1953
Vice Admiral Alfred M. Pride   1 Dec 1953–19 Dec 1955
Vice Admiral Stuart H. Ingersoll   19 Dec 1955–28 Jan 1957
Vice Admiral Wallace M. Beakley   28 Jan 1957–30 Sep 1958
Vice Admiral Frederick N. Kivette   30 Sep 1958–7 Mar 1960

---

* Commander Seventh Fleet changed to Commander U.S. Naval Forces, Western Pacific, 1 January 1947.

** Commander U.S. Naval Forces, Western Pacific with additional duty as Commander Seventh Fleet from 1 August 1949.

COMMANDERS NAVAL FORCES, FAR EAST

Vice Admiral Robert M. Griffin*	21 Jan 1946–9 Jul 1948
Vice Admiral Russell S. Berkey	9 Jul 1948–27 Aug 1949
Vice Admiral C. Turner Joy	27 Aug 1949–4 Jun 1952
Vice Admiral Robert P. Briscoe	4 Jun 1952–2 Apr 1954
Vice Admiral William M. Callaghan	2 Apr 1954–14 Sep 1956
Vice Admiral Roscoe F. Good**	14 Sep 1956–30 Jun 1957

---

* Commander U.S. Naval Activities, Japan changed to Commander U.S. Naval Forces, Far East, 1 January 1947.

** Commander U.S. Naval Forces, Far East changed to Commander U.S. Naval Forces, Japan, 1 July 1957.

CHIEFS OF THE NAVY SECTION, MILITARY ASSISTANCE ADVISORY GROUP

Commander John B. Howland*	Aug 1950–Dec 1950
Commander James B. Cannon	Dec 1950–Feb 1954
Captain Samuel Pattie	Feb 1954
Captain James D. Collett	Mar 1954–May 1955
Captain Harry E. Day	May 1955–Apr 1956
Captain Kenneth S. Shook	Apr 1956–Mar 1957
Captain Theodore T. Miller	Mar 1957–Jan 1958
Captain John J. Flachsenhar	Jan 1958–Jul 1960

---

* The MAAG operated on an *ad hoc* basis until it was formally established in December 1950 as a result of a multilateral agreement for Mutual Defense Assistance signed by the United States, France, Laos, Cambodia, and Vietnam.

APPENDIX II

List Of Abbreviations And Terms

ACNO	Assistant Chief of Naval Operations
ACOS	Assistant Chief of Staff
ADM	Admiral
AF	Store Ship
AGC	Amphibious Force Flagship
AH	Hospital Ship
AK	Cargo Ship
AKA	Attack Cargo Ship
AKL	Light Cargo Ship
AKS	Stores Issue Ship
AMS	Motor Mine Sweeper
AO	Oiler
AOG	Gasoline Tanker
AP	Transport
APA	Attack Transport
APB	Self-propelled Barracks Ship
APD	High-speed Transport
AR	Repair Ship
ARL	Landing Craft Repair Ship
ARS	Salvage Ship
ASD(ISA)	Assistant Secretary of Defense (International Security Affairs)
ASROC	Antisubmarine Rocket
ATOM	Advisory Training and Organization Mission
AV	Seaplane Tender
BB	Battleship
BK	Book
BUMED	Bureau of Medicine and Surgery
CA	Heavy Cruiser
CAG	Aircraft Carrier Air Group
CAG	Guided Missile Heavy Cruiser
CAPT	Captain
CARDIV	Carrier Division
CCS	Combined Chiefs of Staff
CDR	Commander

CG, US FORCES	Commanding General, U.S. Forces
CHMAAG	Chief, Military Assistance Advisory Group
CIA	Central Intelligence Agency
CINCAFPACADV	Commander in Chief, U.S. Army Forces, Pacific, Advance Headquarters
CINCLANT	Commander in Chief, Atlantic
CINCNELM	Commander in Chief, Eastern Atlantic and Mediterranean
CINCPAC	Commander in Chief, Pacific
CINCPACFLT	Commander in Chief, U.S. Pacific Fleet
CINCPAC/POA	Commander in Chief, Pacific and Pacific Ocean Areas
CINCPOA	Commander in Chief, Pacific Ocean Areas
CL	Light Cruiser
CMH	Center for Military History, U.S. Army
CNO	Chief of Naval Operations
COMAR	Commander Naval Forces (French)
COM1STFLT	Commander First Fleet
COM7THFLT	Commander Seventh Fleet
COM8THFLT	Commander Eighth Fleet
COMINCH	Commander in Chief, U.S. Fleet
COMINRON	Commander Mine Squadron
COMINTERN	Communist International
COMNAVEU	Commander Naval Forces, Europe
COMNAVFE	Commander Naval Forces, Far East
COMNAVFORV	Commander Naval Forces, Vietnam
COMNAVFORWEST PAC	Commander Naval Forces, Western Pacific
COMNAVPHIL	Commander Naval Forces, Philippines
COM7THPHIBFOR	Commander Seventh Amphibious Force
COMPHIBGRU1	Commander Amphibious Group One
COMTRANSRON	Commander Transportation Squadron
CTF	Commander Task Force
CV	Aircraft Carrier
CVA	Attack Aircraft Carrier
CVE	Escort Aircraft Carrier
CVL	Small Aircraft Carrier
CVS	Antisubmarine Warfare Support Aircraft Carrier
DCNO	Deputy Chief of Naval Operations
DD	Destroyer
DEPSECDEF	Deputy Secretary of Defense
DESDIV	Destroyer Division
DINASSAUTS	French Naval Assault Divisions
DOD	Department of Defense
DRV	Democratic Republic of Vietnam

FAVN	Armed Forces of Vietnam
FIC	French Indochina
FRC	Federal Records Center, Suitland, Maryland
FY	Fiscal Year
GB	General Board
HQ	Headquarters
ICC	International Control Commission
IFS	Inshore Fire Support Ship
JCS	Joint Chiefs of Staff
JN	Job Number
JUSMAAG	Joint U.S. Military Assistance Advisory Group
LCA	Assault Landing Craft
LCDR	Lieutenant Commander
LCI	Landing Craft, Infantry
LCM	Landing Craft, Mechanized
LCU	Landing Craft, Utility
LCVP	Landing Craft, Vehicle, Personnel
LSD	Dock Landing Ship
LSIL	Landing Ship, Infantry, Large
LSSL	Support Landing Ship, Large
LST	Tank Landing Ship
MAAG	Military Assistance Advisory Group
MDAP	Mutual Defense Assistance Program
MIG	Russian-made Fighter Aircraft
MSM	Military Support Mission
MSTS	Military Sea Transportation Service
NA	Naval Attache
NAVMED	Naval Forces, Mediterranean
NSC	National Security Council
OINCEOD	Officer-in-Charge, Explosive Ordnance Disposal Unit
ONI	Office of Naval Intelligence
OPD WD	Operations Division, War Department
OP-ORDER	Operation Order
OP-PLAN	Operation Plan
OSS	Office of Strategic Services
PBY	Catalina Aircraft
PC	Submarine Chaser
PHIBFORWESTPAC	Amphibious Force, Western Pacific
RADM	Rear Admiral
RN	Royal Navy
RVN	Republic of Vietnam
SACO	Sino-American Cooperative Organization
SACSEA	Supreme Allied Commander, Southeast Asia
SEA	Southeast Asia

SEABEES	Navy Mobile Construction Battalions
SEATO	Southeast Asia Treaty Organization
SECDEF	Secretary of Defense
SECNAV	Secretary of the Navy
SECSTATE	Secretary of State
SS	Submarine
SSK	Antisubmarine Submarine
SSN	Submarine (nuclear-powered)
SURMAR	Commander Maritime Surveillance Force (French)
TERM	Temporary Equipment Recovery Mission
TF	Task Force
TG	Task Group
TRIM	Training Relations Instruction Mission
TU	Task Unit
UK	United Kingdom
UDT	Underwater Demolition Team
VADM	Vice Admiral
VC	Viet Cong
VCNO	Vice Chief of Naval Operations
YMS	Auxiliary Motor Mine Sweeper
YO	Fuel Oil Barge (self-propelled)
YOG	Gasoline Barge (self-propelled)

Bibliographic Note

Official Records

Unless otherwise indicated, all documents cited in this work are located in the Operational Archives of the Naval History Division. The Archives's collections of operation plans, operation orders, action reports, and files of histories and miscellaneous documents arranged by command were particularly valuable. These records provided information on such topics as naval ship visits, the withdrawal of Chinese troops from Indochina in 1945 and 1946, Fleet operations during the crisis of 1954, the evacuation of refugees from North Vietnam in 1954 and 1955, and Fleet exercises in the South China Sea during the years after Geneva. Several groups of records from the Office of the Chief of Naval Operations, also contained in the Operational Archives, provided insights into naval policy regarding Indochina. Among aspects covered in these sources were the Navy's participation in the program of aid to the French and Vietnamese and in the Melby-Erskine Mission of 1950.

Series of naval attache reports from Saigon, held in the Washington National Records Center, Suitland, Maryland, proved useful in tracing events after the establishment of that office in 1950. For the earlier period, naval attache reports from Paris (also located in Suitland) provided some coverage on Indochina subjects.

The files of the Military Assistance Advisory Group are in the Washington National Records Center, Suitland, Maryland. These records primarily relate to matters of Army concern. However, several items, particularly the Annual Country Statements and the Monthly MAAG Reports, were of some help in tracing the development of the Vietnamese Navy.

Two other groups consulted were the records of Commander in Chief, U.S. Pacific Fleet and Commander Seventh Fleet. These originally were held in the Federal Records Center, Mechanicsburg, Pennsylvania, but later were transferred to the Washington National Records Center in Suitland, Maryland. For the period of this volume, the records contained surprisingly little information on Vietnam. However, they did provide some insight into high-level naval thinking.

Published Documents

The most important published documentary source was the U.S. Defense Department Study, *United States-Vietnam Relations: 1945-1967* (Washington: GPO, 1971). Known popularly as the Pentagon Papers, this twelve-book series was used extensively for background on American naval policy. The narrative section of this publication was of very little use in comparison to the sections providing published texts of official documents relating to Indochina.

The background documents in the Pentagon Papers were augmented by published State Department sources. For diplomatic background, the volumes of the *Foreign Relations of the United States* were indispensible. Many of the key documents on Indochina relating to the 1945-1949 period, which appear in the *Foreign Relations* series, also were reproduced by the compilers of the Pentagon Papers. The periodic *Department of State Bulletins* contain most of the major public policy statements of Secretaries of State Dean Acheson and John Foster Dulles. Also published by the State Department was *American Foreign Policy 1950–1955: Basic Documents* (Washington: GPO, 1957), which contains a number of key papers for the period of the French-Viet Minh War.

Two additional collections were particularly useful. The first, edited by Allan B. Cole, *Conflict In Indochina and International Repercussion: A Documentary History 1945–1955* (Ithaca: Cornell University Press, 1956), published a number of basic documents on events in the turbulent post-World War II years that do not appear elsewhere. Alan W. Cameron's *Viet-Nam Crisis: A Documentary History* (Ithaca: Cornell University Press, 1971) started as an attempt to update Cole's work but evolved into a complete revision, focusing almost entirely on Vietnam. These two collections contain many of the basic materials covering the French and Vietnamese negotiations for independence, including the Geneva Conference.

Executive and Congressional Documents

The annual reports of the Secretary of Defense, the Secretary of the Navy, and the Chief of Naval Operations summarized the major activities and problems of these leaders. The first Secretary of Defense report was published in 1948. The next year the Secretary of the Navy's report ceased to be published separately and became a part of the former document. Not only did these reports give highlights of naval involvement in Indochina; they also set the Indochina question in an international context alongside naval operations in other parts of the world.

Congressional hearings throw light on the naval aid program to the French and later to the South Vietnamese. Extensive background information on the organizational evolution of the American military establishment also appears in these sources. For example, the key defense reorganization acts of 1947, 1949, and 1958 were preceded by lengthy hearings by the House and Senate Armed Services Committees, which included witnesses from the Navy.

Papers of Individual Officers

Among the collections consulted for this history were those of Brigadier General Philip E. Gallagher, who advised the Chinese troops accepting the Japanese surrender in North Vietnam. A small collection of his papers, held by the Army's Center for Military History, helped to explain events at the end of World War II. The Navy Operational Archives's collection of Vice Admiral Lorenzo Sabin's papers added information to the official reports of the Passage to Freedom.

Oral Histories

Several participants in the early years of U.S. involvement in Vietnam were interviewed by Dr. Oscar Fitzgerald of the Naval History Division to fill gaps in the record. Captain James D. Collett described his experiences as the Chief of the Navy Section of the Military Assistance Advisory Group from March 1954 to May 1955. Captain Ray Kotrla discussed his role as the first naval attache in Saigon in 1950. Captain Kotrla also served with Commodore Milton E. Miles in China during World War II and was involved with mining operations in Indochina. The oral histories done by Dr. John Mason of the U.S. Naval Institute, Annapolis, Maryland, with Admiral Felix B. Stump and Admiral Thomas C. Kinkaid, also were consulted.

Aside from standard reference sources, the following additional works are cited in this volume:

Memoirs and Autobiographies

Acheson, Dean, *Present at the Creation: My Years in the State Department.* New York: W.W. Norton, 1969.

Barbey, Daniel E., *MacArthur's Amphibious Navy: Seventh Amphibious Force Operations: 1943–1945.* Annapolis, Md.: U.S. Naval Institute, 1969.

Chennault, Claire L., *Way of a Fighter: The Memoirs of Claire Lee Chennault.* New York: G.P. Putnam's Sons, 1949.

Dooley, Thomas A., *Deliver Us From Evil: The Story of Viet Nam's Flight to Freedom.* New York: Farrar, Strauss and Cudahy, 1956.

Eisenhower, Dwight D., *Mandate for Change, 1953–1954.* Garden City, N.Y.: Harper and Brothers, 1956.

Ély, Paul, *Indo-China in Turmoil,* trans. ACOS (Intelligence), Department of the Army. Paris: Plon, 1964.

de Gaulle, Charles, *The Complete War Memoirs of Charles de Gaulle.* New York: Simon and Schuster, 1959.

Ho Chi Minh, *On Revolution: Selected Writings, 1920–66,* ed. Bernard B. Fall. New York: Frederick A. Praeger, 1967.

Hull, Cordell, *The Memoirs of Cordell Hull.* New York: The Macmillan Co., 1948.

Joy, C. Turner, *How Communists Negotiate.* New York: The Macmillan Co., 1955.

Khrushchev, Nikita S., *Khrushchev Remembers*, ed. Strobe Talbot. Boston: Little, Brown and Co., 1970.

King, Ernest J. and Walter M. Whitehill, *Fleet Admiral King: A Naval Record.* New York: W.W. Norton and Co., 1952.

Laniel, Joseph, *Le Drame Indochinois de Dien-Bien-Phu au pari de Geneve.* Paris: Plon, 1957.

Leahy, William D., *I Was There: The Personal Story of the Chief of Staff to Presidents Roosevelt and Truman Based on His Notes and Diaries Made at the Time.* New York: Whittlesey House, 1950.

Lenin, Vladimir I., *Selected Works.* New York: International Publishers, 1943.

Miles, Milton E., *A Different Kind of War: The Little-Known Story of the Combined Guerrilla Forces Created in China by the U.S. Navy and the Chinese During World War II.* Garden City, N.Y.: Doubleday and Co., 1967.

Millis, Walter, ed., *The Forrestal Diaries.* New York: Viking Press, 1951.

Navarre, Henri, *Agony of Indochina.* Paris: Plon, 1957, trans. Naval Intelligence Command.

O'Daniel, John W., *The Nation that Refused to Starve: The Challenge of the New Vietnam.* New York: Coward-McCann, Inc., 1960.

Pham Van Dong, *25 Years of National Struggle and Construction.* Hanoi: Foreign Languages Publishing House, 1970.

Roosevelt, Elliott, *As He Saw It.* New York: Duell, Sloan and Pearce, 1946.

Truman, Harry S., *Year of Decisions*, Vol. I of *Memoirs.* Garden City, N.Y.: Doubleday and Co., 1955.

———————, *Years of Trial and Hope*, Vol. II of *Memoirs.* Garden City, N.Y.: Doubleday and Co., 1956.

Vo Nguyen Giap, *Banner of People's War, The Party's Military Line.* New York: Praeger Publishers, 1970.

———————, *The Military Art of People's War: Selected Writings of General Vo Nguyen Giap.* New York: Monthly Review Press, 1970.

———————, *People's War, People's Army: The Viet Cong Insurrection Manual for Underdeveloped Countries.* New York: Frederick A. Praeger, 1962.

Wedemeyer, Albert C., *Wedemeyer Reports!* New York: Henry Holt and Co., 1958.

Secondary Works

Allan, Richard, *A Short Introduction to the History and Politics of Southeast Asia.* New York: Oxford University Press, 1968.

Auphan, Paul and Jacques Mordal, *The French Navy in World War II.* Annapolis, Md.: U.S. Naval Institute Press, 1959.

Barjot, Pierre, *Histoire de la Guerre Aeronavale.* Paris: Flammarion, 1961.

Bator, Victor, *Vietnam, A Diplomatic Tragedy: The Origins of United States Involvement.* Dobbs Ferry, N.Y.: Oceana Publishers, 1965.

Braisted, William R., *The United States Navy in the Pacific, 1897–1909.* Austin, Tex.: University of Texas Press, 1958.

——————————, *The United States Navy in the Pacific, 1909–1922.* Austin, Tex.: University of Texas Press, 1971.

Brodie, Bernard, *The Atomic Bomb and American Security.* New Haven, Conn.: Yale Institute of International Studies, 1945.

——————————, ed., *The Absolute Weapon: Atomic Power and World Order.* New York: Harcourt Brace and Co., 1946.

Buttinger, Joseph, *The Smaller Dragon: A Political History of Vietnam.* New York: Frederick A. Praeger, 1958.

——————————, *From Colonialism to the Vietminh*, Vol. I of *Vietnam: A Dragon Embattled.* New York: Frederick A. Praeger, 1967.

——————————, *Vietnam at War*, Vol. II of *Vietnam: A Dragon Embattled.* New York: Frederick A. Praeger, 1967.

——————————, *Vietnam: A Political History.* New York: Frederick A. Praeger, 1968.

Carter, Worrall R., *Beans, Bullets, and Black Oil: The Story of Fleet Logistics Afloat in the Pacific During World War II.* Washington: Navy Department, GPO, 1952.

Chen, King C., *Vietnam and China, 1938–1954.* Princeton, N.J.: Princeton University Press, 1969.

von Clausewitz, Karl, *On War.* London: Kegan Paul, French, Trubner and Co., 1908.

Clemens, Diane S., *Yalta.* New York: Oxford University Press, 1970.

Commander in Chief, United States Fleet, "Commander in Chief, United States Fleet, Headquarters." Unpublished history in Naval History Division, 1946.

Commander Naval Forces, Europe, "Administrative History of U.S. Naval Forces in Europe, August 1945 to March 1947." Unpublished history in Naval History Division, 1947.

Commander Naval Forces, Vietnam, "The Naval War in Vietnam." Unpublished history in Naval History Division, 1970.

Crawford, Ann C., *Customs and Culture of Vietnam*. Rutland, Vt.: Charles E. Tuttle Co., 1966.

Davis, Vernon E., "The History of the Joint Chiefs of Staff in World War II: Organizational Development." Unpublished history in Naval History Division, 1972.

Davis, Vincent, *Postwar Defense Policy and the U.S. Navy, 1943–1946*. Chapel Hill, N.C.: University of North Carolina Press, 1962.

Devillers, Philippe and Jean Lacouture, *End of a War: Indochina, 1954*. New York: Frederick A. Praeger, 1969.

Fall, Bernard B., *Street Without Joy*. Harrisburg, Pa.: Stackpole Co., 1964.

——————, *Hell in a Very Small Place: The Siege of Dien Bien Phu*. New York: J. B. Lippincott Co., 1967.

——————, *The Two Viet-Nams: A Political and Military Analysis*. New York: Frederick A. Praeger, 1967.

Field, James A., Jr., *History of United States Naval Operations: Korea*. Washington: Naval History Division, GPO, 1962.

FitzGerald, Charles P., *A Concise History of East Asia*. New York: Frederick A. Praeger, 1966.

——————, *The Southern Expansion of the Chinese People*. New York: Praeger Publishers, 1972.

Frank, Benis M. and Henry I. Shaw, *Victory and Occupation*, Vol. V of *History of U.S. Marine Corps Operations in World War II*. Washington: U.S. Marine Historical Branch, GPO, 1968.

Furer, Julius A., *Administration of the Navy Department in World War II*. Washington: Naval History Division, GPO, 1959.

Gaddis, John L., *The United States and the Origins of the Cold War, 1941–1947*. New York: Columbia University Press, 1972.

George, Alexander L. and Richard Smoke, *Deterrence in American Foreign Policy: Theory and Practice*. New York: Columbia University Press, 1974.

Gerson, Louis L., *John Foster Dulles,* Vol. XVII of *The American Secretaries of State and their Diplomacy,* ed. *Robert H. Ferrell*. New York: Cooper Square Publishers, 1967.

Gorshkov, Sergei G., *Red Star Rising at Sea*. Annapolis, Md.: United States Naval Institute, 1974.

Gurtov, Melvin, *The First Vietnam Crisis: Chinese Communist Strategy and United States Involvement, 1953–1954.* New York: Columbia University Press, 1967.

Hall, Daniel G. E., *A History of South-East Asia.* London: Macmillan and Co., 1964.

Hammer, Ellen J., *The Struggle for Indochina, 1940–1955.* Stanford, Cal.: Stanford University Press, 1954.

——————————, *Vietnam: Yesterday and Today.* New York: Holt, Rinehart and Winston, 1966.

Hammond, Paul Y., *Organizing for Defense: The American Military Establishment in the Twentieth Century.* Princeton, N.J.: Princeton University Press, 1961.

Hayes, Samuel P., ed., *The Beginning of American Aid to Southeast Asia: The Griffin Mission of 1950.* Lexington, Mass.: D. C. Heath and Co., 1971.

Hewlett, Richard G. and Francis Duncan, *Nuclear Navy.* Chicago: University of Chicago Press, 1974.

Hooper, Edwin B., *Mobility, Support, Endurance: A Story of Naval Operational Logistics in the Vietnam War, 1965–1968.* Washington: Naval History Division, 1972.

Hovey, Harold N., *United States Military Assistance: A Study of Policies and Practices.* New York: Frederick A. Praeger, 1965.

Howe, Jonathan Trumball, *Multicrises, Sea Power and Global Politics in the Missile Age.* Cambridge, Mass.: The Massachusetts Institute of Technology Press, 1971.

Johnson, Ellis A., and David A. Katcher, *Mines Against Japan.* Washington: Naval Ordnance Laboratory, GPO, 1973.

Kilian, Robert, *History and Memories: The Naval Infantrymen in Indochina.* Paris: Editions Berger-Levrault, 1948.

Kirby, S. Woodburn, *The Surrender of Japan,* Vol. V of *The War Against Japan* in *History of the Second World War: United Kingdom Military Series.* London: Her Majesty's Stationery Office, 1969.

Lacouture, Jean, *Ho Chi Minh: A Political Biography.* New York: Random House, 1968.

Lancaster, Donald, *The Emancipation of French Indochina.* London: Oxford University Press, 1961.

Leonhard, Wolfgang, *The Kremlin Since Stalin.* New York: Praeger Publishers, 1962.

Leopold, Richard W., "Fleet Organization, 1919–1941." Unpublished history in Naval History Division, 1945.

————————————, *The Growth of American Foreign Policy: A History*. New York: Alfred A. Knopf, 1962.

Lindholm, Richard W., ed., *Viet-Nam: The First Five Years*. East Lansing, Mich.: Michigan State University Press, 1959.

Mahan, Alfred Thayer, *The Influence of Sea Power Upon History, 1660–1783*. Boston: Little, Brown and Co., 1928.

Marder, Arthur J., *The Anatomy of British Sea Power: A History of British Naval Policy in the Pre-Dreadnought Era, 1880–1905*. New York: Alfred A. Knopf, 1940.

Marr, David G., *Vietnamese Anticolonialism: 1885–1925*. Berkeley, Cal.: University of California Press, 1971.

Mauclère, Jean, *Sailors on the Canals*. Paris: J. Peyronnet, 1950.

McAlister, John T., Jr., *Viet Nam: The Origins of Revolution*. New York: Alfred A. Knopf, 1969.

Moore, Withers, "Navy Chaplains in Vietnam, 1954–1964." Washington: Bureau of Naval Personnel, 1968.

Mordal, Jacques, *The Navy in Indochina*. Paris: Amiot-Dumont, 1953, trans. N.L. Williams and A. W. Atkinson.

Morison, Samuel E., *The Rising Sun in the Pacific, 1931–April 1942*, Vol. III of *History of United States Naval Operations in World War II*. Boston: Little, Brown and Co., 1948.

————————————, *New Guinea and the Marianas: March 1944–August 1944*, Vol. VIII of *History of United States Naval Operations in World War II*. Boston: Little, Brown and Co., 1953.

————————————, *The Liberation of The Philippines, 1944–1945*, Vol. XIII of *History of United States Naval Operations in World War II*. Boston: Little, Brown and Co., 1959.

Murti, B. S. N., *Vietnam Divided: The Unfinished Struggle*. New York: Asia Publishing Co., 1964.

Nutt, Anita Lauve, "Troika on Trial: Control or Compromise?" Unpublished history in Naval History Division, 1967.

O'Ballance, Edgar, *The Indo-China War, 1945–1954: A Study in Guerilla Warfare*. London: Faber and Faber, 1964.

Pogue, Forrest C., *Ordeal and Hope, 1939–1942*, Vol. II of *George C. Marshall*. New York: Viking Press, 1965.

————————————, *Organizer of Victory, 1943–1945*, Vol. III of *George C. Marshall*. New York: Viking Press, 1973.

Polmar, Norman, *Aircraft Carriers: A Graphic History of Carrier Aviation and Its Influence on World Events.* Garden City, N.Y.: Doubleday and Co., 1967.

Power, Thomas F., Jr., *Jules Ferry and the Renaissance of French Imperialism.* New York: Kings Crown Press, 1944.

Reis, John C., *The Management of Defense: Organization and Control of the U.S. Armed Services.* Baltimore, Md.: The Johns Hopkins Press, 1964.

Reynolds, Clark G., *Command of the Sea: The History and Strategy of Maritime Empires.* New York: William Morrow and Co., 1974.

Roberts, Edmund, *Embassy to the Eastern Courts of Cochin-China, Siam and Muscat.* New York: Harper and Brothers, 1837.

Rockefeller Brothers Fund, Special Studies Project, Panel II, *International Security: The Military Aspect* in series *America at Mid-Century.* Garden City, N.Y.: Doubleday and Co., 1959.

Romein, Jan, *The Asian Century: A History of Modern Nationalism in Asia.* Berkeley, Cal.: University of California Press, 1962.

Roscoe, Theodore, *United States Submarine Operations in World War II.* Annapolis, Md.: United States Naval Institute, 1949.

Rozek, Edward J., *Allied Wartime Diplomacy: A Pattern in Poland.* New York: John Wiley and Sons, 1958.

Rozow, Arnold A., *James Forrestal: A Study of Personality, Politics, and Policy.* New York: Macmillan, 1963.

Shigenori, Togo, *The Cause of Japan.* New York: Simon and Schuster, 1959.

Smith, R. Harris, *OSS: The Secret History of America's First Central Intelligence Agency.* Berkeley, Cal.: University of California Press, 1972.

Smith, Ralph, *Viet-Nam and the West.* Ithaca, N.Y.: Cornell University Press, 1971.

Stanley, Timothy W., *American Defense and National Security.* Washington: Public Affairs Press, 1956.

Staunton, Sydney A., *The War in Tong-King: Why the French are in Tong-King and What They are Doing There.* Boston: Cupples, Upham and Co., 1884.

Steinberg, David J., *et al, In Search of Southeast Asia: A Modern History.* New York: Praeger Publishers, 1971.

Teston, Eugene and Maurice Percheron, *L'Indochine Moderne.* Paris: Librairie de France, 1931.

Thomas, Hugh, *Suez.* New York: Harper and Row, 1966.

Thompson, Robert, *Revolutionary War in World Strategy, 1945–1969.* New York: Taplinger, 1970.

—————————, *Defeating Communist Insurgency.* New York: Praeger, 1966.

Trager, Frank N., *Why Viet Nam?* New York: Frederick A. Praeger, 1966.

U.S., Bureau of Medicine and Surgery, "History of the Medical Department of the United States Navy 1945–1955." Washington: Government Printing Office, 1958.

U.S., Defense Department, Joint Logistics Review Board, *Logistic Support in the Vietnam Era: A Report,* Washington, 1970.

Xydis, Stephen G., *Greece and the Great Powers, 1944–1947: Prelude to the "Truman Doctrine."* Thessalonicki, Greece: Institute for Balkan Studies, 1963.

Articles

Bui-kong-Chyng, "Pomoshch'stran sotsialisticheskogo lageria v vosstanovlenii i razvitii narodnogo khoziastra DRV," in *Demokraticheskara Respublika V'etnam, 1945–1960,* ed. A.A. Guber and Nguyen-khan'-Toan. Moscow: Publishing House of Eastern Literature, 1960.

Burke, Arleigh, "The Lebanon Crisis," *Proceedings, Naval History Symposium.* Annapolis, Md.: United States Naval Academy (1973).

Bush, Vannevar, "Scientific Weapons and a Future War," *Life Magazine,* XVI (14 November 1949).

Chen, King C., "Hanoi's Three Decisions and the Escalation of the Vietnam War," *Political Science Quarterly,* XC, No. 2 (Summer 1975).

Connery, Robert H. and Paul T. David, "The Mutual Defense Assistance Program," *The American Political Science Review* (June 1951).

Croizat, Victor J., "Vietnamese Naval Forces: Origin of the Species," *United States Naval Institute Proceedings,* IC (February 1973).

Esthus, Raymond A., "President Roosevelt's Commitment to Britain to Intervene in a Pacific War," *The Mississippi Valley Historical Review,* L, No. 1 (June 1963).

Fall, Bernard B., "The History and Culture of Vietnam," *Naval War College Review,* XXIII (February 1971).

Gittinger, J. Price, "Communist Land Policy in North Viet Nam," *Far Eastern Survey,* XXVIII (August 1959).

Gould, James W., "American Imperialism in Southeast Asia Before 1898," *Journal of Southeast Asian Studies,* III (September 1972).

Haight, John McVickar, Jr., "Franklin D. Roosevelt and a Naval Quarantine of Japan," *Pacific Historical Review*, XL (May 1971).

Hamilton, William A., "The Decline and Fall of the Joint Chiefs of Staff," *Naval War College Review*, XXII (April 1972).

Hammond, Paul Y. "Super Carriers and B–36 Bombers: Appropriations, Strategy and Politics," in *American Civil-Military Decisions, A Book of Case Studies*, ed. Harold Stein. Birmingham, Ala.: University of Alabama Press, 1963.

Hébert, Guy, "The Birth of a Flotilla," trans. Remote Area Conflict Information Center, *La Revue Maritime*, XLII (October 1949).

Hess, Gary, "Franklin Roosevelt and Indochina," *Journal of American History*, LIX (September 1972).

Jung-Pang Lo, "The Emergence of China as a Sea Power During the Late Sung and Early Yuan Periods," *The Far Eastern Quarterly*, XIV (August 1955).

Knight, Jonathan, "American Statecraft and the 1946 Black Sea Straits Controversy," *Political Science Quarterly*, XC (Fall 1975).

LaFeber, Walter, "Roosevelt, Churchill, and Indochina: 1942–1945," *American Historical Review*, LXXX (December 1975).

Le Breton, E., "The Marines in Indo China," trans. Remote Area Conflict Information Center, *La Revue Maritime*, XXX (October 1948).

Martin, James V., "Thai-American Relations in World War II," *The Journal of Asian Studies*, XXII (August 1963).

U.S., Office of Naval Intelligence, "Disputed Islands in the South China Sea: Part I," *The ONI Review*, XI (May 1956).

—————————, "Disputed Islands in the South China Sea: Part II," *The ONI Review*, XI (June 1956).

—————————, "Development of and Plans for the Vietnamese Navy," *The ONI Review*, VIII (March 1953).

—————————, "Operations of the French CVL *Arromanches* in Indochina," *The ONI Review*, VIII (January 1953).

—————————, "French Naval and Air Operations in Indochina," *The ONI Review*, VI (November 1951).

—————————, "The Dinassaut Units of Indochina," *The ONI Review*, Supp. (Autumn 1952).

Ortoli, P., "The French Navy in Indochina," trans. Remote Area Conflict Information Center, *La Revue Maritime*, LXXX (December 1952).

Roberts, Chalmers M., "The United States Twice Proposed Indochina Air Strike," in *The Washington Post*, 9 July 1954. Reprinted in *The Congressional Record*, Senate, 83rd Congress, 2nd Session, Vol. C.

Sabin, Lorenzo S., "South Vietnam—An Exercise in Tragedy," *Shipmate*, XXVIII (April 1965).

Sander, Alfred D., "Truman and the National Security Council: 1945–1947," *The Journal of American History*, LIX (September 1972).

Shaplen, Robert, "The Cult of Diem," *New York Times Magazine* (14 May 1972).

Spector, Ronald, " 'What the Local Annamites are Thinking': American Views of Vietnamese in China, 1942–1945," *Southeast Asia*, III (Spring 1974).

——————————, "The American Image of Southeast Asia, 1790–1865, A Preliminary Assessment," *Journal of Southeast Asian Studies*, III (September 1972).

Stevens, Benjamin E., "Around the World in the United States Frigate Constitution in the Days of the Old or Wooden Ships," *The United Service*, VII (May 1905).

Westcott, Allan, "Captain 'Mad Jack' Percival," *United States Naval Institute Proceedings*, LXI (March 1935).

Xydis, Stephen G., "The Genesis of the Sixth Fleet," *United States Naval Institute Proceedings*, LXXXIV (August 1958).

Index

Unless otherwise indicated, all military personnel are USN and all ships are USS.

☆ U.S. GOVERNMENT PRINTING OFFICE: 1977 0—507–602